THE EGO
AND
THE DYNAMIC GROUND

SUNY Series in Transpersonal and Humanistic Psychology
Richard D. Mann and Jean B. Mann, Editors

THE EGO
AND
THE DYNAMIC GROUND

A Transpersonal Theory
of Human Development

Michael Washburn

STATE UNIVERSITY OF NEW YORK PRESS

Tables 1-4 and 1-5 adapted from *Eye to Eye: The Quest for a New Paradigm* by Ken Wilber. Copyright © 1983 by Ken Wilber. Reprinted by permission of Doubleday, a division of Bantam, Doubleday, Dell Publishing Group, Inc.

Published by
State University of New York Press, Albany

© 1988   State University of New York

For information, address State University of New York
Press, State University Plaza, Albany, N.Y., 12246

Library of Congress Cataloging-in-Publication Data

Washburn, Michael, 1943-
    The ego and the dynamic ground.

    (SUNY series in transpersonal and humanistic
psychology)
    Bibliography: p.
    Includes index.
    1. Transpersonal psychology. 2. Ego (Psychology)
I. Title. II. Series.
BF204.7.W37   1987   150.19   87-9938
ISBN 0-88706-611-9
ISBN 0-88706-612-7 (pbk.)

10 9 8 7 6 5 4 3 2

FOR

Ione Rich Washburn
My Mother, My Friend

CONTENTS

PREFACE

IN TERMS OF THE DISCIPLINARY categories currently in use, this study falls within the field of transpersonal psychology. Transpersonal psychology is the study of human nature and development that proceeds on the assumption that human beings possess potentialities that surpass the limits of the normally developed ego. It is an inquiry that presupposes that the ego, as ordinarily constituted, can be transcended and that a higher, transegoic plane or stage of life is possible. The present study falls within this field of investigation because it postulates that the ego, despite pretensions of independence, is a grounded existent and, consequently, that the highest plane or stage of life is not the usual egoic one but rather one in which the ego is properly rooted in its ground. Specifically, the present study postulates that the ego exists in essential relation to a superior *Dynamic Ground* and that the highest possible psychic organization is one in which the ego, itself fully developed and self-responsible, is a faithful instrument of this Ground.

Transpersonal psychology is less a subdiscipline of psychology than it is a multidisciplinary inquiry aimed at a holistic understanding of human nature. It is a synthesis of several disciplines, including most importantly not only the larger discipline of psychology but also the disciplines of religion and philosophy. Transpersonal psychology is concerned not only with psychological notions such as ego, unconscious, and integration but also with religious notions such as fallenness, transcendence, and spiritual realization and with philosophical notions such as selfhood, existential project, and lifeworld. Transpersonal psychology is a comprehensive enterprise; it is a *Geisteswissenschaft* that draws upon several humanistic disciplines without itself being strictly subsumable under any of them. In light of this multidisciplinary character of transpersonal psychology, it would perhaps be better if transpersonal inquiry were to change its name from transpersonal *psychology* to, simply, transpersonal *theory*.

I have approached transpersonal theory from a dynamic and phenomenological orientation. For this reason my thinking, in drawing upon psychology, religion, and philosophy, has drawn most heavily upon dynamic depth psychology (especially Jung), psychospiritually oriented religion (e.g., ascetical and mystical theology, yoga, alchemy), and existential-phenomenological philosophy (especially Kierkegaard, Nietzsche, and Sartre). I trace the unfolding interaction between the ego and the Dyanmic Ground from the ego's initial differentiation from the Ground (the period of the pre-Oedipal body-ego), through the ego's repressive dissociation from the Ground (the period of the Cartesian ego and the dynamic unconscious), to, finally, the ego's return to and reconstitution by the Ground (the period of spiritual regeneration and higher integration). And in tracing these stages of the ego/Ground interaction, I also speak to the different senses of selfhood, the different existential projects, and the different experiential life-worlds that correspond to the stages.

I am aware of the ambitious nature of any attempt to formulate an encompassing transpersonal theory, so acutely aware, in fact, that I have been plagued with self-doubts throughout the writing of this book. There were countless times when, for lack of understanding or learning, I felt inadequate to the task and unable to proceed. Nevertheless, I persevered to the end. And on the whole I am pleased with the way the book has turned out. The book suffers from many weaknesses, I am sure. In particular, since my professional training is confined to philosophy, it is likely that my treatment of psychological and theological notions will in some cases seem unsophisticated to experts in these fields. However, notwithstanding these, and other, shortcomings, I am confident that the book at least presents a distinctive and fully developed point of view, and I am hopeful that it will make some significant contributions to transpersonal theory.

This book has been six years in preparation. During this time there have been many people who have given generously of their time and understanding in helping me. Richard Allen, Arthur Bohart, William Borden, David Eastman, James McGrath, Richard D. Mann, James Mosel, George Nazaroff, Pamela Washburn, and Ken Wilber all read and commented on portions of the book at various stages of its evolution. Their encouragements have sustained me, and their constructive criticisms have saved me from many errors and have challenged me to state my ideas as clearly and as rigorously as I am able. The readers for the State University of New York Press offered many acute suggestions, almost all of which have been followed. I would like to thank them for helping me make this a considerably better book than it otherwise would have been. Of the people mentioned so far, I am especially indebted to Richard Mann and to Ken Wilber. Richard Mann warmly received the manuscript of this book and offered sage advice as to how it could be improved. And Ken Wilber has been an inspiring intellectual model. Wilber's books are powerful beacons that have led the way in the early years of transpersonal inquiry.

I am grateful to my school, Indiana University at South Bend, for providing me with a Summer Faculty Fellowship (1981) and a sabbatical leave (1983-84) at crucial junctures in this project. Also, my colleagues in philosophy at IUSB—Andrew Naylor, Jon Ringen, and J. Wesley Robbins— have been a valued resource. They have all read parts of the book and have given me insightful feedback and suggestions. And appreciative acknowledgement is due, too, to Peter Blum, Craig Schroeder, and Michael van de Viere, friends in philosophy at IUSB with whom I have enjoyed many stimulating conversations on topics related to those dealt with herein.

I would like finally to thank the members of my family for their understanding and support, especially during the last year when I was so preoccupied with finishing the book. Kirsten, Tracy, and Alison, my daughters, were always willing to listen when I needed to express my hopes for the book or my frustrations in trying to write it. Pamela, my wife, helped me in all phases and aspects of the project. And Ione, my mother—to whom the book is dedicated—provided me with vital encouragements and insights.

Michael Washburn

INTRODUCTION

A CHIEF OBJECTIVE OF TRANSPERSONAL theory[1] is to integrate spiritual experience within a larger understanding of the human psyche. Transpersonal theory thus is committed to the possibility of unifying spiritual and psychological perspectives. In being committed to such a unification, however, transpersonal theory is not advocating a program of reduction, of the spiritual to the psychological (or of "promotion," of the psychological to the spiritual, for that matter). Transpersonal theory is not just psychology of religion or spiritual psychology. Rather, it is a project that attempts a true synthesis of spiritual and psychological approaches to the psyche, a synthesis that involves a thorough rethinking of each of these approaches in the terms of the other.

Although transpersonal theory aims at a genuine synthesis of psychological and spiritual perspectives rather than a one-sided reduction or promotion, it does not consider these two perspectives to be absolutely on a par. Rather, it accords a higher status to the spiritual standpoint. For transpersonal theory assumes that spiritual experience is expressive of humanity's highest potentialities. Transpersonal theory assumes that human development aims ultimately at a spiritual fulfillment, and therefore that it is only from the spiritual perspective that human nature can be fully understood. Accordingly, it is fundamental to transpersonal theory that spirituality or religion (understood experientially rather than doctrinally or institutionally) should play the leading role in a unified science of humankind.

Transpersonal theory was pioneered by Carl Jung, who parted company with the original Freudian circle when he stressed that psychology should seek (nonreductively) to understand the spiritual strivings of our race. Jung's analytical psychology, which stresses the depth and dynamic dimensions of psychology and the mythic dimension of religion, maintains that the drama of human development is fully intelligible only in light of the spiritual symbols

1

that prefigure it. According to Jung, the symbols of religion speak so powerfully to us because they are embodiments of the numinous archetypes that, rooted in the unconscious, guide us on our odyssey of self-realization. Religious symbols point to the future and highest stages of the developmental process; they are signposts along the way to full spiritual humanness.

Jung's contribution to transpersonal theory is immense. Not only was he the chief pioneer of transpersonal thought, but he remains a towering figure in the field. The Jungian dynamic and archetypal approach to understanding human spiritual potentialities is presently one of the two major perspectives within transpersonal theory. Ken Wilber's structural-hierarchical approach is the other. (More on Wilber in a moment.)[2]

A second major figure in the history of transpersonal theory is Roberto Assagioli, the Italian psychiatrist and founder of psychosynthesis. Assagioli's chief contribution to transpersonal thought is his view that human beings have not only a lower unconscious but also a higher superconscious, and, consequently, that psychotherapy needs to focus not only on remedying pathologies connected with the former but also on realizing spiritual potentialities connected with the latter. Also, in his main work, *Psychosynthesis* (1971), Assagioli defended the position that not all psychological disturbances, even very serious ones, are to be understood as symptoms of psychopathology, but rather that some are to be understood as crises of spiritual awakening. For Assagioli, then, it is the proper business of psychotherapy not only to treat ills connected with the unconscious but also to foster spiritual awakening and to deal intelligently with the difficulties that such awakening can incur.

Finally, a third major contributor to transpersonal theory is Abraham Maslow, a founding father of both humanistic and transpersonal psychology. In relation to transpersonal theory, Maslow's greatest importance lies in his advocacy of the view that the capacity for religious experience is a higher or transcendent potentiality of human nature, a potentiality which belongs to us inherently as a biological species that has evolved (1970, 1971). For Maslow, the capacity for religious experience is innate, and religious experiences are "peak" or "plateau" experiences occurring at the "farthest reaches of human nature." For Maslow, as for transpersonal theory generally, spirituality corresponds to the highest of human possibilities. For this reason it was Maslow's view that psychology, including humanistically oriented psychology, cannot be complete until it has been refocused and brought under a spiritual or transpersonal point of view. For example, Maslow (1968, iii-iv) said:

> I should say also that I consider Humanistic, Third Force Psychology to
> be transitional, a preparation for a still "higher" Fourth Psychology,
> transpersonal, transhuman, centered in the cosmos rather than in human

needs and interests, going beyond humanness, identity, self-actualization, and the like.

Transpersonal theory came into its own as a self-conscious movement with the founding of *The Journal of Transpersonal Psychology* in 1969. In the early years, transpersonal psychology (as transpersonal theory, somewhat narrowly, has come to be called) was predominantly humanistic in its psychology and Eastern in its religion, a synthesis of Maslow and pop Buddhism (mostly Zen). These identifications, however, have loosened over the years, and transpersonal psychology is now more open to a diversity of psychological and religious perspectives. Besides Jung, the principal figure in the field at this time is Ken Wilber (1980a, 1981b, 1983a, 1983b), whose theory of the spectrum of consciousness draws on vast amounts of material from contemporary psychology and comparative religion. Unlike Jung's work, which arose primarily out of the psychodynamic school of psychology and the Christian religious tradition, Wilber's work is situated primarily in the structural (mainly cognitive-developmental) school of psychology and the Indian (principally Buddhist) religious tradition. But these chief influences on Wilber's thought are not rigid allegiances. They are, rather, guiding frameworks for Wilber's wide-ranging explorations.

Transpersonal theory is still in its infancy—even though, in another sense, it is a very old quest: the *philosophia perennis*. There are exciting possibilities for significant new understanding, especially as scientific methods of investigation are applied to such things as meditation, spiritual practice, altered states of consciousness, and exceptional experiences and exceptional individuals. Stanislav Grof (1975, 1985), for example, in his work in LSD psychotherapy, has made some fascinating discoveries about the nature of the unconscious, and about its transpersonal potentials in particular. And on the level of metatheory, the introduction of the holographic paradigm into transpersonal inquiry must be counted as a noteworthy occurrence.[3] The holographic model, stressing internal over external relations and interconnection over independence, opens up ways of explaining aspects of human experience that otherwise might not be amenable to scientific consideration. There are at present many promising prospects for transpersonal theory, which is an inquiry that perhaps more than any other is extending the frontiers of our understanding of human nature and human potentialities.

In light of this overview, the purpose of the present book can be situated within the larger transpersonal enterprise. The purpose is, namely, to advance the cause of the psychodynamic paradigm within transpersonal theory by presenting a new formulation of that paradigm as it bears upon transpersonal issues. Specifically, the book presents a formulation that is at once *dynamic*, *triphasic*, and *dialectical*. Let me explain.

The perspective of this book is *dynamic* in that the primary focus is on the ego's interaction with dynamic life, the source of which is referred to as the *Dynamic Ground*.[4] Accordingly, I will be focusing, in the domain of psychology, on the relation of the ego to the dynamic unconscious and, in the domain of spirituality, on the relation of the ego to possible religious (e.g., numinous, infused, charismatic, illumined) experience. In what follows, it is a fundamental assumption that these two main expressions, psychological and spiritual, of our dynamic life derive from a single source. It is assumed that these two expressions are not effects of two different dynamic realities but are rather two different modes of appearance of the same power, the power of the Dynamic Ground. Libido and spirit, I will argue, are ultimately one.[5]

The perspective of this book is *triphasic* in that it divides human development into three principal stages. These are the pre-egoic, egoic, and transegoic stages. Such a broad tripartite division is inherent to any transpersonal theory that, in treating human development, accepts Wilber's (1980b) "pre-/trans-" distinction. What is distinctive about the triphasic scheme set forth in this book is that it conceives the three stages of development as reflecting three different positions in the ego's unfolding interaction with dynamic life. Accordingly, the pre-egoic stage, which corresponds roughly to pre-Oedipal childhood, is seen as a period during which the Dynamic Ground dominates a weak and undeveloped ego. The egoic stage, which corresponds to the years extending from later childhood to middle adulthood, is seen as a period during which a maturing ego is repressively dissociated from the Dynamic Ground. And the transegoic stage, which corresponds to later adulthood (i.e., in those cases in which the stage appears), is seen as a period in which a strong and mature ego is resubmitted to and integrated with the Dynamic Ground. In sum, the three stages of life are understood as reflecting three basically different forms of relationship between the ego and the Dynamic Ground.

Conceived in this fashion, the three stages of development can be said to have the following basic features.

1. The pre-egoic stage. This stage, which will also be called the stage of the *body-ego*, is the stage of pre-Oedipal childhood. It is distinguished by: (1) a predominantly somatic, instinctual, and (polymorphously) sensuous character; (2) intimacy with the maternal presence, understood in both outer (parental) and inner (dynamic, archetypal) senses; (3) openness both to the world without and to the deepest sources of life within; (4) dynamically charged experience; (5) a sense of the numinous; and (6) a creative but crude cognitive life, conducted in the medium of concrete images.

2. The egoic stage. This stage, which will also be called the stage of the *mental ego*, is the stage that by far is of the longest duration. Commenced very early in life (during what Freud called the latency period), the egoic stage is consolidated near the end of adolescence, after which, for most people, it continues in more or less stable fashion until the end of life. Principal among the features of the egoic, or mental-egoic, stage are: (1) a deeply underlying repressive infrastructure, which insulates the mental ego from the dynamic unconscious, and therefore also from the Dynamic Ground; (2) a predominantly mental—and antiphysical, anti-instinctual—character; (3) apparent ego independence, self-control, autonomous command of will; (4) a developed personality, shaped in response to social roles, norms, and values; (5) secondary process or formal operational cognition; and, in the later phases of its unfolding, (6) a sense of emptiness and alienation together with a corresponding impetus toward transcendence.

3. The transegoic stage. This stage, which will also be called the stage of integration, is a stage that usually begins—in those cases in which it does begin—only in the middle or later years of life. The first turn toward the transegoic or integrated stage typically is expressed in the form of a conversion experience. The conversion presages spiritual awakening (i.e., the reopening of the Dynamic Ground) and, thereby, the initiation of a process of psychic reorganization that, if seen through to the end, culminates in a higher synthesis of psychic resources. Principal among the features of the transegoic, or integrated, stage are: (1) transcendence of the major dualisms that plague the mental ego—e.g., the dualisms of mind and body, thought and feeling, logic and creativity, civilization and instinct, and, most basically, ego and Ground— and the transformation of these dualisms into harmonious dualities, higher syntheses of opposites; (2) rooting of the ego in the Ground and felicitous infusion of the ego by the Ground; (3) spiritual presence, charisma; (4) fully realized intuitive, contemplative, and creative capacities; (5) refound openness, dynamism, and spontaneity; and (6) an agapeic sense of love, kinship, and community. To these facts about the transegoic or integrated stage should be added one more, namely, that it is the stage that is least frequently attained. Many people come to the threshold of the transegoic stage, and some begin the process of reconstitution and regeneration that spiritual awakening initiates. But for whatever reason, few people are awakened soon enough or with sufficient power to get very far beyond the stage of the mental ego.

As this brief sketch indicates, the triphasic division of human development is a markedly disproportionate one. The first stage is short; it is soon over and forgotten. And the third stage is rare; it is only infrequently commenced, and even more infrequently completed. In contrast to these two stages, the second, egoic, stage lasts for most people very nearly the whole of their lifetimes. Given this disproportion, it is understandable that the triphasic conception should not have stood out as the most evident way of dividing human development.

Finally, the perspective of this book is dialectical in that movement through the three stages of life is seen as observing a pattern not of straightforward ascent to higher levels, but rather of negation, return, and higher integration. Specifically, development is seen as involving a *negation* in the form of a repressive submergence of the Dynamic Ground perpetrated by the very young ego—which negation brings the pre-egoic stage to an end and commences the egoic stage. Second, development is seen as involving a *return* in the form of a regressive reconnection of the (now mature) ego with the Dynamic Ground—which return, passing beyond the egoic stage, leads the ego through such transitional experiences as conversion, descent into the underworld, and the dark night of the soul. And third, development is seen as involving a *higher integration* in the form of a transcending synthesis of the ego with the Dynamic Ground—which integration proceeds through a period of spiritual regeneration and culminates in full transegoic realization. According to the dialectical view to be presented here, then, triphasic development is not a unidirectional ascending process; it is rather a dialectical interplay between the ego and the Dynamic Ground.

As parts of a dialectical process, the three stages of the triphasic framework are related in a way that is expressed in the formula *thesis-antithesis-synthesis*.[6] Accordingly, the pre-egoic stage sets forth the basic potentials of life (thesis). The egoic stage, in order to allow for the unhindered development of egoic structures and functions, then negates many of the potentials developed in the pre-egoic stage (antithesis). Finally, the transegoic stage, in order to surmount the limitations of the egoic stage, then restores the lost potentials of the pre-egoic stage and integrates them with the structures and functions developed in the egoic stage (synthesis).

These dialectical countermovements can be stated in the following more precise manner: (1) The body-ego gives initial, and very rudimentary, expression to both the nonegoic (e.g., somatic, instinctual, dynamic, numinous, creative) and egoic (e.g., organizing, controlling) dimensions of life (thesis). (2) The mental ego, in order to master rational thought and civilized behavior, then represses many nonegoic potentials, submerging them into unconsciousness (antithesis). Finally, (3) the integrated self, in order to surmount the one-sidedly abstract forms and repressive controls of the mental ego, then resurrects buried nonegoic potentials and allows these potentials to fuse with the mature structures and functions of the egoic sphere, thereby bringing into being an integrated whole that is greater than the sum of its egoic and nonegoic parts (synthesis). This synthesis is a wedding of opposites in which nonegoic potentials acquire the rational and practical discipline of egoic life and in which the ego is reunited with the substance, eros, vision, and spirit of nonegoic life. However, as a wedding of opposites, this synthesis is not a union of equals; rather, the ego, in submitting to nonegoic life, is rerooted in the Ground and becomes a servant of spirit.

This statement of the triphasic dialectic is extremely abstract and condensed. Nevertheless, it should suffice as a preliminary indication of the basic perspective to be followed in this book. The triphasic dialectic is treated more fully in Chapter 1.

In approaching transpersonal theory from a dynamic and dialectical perspective, this book to a large extent follows in the footseps of Jung. For example, following Jung, human development is explained as involving a rise, fall, and higher rebirth of the ego. Also following Jung, the ego's fall and higher rebirth are explained as involving a redemptive return to origins, and specifically a return to dynamic and creative potentials that function as both the alpha and omega of life. However, if Jung is followed in these fundamental regards, he is not followed in many of the specifics of his transpersonal theory. I have borrowed extensively from Jung, as I have as well from Freud and from other representatives of psychodynamic thought. However, in drawing heavily on thinkers such as these, I have not adhered closely to any of them, but rather have gone my own way.

In light of the debts just mentioned, the transpersonal theory presented in this book can be classified as falling within the classical psychodynamic, depth-psychological tradition. In dealing primarily with the dynamic depths and possible spiritual heights of life, the theory presented here is most closely tied with early psychoanalytic thought and its Jungian revision. Consequently, the concerns of this book are significantly different from those of contemporary psychoanalytic schools, which downplay intrapsychic dynamics and stress either autonomous ego functions (psychoanalytic ego psychology) or interpersonal and social factors (object-relations theory). Now, while I fully affirm the importance of the ego-psychological and object-relations perspectives, I do not myself emphasize these perspectives. Thus, although I make good use of a number of postclassical psychoanalytic sources (especially Heinz Hartmann, Erik Erikson, and Margaret Mahler), my chief sources remain Freud and Jung, the two great theorists of the dynamic unconscious.

A note should be added here on my use of religious sources, since I have exercised selectivity with them as well. I have not been selective in any doctrinal or cultural (e.g., Eastern versus Western) sense—or at least I have tried very hard to avoid such leanings. But I have been selective in utilizing primarily sources that treat of religious *experience*, and in particular of spiritual development and spiritual dynamics (e.g., ascetical and mystical theology, classical and tantric yoga, alchemy). Just as my chief debt in the field of psychology is to classical psychodynamic sources, so my chief debt in the field of religion is to traditional psychospiritual sources. In general, it is upon dynamically oriented sources in both psychology and religion that I have chiefly relied.

A final caveat: There is a good deal of (disciplined) speculation in this book, especially in the last few chapters, which explore the farther frontiers of transpersonal development. I hope the reader will be tolerant of this. I have tried, to the best of my knowledge, to ground speculation in the literatures of the several disciplines that enter into transpersonal theory. But still, the book is not an intellectual reconstruction of scholarly materials. It is rather an attempt to give rigorous articulation to an intuition.

CHAPTER 1

Transpersonal Theory: Two Basic Paradigms

THIS CHAPTER WILL DISCUSS two basic and competing paradigms within transpersonal theory. The essential contours of these paradigms will be set forth, and then the paradigms will be contrasted on key issues so that the stakes involved in choosing between them can be clearly understood.

The two paradigms in question are the psychodynamic or, more precisely, the *dynamic-dialectical* paradigm and the *structural-hierarchical* paradigm. The former of these two paradigms was introduced in a preliminary way in the Introduction. It is the paradigm upon which the ideas of this book are based. The discussion of the dynamic-dialectical paradigm that follows in this chapter can therefore serve as a condensed preview of the perspective to be developed in later chapters. Accordingly, it should be understood that the ensuing formulation of this paradigm is my own and is not intended to be an exposition of any other, already existing formulation (e.g., Jung's).

The version of the structural-hierarchical paradigm to be presented here, on the other hand, is closely geared to an already existing formulation, namely, that of Ken Wilber.[1] Wilber is presently the leading figure in the transpersonal field, and justifiably so, since his contributions are exceptional in both range and originality. Wilber's work is distinctive in its coherent integration of highly diverse psychological and religious materials within a single theoretical framework: the structural-hierarchical paradigm. This paradigm is one that, in its basic conception, combines structurally oriented psychology (in particular of the Piagetian, cognitive-developmental type) and hierarchically oriented metaphysics (especially in Indian—e.g., Buddhist and Vedanta—variations). This combination is in itself a powerful one, and Wilber presents it in a particularly lucid and forceful way.

Both the dynamic-dialectical and the structural-hierarchical paradigms divide human development along triphasic (pre-egoic, egoic, and transegoic) lines. However, in doing so, they have very different conceptions of the

9

psychic constitution that underlies the stages of the triphasic sequence. Consequently, they also have very different conceptions of how these stages are related to each other.

The dynamic-dialectical paradigm is based on a bipolar conception of the psyche, and it sees triphasic development as proceeding by way of a dialectical interplay between the two psychic poles. First one pole is dominant (thesis), then the other (antithesis), and then there occurs a higher integration of the two poles, a higher conjunction of opposites (synthesis). According to the bipolar conception, the ego is the seat of one of the two psychic poles, the Dynamic Ground the seat of the other. The dialectical interplay governing triphasic development is thus most fundamentally an interplay between the ego and the Dynamic Ground. The interplay is one according to which: (1) the ego first emerges from the Ground and is still under the dominating influence of the power of the Ground (the pre-egoic or body-egoic stage); (2) the ego differentiates itself from the Ground and develops the structures and functions of the egoic pole, but only by dissociating itself from the Ground (the egoic or mental-egoic stage); and (3) the ego undergoes a regressive return to the Ground followed by a higher synthesis with the Ground, which synthesis is at the same time a transcending integration of the two corresponding poles of the psyche along with their collective potentials, structures, and functions (transegoic stage).

The structural-hierarchical paradigm, in contrast, is based on a multi-leveled structural conception of the psyche, and it sees triphasic development as proceeding by way of a tier-by-tier movement through the ascending structural levels. First the structures of the lowest level are developed. Then the structures of the next higher level are developed, incorporating and reorganizing within themselves the structures of the preceding level. Then the structures of the next higher level are developed, incorporating and reorganizing within themselves the structures of the preceding two levels. And so the process unfolds, level by level, each level at once developing its own structures and incorporating and reorganizing within itself the structures of the preceding levels. Development proceeds in this fashion in principle until the structures of the highest level have been developed and, thereby, complete psychic differentiation and integration have been accomplished. According to Wilber, there are many different psychic levels and stages—ten or eleven, depending on how they are counted (see Tables 1-4 and 1-5, below). The triphasic division is therefore only a very broad one, as each of its stages really spans several sublevels and substages.

Both of the transpersonal paradigms here under consideration divide development along broad triphasic lines while at the same time diverging considerably in their interpretations of what triphasic development is really about. The dynamic-dialectical paradigm interprets triphasic development as a negation-and-higher-return countermovement between two psychic poles; the structural-hierarchical paradigm interprets it as a stepwise climb through ascending psychic levels.

THE DYNAMIC-DIALECTICAL PARADIGM

In presenting the dynamic-dialectical paradigm, the order of discussion will be: (1) the bipolar constitution of the psyche, (2) the dialectical interplay between the two psychic poles, and (3) unfolding selfhood according to the bipolar and dialectical perspectives.

1. The bipolar constitution of the psyche. Table 1-1 sets forth the bipolar conception of the psyche. This conception, as the term itself implies, divides the psyche into two opposite poles, namely, the nonegoic and egoic poles or, more fully, the physico-dynamic and mental-egoic poles. As indicated in Table 1-1, the nonegoic pole is the source of all dynamic, biophysical, instinctual, and affective potentials, and it is the point of origin of creatively spawned images and symbolic meanings as well. In contrast, the egoic pole is the center of operational cognition and rational volition. The egoic pole is the part of the psyche that is responsible for forging concepts, performing analyses and inferences, formulating and executing decisions, and, in general, operating in a logical, discursive, deliberate, linear, and durational manner. In sum, the nonegoic or physico-dynamic pole of the psyche is the seat of dynamism,

Table 1-1

THE BIPOLAR CONSTITUTION OF THE PSYCHE

Nonegoic or Physico-Dynamic Pole	Egoic or Mental-Egoic Pole
1. Dynamic Ground: energy, libido, spirit	1. Ego: individuated selfhood
2. Sensuous bodily life	2. Inner, reflexive mental life
3. Instincts	3. Cultivated personality
4. Spontaneous feelings	4. Self-control, deliberate will
5. Imaginal, autosymbolic cognition	5. Abstract, operational cognition
6. Nontemporal experience	6. Temporal, durational experience

bodily substance, feeling, and creative vision, and the egoic or mental-egoic pole is the seat of rational, organizing and controlling functions. The bipolar structure, then, encompasses many of the basic dualities of life: body and mind, heart and head, passion and will, vision and logic, dynamism and form.[2]

In classical psychodynamic theory the bipolar structure is implicit in Freud's so-called structural (id/ego/superego) model of the psyche.[3] Freud's structural model—which is not to be confused with the structural-hierarchical paradigm—is in many respects congruent with the bipolar conception just set forth. But there are at least two apparent discrepancies. One is that the structural model seems quite evidently to divide the psyche into three, rather than two, basic constitutional components. This discrepancy is, however, only a surface difficulty, since one of the three parts of the structural model, the superego, does not constitute a psychic sphere or region unto itself but is rather a structure that exists within the larger egoic sphere. The superego, Freud maintains (1923), exists on the ego side of the id/ego duality. Moreover, the superego is more a developmental than a constitutional structure; it is the "heir to the Oedipus complex." The superego is not part of the original equipment of the psyche in the sense of being a genetically inherited structure needing only the proper developmental moment to unfold into actuality. Although there may be inherited predispositions leading in the direction of superego formation (Hartmann and Loewenstein 1962), the superego itself, as a psychic structure, is not inherited. It is rather something that is constructed out of adventitious elements, which are introjected at the time of the resolution of the Oedipus complex. The superego is created when the child, in order to resolve the Oedipal conflict, identifies with parental authority, and with the social prohibitions, norms, and values that the parental figures represent. The superego is thus a locus of developmental identifications or introjects, not an inherent fixture of the psyche. Therefore, if Freud's structural model is to be reformulated to include only basic constitutional elements, the superego can and should be deleted from it. And if the superego is deleted, then the structural model, as an id/ego duality, is indeed a type of bipolar structure.[4]

Reformulated in this fashion, the id can of course be said to correspond to the nonegoic pole of the bipolar structure. For like the nonegoic pole (as described in Table 1-1), the id is the seat of dynamic, biophysical, and instinctual potentials: it is a field of somatically generated libido. The id is also the point of origin of affective upwellings (governed by the pleasure principle) and of autogenerated images (which are the medium of the primary process). Moreover, the id represents the nonegoic pole in being a source or region of timeless experience: the id knows nothing of reality or duration.

As the id corresponds in these ways to the nonegoic pole of the bipolar structure, so the ego as conceived by Freud corresponds to the egoic pole. Like the egoic pole, the ego of Freud's structural model is an individuated subject with an inner, reflexive mental life (accessed via introspection and free association); it is the seat of cultivated personality (as judged by the superego);it is the agency of self-control and rational will (as governed by the reality principle); and it is the executor of abstract operational cognition (the secondary process). Moreover, the ego of the structural model, like the egoic pole, is bound by time, since, in confronting reality and exercising rational will, the ego is forced to postpone gratification and to deliberate about future possibilities.

Freud's structural model, pared down to an id/ego duality, is congruent with the bipolar structure in all these ways. But there is still one major difference, which is the second discrepancy aforementioned, and that is that the id is a one-sidedly pre-egoic, or subegoic, interpretation of the bipolar structure's nonegoic pole. Table 1-1 describes the nonegoic pole in neutral terms, leaving it unspecified whether that pole is to be interpreted in a lower or higher, primitive or ego-transcending manner. Freud, however, is emphatic in describing the id as something exclusively lower and primitive. The id is inherently unconscious; its dynamism consists solely of sexual or aggressive energies; its affective movements are basically instinctual impulses; and its primary process is a creative but crude mode of cognition. Freud, then, in effect reduces the nonegoic pole to the pre-egoic level, which means that Freud's id/ego duality can more accurately be said to be a pre-egoic/egoic than a nonegoic/egoic bipolar structure.

In Jung's theory, the bipolar structure is reflected in the fundamental distinction between the collective unconscious or objective psyche on the one hand and the ego and consciousness on the other.[5] The collective unconscious of course corresponds to the nonegoic pole of the bipolar structure, since, like the nonegoic pole, the collective unconscious is the source of psychic energy, the basis of instinctual life, the procreator of emotions, and the spawner of timeless archetypal images. In turn, the ego as conceived by Jung corresponds to the egoic pole of the bipolar structure, since, like the egoic pole, the Jungian ego is the agency that monitors and makes adjustments to the environment and the subject that bears the socially tailored personality (the *persona*).

The Jungian collective unconscious is a truer rendering of the bipolar structure's nonegoic pole than is the Freudian id, because the collective unconscious is by no means merely pre-egoic in nature. The collective unconscious is not only a sphere of energy and instinct; it also is the source from which spring higher symbolic meanings and spiritual possibilities. Nevertheless, although Jung's conception of the nonegoic pole is not reductionistically one-sided in the manner of Freud's, it still differs from the formulation presented in Table 1-1. For if Jung does not reduce everything nonegoic to a merely pre-egoic level, he does tend (rather confusedly) to describe nonegoic potentials in ways that make them simultaneously pre-egoic and transegoic, e.g., at once instinctual and spiritual, subhuman and transhuman. That is, he tends to attribute both "pre-" and "trans-" aspects to the collective unconscious without clearly distinguishing which is which, or without clearly specifying whether these aspects are to be understood in constitutional or merely developmental senses. Properly conceived, I believe, the nonegoic pole of the psyche is a constitutional structure which, as such, is to be distinguished from both its pre-egoic and transegoic expressions, which themselves are to be understood developmentally rather than constitutionally. Jung, however, makes no such distinctions, and therefore his notion of the collective unconscious, although not as one-sided as Freud's notion of the id, still falls short of being a fully adequate conception of the nonegoic pole. The Jungian notion of the collective unconscious is, in my opinion, plagued by a number of developmental misreadings of constitutional matters.

A psychic duality that should be distinguished from the bipolar structure is a duality that Deikman (1971) has designated the *bimodal* structure of consciousness. The distinction upon which the bimodal duality is based is that between engaged activity and open receptivity. Accordingly, the two modes of the bimodal structure can aptly be called the active and receptive modes of consciousness. Some important features of the bimodal structure are listed in Table 1-2.

Table 1-2

THE BIMODAL STRUCTURE

Receptive Mode	Active Mode
1. Receptive openness	1. Active control
2. Subjectless absorption	2. Detached subjecthood
3. Intuitive	3. Operational
4. Impassioned or infused surrender	4. Dispassionate reserve

The dynamic-dialectical paradigm assigns the bimodal structure to the egoic side of the bipolar division: it is the ego or egoic pole that has two basic modes, active and receptive. It is the ego that is either engaged and in command of operational functions (active mode) or that is disengaged and thereby open to nonegoic influences (receptive mode). It is the ego that is either in control or surrendered, detached or immersed, self-contained or open, active or receptive.

14

The dynamic-dialectical paradigm not only assigns the bimodal structure to the egoic pole; it also explains the existence of the bimodal structure in terms of the ego's distinctive status as a side of a bipole. This explanation is advanced because, assuming that the ego possesses such a status, it follows that the ego is something that is at once individuated *and* ontologically dependent. That is, it follows that the ego is a distinct existent but not a self-subsistent one—a semi-entity rather than a true substance (e.g., a Cartesian "thinking thing"). And it follows from this in turn that the ego has two different stances that it can adopt: it can either assert itself in its status as an individuated existent or surrender itself in its status as a dependent one. In doing the former, the ego exercises its distinctively egoic operations in relative independence from nonegoic influences. In doing the latter, the ego lets go of its operational controls and opens itself to the play of nonegoic forces. Or in bimodal terms, in doing the former, the ego functions in the active mode; in doing the latter, it "switches off" the active mode and enters the receptive mode.[6]

To summarize, the dynamic-dialectical paradigm interprets the bimodal structure as an egoic structure deriving from the ego's status as a side of a bipolar psyche.[7] So interpreted, the active mode of the bimodal structure is the mode in which the ego exercises the cognitive and practical functions that reside in its own pole. The active mode is the mode in which the ego asserts its operational autonomy within the limits of its semi-independence. The receptive mode, in contrast, is the mode in which the ego opens itself to influences deriving from sources beyond its own pole, and in particular to influences deriving from the nonegoic pole of the psyche. According to Table 1-1, the ego, in doing this, can be affected in a variety of ways. For example, the ego might be (1) entranced, absorbed, dissolved, infused, ecstatically inflated, or inspired by the power of the Dynamic Ground; (2) brought under the sway of instinctual complexes; (3) made witness to images generated by the autosymbolic process; or (4) moved, if not overswept, by feelings. In the dynamic-dialectical conception, the ego, in entering the receptive mode, yields itself to the diverse potentials of the nonegoic pole of the psyche, and is affected accordingly.

2. The dialectical interplay between the two psychic poles. The dynamic-dialectical paradigm holds that triphasic development is governed by a dialectical interplay between the two poles of the bipolar structure. This bipolar dialectic is schematized in Figure 1-1.

According to the bipolar dialectic, life begins with only one active pole. The nonegoic pole of the psyche alone is active at the very outset of development (the neonatal period); the egoic pole is at first dormant and undifferentiated. The dynamic-dialectical paradigm, in agreement with psychodynamic thought generally, takes the position that the beginning weeks of

15

life are a time during which the ego is still latent, and, therefore, during which experience is of a purely nonegoic character: an undifferentiated dynamic matrix. This original condition will hereafter be referred to as *original embedment.*

Figure 1-1 indicates that, soon after original embedment, the egoic pole of the psyche is activated and begins to differentiate itself, with the result that both poles are soon involved in the developmental process, and remain involved thereafter. However, if both poles participate throughout virtually the whole of the developmental process, they do not always do so in a balanced or harmonious way. On the contrary, the dynamic-dialectical view is that the two poles are never in a state of parity or equipollence. Specifically, the pre-egoic stage is a period during which the physico-dynamic potentials of the nonegoic pole dominate a weak and undeveloped egoic pole. The egoic stage, in turn, is a period during which the nonegoic dominance of the pre-egoic period is reversed. The egoic pole frees itself from the domination of the nonegoic pole, but it accomplishes this only by alienating the nonegoic pole and banishing its potentials from consciousness. The egoic stage is for this reason one of ego dominance, a period that is unbalanced in the favor of the ego. The egoic pole is developed and operates in apparent independence of the nonegoic pole, which is covered over and submerged. Finally, the transegoic stage is a period during which the dominance of the egoic pole is itself overturned. The egoic pole loses its ascendancy and, at last, is brought into a state of harmonious integration with the nonegoic pole.

Even this harmonious unity of integration, however, is not a balanced unity in the sense of a unity of equals. For the dynamic-dialectical paradigm stipulates that the two psychic poles are inherently of unequal status: the non-egoic pole is the superior of the two. The nonegoic pole is basic and prior not only developmentally and in the order of time but also intrinsically and in the order of right. Consequently, the transegoic stage is a stage in which the nonegoic pole, without being dominant, is nonetheless sovereign and in which the (now mature) egoic pole, without being subjugated, is nonetheless subject. The transegoic stage is one in which the ego is rooted in the Ground, such that the power of the Ground rightfully rules over the ego and the ego faithfully serves the power of the Ground.

Given the dialectical view that the stages of triphasic development embody reversals in polar ascendancy, it follows that the transitions between the triphasic stages are the temporal intervals during which these reversals occur. For the bipolar dialectic, then, the transition from the pre-egoic to the egoic stage is the interval during which the original dominance of the nonegoic pole is brought to an end and the dominance of the egoic pole begins. In turn, the transition from the egoic stage to the transegoic stage is the interval during which the dominance of the egoic pole is brought to an end and the true

Figure 1-1

TRIPHASIC DEVELOPMENT: THE BIPOLAR VIEW

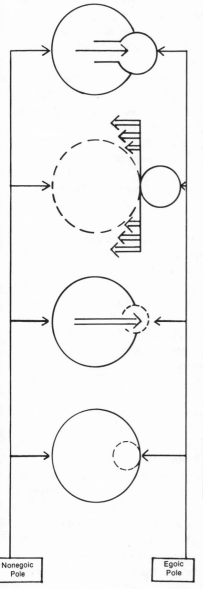

Transegoic Stage: Integration. Egoic pole, rerooted in nonegoic pole, is instrument of Dynamic Ground. The power of the Ground (as spirit) is sovereign, the ego subject.

———→ = sovereignty of nonegoic pole.

Egoic Stage: Ego establishes independence from nonegoic pole, but only by dissociating itself from the nonegoic pole by means of *original repression.* The nonegoic pole is arrested and submerged, becoming the dynamic unconscious, and the ego assumes airs of a Cartesian self: an immaterial thinking thing,

·············· = nonegoic pole submerged and unconscious; ═══⟹ = original repression.

Pre-Egoic Stage: Egoic pole begins differentiating itself from nonegoic pole. But egoic pole is weak and undeveloped, and is therefore dominated by physico-dynamic potentials.

·············· = egoic pole weak and undeveloped; ═══⟹ = dominance of nonegoic pole.

Neonatal State: Egoic pole is not yet differentiated from nonegoic pole. Ego exists only preactively, as a psychic potential within an undifferentiated dynamic matrix: *original embedment.*

·············· = egoic pole not yet differentiated from nonegoic pole.

Nonegoic Pole

Egoic Pole

sovereignty of the nonegoic pole, and of the Dynamic Ground in particular, is inaugurated.

To repeat, the shift from nonegoic to egoic dominance occurring at the transition to the egoic stage is said to be due to alienation or dissociation: the very young ego divorces itself from the potentials of nonegoic life. This psychic split has been treated in different ways in the major psychodynamic theories. For example, in classical psychoanalysis the split is said to be primarily a result of primal repression, which is a response of the very young ego to the traumatic anxiety caused by excessive libidinal excitation and instinctual demand.[8] Owing both to its undeveloped state and to its proximity to the id, the fledgling ego is frequently overwhelmed by impulses arising from the id. The immature ego is helpless to deal with these impulses in any way other than to perpetrate a massive repression. This repression blocks impulses originating from the id and, once solidified, serves as a permanent buffer that insulates the ego from the id. Freud states that this initial repressive reaction by the ego likely occurs even before the resolution of the Oedipus complex (1926, 94). The termination of the Oedipal predicament, however, which carries with it the introduction of the superego, is held to reinforce the id/ego disjunction initiated by primal repression.

Jung, whose focus was more on the second than the first half of life, dispensed with the notion of primal or early childhood repression. Nevertheless, it is part of the general Jungian perspective (especially as articulated by Erich Neumann 1954, 1973) that there occurs at a very early age, if not a repression, at least a decisive turning away of the ego from its dynamic-archetypal origins. This forsaking of origins is usually explained in terms of a conflict between the young ego and the interpersonal and intrapsychic forces constellated under the archetype of the Great Mother—in her "Terrible Mother" guise. Following this initial departure of the ego from nonegoic sources, there is said to occur, progressively throughout the first half of life, a further distancing of the ego from these sources, which together make up the collective unconscious.

Departing from Jung, the position that I defend in this book is that the act by which the young ego separates itself from the nonegoic pole is definitely of a repressive character. Accordingly, I introduce the notion of *original repression*, which is similar in many respects to Freud's concept of primal repression. Freud is here followed in the view that the young child is forced to commit an act of repression, an act which is the most fundamental and serious act of its kind, on which all subsequent repressions are based. But if Freud is followed to this extent, Jung is followed as well, since many Jungian ideas are utilized in explaining the *causes* of this first repressive act. Specifically, I argue that the immature ego of the pre-egoic stage is so under the sway of nonegoic potentials, which are perceived as dimensions of the archetypal maternal power, that the ego eventually has little choice but to lay down a repressive barrier to shield itself from the nonegoic pole. This repressive barrier protects the vulnerable ego and wins for it a significant degree of independence, allowing the ego thereby to develop its own distinctive functions in a relatively free and unimpeded manner. This, in the dynamic-dialectical conception, is the positive side of the transition to the egoic stage, the side by virtue of which the transition counts as a real developmental advance.

But the negative side of the transition is that nonegoic potentials are forsaken. They are disconnected from consciousness, which means not only that they are prohibited further expression but also, therefore, that they are arrested at the pre-egoic level of development. It is the dynamic-dialectical view, then, that the movement to the egoic stage, although a real developmental advance, is nonetheless an advance paid for by an alienation and developmental retardation of nonegoic life, which is submerged and becomes the *dynamic unconscious.*[9]

Most psychodynamic theories hold that this state of egoic dominance and nonegoic submergence continues for the majority of people throughout most of the rest of their lives. In Freud's thinking, of course, this state of affairs is considered an irreversible psychic structure. In Jung's view, on the other hand—and in any psychodynamic theory of a transpersonal orientation—it is thought that this unbalanced and estranged relation between the two psychic poles in some cases begins to reverse itself, typically in the second half of life. Jung believed that this reversal is part of the natural oscillation of life, the first half of which is devoted to ego development and the second half of which is devoted to a return of the ego to its underlying psychic sources: nonegoic dynamisms and archetypes. In contrast to Jung's view, the position that I propose is that the reversal away from egoic dominance is due primarily to a loosening or lifting. of original repression. I argue that in some cases original repression eventually gives way, gradually or suddenly, and consequently the ego is divested of its shielding from the nonegoic pole and is brought back into contact with nonegoic potentials. The repressive infrastructure of the mental-egoic system is dismantled and the mental ego is forced to submit to a reversion, indeed a regression, to the Dynamic Ground. The mental ego loses its protective undergirding and is drawn into the stormy underworld of the dynamic unconscious.

It is distinctive of the dynamic-dialectical perspective that the ego's return to nonegoic sources is considered not only a radical, and sometimes pathological, reversion but also, potentially, a redemptive process. Specifically, this return is seen as the first segment of a psychic metamorphosis that, in reuniting egoic and nonegoic poles, leads potentially to a creative synthesis of the structures and potentials of these two poles.[10] That is, it is seen as the first phase of a two-phase, return-then-higher-synthesis process. Jung recognized this phase of development, which, following Frobenius (1904), he referred to as the night sea journey, the period during which the sun god (ego) descends into the sea and is devoured by a water monster, a whale-dragon, only later to be reborn for the dawn of a new day. In Jung's interpretation of the night sea journey, the sun's descent beneath the sea is the ego's descent into the collective unconscious, wherein the ego is engulfed, only later to be reborn on a higher level (Jung 1912/1952/1967). In other mythic or symbolic expressions, this regressive return is depicted as an odyssey of a hero into the underworld, as a journey of a saint into the bowels of hell, and as an alchemical reduction of base metal to prime matter. In the words of St. John of the Cross, it is the dark night of the soul. In this book, the mental ego's regression into the nonegoic sphere will be called *regression in the service of transcendence*.

Once the ego has been returned to the Ground, the second, redemptive phase of the return-then-higher-synthesis process begins. This is the turning point at which, according to the dynamic-dialectical paradigm, descent gives way to ascent, darkness to light, regression to regeneration. Having survived the violent encounter with nonegoic potentials and having made peace with them, the ego here begins to be affected more and more positively by nonegoic potentials. The storm and stress experienced during regression to the Ground abate, and the ego, reconnected with the Ground, begins to be infused and transfigured by the power of the Ground. In general, the completion of regression in the service of transcendence is the turning point at which, it is held, nonegoic potentials cease assailing egoic structures and faculties and begin combining creatively with them instead. This higher rebirth of the ego has been described in many ways—for example, as the liberation and ascent of the sun god from the belly of the sea monster, as the triumphant return of the hero or saint from infernal regions, and as the alchemical transubstantiation of base metal into gold. In this book, the higher rebirth of the ego will be called *regeneration in spirit*.

The higher synthesis of opposites aimed at by the regenerative process (viz., the state of transegoic integration) is conceived as a condition of fully actualized and unified bipolarity. This is a condition in which the two poles of the psyche are finally fused into a true two-in-one, and all of their opposing potentials, structures, and faculties are fused as well and begin functioning harmoniously and on a higher plane. It is a union of opposing psychic poles that is greater than the sum of its parts, a *coincidentia oppositorum* that surpasses all of the elements that enter into it. However, the stipulation needs to be added that, as a higher unity of opposites, such a bipolar integration is not a unity of equals. For, again, it is the dynamic-dialectical view that the nonegoic pole of the psyche is the basic pole, and, in particular, that the power of the Dynamic Ground (as spirit) is the sovereign power of the psyche. The egoic pole, then, in being wedded to the nonegoic pole, at the same time accedes to the authority of the nonegoic pole. The ego, in being rerooted in the Ground, at the same time surrenders itself to spirit.

3. *Unfolding selfhood according to the dynamic-dialectical paradigm.* The bipolar dialectic is at the same time a dialectic of unfolding selfhood. This is so because both psychic poles are held to have a share in selfhood, the nonegoic pole being the ultimate and higher self, the egoic pole being the subordinate and lesser self. The unfolding relationship between these polar selves is schematized in Figure 1-2.

As we know, the bipolar dialectic begins with original embedment, which is a preindividuated state in which the egoic pole of the psyche is not yet active. The ego is at first undifferentiatedly at one with the Ground, which is the aboriginal source of life, prior to all selfhood. This initial unity, however, is short-lived, as the egoic pole soon becomes active and begins to exert itself, dividing the oneness of original embedment into a primitive and lopsided duality: a Ground-dominant bipole. Correspondingly, since both psychic poles are thought to have a share in selfhood, the breakup of original embedment results as well in a primitive and lopsided duality of selfhood: a Ground-dominant dyadic self. The unbalanced bipolarity of the pre-egoic period is at the same time an unbalanced bipolarity of selfhood. The ego is at this point only beginning to emerge as an individuated subject or self, which in bipolar terms means that it is still to a large extent enfolded in the Dynamic Ground. The Ground remains the principal reality of the ego's life, not only as the aboriginal source from which the ego sprang but also, now, as the primordial Self out of which the ego grows and to which the ego, dissolubly, frequently returns. This continuing dominance of the Ground as primordial Self is, in the dynamic-dialectical view, one of the reasons why the ego only slowly achieves a sense of its own self-boundaries, namely, as a bodily self or body-ego.

The dominance of the Ground comes to an end only when the ego finally perpetrates the act of original repression and thereby divorces itself from its nonegoic origins. In making the transition to the egoic stage, the ego asserts its independence, but only by dissociating itself from the nonegoic pole, which is arrested at the "pre-" level and submerged beneath consciousness, becoming the id or not-self. According to the dynamic-dialectical paradigm, then, the ego becomes an individuated self only by assuming the posture of an exclusive self. The ego alienates the primordial Self and takes on airs of being the sole, and hence supreme, self of the psyche. The egoic, or mental-egoic, stage of development is therefore a period during which the ego fancies itself to be the exclusive owner and controller of psychic life. It is a period during which there is an appearance of a completely independent and autonomous self: the mental ego or Cartesian self, a "thinking thing" (*res cogitans*).

But the emphasis needs to be put on the *apparentness* of this independence

21

Figure 1-2

UNFOLDING SELFHOOD ACCORDING TO THE
DYNAMIC-DIALECTICAL PARADIGM

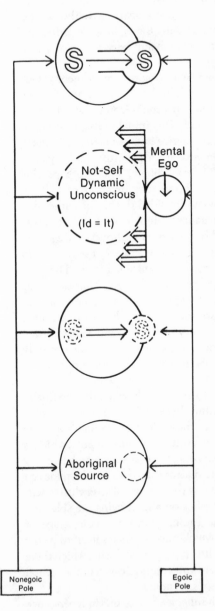

The Ego Subject and Sovereign Spirit: The ego, rooted in and aligned with the Ground, is the loyal subject of spirit, which is sovereign.

S, s = the poles of fully developed selfhood; ——> = sovereignty of spirit.

The Mental Ego and the Not-Self: The two poles of the psyche are disconnected. The egoic pole, as mental ego, takes itself to be an exclusive self, the sole owner and controller of psychic life: the Cartesian immaterial self. The nonegoic pole is alienated from consciousness and demoted to not-self: the id, the nonegoic pole in arrested, "pre-" form.

·············· = nonegoic pole submerged and unconscious; ====> = original repression.

The Body-Ego and the Primordial Self: The egoic pole begins to differentiate itself from the Dynamic Ground and, identified with the body, is a bodily self or body-ego. The body-ego is not a well-defined or complete self. It is rather one side of a Ground-dominant dyad. The Ground, as the other side of the dyad, also participates in selfhood, namely, as the underlying primordial Self.

🌑 , 🌑 = poles of emerging but incomplete selfhood; ====> = dominance of nonegoic pole as primordial Self.

The Aboriginal Source: Prior to the activation of the egoic pole, the Dynamic Ground is the aboriginal source from which selfhood emerges.

·············· = egoic pole not yet differentiated from nonegoic pole.

and autonomy, for, given that the mental ego is a pole of a bipole, it follows that the mental ego remains all the while internally related to its nonegoic counterpole, which is the mental ego's superior "other half." Hence, notwithstanding its airs of independence, the mental ego is inherently vulnerable to feeling unwhole, to feeling that it is somehow out of touch with a higher part of itself. The mental ego thus maintains the posture of exclusive selfhood while at the same time suffering from doubts that this posture may be only a false pose, a pose that hides a higher power and a truer self.

Although the mental ego's posture of self-sufficiency is plagued with uncertainties, it is not for that reason a stance that is quickly or easily relinquished. On the contrary, it is a posture that, in the dynamic-dialectical view, is very deeply entrenched and only rarely reversed. Reversals are, however, acknowledged. As noted above, these reversals are explained in terms of a loosening or lifting of original repression: original repression sometimes gives way, undermining the mental ego's standing in being and setting the mental ego on the course of regression in the service of transcendence. No longer supported by the false ground of original repression, the mental ego is exposed to the Dynamic Ground, which reclaims the mental ego and disabuses it of its pretensions of independence. The mental ego, facing this situation, has no choice but to confess the falseness of its posture of self-sufficiency and to submit to the conversion of faith. No longer undergirded by original repression, the mental ego loses its self-possession; it is drawn out of its own sphere and begins the odyssey of return to the Dynamic Ground, the power of which is the ego's higher self.

The ego's return to the Ground involves a regression: regression in the service of transcendence. It does so because original repression, in arresting nonegoic potentials at the "pre-" level, determines that any return to the nonegoic (including movement to the transegoic) must at first be a re-encounter with the pre-egoic. The lifting of original repression therefore re-exposes the ego not just to previously submerged nonegoic potentials, but to *retarded* (i.e., primitive and primarily instinctual) nonegoic potentials. These potentials, loosed from the bonds of original repression, recoil upon their repressor in dark and menacing fashion. This is the fury of the return of the repressed. In particular, the power of the Ground, in being derepressed, asserts itself against the ego, challenging the (mental) ego's claim on psychic supremacy. From the dynamic-dialectical perspective, then, the ego's return to the Ground involves a regression that brings the ego into conflict with what appear to be alien and hostile forces.

This conflict lasts until the power of the Ground (along with other nonegoic potentials) has fully asserted itself and the ego has finally overcome its resistance to the power of the Ground. Then the transition from regression to regeneration occurs: the power of the Ground gradually ceases manifesting

Table 1-3

THE DYNAMIC-DIALECTICAL PARADIGM
OF TRIPHASIC DEVELOPMENT

INTEGRATION	The two poles of the psyche, having been reunited and their resources fused into higher forms, are integrated as a true bipolar system, a true two-in-one or *coincidentia oppositorum*. The power of the Ground, as spirit, is sovereign; the ego is subject.
REGENERATION IN SPIRIT	The ego, having ceased its resistance to nonegoic potentials, is now enhanced rather than assailed by these potentials; it begins to be regenerated by the power of the Ground: spirit.
REGRESSION IN THE SERVICE OF TRANSCENDENCE	Original repression gives way and the ego is resubmitted to the nonegoic pole, to which it regresses. The ego is assailed by resurging nonegoic potentials in their arrested, "pre-" form.
EGOIC OR MENTAL-EGOIC STAGE	The ego develops its operational functions in relative independence from the nonegoic pole, which, repressed and submerged, underlies the ego as the dynamic unconscious. The nonegoic pole is the not-self or id; the egoic pole is the mental or Cartesian ego.
ORIGINAL REPRESSION	At this turning point, the ego wins its individuated selfhood but only by repressively dissociating itself from the nonegoic pole, the potentials of which are arrested at the pre-egoic level and submerged into unconsciousness.
PRE-EGOIC OR BODY-EGOIC STAGE	Pre-Oedipal childhood is a period during which the ego begins to be differentiated from the Great Mother but is still under the sway of nonegoic forces. The nonegoic pole is a primordial Self; the egoic pole is a body-ego.
ORIGINAL EMBEDMENT	The neonatal condition is a state prior to any differentiation of the egoic from the nonegoic pole, of the ego from the Dynamic Ground. The Dynamic Ground is here the aboriginal source prior to all selfhood.

itself as an alien force and begins manifesting itself, in its true nature, as a higher kindred spirit. It begins revealing itself as a force that is both superior and essential to the ego. The ego, having been regressed to the Ground, here begins to participate in a regenerative transformation that unites the ego with the Ground, and that in general integrates the egoic pole of the psyche with its nonegoic counterpole. This regenerative process leads ultimately to complete bipolar integration, to a union of egoic and nonegoic poles that is at the same time a wedding of ego (as lesser self) and spirit (as greater Self). Full self-realization conceived in dynamic-dialectical terms is thus a condition of perfected bipolarity: two psychic poles function as one and the two selves that correspond to these poles are joined as one. The ego, as subject, becomes the instrument of sovereign spirit.

Table 1-3 reviews the dynamic-dialectical conception of psychic development and the unfolding of selfhood.

THE STRUCTURAL-HIERARCHICAL PARADIGM

The structural-hierarchical paradigm differs from the dynamic-dialectical both in its conception of the psychic constitution and in its conception of how the stages of development are related to each other. Moreover, as a consequence of these differences, the structural-hierarchical paradigm has a very different conception of unfolding selfhood as well. The structural-hierarchical paradigm shares with the dynamic-dialectical paradigm the triphasic, transpersonal perspective. But beyond this it has little in common with the dynamic-dialectical view, as will become evident in what follows.

To repeat, the account of the structural-hierarchical paradigm to be presented here is based on the work of Ken Wilber. Wilber's first full-scale formulation of the structural-hierarchical paradigm was in *The Spectrum of Consciousness* (1977). Wilber has since reformulated the paradigm in a number of different places (Wilber 1980a, 1980b, 1981a, 1981b, 1983b; Wilber et al. 1986). The ensuing exposition draws on all of these sources, but especially on the statement of the paradigm in the collection of papers published under the title *Eye to Eye* (1983b).

1. The hierarchical constitution of the psyche. The structural-hierarchical paradigm conceives of the psyche as a hierarchy of structural levels, each higher level of which surpasses the ones below it in representing both greater psychic differentiation and greater psychic integration. Each higher level represents greater psychic differentiation in that, once a higher level emerges, it adds its own structures to the structures of the levels beneath it and therefore increases the overall psychic inventory or capacity. And each higher level represents greater psychic integration in that each such level has a significant

25

degree of access to and command over the structures of lower levels and therefore effectively integrates those structures within itself.

Wilber holds that each level of the psychic hierarchy is distinguished by a set of basic or defining structures (faculties, potentials, etc.). These basic structures, in being inherent to a level of the psychic hierarchy, are thereby inherent to the psyche itself. They are deep structures which are part of the psyche's original endowment and which, as such, are transcultural: universal to human experience. As deep structures, these basic structures are to be distinguished from surface structures, which are the merely contingent ways in which the psyche's basic structures happen to be expressed and applied in life. Whereas basic structures are the innate underlying patterns of life, surface structures are the particular social and thematic manifestations of those patterns. Unlike basic structures, which are original and universal, surface structures are derivative and variable, differing widely in cultural form and focus.

The most fundamental ways in which the levels of the psychic hierarchy are said to be interrelated are: (1) that lower levels support and subserve higher levels and (2) that higher levels subsume and control lower levels. Lower levels support and subserve higher levels in that the structures of lower levels are prerequisites of the structures of higher levels. Lower levels serve as the necessary foundations upon which higher levels are built. Lower levels, however, are not only prerequisites and foundations; they also are integral parts of higher levels. Higher levels subsume the structures of lower levels, utilizing them as elements of higher-level functions. In doing this, higher levels reorganize lower levels and exercise control over them. Lower levels retain a certain degree of autonomy, but to a significant degree their functioning is subject to the control of the higher level under which they are subsumed. This model is clearly organic and holistic. The levels of the structural-hierarchical paradigm are related in ways that are similar to the ways in which the levels of an organic hierarchy (e.g., cell, organ, organ system) are related.

Given that higher psychic levels incorporate lower levels, it follows that the highest active psychic level is in effect the whole of the psyche. That is, each level (except the lowest) is not only a single psychic layer but also a multilayered totality including within itself all lower levels. Thus the structural-hierarchical paradigm conceives of the psyche not just as a hierarchy, but more specifically as a hierarchy that is unified and organized in a top-down fashion. The psyche is a hierarchy the highest active level of which embraces and superintends the whole.

Table 1-4 schematizes Wilber's account of the principal psychic levels and their corresponding basic structures.[11]

Table 1-4 divides the psychic hierarchy into eleven different levels, which are themselves divided along triphasic lines into pre-egoic, egoic, and

Table 1-4

WILBER'S HIERARCHICAL PSYCHE

	PSYCHIC LEVEL	BASIC STRUCTURES
TRANSEGOIC LEVELS	——— ULTIMATE UNITY ———	Complete part-whole, individual-reality integration: unity of sacred and profane, *samsara* and *nirvana*.
	——— CAUSAL ———	Unitive consciousness; contemplation of unity of human and divine; radiant absorption in godhead.
	——— SUBTLE ———	Paranormal psychic abilities; archetypal, visionary intuition; spontaneous devotional and altruistic feelings.
EGOIC LEVELS	——— VISION-LOGIC ———	Holistic-synthetic thinking; mind-body, thought-feeling integration; existential wholeness and authenticity.
	——— REFLEXIVE/FORMAL MIND ———	Formal operational (Piaget) or secondary process (Freud) cognition: abstract, analytical (inferential, hypothetical, etc.) thinking. Self-consciousness combined with ability to assume perspective of other.
	——— RULE/ROLE MIND ———	Concrete operational thinking (Piaget); initial command of basic laws of the logic of classes and propositions. Ability to assume role but not perspective of other.
PRE-EGOIC LEVELS	REPRESENTATIONAL MIND ———	Highest level of preoperational thinking (Piaget); initial capability for language and concept formation.
	——— PHANTASMIC ———	Rudimentary imaginal cognition; the autosymbolic process.
	——— EMOTIONAL-SEXUAL ———	Basic organismic dynamism (bioenergy, libido, *prana*) and its basic instinctual modes of expression.
	——— SENSORIPERCEPTUAL ———	Simple sensorimotor skills (as described by Piaget).
	——— PHYSICAL ———	Basic physical substratum of organism.

transegoic groups. The rationale for the triphasic division is basically Piagetian: Wilber extends Piaget's distinction between preoperational and operational structures by adding a set of transoperational structures. Accordingly, the pre-egoic levels of the psychic hierarchy, up to and including the phantasmic level (representational mind is a transitional level), correspond to the preoperational rudiments of life: sensorimotor and phantasmic cognition, instinctually governed dynamism and affect. The egoic levels, in turn, up to and including reflexive/formal mind (vision-logic is a transitional level), correspond to the operational functions normally associated with the ego: conceptual and logical thinking, rule-governed and conscientious action. Finally, the transegoic levels, up to and including ultimate unity,[12] correspond to the transoperational possibilities of life: visionary and mystical cognition, devotional and altruistic feeling.

In summary, Wilber conceives of the psychic hierarchy as being at once complexly multitiered and yet fundamentally triphasic in its constitutional organization.

2. Development from lower to higher levels. It is part of the structural-hierarchical view that all of the levels of the psychic hierarchy are implicitly or potentially present at the outset of development. The explicit or actual emergence of the levels of the hierarchy, however, occurs only over time, starting with the lowest level and proceeding step by step to each higher level. The psychic hierarchy is therefore not only a constitutional framework but also a developmental itinerary. Wilber holds that typical human development proceeds through the initial parts of this itinerary up to the level of reflexive/formal mind, or in some cases to the level of vision-logic. However, Wilber holds that in exceptional cases human development, starting at the bottom or physical level, proceeds all the way to the highest transpersonal level, ultimate unity.

Since the structural-hierarchical paradigm stipulates that lower levels are prerequisites of higher levels, it also stipulates that there can be no skipping of steps as development proceeds upwardly through the psychic hierarchy. A higher level cannot be attained until the basic structures of the level below it have emerged and have been established. Or as Wilber states this point, there can be no *transformation* to a new level until the *translations* (i.e., the basic structural manipulations) of the immediately preceding level have been mastered. A developmental transformation occurring before such mastery would be dangerously premature. Lacking the requisite foundations, it would likely fail.

In addition to not skipping levels, normal structural-hierarchical development also does not abandon levels. Since, constitutionally considered, lower levels are functional components of higher levels, movement to higher levels must normally assimilate rather than alienate lower levels. This means that

28

developmental transformation or transcendence must normally be of an incorporative rather than dissociative sort. It would be an exception to the rule if some part of a lower level were alienated or repressed. Moreover, if and when such exceptions should occur, the higher level that would be attained would be only tenuously or faultily attained, since it would be missing an ingredient integral to its functioning.

Normal structural-hierarchical development, then, neither skips nor abandons psychic levels but rather preserves them in higher form within the most recent level to have emerged. This is simply a developmental corollary of the constitutional fact, mentioned a moment ago, that the psychic hierarchy is unified and organized in a top-down manner. Each succeeding stage of development integrates and restructures the already existing psychic totality on a new and superior plane, which plane therefore becomes the de facto, if not ultimate, seat of psychic operations.

The structural-hierarchical account of development closely mirrors the structural-hierarchical account of the psychic constitution. The former is simply the temporal, sequential unfolding of the latter. The succeeding stages of development correspond to the ascending levels of the psychic hierarchy, and the principal developmental relations that obtain between succeeding stages are corollaries of the constitutional connections that obtain between ascending levels.

3. Unfolding selfhood according to the structural-hierarchical paradigm. Just as each succeeding level is a new center of psychic operations, so, too, according to the structural-hierarchical paradigm, is it a new locus of selfhood. Selfhood is relative to psychic level; each psychic level, in being attained, reconstitutes the sense of self. Conceived in this fashion, the self is what Wilber (1981a, 1983b) calls a *transition* structure.

Transition structures are structures that come into existence when life is lived at a certain level of the psychic hierarchy, namely, whichever one, developmentally, happens to be the highest active level. Transition structures are not inherent to the psychic level to which they correspond, but rather result from seeing and acting upon the world through the basic structures of that level. Transition structures therefore exist only when their corresponding psychic level is the highest active level. Once this level is developmentally superseded, the transition structures that obtained during its ascendancy are dissolved and new transition structures, appropriate to living at the next higher level, come into being.

Transition structures are to be distinguished from both basic structures and surface structures. They differ from basic structures in being derivative rather than constitutional structures. Whereas basic structures are innate and hence present (in actual or potential, enfolded form) at the outset of development, transition structures do not exist in any sense until the psychic level with which they are associated emerges and becomes developmentally ascendant. And even then, transition structures come into existence only in a virtual, not a real, sense, namely, as "the ways things seem" when the world is engaged through the basic structures of the ascendant psychic level. Unlike basic structures, then, transition structures are developmental epiphenomena; they exist only derivatively, temporarily, and virtually.

Transition structures differ from surface structures in that, whereas surface structures are merely contingent, transition structures are necessary in the sense that they perforce obtain when their corresponding psychic level is the level at which life is lived. Transition structures, although merely derivative, are nonetheless developmentally unavoidable; they are appearances that necessarily exist during the ascendancy of a particular psychic level. Transition structures also differ from surface structures in that transition structures are in all cases merely temporary. Many surface structures, notwithstanding their contingency, are frequently retained in later stages of development. Transition structures, on the other hand, as the term itself implies, are not retained; they are exclusively stage-specific, and therefore impermanent. Transition structures are always dissolved and replaced when their psychic level is superseded.

Among the transition structures discussed by Wilber are: (1) *world view*: the fundamental character of the world as it happens to appear when seen through the basic cognitive structures of a particular level; (2) *needs*: the primary types of felt needs that are distinctive of life at a particular level; (3) *morality*: the kinds of behaviors and values that are implied by the basic structures of a particular level; and (returning to our main topic) (4) *selfhood*: the organization of self that is characteristic of a particular level.

All of these structures have been subjects of developmental studies, to which Wilber defers. For example, regarding world view, he draws on the well-known cognitive-developmental studies of Piaget, as well as on, among other sources, the psychoanalytically oriented work of Silvano Arieti (especially 1967). Regarding needs, he accepts the hierarchical framework constructed by Abraham Maslow (1968). Regarding morality, he adopts the developmental scheme of Lawrence Kohlberg (1969, 1976, 1984). And regarding selfhood, he utilizes the timetable of ego growth formulated by Jane Loevinger (1976). Wilber provides many different tables that correlate these developmental accounts with his own model of structural and developmental levels. Table 1-5 is one such table, slightly recast.[13]

For Wilber, then, world views, needs, moralities, and self-structures change with each transition to a higher level. For example, in the transition from the level of representational mind to that of rule/role mind, the world view is said to change from being mythical (i.e., protoconceptual, prelogical) to being rational (i.e., rule-governed, logical) in character. Correspondingly,

Table 1-5

WILBER'S DEVELOPMENTAL HIERARCHY
AND RELATED TRANSITION STRUCTURES

	LEVELS	AGES	MASLOW (NEEDS)	LOEVINGER (SELF-SENSE)	KOHLBERG (MORAL SENSE)
TRANSEGOIC STAGE	ULTIMATE	Begins ??	Self-transcendence		
TRANSEGOIC STAGE	CAUSAL	Begins ??	Self-transcendence		
TRANSEGOIC STAGE	SUBTLE	Begins ??	Self-transcendence	Integrated	
EGOIC STAGE	VISION-LOGIC	Begins 21 yr. ??	Self-actualization	Autonomous / Individualistic	
EGOIC STAGE	REFLEXIVE/ FORMAL MIND	Begins 11-15 yr.	Self-esteem	Conscientious / Conscientious-Conformist	6. Individual conscience / III. Postconventional / 5. Individual rights
EGOIC STAGE	RULE/ROLE MIND	Begins 6-8 yr.	Belongingness	Conformist / Self-protective	4. Law and order / II. Conventional / 3. Approval of others
PRE-EGOIC STAGE	REPRESENTATIONAL MIND	Begins 15mo.-2yr.	Safety	Impulsive	2. Naive hedonism / I. Preconventional / 1. Punishment/ obedience
PRE-EGOIC STAGE	PHANTASMIC	Begins 6-12mo.		Beginning impulsive	
PRE-EGOIC STAGE	EMOTIONAL-SEXUAL	Begins 1-6 mo.	(Physiological)		
PRE-EGOIC STAGE	SENSORI-PERCEPTUAL	Begins 0-3 mo.		Symbiotic	
PRE-EGOIC STAGE	PHYSICAL	Birth		Autistic	

the primary felt need is said to change from being one for safety to one for belonging. Morality is said to change from a preconventional standpoint (stressing desires and self-interested consequences of behavior) to a conventional standpoint (stressing moral rules and social norms). And the self-structure is said to change from what Loevinger calls the impulsive self (identified chiefly with the impulses and feelings of immediate bodily life) to the conformist self (identified chiefly with stereotypical social labels, which confer a definition and sense of belonging). In each of these examples, the transition involves a dissolution of structures that had existed when development was at the level of representational mind and a replacement of those structures with completely new ones that are congruent with living at the level of rule/role mind. The basic structures of the level of representational mind are preserved in the movement to the level of rule/role mind, but the transition structures just considered are not.

Concentrating now on the case of selfhood, the most salient implication of Wilber's analysis is that the self is not part of the psychic constitution as such. As a transition structure, the self is not part of the inherited psychic apparatus. It is not a pregiven structure, actual or potential, but rather something that is merely derivative. Moreover, as a transition structure, the self is not anything real in the sense of being part of the furniture of existence. The self is not an actually existing entity (or even semi-entity, such as a pole of a bipole); it is rather something that exists only in a virtual sense, as a subjective experience accompanying different levels of development. The self is not part of the furniture of existence; it is rather a mere, albeit developmentally unavoidable, appearance. On this point Wilber and the structural-hierarchical paradigm concur with the principal Eastern view espoused by Buddhism and (non-dualistic) Vedanta: separate selfhood, although seemingly real, is ultimately illusory.

If the self is not an existing basic structure, what it is, according to Wilber, is *identification* with such structures. Specifically, it is the identification that naturally obtains with the basic structures of a psychic level when life is lived at that level. Since the highest active level of the psychic hierarchy is the de facto center of psychic operations, it is therefore also the vantage point from which life is lived, which means that the highest active level is the natural residing point of the sense of self. In living at a certain level, one inevitably identifies with that level; one effectively *is* the basic structures of that level. For the structural-hierarchical paradigm, then, the self is a psychic identification rather than a part of the psychic apparatus. The self exists only as self-identity, the boundaries of which are determined at each psychic level by the basic structures of that level.

It is clear that the self, so conceived, is a transition structure, something merely derivative and temporary rather than original and permanent. For if the self exists only as a level-specific identification, then the self must be dissolved when, in developmental transformation, that identification is dissolved. Developmental transition from one psychic level to another breaks the identification that had obtained with the basic structures of the transcended level and brings about a new identification with the basic structures of the transcending level. And since the self exists only as such succeeding

32

identifications, this process of disidentification and reidentification is tanta-mount to a process of negation and recreation. The old self is not carried over, as basic structures are; instead, the old self is dissolved and replaced by a new self. Wilber holds that self-unfolding can in principle proceed in this fashion all the way to the highest psychic level, ultimate unity. Then, in arriving at ultimate unity, the process necessarily comes to an end. It does so not only for the obvious reason that ultimate unity is the highest and therefore last psychic level to be attained but also because ultimate unity transcends all possible boundaries of separate selfhood. The basic structure of ultimate unity is universal in scope: it is coincidence with reality itself. Any sense of identity based on this basic structure hence would be equally universal; it would be a sense of identity with all that exists. But clearly, such an all-inclusive identity is not really a *self*-identity in any normal meaning of the term, since it is altogether without limits and is therefore undefined. If there is nothing that is not-self, then neither is there anything that is self. The notion of selfhood is based on the self/other distinction, and from the universal standpoint of ultimate unity this distinction does not exist. It is a root illusion that has finally been dispelled. In the transition to ultimate unity, then, not only is an old self transcended and dissolved, but so too is the very basis on which the notion of selfhood rests. Consequently, the old self is not replaced by a new one. Rather, the inherent selflessness of existence is at last realized. Such, at any rate, is the structural-hierarchical view.

CHOOSING BETWEEN THE PARADIGMS

Having set forth the basic features of the dynamic-dialectical and structural-hierarchical paradigms, I would like in this final section to sharpen the contrast between them by considering five main points of disagreement. This will help clarify exactly what is at stake in choosing between the two paradigms.

1. *The pre-egoic stage: How central a role does conflict play?* The two paradigms disagree on whether the pre-egoic stage is normally plagued, indeed vitiated, by intrapsychic conflict. The dynamic-dialectical position is that such conflict is the primary theme of the pre-egoic period. The structural-hierarchical position, in contrast, is that the primary theme of the pre-egoic stage is not conflict, but rather the development of lower-level basic structures and the establishment, thereby, of a solid structural foundation for later life.

In the dynamic-dialectical view, early childhood is a period during which the psyche is volatile and unstable. Nonegoic potentials dominate the ego, which is weak and undeveloped, and consequently the ego must struggle against the influence of these potentials—even though, at the same time, the ego remains strongly attracted to them. The pre-egoic stage therefore is seen as a time of intense interpolar conflict, which is expressed in a variety of interpersonal ways, for example, in acute ambivalences toward both (archetypal) parental figures: the Great Mother and the Oedipal Father. Accordingly, the dynamic-dialectical perspective focuses on dilemmas and contradictions in the early childhood years and recommends a parenting style that is especially sensitive to such conflicts so that the child can be steered safely through a precarious developmental period.

In the structural-hierarchical view, in contrast, conflict is de-emphasized. Difficulties inherent to the pre-egoic stage are acknowledged, but these difficulties are not placed at the center of the developmental stage. Instead, the focus is on structural, and especially cognitive, development. Early childhood is seen as the time during which the most fundamental of all the psyche's basic structures are articulated, as the time during which the foundations of all subsequent development are laid down. Given this perspective, the structural-hierarchical view agrees with the dynamic-dialectical view that the pre-egoic stage is a critically important period in need of sensitive supervision. However, whereas the dynamic-dialectical paradigm explains this fact as being due primarily to the dangers of intrapsychic conflict, the structural-hierarchical paradigm explains it as being due primarily to the momentous and enduring effects that foundations have upon superstructures. Accordingly, whereas exponents of the dynamic-dialectical paradigm typically recommend a parenting style focusing on the negotiation of conflicts, exponents of the structural-hierarchical paradigm typically advise a parenting style focusing on the proper order and full mastery of basic life skills and abilities.

2. *The transition to the egoic stage: Are pre-egoic potentials lost or retained?* The two paradigms disagree on whether potentials distinctive of the pre-egoic period are lost or retained in the transition to the egoic stage. The dynamic-dialectical position is that the transition to the egoic stage is normally of a dissociative sort, involving a forfeiture of many of the psychic resources available during the pre-egoic stage. The structural-hierarchical position, in contrast, is that the transition to the egoic stage, like all other developmental transitions, is rather normally of an incorporative sort, involving the retention and higher integration of pre-egoic (basic) structures.

The dynamic-dialectical paradigm explains the transition to the egoic stage in terms of conflict resolution: the interpolar conflict of the pre-egoic stage is brought to an end by means of a repressive alienation of the nonegoic pole. The ego finally frees itself from the dominating influence of nonegoic (qua pre-egoic) potentials by dissociating itself from those potentials. The ego commits the act of original repression, which divorces the ego from the nonegoic pole by submerging the potentials of that pole into unconsciousness. In the dynamic-dialectical view, then, the transition to the egoic stage is the

34

developmental point at which interpolar conflict is resolved, but only at the cost of banishing many of the physico-dynamic potentials of life.

The structural-hierarchical paradigm, in contrast, explains the transition to the egoic stage in terms of structural development. Accordingly, it sees this transition as a movement that builds upon pre-egoic foundations rather than as one that submerges pre-egoic influences. The structural-hierarchical view, not deeming conflict to be central to the pre-egoic stage, also does not deem repression to be a necessary, or even normal, part of the transition to the egoic stage. Rather, repression and alienation are the exception. Under normal conditions, the basic structures developed during the pre-egoic stage are preserved as supporting structures on which the higher structures of the egoic plane are built. The structural-hierarchical view does not deny that the transition to the egoic stage requires a forsaking of some of the structures of the pre-egoic stage. But the structures forsaken are ordinarily *transition*, not basic, structures. The world view, distinctive felt needs, morality, and sense of self that prevailed during the pre-egoic stage are ordinarily dissolved and hence "lost." But this "loss" is really a net gain, since basic structures are preserved and augmented and since transition structures are replaced.

3. The egoic stage: Is the mental ego alienated from its origins and true foundations? The two paradigms disagree on whether the mental ego is alienated from or rooted in the proper foundations of its being. The dynamic-dialectical position is that the transition to the egoic stage involves a dissociation of the two poles of the psyche and, therefore, that the ego of the egoic stage, the mental ego, is out of touch with its origins and true foundations. The structural-hierarchical position, in contrast, is that the mental ego, in rising above the pre-egoic level, continues to stand upon the foundations laid down during the pre-egoic period.

The dynamic-dialectical paradigm has affinities with the existentialist perspective in that both see humanity as suffering from alienation and "nothingness," and as prone to guilt and despair. The difference is that most existentialists consider these difficulties to be inherent to the human condition per se, whereas the dynamic-dialectical view holds that these difficulties are inherent only to the ego of the egoic stage of development. In the dynamic-dialectical perspective, it is the *mental ego* that, having divorced itself from the nonegoic pole, is cut off from origins (alienation), is vulnerable to the feeling that it is without foundations in existence ("nothingness"), is plagued by a sense of being untrue to its own higher self or to a higher power (guilt), and consequently is prone to the mood of hopelessness (despair). To be sure, the mental ego is not always aware of these existential woes—especially in its early years, during which the mental ego is thought to be more buoyed by a sense of freedom from nonegoic potentials than afflicted by a sense of loss of these potentials. That is, the mental ego may not always be cognizant that its basic (repressed, alienated) posture is inauthentic and insecure. But such lack of awareness does not mean that the posture in question does not exist. The fact remains, in the dynamic-dialectical view, that the mental ego's posture *is* inauthentic and insecure, and therefore that the mental ego is constitutionally susceptible to existential concerns.

The structural-hierarchical paradigm sees things very differently. It sees the mental ego as being in touch with its pre-egoic foundations. Therefore this paradigm does not see the mental ego as being liable to existential problems as a consequence of its basic posture or stance in being. Nevertheless, the structural-hierarchical paradigm does have a way of accommodating much of the existentialist perspective. Specifically, it can explain existential difficulties as problems arising not from disconnection from prior foundations, but rather from lack of fulfillment of future, higher possibilities. That is, it can explain existential difficulties as growth pains of the mature mental ego, which, still confined within egoic boundaries, is driven toward transcendence. This is the view that Wilber defends, most forcefully in *Up from Eden* (1981). In this view, the mental ego's problem is not that it has alienated itself from a pre-egoic Eden, but rather that it has not yet attained transegoic heaven. The mental ego's alienation exists in relation to future possibilities, not past actualities.

Despite this accommodation, the two paradigms remain sharply divided in their explanations of the mental ego's existential condition. The dynamic-dialectical paradigm sees the mental ego as having turned its back on its sources in being. It holds that the mental ego has "sinned" against its origins and consequently is liable to the existential burdens of "fallen" existence: forsakenness, rootlessness, guilt, and despair. The structural-hierarchical paradigm, on the other hand, sees the mental ego not as having fallen from origins but rather as being only "half risen" to its proper higher destiny. Accordingly, the structural-hierarchical paradigm sees the mental ego's problems as being chiefly those arising from a frustration of the drive toward transcendence.

4. The transition to the transegoic stage: Does movement to the "trans-" involve a restoration of the "pre-"? The two paradigms disagree on whether the transcendence of the mental ego involves a return to pre-egoic potentials. The dynamic-dialectical paradigm, given its bipolar conception of the psyche and its view that the mental ego is alienated from the nonegoic pole, holds that ego transcendence necessarily involves a re-encounter with nonegoic potentials (in retarded, "pre-" form). It holds that the ego must be regressed through the "pre-," and thereby rerooted in the nonegoic, before the ego can be reborn on the level of the "trans-." In contrast, the structural-hierarchical paradigm, given its hierarchical conception of the psyche and its view that the mental ego is well integrated with the pre-egoic, holds that ego transcendence is a straightforward ascent to a new and higher psychic level. It holds that ego transcendence is a unidirectional ascending movement, from the egoic to the transegoic plane. In sum, it is implied by the dynamic-dialectical paradigm that the transcendence of the mental ego is a spiraling movement consisting of regression, restoration, and higher integration; and it is implied by the structural-hierarchical paradigm that this transcendence is a linear movement consisting of a direct progression to a higher plane.

The choice between these two conceptions of ego transcendence is laden with consequences. In practical terms, the choice is one between a risky and a safe view. The dynamic-dialectical view holds that ego transcendence is fraught with danger: the ego must regress through the "pre-" (i.e., the dynamic unconscious) before the ego can be rerooted in the Dynamic Ground and regenerated in spirit. The ego must submit to a radical regression with an uncertain outcome, a regression that can lead to psychosis as well as transcendence, disintegration as well as higher integration. The structural-hierarchical view, on the other hand, sees ego transcendence as being a much less perilous venture, since it is conceived as a purely progressive movement. The structural-hierarchical paradigm acknowledges that ego transcendence, like all developmental transformations, can be a very unsettling and frightening affair—one must die to an old level before one can ascend to a new level. But, according to this paradigm, however unsettling ego transcendence may be, it is not a process that incurs the risks attendant to radical regression.

It is Wilber's contention (1980b) that the choice between the dynamic-dialectical and structural-hierarchical views on ego transcendence can be decided in favor of the latter. This is so, Wilber argues, because the dynamic-dialectical view is based on a fallacy: the "pre-/trans-" fallacy.[14] The "pre-/trans-" fallacy is quite simply the confusion of pre-egoic with transegoic correlates, and vice versa. For example, it is the confusion of narcissism (pre-egoic) with true selflessness (transegoic), of the primary process (pre-egoic) with visionary cognition (transegoic), of impulsivity (pre-egoic) with spontaneity (transegoic), of temporal oblivion (pre-egoic) with eternity within time (transegoic). Wilber allows that confusions such as these are understandable in that pre-egoic and transegoic correlates are both nonegoic in nature and therefore remote from and unfamiliar to the mental ego, which makes these correlates appear similar simply by ignorance or by default. But if these correlates appear similar by default, they are not, Wilber believes, similar in fact. On the contrary, in his view they are in fact more distant in nature from each other than either is from the mental ego. To intertwine them, then, as does the dynamic-dialectical conception of regression in the service of transcendence, is, according to Wilber, to commit a dangerous fallacy. It is to mistake the lower for the higher, and thus to court regression in the name of transcendence or, even worse, psychosis in the name of salvation.

But there is a rejoinder to Wilber's argument, since it rests on an unproved assumption, namely, that pre-egoic and transegoic correlates are similar only in appearance. This assumption can be challenged. And of course it is just this assumption that is rejected by the dynamic-dialectical paradigm, which affirms the opposite assumption that such correlates are instead similar in inherent nature. Specifically, the dynamic-dialectical view is that these correlates are two different developmental expressions of the same nonegoic potentials. Pre-egoic correlates are nonegoic potentials in arrested, still primitive-infantile form and transegoic correlates are the same nonegoic potentials once they have been liberated from original repression and fused with developed egoic forms.

Challenging Wilber's assumption in this way clears the dialectical or spiraling conception of ego transcendence of the "pre-/trans-" fallacy. For if there is nothing conceptually mistaken in the view that the pre-egoic just is the nonegoic in arrested form (and the view, whether true or not, seems entirely possible), then there need be no error in the corresponding view that movement to the transegoic requires resurrection of the pre-egoic. If it is possible that the pre-egoic is potentially the transegoic, it also is possible that return to the "pre-," rather than always being a merely regressive U-turn toward origins, is in some cases a regressive-regenerative spiral toward transcendence. Proponents of the dynamic-dialectical paradigm, then, while perhaps agreeing with Wilber that Jung's account of this spiral movement is guilty of the "pre-/trans-" fallacy,[15] need not agree that all theories combining regression with transcendence are so guilty.

This of course is not to say that the dynamic-dialectical conception of ego transcendence is correct and Wilber's incorrect—although I believe that this is the case. The point is simply that "pre-" and "trans-" need not be as disconnected as Wilber contends, and therefore that there need be no fallacy involved in holding that regression is integral to ego transcendence. The point is that the two paradigms under consideration offer equally coherent conceptions of the process of ego transcendence. The dynamic-dialectical and the structural-hierarchical conceptions of ego transcendence are indeed highly discrepant and pose some very difficult choices. But neither conception can be ruled out on nonempirical or logical grounds.

5. The transegoic stage: Are there two selves or none? The two paradigms agree that the ego of the egoic stage of development is a small s self that needs ultimately to be transcended. However, whereas the dynamic-dialectical paradigm conceives of this small self as a real thing that needs to be transformed (i.e., a psychic pole that needs to be returned to and integrated with its counterpole), the structural-hierarchical paradigm conceives of this small self as an illusion that needs to be dispelled (i.e., a transition structure that needs to be dissolved).

In the dynamic-dialectical conception, the small s self of the egoic stage, the mental ego, is an actually existing self but not a complete self. It is a pole of a bipole, which, as such, is something that possesses real but not self-subsistent existence. True, the mental ego may *believe* itself to be an independent and complete self, but this is a false pose based on a repressive submergence of the nonegoic pole of the psyche. Beneath, then, the mental ego's pose of independence there invisibly exists the nonegoic pole, which is at once the mental ego's prior and ultimate Ground, and self: the big S Self. The ego of the egoic stage is therefore something that is real; it is not an illusion. But although a reality, it is a merely partial and distorted reality, since it is out of touch with its proper Ground and contorted in the false stance of ontological independence.

Wilber's formulation of the structural-hierarchical paradigm advances the contrasting view that the small s self of the egoic stage is not a real thing. It is not among the basic structures that make up the psychic constitution. Rather, this self is merely a transition structure, something that exists only virtually, as a developmental epiphenomenon. Specifically, the mental ego exists only as a level-specific identification with egoic basic structures. And this identification, it should be added, is in fact a false one, since the only ultimately true identification is the all-inclusive identification of ultimate unity, which transcends all selfhood. For the structural-hierarchical paradigm, then, there is no separate self, because one's true existence coincides with reality itself. One's true existence is none other than the Brahman of Upanishadic Hinduism, the Void of Mahayana Buddhism, the Godhead behind God of Judeo-Christian mysticism. The mental ego, qua separate self, is an illusion. It is not any existing thing, not even, as in the dynamic-dialectical view, an incomplete and distorted thing. It is rather only a case of mistaken identity. It is a case of developmentally necessary and warranted mistaken identity, to be sure, but a case of mistaken identity nonetheless.

Following from these differences concerning the mental ego as a small s self, the two paradigms have correspondingly different prescriptions for ego transcendence. The dynamic-dialectical paradigm, viewing the egoic self as a real but pseudo-independent self, prescribes a transcendence that would reunite and "alchemically" bond the egoic self with its missing, superior half. Such a reconnection and fusion would bring into existence a higher synthesis of the egoic and nonegoic poles of the psyche. This synthesis would be a union of opposites, a unity-in-duality of small and large s selves, of ego and spirit.

The structural-hierarchical paradigm, on the other hand, viewing the egoic self as a transition rather than a "real" or basic structure, does not prescribe any such realignments of the psychic constitution. The small s self is not considered a part of the psychic apparatus that needs somehow to be righted or redeemed. It is rather only an identification that needs to be outgrown. Thus, ego transcendence, for the structural-hierarchical paradigm, is not a matter of grounding and transforming a small s self but rather of awakening to the fact that there is no such self to ground or transform. Self-realization is not a matter of yoking a lesser to a superior self but rather of seeing that the very notion of selfhood has no basis in reality. Granted, such an insight is by no means easily attained, since there is a whole sequence of transition selves that must be formed and dissolved before the selflessness of ultimate unity can be appreciated. But still, the highest attainment of selfhood coincides with the understanding that, truly, there is no self.

The choice between the dynamic-dialectical and structural-hierarchical paradigms, therefore, is a choice between two selves or none. The dynamic-dialectical paradigm sees development as leading ultimately to a goal in which two selves are united as one, the higher self of spirit and the lower self of the ego-subject. The structural-hierarchical paradigm, on the other hand, sees development as leading ultimately to a goal that lies beyond all selfhood, a goal at which the root illusion of selfhood has been dispelled.

CONCLUSION

In presenting the foregoing account of the dynamic-dialectical and structural-hierarchical paradigms, my purpose has been to sketch their essential lineaments, to point out their most important differences, and thereby to indicate what is at stake in choosing between them. Both of these are coherent and defensible frameworks or points of view, and each has its distinctive advantages and difficulties. Choosing between them is not easy.

I, of course, have chosen the dynamic-dialectical paradigm. I have done so not because I can prove that this paradigm presents the only correct or viable view, but rather primarily because I believe that it offers the more sensitive reading of the nonegoic bases and higher potentialities of life. I hope this is borne out in the chapters that ensue, in which I will be following out the dynamic-dialectical paradigm as rigorously as I am able. I will be plotting the course of triphasic development as if that course were entirely true to the dynamic-dialectical paradigm, which hereafter will be assumed.

CHAPTER 2

The Body-Ego: The Dynamics of its Development

H UMAN LIFE BEGINS IN a state of pre-egoic embedment. The neonatal
condition is one of immersion in the Dynamic Ground prior to the
articulation of any sense of individuated selfhood. The infant is at first entirely
unaware of his own existence; he has no cognizance of himself or of a world
distinct from himself. In the state of original embedment, the neonate is, in
effect, in a womb outside the womb. He is in a state of psychic gestation
antecedent to the delivery and development of the ego.

In time, the ego begins to emerge. And since it is body boundaries that
most conspicuously mark off the ego-qua-infant from the surrounding
environment, it is natural that the body would be the first locus of the ego's
identity. The first self, therefore, is a bodily self, a self wholly and exclusively
identified with concrete somatic existence. In other words, the first self is a
corporeal subject or, as I will call it, a body-ego.

The body-ego goes through several phases of development. These phases
are governed by many different factors. In this chapter, I will concentrate on
the psychodynamic and interpersonal factors, giving specific consideration to
the following: (1) the pre-egoic fusion state, i.e., original embedment,
immersion in the Dynamic Ground; (2) the body-ego's ambivalence toward
the Ground and the maternal parent, and the differentiation of the Ground/
mother complex (the Great Mother) into positive and negative poles (viz., the
Good Mother and the Terrible Mother); (3) the dynamically charged
character of the body-ego's experience, which is manifested diversely as
polymorphous sensuousness, overall intensity, and numinosity; (4) the
phases of psychosexual development, culminating in the Oedipal conflict; and
(5) the conflict with the maternal and paternal powers (as Terrible Mother and
Oedipal Father), leading to original repression.

41

ORIGINAL EMBEDMENT

In the neonatal state, the ego exists only germinally and preactively. The newborn's ego is dormant; it exists, but it has not yet been differentiated or engaged. Although the infant's body has been delivered from the mother's womb, the infant's ego is still *in utero*: it gestates in the Ground.

The neonate thus begins life in a state of subjectless immersion and absorption in the Dynamic Ground. The newborn, when awake, is no doubt keenly aware; however, lacking an activated ego, he is without an individuated self that is aware. Rather, the neonate's awareness is ownerless; it is but a stream of unpossessed and uncoordinated experiences. Moreover, since it is an egoic function to control the direction and scope of awareness, the fact that the newborn is without an activated ego means that his attention is both unselective and unrestrictedly open.[1] It means, that is, that the infant exercises no self-determination with respect to experience. His consciousness is choicelessly and unguardedly open; it is both "unaimed" and "fully dilated." Like a mirror, the consciousness of the newborn unselectively registers everything that comes within its range.

But, paradoxically, the infant's awareness is as closed as it is open, for it is an undivided sphere, a world unto itself. The newborn, being without a functioning ego, is therefore without self-boundaries; he senses no difference between self and other, inner and outer. The newborn makes no distinctions or exclusions. Hence, his experience is, if only by default, a seamless and omni-inclusive whole; it is a "one without a second," a fusion state that is utterly wrapped, and rapt, in immediate experience. So far as the infant knows, there is nothing that exists beyond the stimulus of the moment; for him, the contents of present awareness exhaust the contents of the world. It is for this reason that Freud described the state of original embedment as a condition of primary narcissism, i.e., of pre-egoic self-absorption. And it is for the same reason that Margaret Mahler, in her reading of early object-relations (Mahler et al. 1975), calls the neonatal state a state of normal autism, i.e., a state of self-encapsulated consciousness.

In sum, original embedment has a paradoxical open-closed character: it is a condition that is at once completely (and defenselessly) open to whatever might emerge within itself and completely closed to the fact that there is a world beyond itself. Since original embedment lacks an ego-subject, it is without a center, and consequently it also is without a delimited circumference. Original embedment is altogether without limits or boundaries; in effect, it is a domain of experience into which anything can enter and outside of which nothing can exist.

Also distinctive of original embedment is dynamic plenitude. Original embedment, as a state of enfoldment in the Dynamic Ground, is a state that

42

is full, indeed overflowing, with the power that wells up from the Ground. The newborn is bathed in this power, which rises from the Ground and circulates freely throughout the body. The newborn, suffused with the power of the Ground, is a fount of life, and his condition is thus one of dynamic saturation. The circulation of the power of the Ground affects the infant in two main ways. First, since the power of the Ground is an energy that amplifies psychic processes, its unimpeded flow quickens and enhances the infant's experience across all dimensions. And second, since the power of the Ground is a force of a magnetic and fluidic nature, its free ascent buoys, lulls, and entrances the infant, keeping him in a state of unmindful absorption. Viewed in this light, original embedment is a state analogous to the intrauterine condition. It is a womb outside the womb, a condition sustained and suspended in "maternal fluid." It is a condition of immersion and dissolution, which, as such, is aptly called an oceanic state. Original embedment, then, to put it succinctly, is a liquidlike plenum or, as Neumann calls it, a pleroma, a condition of dynamic fullness and fulfillment. He says (1954, 276-77):

> the ego germ still exists in the pleroma, in the "fullness" of the unformed God, and, as consciousness unborn, slumbers in the primordial egg, in the bliss of paradise.

It follows from the fact that original embedment is a condition of dynamic plenitude that it is a condition that, literally, is content (i.e., content-full) and fulfilled, without felt lack or need, and therefore that it is a condition that is psychically (although of course not physically) independent. Original embedment is then a state that, subjectively speaking, is self-sufficing as well as singular, autarkic as well as autistic. The metaphor that best captures this self-contained independence of original embedment is that of the fertilized egg. Neumann uses this metaphor in the passage just cited, as too does Mahler in her description of the "hatching" of the ego during the separation-individuation process. Freud also acknowledged the appropriateness of the metaphor. For example, in a frequently quoted passage, he observed (1911a, 220):

> A neat example of a psychical system shut off from the stimuli of the external world, and able to satisfy even its nutritional requirements autistically...is afforded by the bird's egg with its food supply enclosed in its shell; for it, the care provided by its mother is limited to the provision of warmth.

To be sure, the human infant must rely upon the mothering parent for a good deal more than warmth. He must rely upon her for all of his physical needs. But the newborn is entirely unaware of this. For him, the nurturance provided by the caretaker is an unrecognized given. Thus, although the newborn, as a physical being, is utterly dependent, he is, as a psychic system, completely independent. Immersed in the Dynamic Ground, his experience contains a superabundant source within itself. The experience of the newborn is an entirely self-supporting sphere, a self-subsistent monad.

Although the state of original embedment is soon abandoned by the developing ego, traces of it remain as an archetype of the collective unconscious. The images issuing from this archetype are many and varied. Among them, the egg image, owing to its particular fittingness, is perhaps the most common. The picture of a cosmic egg out of which is hatched the world of multiplicity and change appears in mythologies around the world. Other images in which the archetype frequently has been expressed are those of (1) a primordial chaos preceding the separation of heaven (ego) and earth (unconscious); (2) an enveloping darkness prior to the dawning of light (ego) and, therefore, prior to the alternation of day (consciousness) and night (unconsciousness, sleep); (3) an oceanic depth out of which are born the myriad forms of life; and (4) the uroboros (a snake eating its own tail) and other symbols portraying self-containment and self-sustenance.

Although consideration of the cognitive and affective dimensions of pre-egoic development is the task of the next chapter, it would be good here briefly to indicate what is distinctive of the originally embedded state in these regards.

Being without a functioning ego, the originally embedded state is, properly speaking, devoid of cognition. Cognition requires, however minimally, a synthetic unity of consciousness, i.e., a grasping or holding together (a com-prehension) of the elements of experience. Accordingly, there can be no cognition when there is no ego-subject to unify experience in this way. Without an ego, there is, as was noted a moment ago, no distinction between self and world or between present and past or future. In fact, in the originally embedded state, there probably are no conscious discriminations whatsoever. It is unlikely that any of the sensations or feelings that pass through awareness is distinguished from any other; all of the contents of experience are probably experienced only in the barest way. Moreover, it is implausible even that anything is recognized in the sense of being seen as a reappearance of a thing or type of thing.[2] Rather, it is likely that the data of the moment are absolutely new. In the absence of a temporal horizon, it would seem that the data of the moment are, for all the newborn knows, the only things in existence. For the newborn, then, everything may be said to exist out of relation to everything else. Or as Philip Cowan—giving expression to Piaget's view—has described it (1978, 86):

Sights are unrelated to sounds, sounds to kinesthetic sensations, muscle movements to visual cues, and so on. The perceived world is something like a living movie being shown without synchronization of events in space and time.

The neonate's experience is a virgin manifold. It is a bare succession of stimuli, which are unowned, unintegrated, and uncomprehended.

However, if the newborn does not actively distinguish one thing from another, this does not mean that he does not *attend* to some things more than others. Although the newborn, lacking an ego-subject, is unable to monitor experience, and thus to exercise conscious choice in his response to things, he is biologically programmed in such a manner as to respond automatically to certain key stimuli.[3] Certain sensory stimuli (e.g., tactile sensations connected with feeding, moving visual stimuli, specific patterns and colors) engage the neonate's awareness and, without the mediation of any memories or concepts, sometimes trigger inherited reaction routines (e.g., turning of the face in the direction of touch, sucking, movement of eyes to track visual signals or to select preferred patterns or colors). Hence, although originally embedded experience is altogether preconceptual, it is to a certain extent, to use Arieti's (1967) term, *exoceptual*: it involves forms of predetermined selective attention and response.

The affective dimension of the originally embedded condition, like the cognitive, is extremely rudimentary, but it is nonetheless of capital importance, both in itself and in relation to subsequent development. Without any real degree of cognitive differentiation, only the most diffuse and global feelings are possible. Most of these are transient feelings brought about by physical causes, for example, generalized relaxation/tension, comfort/discomfort, and pleasure/pain. But there is one feeling that differs from all the rest and should be singled out as being especially distinctive of original embedment, namely, exuberance, or overflowing well-being. This feeling is intrinsic to original embedment because, as was explained, original embedment is a condition of dynamic saturation or plenitude. The power of the Ground, released from the sexual system, pulsates through the infant's body in rising and expanding waves of bliss. The very power that on rare occasions induces euphoric inflations in the ego is a constant ingredient of the neonate's egoless experience. This power continuously wells up and through the neonate's being, buoying it, lulling it, and rendering it felicitously content. The newborn is a conduit through which the waters of life freely flow, and for this reason the affective tone characteristic of the newborn's experience is one of superabundant well-being.

The well-being experienced during original embedment is never entirely forgotten, and the ever-so-faint memory of it lives on to haunt us in later life. Our nostalgia for paradise reflects a longing for this original state, the undividedness and ebullience of which constitute for us an implicit paradigm of wholeness and happiness. However, this nostalgia can be misleading if it is taken to imply that original embedment is the proper standard of fulfilled existence. For original embedment is only a foreglimpse of the truly fulfilled state; it is the pre-egoic correlate of the transegoic state that is the proper goal of life. It is true that original embedment is a condition of unqualified unity and bliss, but it is equally true that it is a condition that is wholly undeveloped and therefore primitive. Specifically, original embedment is a state the unity of which is completely undifferentiated: it is a state of at-one-ment without an ego that is at one. And original embedment is a state the bliss of which, although real and of lasting importance, is completely blind, i.e., unpossessed and unappreciated.

Original embedment is, then, only a primitive precursor of (transegoic) paradise, not paradise itself. This means that the real point of the nostalgia for paradise is not that the ego should return to its original predifferentiated unity with the Dynamic Ground, but rather that the ego should reroot and thereby regenerate itself in this Ground. Hence, if regression in the service of transcendence would draw the ego back toward the first source of its being, it does so not to dissolve and re-embed the ego in the Ground, but rather to open a permanent channel to the Ground so that the ego can be replenished by the power-spirit that issues from the Ground.

THE EMERGENCE OF THE EGO FROM THE DYNAMIC GROUND AND THE FIRST APPEARANCE OF THE GREAT MOTHER

The ego soon begins to emerge from the matrix of original embedment. And quite naturally the first locus of its identity is the body. In the beginning, this somatic identity is vague; it is made up of little more than undefined physical sensations and pervasive feeling states. Time and experience, however, articulate the ego's bodily self-identity. The boundaries of the body are outlined in images; its motor and perceptual capabilities are learned; its limbs and parts are explored; and its basic desires and feelings are recognized. These aspects of embodied existence constitute what the ego at this point is. For the ego at this stage, although now distinct from the Dynamic Ground, is in no way distinct from the body. The ego at this stage relates to the body as self and not at all as an object for self. The ego is wholly identified with the body; the body's life is the ego's own life.

The emergence of the body-ego occurs in relation to the all-embracing reality of the maternal principle: the Great Mother.[4] This maternal principle is primarily and at first the environment of original embedment itself, with its total envelopment of selfhood and its fluid energies of life. That is to say, it is the Dynamic Ground in its original capacity as psychic womb. Derivatively and later, when the infant begins dimly to apprehend the world beyond himself, the maternal principle becomes instantiated in the person of the mothering parent, with her physical embrace and lactic fluids. The maternal principle therefore is essentially bifaceted. It is both an inner source and an outer personal presence; it is at once the body-*ego's* psychic Ground and the *body*-ego's principal material support. And for the body-ego, it is both of these at once and without distinction.

The inner and most basic side of the Great Mother, the Dynamic Ground, is a source that, for the nascent body-ego, is still immediately at hand. The newly emerged body-ego has not yet separated itself by any great distance from the state of original embedment, and it regularly returns to that state, not only during sleep but also during waking experience. The fledgling ego is relatively unindividuated and has little strength with which to stand on its own; consequently, it is ever liable to relapse into its original condition. It is easily drawn back to the Ground, as it is irresistibly attracted to the Ground—both by virtue of the magnetic character of the Ground and by virtue of the blissful dissolution that results from immersion in the Ground. And what holds in these respects for the ego in its relation to the inner side of the Great Mother holds as well, in analogous fashion, for the ego in its relation to the outer side of the Great Mother, the mothering parent. For the mothering parent too is a source from which the body-ego derives and to which, as provider of love and life necessities, it is ineluctably drawn. She too is an ever-present reality that can at any moment take hold of the body-ego, envelop it, and melt its tenuous self-boundaries.

The inner and outer sides of the Great Mother thus have the same effects upon the body-ego. They are etiologically equivalent: both are magnetic-solvent powers. Both affect the body-ego by attracting it in ways that it cannot resist and then by dissolving it. Both exert a tractional force that entrances and then engulfs the body-ego, reabsorbing it in the preindividuated, originally embedded state. Inwardly, it is the power of the Dynamic Ground that has these effects upon the body-ego; outwardly, it is the loving attentions of the mothering parent. By the combined influence of these forces, the Great Mother holds the body-ego in sway. She keeps the body-ego within the orbit of her influence and frequently re-embeds it within the primordial unity of her being.

In addition to having identical effects upon the body-ego, the inner and outer sides of the Great Mother are themselves causally interactive. The power of the Ground and the love of the mother are confluent, mutually stimulating forces. They are forces that, in affecting the body-ego, also affect each other, in somewhat the following way: The Dynamic Ground releases effluences which well up in the body-ego as eddies or waves of bliss. The body-ego responds with cooing sounds and gestures of delight. These behaviors prompt the

47

mother to bestow playful affections upon the body-ego. The affections of the mother in turn captivate and dissolve the body-ego, penetrating it to the core: the Dynamic Ground. The Dynamic Ground, in being stirred in this way by the love of the mother, again releases blissful effluences—which effluences in turn cause the body-ego to coo and gesture with delight, which behaviors again cause the mother to ply loving attentions, and so on. In this way a circuit is established between the inner and outer sides of the maternal reality; the power of the Ground and the mother's love work in turn to stir and elicit each other.

Given their similarity and interactivity, the inner and outer sides of the maternal reality cannot help but appear as one to the body-ego. The body-ego, which in any case is capable of only the most rudimentary cognitions, has no way of knowing that its principal other, the Great Mother, is in fact a fusion of distinct (psychic and physical) sources. Accordingly, the body-ego's "concept" of the Great Mother—which is our archetype of her—consists of a primitive grouping of perceptions, images, and feelings in which aspects of both the inner and outer sides of the maternal principle are condensed without distinction. It is a configuration of meanings in which are intermingled the most important features of both the Dynamic Ground and the mothering parent.

The life of the body-ego is played out against the background of the maternal principle. The Great Mother has a bearing upon virtually everything the body-ego says and does. So much, in fact, does the body-ego partake of the Great Mother that it is more accurate to conceive of the body-ego as a lesser member of a binary system than as an entity in its own right. The emergence of the body-ego thus breaks up the monadic world of original embedment and divides that world not into two self-contained spheres, but rather into a lopsided dyad, a dyad in which the Great Mother is the central reality, the body-ego merely a satellite.

To tie threads together, the Great Mother can be said to be at once the source, foundation, and center of gravity of the body-ego's life. She is the womb, physical and psychic, from which the body-ego is delivered. As provider and enlivener, she is the body-ego's continuing support, indeed the very basis of its being. And as a magnetic-solvent power, she is an attractive force that keeps the body-ego in tow and that frequently regresses it to the originally embedded condition.

It is by virtue of its intimate relation with the Great Mother that the body-ego at first lives a life full of grace.[5] The body-ego is physically provided for and protected by the mothering parent, who also showers the body-ego with "unmerited" love. And the body-ego is psychically sustained by the Dynamic Ground, the power of which fills the body-ego with delight, magnifies and quickens its experience, and enchants its world with an aura of the miraculous.

The nascent body-ego is ministered to both from without and from within, and the result is that its life is a blessed one, unburdened by work and worry and full of love, power, and wonder.

The graces bestowed upon the body-ego by the mothering parent are fairly obvious. The benefits contributed by the Dynamic Ground are more subtle. Regarding the latter, I have already spoken of the felicitous feelings caused by pulsations issuing from the Ground. These pulsations, which are inherent to original embedment, occur in the body-egoic period as well. Like the infant, the body-ego is inwardly caressed by effluences which arise from the Ground and ascend through the body as ripples or waves of bliss. In addition to these effluences, there are three other noteworthy benefits conferred upon the body-ego by the Dynamic Ground. These are: (1) polymorphous sensuousness, (2) superaliveness in all dimensions of experience, and (3) numinosity.

In saying that the body-ego is polymorphously sensuous, I am agreeing in substance with Freud—disagreeing only with Freud's narrowly sexual conception of sensuous experience. The body-ego, owing to its direct openness to the Dynamic Ground, is energized throughout by the power of the Ground. The body-ego's entire physical being is electrically charged, which means that any of its bodily limbs, parts, or "zones," upon being caressed or manipulated, can become a seat of somatic ecstasy. This of course is especially true of the erogenous zones, which are sequentially dominant according to the pattern described in Freud's theory of psychosexual development. The body-ego's capacity for somatic ecstasy, however, is not limited to the erogenous zones. The body-ego is supercharged from head to toe, and any area or appendage of its surface can be a vehicle of transport and delight.

The beneficial effect of the power of the Ground is manifested as well in the all-around abundance and aliveness of the body-ego's experience. All dimensions of the body-ego's life are amplified by the power of the Ground. For example, the body-ego's perceptions are rich and variegated, full of colors that scintillate, sounds that reverberate, smells that penetrate, and so on. The body-ego's feelings are potent and deeply moving, as currents of affect ripple, roll, or crash through its body. And the body-ego's thoughts, although primitive, are insights that arrive with great impact and sense of significance, sometimes assuming the proportion of astounding realizations. Every aspect of the body-ego's awareness is accentuated by the power of the Ground, which functions as a fuel, and thus enhancer, of experience.

Finally, the power of the Ground graces the young body-ego by imbuing its world with a numinous aura. The body-ego's world, overlaid with the power of the Ground, is animated and rendered wondrous: alluring, hypnotic, awesome, mysterious, full of hidden depths and meanings. The body-ego's world is magical and enchanted—and, correspondingly, the body-ego itself is enthralled. The body-ego is prone to being seized and captivated, as everything in its world is charged with and magnetized by psychic energy. The environment in general shimmers with aliveness, and the specific objects that populate the environment—especially those that are primary targets of cathexes—emanate a power that beckons, and sometimes commands, the body-ego's attention. The body-ego's world is full of *mana*; it is permeated by an invisible power that, proceeding from the Dynamic Ground, extends to the farthest reaches of perception.

In bringing this section to a close, it should be noted that what have just been described as benefits bestowed by the Dynamic Ground are really effects that cut two ways. For example, polymorphous sensuousness is a matter not only of somatically generated ecstasies but also of vulnerability, as the body-ego is easily absorbed and dissolved, even against its will, in bodily sensations (e.g., tickling). The amplification of perceptual, affective, and cognitive modalities is a matter not only of experience being enhanced but also, sometimes, of it being made painfully acute, even overwhelming, in its power and impact. And the numinous quality of the body-ego's world is a matter not only of enchantment and rapture but also, sometimes, of eerie strangeness and bone-chilling dread. These examples show that the Dynamic Ground can affect the body-ego's total experience in a bivalent manner. This fact notwithstanding, however, it is primarily the positive side of the Dynamic Ground that is experienced by the younger body-ego, whose life, as was said, is one full of grace. Accordingly, the Great Mother appears to the younger body-ego for the most part in her Good Mother rather than in her Terrible Mother form. The negative side of the Dynamic Ground and of the maternal principle more generally, although an inevitable counterpart of the positive side, remains in the background at first. The ego/Great Mother relation thus is initially an affair that altogether favors the ego.

But in time the negative side of the maternal principle does begin to move to the fore. For as the body-ego moves in the direction of individuation, it begins to strain against the countervailing influence of the Great Mother, and consequently it begins to experience the magnetic and seductive power of the Great Mother as a threatening force. At this point the Great Mother begins to appear to the body-ego in ominous and frightening guises: the Good Mother begins to give way to the Terrible Mother. Outwardly, the mothering parent gradually changes from a being of gentleness and warmth, a provider of unconditional love and inexhaustible sustenance, to a being who, in ever-greater measure, is harsh and cold, demanding and engulfing—an ogress armed with deceptive enticements. And inwardly, the Dynamic Ground gradually changes from a fount of grace to an abyss from which emanates a dark and dangerous power. The Great Mother remains, for the body-ego, an entrancing and compellingly magnetic being. As time passes, however, she becomes less and less an object of desire and more and more a seemingly inescapable object of dread.

Let us now consider the major factors that bear upon this transformation.

CONFLICT WITH THE MATERNAL POWER AND ORIGINAL REPRESSION

The Great Mother system has two axes, a positive/negative axis and an inner/outer axis. The Great Mother is both positive and negative because, as was just explained, there arrives a point in the body-ego's development at which the Great Mother begins to appear not only as the Good Mother, a soft and loving benefactress, a sustaining and nurturing source, but also as the Terrible Mother, a nagging and deceitful crone, an abysmal and horrific power. And the Great Mother is both inner and outer because she is at once the inner power of the Dynamic Ground and the outer person who is the mothering parent. The Great Mother is, then, a double duality—which makes her very complex indeed. In order to avoid confusion, let us distinguish the two axes of the Great Mother system by referring to the positive/negative axis as the *bivalent* axis and the inner/outer axis as the *bidirectional* axis of the system.

Regarding the bivalent axis, we already know that it is the positive side of the Great Mother to which the newly emerged body-ego is primarily related. In its first year, the body-ego leads a charmed life, enjoying a felicitous relation with both the inner and outer dimensions of the Great (= Good) Mother. However, as the body-ego carves out its own sphere of existence, it begins to experience the Great Mother as an obstacle and, it seems, an adversary to growth. The body-ego begins to be threatened by the Great Mother, and, accordingly, the positive side of the Great Mother begins to recede from the body-ego's experience and the negative side begins to come to the fore, until it begins to dominate. Hence, although the maternal principle is inherently bivalent in its expression to the body-ego, it is not always bivalent in a balanced way. At first, the body-ego is cradled and nursed by the mothering parent and blissfully infused by the power of the Ground. But later the mothering parent becomes the very opposite of her former self (at least in the body-ego's perception, if not also to a certain extent in fact), and so too does the power of the Ground. The mothering parent turns into a guileful tyrant and the power of the Ground turns into a menacing force. To speak the language of fairy tales, the mothering parent becomes an evil witch and the power of the Ground becomes the witch's caldron and fire.

The bivalence of the maternal principle is for the most part a relative, not absolute, property. The maternal principle is bivalent not so much in itself as in its appearance to the body-ego. (There is one exception to this, to be discussed in a moment.) In fact, the bivalence of the maternal principle is at

51

bottom a function of the *ambivalence* of the body-ego toward the maternal principle, and specifically toward the magnetic-solvent character of that principle. The body-ego is ambivalent in face of the Great Mother's attractive, enveloping power, which hypnotizes the body-ego and frequently regresses it to the predifferentiated unity of the originally embedded state.[6] At first, as we know, the body-ego has little stake in separate selfhood and therefore yields to the Great Mother's entrancing solicitations without resistance and welcomes reabsorption in the Great Mother as unmitigated release and joy. In time, however, since the body-ego begins to sense that the Great Mother is an adversary to its growth, it also begins to have mixed feelings for the Great Mother, and for her magnetic-solvent influence in particular. Accordingly, the body-ego begins to find the entrancement-reabsorption experience not only an ecstatic release from self but also, and increasingly, a frightening loss of self. The body-ego, then, is ambivalent toward the Great Mother, and the Great Mother in turn is bivalent in her appearance to the body-ego, because the body-ego is not long in existence before it finds that it is not only strongly desirous of the Great Mother (as magnetic dispenser of graces) but also deeply fearful of her (as seductive subverter of the drive for independence). The body-ego comes to have conflicting feelings for the Great Mother, and, correspondingly, the Great Mother begins to appear to the body-ego in contradictory guises, as a force of both love and hate, light and darkness, life and death. The maternal reality is the central body around which the body-ego orbits, in an ego/Great Mother binary system. However, since the body-ego is programmed for a trajectory of independence, it experiences this body not only as a central sun emitting light and warmth but also as a black hole drawing it, the body-ego, to a dreadful doom.

The bivalence of the maternal principle is captured in a great many archetypal and mythological images. To the extent that the two sides of the bidirectional axis can be separated from each other, the bivalence of the outer or personal side is typically depicted in the form of female figures of either good or evil nature, and the bivalence of the inner or psychic side is typically depicted in the form of elemental forces of either friendly or hostile character.

Outwardly, the bivalence of the Great Mother is expressed in images of good and evil ministresses: fairies, witches, enchantresses. The good ministresses are characteristically portrayed as wise, kind, and graceful maidens who protect and provide for young children. The evil ministresses, in contrast, are characteristically portrayed as ugly crones who gain pleasure in deceiving and destroying young children. As expressions of the Great Mother, both of these types of figures are magnetically alluring. The good ministresses are so by virtue of the reassuring grace of their countenance and by magic charms. The evil ministresses, being repellent in appearance, must rely on magic and deceptions (e.g., the house of candy in the story of Hansel and Gretel).

The bivalence of the inner dimension of the maternal principle, on the other hand, is depicted in terms of elemental forces of clement or inclement character—especially those of water, fire, and wind, which provide the best metaphors for the movement of psychic energy. As archetypal symbols, these forces are always either gentle, soothing, and life-supporting or else violent and destructive; they are never neutral. So, for example, the power of the Ground is pictured as both good and evil waters, as both the water of life (e.g., virgin springs, a fount of youth) and a raging sea full of tempests and dangerous whirlpools. Or the power of the Ground is pictured as both good and evil fires, as both a vital warmth (e.g., the fire of the hearth) and a scorching heat (e.g., infernos, volcanoes). Or again, the power of the Ground is pictured as both good and evil winds, as both a caressing zephyr and a raging whirlwind or gale.[7] These elemental forces are in all cases extreme; they are forces that either assuage or assail, sustain or slay. As expressions of the inner dimension of the Great Mother, they indicate that the body-ego's subjective atmosphere is a hypervolatile one, one that is almost always either dramatically positive or dramatically negative.

Since the bidirectionality of the maternal principle is unknown to the body-ego, many of the images of the Great Mother, and of her bivalent manifestations in particular, stress neither her outer nor her inner dimension, but rather reflect a fusion of features deriving from both of these dimensions. The typical kind of image that results from such a fusion, combining as it does an external life form with an internal force or power, is one of a subhuman animal, characteristically either a furry mammalian comforter or a scaly reptilian devourer. The furry mammalian comforter is, of course, the positive aspect of the maternal principle: the Good Mother. It plays the role of a constant companion and guardian of the body-ego—witness the stuffed animals that accompany children to bed at night. And the scaly reptilian devourer is the negative aspect of the maternal principle: the Terrible Mother. It typically is pictured as a serpent under foot, a dragon under ground, a behemoth under water, or a "creepy-crawly" under the bed—which, it is feared, might rise up at any moment and snatch the ego unawares. Animals such as these constitute perhaps the very best symbols of the Great Mother, who, to the body-ego, is not clearly a person in the full sense or simply a bare force or power, but who nonetheless is something that approaches both of these. The mammal/reptile antithesis may therefore be the most representative expression of the bivalence of the maternal reality.[8]

Because she is both bivalent and bidirectional, the Great Mother assumes an immense number of different forms. She is a person, power, creature, friend, and foe. She is a multifaceted living presence on which is overlaid a complex array of archetypal images. She is, in short, a profusion of diverse and conflicting manifestations. But these manifestations are by no means random.

Understood in light of the Great Mother's biaxial character, they observe an inner logic; they fit together as an ordered series or coherent constellation of forms.

The ambivalence that the body-ego experiences in relation to the Great Mother determines the body-ego's fundamental life project, namely, to be an "independent intimate" of the Great Mother. The body-ego, quite understandably, wants both to be open to the maternal graces and to be an independent existent. It wants both the blissful contentment of the oceanic state and self-possessed life. However, these two desires work against each other; the ends to which they lead are, for the body-ego, mutually exclusive. For the body-ego lacks sufficient strength in being to survive the solvent power of the Great Mother, in whose presence the body-ego tends to disintegrate. Hence, when the body-ego gives way to its desire for intimacy with the Great Mother, the consequence is dissolution, loss of independent existence, regression to the oceanic state. Conversely, when the body-ego holds fast to its independence—as developmental impulses drive it to do—the consequence is alienated aloneness, loss of intimate contact with what, for it, is the primary reality. The body-ego thus wants two things that, for it, are incompatible. It wants both to be intimate with the Good Mother and independent of the Terrible Mother. But since the Good Mother and the Terrible Mother are two facets of a single reality, the body-ego's two basic desires necessarily negate each other. Together, they constitute an impossible project, a double bind that condemns the body-ego to self-defeating endeavors.

The body-ego, then, pursues an impossible fundamental project. However, the impossibility of this project is not evident at first, since it is not until the later stages of the body-ego's development that the body-ego, attached to its emerging selfhood, begins seriously to resist the magnetic-solvent power of the Great Mother. It is hard to say exactly when this corner is turned, although, generally speaking, the event can be said to occur sometime in the second or third year of life. In any case, once the corner is turned, the body-ego's relation with the Great Mother begins seriously to be plagued with approach-avoidance difficulties. The body-ego remains strongly attracted to the Great Mother, but from this point on it also is pronouncedly fearful of her. The body-ego continues to approach the Great Mother because it is drawn to the love and nurturance that flow from her. However, as the body-ego enters more intimately into the Great Mother's sphere of influence, it feels more strongly her magnetic pull, and, now, it begins to sense, however vaguely and prereflectively, that it is in danger of being engulfed, and perhaps destroyed. And so the body-ego retreats and increases its psychic distance from the Great Mother. But in guarding its safety in this way, the body-ego cuts itself off from the maternal graces that otherwise would be bestowed upon it. In want of these, the body-ego again approaches the Great Mother, only again to suffer the anxiety of impending self-loss. The body-ego thus experiences a desire/fear, love/hate, approach/avoidance dilemma in relation to the Great Mother, and this dilemma becomes increasingly acute as the body-ego matures. Because the body-ego's fundamental project is self-defeating, it cannot be endured indefinitely. Eventually the body-ego must choose between its two opposing desires. And since it is the terrible side of the Great Mother that in the long run looms the largest, this choice is really made for the body-ego. In the end, the Great Mother is decidedly more of a threat to the body-ego than she is a source and foundation; consequently, the body-ego is eventually left with no choice but to give up its desire for, and its self-dissolving indulgence in, the maternal Ground. If the body-ego is to be itself, an individuated and self-possessed existent, it must at this point cease being vulnerable to the Great Mother's influence. It must free itself from her magnetic-solvent power. And in order to do this, it must oppose her advances. Accordingly, there here ensues a struggle between the body-ego and the maternal principle that is of decisive importance for the future course of human development.

The body-ego's struggle with the Terrible Mother has two major aspects, corresponding to the bidirectional character of the maternal principle. The struggle is at once an interpersonal conflict by which the child seeks to extricate himself from the dominance of the mothering parent and an intrapsychic conflict by which the ego resists, and finally contains, the power of the Dynamic Ground. The first or interpersonal side of the struggle has as its chief consequences a withdrawal by the child from the mother's affections and, as a means to this, a burying by the child of his needs ("vulnerabilities") for openly flowing and intermingling love. And the second or intrapsychic side of the struggle has as its chief consequences a repressive alienation of the Dynamic Ground and, as a means to this, a repression of the body and of physico-dynamic life. Let us see how these consequences take shape.

On its outer front, the body-ego's battle with the Terrible Mother is waged in response to two threats. One of these has already been discussed, namely, the threat posed by the subversive-engulfing effect of the maternal power. This is a problem that grows larger as the body-ego grows older. Consequently, it is a problem that (1) makes the mothering parent appear progressively more sinister (e.g., ugly, massive, consuming, relentless, inescapable) in the eyes of the body-ego and that (2) impels the body-ego to retreat from and, finally, to do battle with the mother in an effort to free itself from her suffocating ubiquity. But this is just one side of the conflict with the maternal caretaker, for the change that the mother undergoes is a change not only in the body-ego's perception of her but also a change in fact. The mother assumes an increasingly negative appearance not only because the gravity of her presence is increasingly oppressive but also because her *discipline* is increasingly severe. To be sure, owing to the attraction-versus-separation opposition, the body-ego is predisposed to see the mother in a more unfavorable light as time passes. But compounding this perceived change, it also happens that the mother's actual behavior turns, relatively speaking, from light to dark. For the mother, who in the beginning attends to all of the body-ego's needs and blesses the body-ego with unconditional and uninterrupted love, begins in time to adopt definite expectations of the body-ego. That is, she begins to relate to the body-ego not just acceptingly and affectionately but also demandingly and punishingly. The body-ego is expected to behave according to an ever-stricter code of conduct and is expected to take care of more and more of its own needs. And depending upon whether or not the body-ego fulfills these expectations, the mother responds in markedly different ways. Accordingly, the mother ceases being simply an all-loving refuge and becomes in growing measure a coercive power, a power that praises, rewards, and embraces the body-ego when it is "good" and that scolds and perhaps physically punishes the body-ego when it is "bad." To the older body-ego, then, the mothering parent is both a subversive *and* coercive power. She is at once a magnetic force that undermines its independence and a harsh judge who disapproves of, and seeks to change, much of what it says and does.

The body-ego continues to be attracted to the mother and to crave oneness with her even as she undergoes these changes in appearance and behavior. But it is just this need of intimacy with the mother that is the body-ego's Achilles' heel, for it is just this need that leads the body-ego again and again to expose itself to the maternal power. The mother could not have anywhere nearly as great an impact upon the body-ego if the body-ego did not continue to pursue her and submit itself to her. Even her punishments would lose much of their sting if they were not experienced as the opposite of something—interflowing love— that the body-ego both wants and needs. It is therefore attachment to the mother that leads repeatedly to the body-ego's undoing, its dissolution and self-loss. This means that the body-ego, if it is truly to have a life and will of its own, must somehow put a stop to its yearning for loving intimacy with the mother. And this it does. It distances itself; it braces itself; it holds itself back in defensive reserve; it no longer allows itself unconditionally to surrender or "let go." In short, the body-ego escapes from the mother by withdrawing from her and by stifling its desire for her. The body-ego closes itself to the mother's magnetic-solvent influence, and in this way it "wins" the (outer front of the) battle with the Terrible Mother. To be sure, the body-ego continues to need the mother and to interact with her in an affectionate manner. But it never again surrenders itself to her totally; the period of unconditional openness and completely intimate mutuality is over.

What the ego accomplishes externally by effecting a breach of intimacy between itself and the mothering parent it accomplishes internally by effecting a psychic split: it separates itself from the Dynamic Ground. These two acts go hand in hand, since, as was explained, the mothering parent and the power of the Ground are, for the body-ego, inseparable dimensions of a single phenomenon. From the very beginning, it is one and the same experience for the body-ego to yield to the love of the mother and for it to give way to the power of the Ground. The body-ego knows nothing of the independence of these two dimensions of the maternal reality, and even if it did, given the causal interactivity of these dimensions and their etiological equivalence as magnetic-solvent forces, the body-ego would not be able to undertake an action with respect to one dimension without simultaneously undertaking the same action with respect to the other. Moreover, as will be explained presently, the body-ego's action against the mother is of necessity also an action against the Ground because the very same bodily posture that distances the body-ego from the mother also has the consequence of severing the body-ego from the Ground. For these reasons, then, the body-ego's alienation of the mother's affections is perforce also an alienation of the power of the Ground.

The body-ego alienates the Ground by perpetrating a repression that contains the power of the Ground. This power, which from the outset is an integral part of the body-ego's overall experience, changes over time from a force of upwelling well-being and heightened life to a force, seemingly, of dread and doom. Initially, the power of the Ground is the water of life, which, in pulsating through the body-ego, bathes it in waves of delight and which, in enveloping and dissolving the body-ego, gently returns it to the blissful oblivion of the oceanic state. But later, as the body-ego moves further along the course of individuation, this power undergoes an alteration in appearance: it begins to manifest itself as an ominous, menacing force. It becomes volatile, filling the body-ego's subjective atmosphere with violent storms, and, in its magnetism, it becomes an abysmal force that would engulf the body-ego and bring it to an awful death. Hence, notwithstanding the body-ego's continued attraction to the Ground, the power of the Ground inevitably undergoes a reversal from positive to negative. Sensitive to this change, the body-ego begins to feel imperiled by the power of the Ground, so much so, in fact, that the body-ego eventually begins to feel that it has no choice but to remove itself from further contact with the Ground. The body-ego therefore undertakes a repressive action against the Ground, which results in the sealing of the Ground and the submerging of it (together with the nonegoic pole of the psyche generally!) into unconsciousness. This repression of the Ground, which is the ego's first and most basic repressive act, is what in the last chapter was termed *original repression*.

As Neumann (1954, 1963), following Jung (1912/1952/1967), has shown, the ego's battle for independence from the Terrible Mother is depicted archetypally—in mythology and, I would add, in the rudimentary imaginings of the body-ego—as a battle to the death between a young hero (perhaps a brave warrior or knight in shining armor) and a monstrous person or beast.[9] The hero risks his life in a contest with a mighty power. It would seem that all the odds are against the hero. However, by virtue of his courage (and, frequently, by virtue of luck or miraculous intervention as well), the hero prevails, and what had appeared to be an invincible adversary is slain.

Or so it seems. Actually, the monster does not die; it merely is forced to return to the dark and the deep from whence it came and consequently is removed, not from existence, but only from sight. In other words, the dreadful power of the Ground-abyss is not extinguished; it is merely repressed and thereby contained in the nether regions: the unconscious. It waits there to be faced again at a future time, this time by the mature ego, which, in returning to its source, re-enters the arena of battle, not to reconquer the Ground qua Terrible Mother, but rather to surrender to the Ground qua spirit. To use Kierkegaard's term, the power of the Ground waits there to be braved by the knight of faith.

The battle with the Terrible Mother therefore culminates in original repression, which is the act by which the body-ego separates itself from the bidirectional maternal reality. It is the act by which the body-ego simultaneously closes itself to the mothering parent and seals the Dynamic Ground. Original repression is at once an interpersonal and an intrapsychic act; it involves both an alienation of outer affections and a containment of inner dynamism.

It would be well to point out that original repression is a physical as well as psychic event—which inaugurates a chronic physical as well as psychic posture. In committing the act of original repression, the young child *physically* separates himself from the influence of the Great Mother. He does so by tensing the body, especially the anus and abdomen, and thereby holding himself in taut, girded reserve. This rigid stance shields the child from both the outer and the inner dimensions of the maternal power. In relation to the outer dimension, the girdedness of the posture steels the body and renders it untouchable by, and therefore invulnerable to, the seductive-subversive overtures of the mother. And in relation to the inner dimension, the anal, abdominal, and other tensions inherent to the posture constrict the body in a way that blocks pulsations that otherwise would arise from the Ground. Original repression is an act that establishes a posture of defensive self-containment. In bracing the body, it armors the child against emotional solicitations. And in constricting the body, it barricades the child against dynamic upwellings.

Intrapsychically, the posture of original repression is a structure that seals the Ground and, in doing so, dams the power of the Ground. The inner tensions that make up the posture constitute a hierarchy of knots and occlusions that arrest the power of the Ground at its point of release from the sexual system. Original repression thus seals the Ground by transforming the body from a vehicle receptive to the free upflow of the power of the Ground into an impervious barrier by which the ego (now residing in the area of the head: the mental ego) is separated from the Ground. The physical infrastructure of original repression will be described in greater detail in Chapter 5. For the present, suffice it to say that the net effect of this infrastructure is that it confines the power of the Ground within the lower regions of the body and provides the ego with a haven in the mental space associated with the head.

Because it contains the power of the Ground within the sexual system, original repression marks the point at which polymorphous sensuousness ends and genital predominance begins. Polymorphous sensuousness is an expression of the unimpeded circulation of psychic energy. Hence, since original repression steels the body against the movement of psychic energy, it at the same time divests the body of its inherent overall aliveness.[10] Original repression both hardens and deadens the body; it transforms the body from a supple vehicle of the power of the Ground into a rigid barrier, a dam, that keeps the power of the Ground at bay. Original repression, then, involves not only a negation of the Ground but also, as a means to this, a negation of the body and of polymorphously sensuous life. In using the body against the Ground, original repression effects a thoroughgoing psychosomatic split. It effects a split not only between the ego and the Ground but also between mind and body and in general between consciousness and the physico-dynamic potentials of life.

It is evident that there is no longer a *body*-ego once the repression of the body has occurred. The final victory over the Terrible Mother, and the psychosomatic split that ensues from it, brings an end to the ego's bodily identification. In separating itself from the maternal power, the ego also separates itself from the body, especially the lower dynamic and instinctual regions. The body is demoted in status from self to object, and the ego now assumes an exclusive identification with the mind (and the mind's self-*concept*). The ego ascends into cerebral realms and begins to command the body from on high. In other words, the body-ego here gives way to the mental ego, a disincarnate "thinking thing" (Descartes' *res cogitans*). The period of Cartesian dualism begins.[11]

To this point we have considered the body-ego's battle with the maternal power only in terms of the emerging negativity of the maternal power in its guise as Terrible Mother. But the very same battle can be looked at the other way around, that is, in terms of an emerging sense by the body-ego of its *own* negativity, i.e., as "terrible child." And, in fact, it works both ways, since, as Mahler (Mahler et al. 1975) explains, the young child's splitting of the object representation (viz., the mother) is at the same time a splitting of the self representation. Thus, in addition to perceiving the Great Mother in increasingly menacing forms, the body-ego at the same time perceives itself in increasingly unfavorable light. It perceives itself not only as the center of the mother's loving attentions but also, and increasingly, as a being that is "bad" or "naughty," i.e., unworthy of the maternal graces that are now frequently being withheld from it and deserving of the demands and punishments that are now frequently being inflicted upon it.

This is a tragic dimension of the early childhood years. Owing simply to the dynamic of ego-versus-Ground and to the fact that the mothering parent must discipline the child if he is to grow, a change occurs that the child can understand only as meaning that he is no longer a being worthy of the unconditional love and support that once were lavished upon him. The Great Mother, which at first gives all to the body-ego and expects nothing in return, is inexorably transformed into a predominantly negative power that punishes the body-ego for acts that are natural expressions of its being (e.g., defecation, crying, anger, destructiveness) and that uses love as an instrument of coercion, i.e., as a reward when the body-ego alters its behavior to conform to ever-more-exacting standards and expectations. Operating on the prereflective assumption that the mother's treatment of it is a statement of its inherent value, or lack thereof, the body-ego at this point concludes that it is not a good child. The emergence of the Terrible Mother therefore means to the body-ego that it is a "terrible child." Tragically, it means to the body-ego that it is not a being inherently deserving of love. The body-ego feels that it is inherently "bad" or "naughty" and that it can *become* good only if this original self-nature is denied and replaced by traits and habits of conduct that live up to the standards and expectations now being imposed.

Viewed from this perspective, the battle between the body-ego and the Terrible Mother shows itself also to be a battle that the body-ego wages against itself. And the act by which the body-ego finally bests the Terrible Mother shows itself also to be an act by which the ego represses its own inner life. This act, original repression, thus is not only a banishment of an other, the Terrible Mother; it also is an act of *self*-alienation. It is an act of self-closing by which the child buries nonegoic potentials and, in doing so, stifles his own spontaneity and subdues his own inner spirit.

To summarize, the maternal power or Great Mother can be said to have many aspects and expressions. Specifically, the maternal power is a dynamic reality that is at once bidirectional and bivalent. Accordingly, the body-ego's relation to the maternal power is extremely complex. The body-ego relates to the maternal power simultaneously in two, outer and inner, directions, and the body-ego's experience of the maternal power, in both of these directions, is thoroughgoingly ambivalent. The body-ego has a love/hate, approach/avoidance relation with both the mothering parent and the Dynamic Ground. In the early period of its development, the body-ego experiences mostly the positive aspect of the Great Mother, who, as Good Mother, protects the body-ego and showers it with blessings. But as the body-ego matures, it begins to experience the negative dimension of the Great Mother, who, as Terrible Mother, subverts the body-ego's independence, coerces its behavior, and punishes it, leading it to believe that it is a "terrible child." Owing to this change in character of the body-ego's relation with the Great Mother, there ensues a battle between the body-ego and the maternal power that terminates in original repression: the dissociation of the ego from the maternal power, which is at the same time a dissociation of the ego from its own instinctual, affective, creative, and spiritual life.

Original repression is the last act of the body-ego. And like every other aspect of the body-ego's life, it too is two-sided. Original repression is indeed a conquest over a menacing power, but it is a conquest that is also a defeat. It is true that original repression is a victory that is essential to the ego's continued development, since original repression earns the ego self-possession and freedom to conduct its own activities without the overawing influence of nonegoic potentials. However, original repression at the same time incurs a profound loss, since the nonegoic pole of the psyche, half of the human endowment, is forfeited from consciousness. The ego loses contact with upwelling life. The nonegoic pole of the psyche is buried and rendered invisible. Arrested at the pre-egoic level, it becomes the dynamic unconscious.

THE BODY PROJECT, THE OEDIPAL CONFLICT, AND ORIGINAL REPRESSION

To repeat, the body-ego's fundamental project is to be an "independent intimate" of the Great Mother. In the body-ego's interaction with the mothering parent, this project takes the form of the *body project*, which is the attempt on the part of the body-ego to use its body as a means of achieving both closeness to and safe distance from the mother. The body project, in my opinion, is a major factor in early psychosexual development.

The stages of psychosexual development are rooted in bodily areas that bear a twofold relation to the maternal principle. On the one hand, these areas, as erogenous zones, are avenues of access to the originally embedded condition. The mouth, anus, and genitals are made of sensitive tissue that normally bears a high energic charge. The stimulation of these zones, therefore, releases concentrated doses of energy, potent outpourings which induce euphoria in the body-ego and allow it to lose itself in an ecstatic return to original embedment. The body-ego is polymorphously sensuous, which means that it can be enraptured by means of any bodily surface or member. Nevertheless, it is the erogenous zones that are the most compelling in this regard. Stimulation of them usually effects an immediate melting of the body-ego's self-boundaries.

However, the psychosexual zones are not given to the child to enjoy at will. They are under the supervision and restraint of the mothering parent. It is the mother who gives or refuses the breast, who stipulates the times and places for defecation, and who mandates that the genitals be covered and, in many cases, not touched. In short, it is the mother who guards the gates of her own paradisiacal domain. The child is allowed to dissolve himself in erogenous euphoria only on her conditions and at her discretion.

But the situation is more complicated than this. For we have already seen that the child is not only attracted to but also threatened by the self-dissolution that goes with re-embedment. Therefore, the temptation to let go and give way to the energies that are released from the erogenous zones is overlaid with anxiety, especially for the older body-ego. Letting go is experienced as self-loss. On the oral level, the body-ego likely senses that the loss will be by being swallowed; on the anal level, by being emptied of self; and on the phallic level, by suffering some vague calamity—for the child quickly infers from the adult's concern that the genitals be covered that the genitals are taboo and dangerous in some way.

The psychosexual zones are, then, double-edged. And so too is the mother's superintendence of them. From the point of view of the body-ego, the mother uses these zones both to bar access and to solicit approach to original embedment, which is a state that the body-ego both does and does not want to enter. Accordingly, the body-ego responds to the maternal injunctions and enticements with an inconsistency that expresses the vicious ambivalences and contradictions of its situation. It responds both obediently and defiantly. Oral aggression can in this way be seen as the other side of oral submission—as, correspondingly, "bad" and "good" breasts can be seen as instantiations of the Terrible Mother and the Good Mother. Anal sadism can be seen as the other side of anal conformity. And phallic rebelliousness—e.g., exhibitionism, public urination—can be seen as the other side of phallic propriety. For the most part, the child tries to remain in the good graces of the mother, but her threatening guise prompts frequent defensive-aggressive attacks. The body-ego wants to be an "independent intimate" of the mother. However, independence and intimacy are incompatible for the body-ego, and, consequently, it tends to interact with the mother in flagrantly contradictory ways, shifting dramatically between submission in search of intimacy and defiance in defense of independence.

The body-ego's fundamental project culminates in the Oedipal conflict. This happens because, around the age of four or shortly thereafter, it dawns upon the child that there is someone who enjoys just the sort of relationship with the mother for which the child impossibly strives: the father. The father is on intimate terms with the mother and yet is also a fully independent being. Given this model, the body-ego's fundamental project develops into the fantasy of displacing the father. The body-ego senses that if it could but assume the father's role vis-a-vis the mother, it could succeed in its desire to be at one with the mother without thereby suffering self-loss. Therefore, a rivalry with the father ensues—or at least this is what happens in the eyes of the body-ego.

It is implied in this interpretation of the Oedipal conflict that the child-mother relationship at the Oedipal stage is not one of a *boy* child desiring to experience *sexual* intimacy with the mother. It is rather one of a boy *or girl* child desiring to *usurp the father's special relationship* with the mother. This means that the Electra complex, if there is such a thing, is not the little girl's version of the Oedipus complex. Male and female children, I suggest, share the same fundamental project. Both seek to be an "independent intimate" of the mother, and both pursue the same basic strategies toward this end.[12]

Another implication of this interpretation of the Oedipal conflict is that the child need harbor no fantasies of genital sexuality or fears of genital mutilation. The child need have no fixation on, or even any comprehension of, the mechanics of sexual intercourse. Nor need he or she have any apprehensions about castration, better yet clitoridectomy. The fantasy, rather than being focused on sex, is an undefined one of personal closeness with the mother. And the fear, rather than being focused on a particular organ, is the general one of provoking the wrath of the father. The child indulges fantasies of besting the father in a competition for the mother's favor. This may or may not lead to a real antagonism with the father. But in any case, given the father's virtual omnipotence in the child's eyes, the mere prospect of such an antagonism is sufficient to cause the child to fear for his life.

In tendering this interpretation of the Oedipal conflict, I am also taking exception to the existentialist view—advocated by N.O. Brown (1959), Ernest Becker (1973), and (in modified transpersonal form) Ken Wilber (1980a)[13]—according to which the desire for the mother is the desire for godlike independence, the desire to be parent or cause of oneself, *ens causa sui*. This view is ingenious, but it suffers from insuperable difficulties. For example, it shares with the orthodox psychoanalytic view the problem of explaining how a child as young as four can have knowledge of sexual intercourse. And it compounds this problem by additionally assuming that the four-year-old has knowledge of the causality of procreation. The body-ego just does not aspire to the kind of independence that existentialists like Sartre extol. True, the body-ego does aspire to independence, but not unconditionally so, since it also longs for intimacy and support. The body-ego does not want absolute independence; rather, it wants to be an "independent intimate" of the mother. The existentialist perspective is misapplied to the body-ego. However, this perspective does have a proper sphere of application: the mental ego. It is the mental ego that, in separation from the nonegoic pole of the psyche, is embarked upon a project of absolute independence. It is the mental ego that strives to be *ens causa sui*. The mental ego's project of independence will be discussed in Chapter 4.

To return now to the predicament of the child in the Oedipal situation, it is evident that the child cannot win in his competition with the father; eventually the child must capitulate. And the terms of surrender are clear: the child must relinquish all hopes of or claim to intimacy with the mother, who now belongs, in this way, to the father alone. In other words, the child at this point must concede half of his fundamental project; he must forfeit intimacy and pursue independence as his exclusive goal. But if we remember, this is precisely the outcome of the child's struggle with the Terrible Mother. What this means, then, is that the child's capitulation to the father and conquest of the mother are contemporaneous and functionally equivalent events. They are events that occur concurrently and that arrive at the same end, to wit, dissociation from the mother and all that she represents (viz., nonegoic potentials: body, dynamism, instinct, feeling, creativity) and exclusive identification with the father and all that he represents (viz., egoic functions and concerns: self-control, reason, personality, civilization). In the case of both events, the same sacrifices are made and the same things are won, or at least consolidated. The battle with the Terrible Mother and the rivalry with the Oedipal Father, then, go hand in hand. They work in concert to bring about a single result.[14]

It has already been explained that dissociation from the maternal principle carries with it the alienation of the body, which must be repressed in order to dam the maternal energies that otherwise would overwhelm or dissolve the ego. It can now be said that the same result is arrived at as a consequence of the Oedipal competition with the father. This follows from the fact that the child senses that the father is likely to do violence not just to the child's genitals, but to his very being. The child fears that his bodily existence is in danger, and for this reason he takes flight from the bodily plane, as if from lost ground. He retreats into himself, and as he does so he discovers that his subjectivity is a world unto itself. That is, in escaping from the body, the child comes suddenly to realize that he is not just an outer physical thing but also a mind, a private inner space. And this insight comes as a great relief. For the privacy of the mind is taken by the child to mean that the mind or subjectivity is an inviolable refuge, a place in which the child is safe from the father, and from the outer public world generally. Fear of the Oedipal Father leads in this way to the disclosure of subjectivity as a distinct level or domain of existence. The ego retreats into this sanctuary and begins to define itself in mentalistic terms. It secedes from the body and begins a new life and identity as a mental being.

So we arrive at original repression and Cartesian dualism once again. Whether by victory over the Terrible Mother or surrender to the Oedipal

Father, the body is alienated and reduced to the status of a thing and, simultaneously, the mental sphere is occupied and accorded the status of (exclusive) self. This mental self or ego now assumes ownership of the body and relates to it as a pure subject would relate to a mere object. Accordingly, the mental self or ego considers itself to be altogether independent of and superior to the body. Physically, for example, the mental ego, associated with the head, sits atop the body and commands it from on high. Metaphysically, the mental ego thinks of itself as being invulnerable to the dependencies, and even mortality, of bodily existence. Practically, the mental ego fancies itself to be completely autonomous and self-possessed, and therefore unaffected by impulses arising from beneath its own sphere. And morally, the mental ego stands in judgment of the flesh as making up our "lower nature." However, since this so-called lower nature is a central part of our total self-nature, the rule of the mental ego, however warranted it may be for developmental reasons, is ultimately a species of self-negation. It is a negation of the nonegoic pole of the psyche—which negation must itself be negated before the self can be whole and true.

In drawing to a close, it should be acknowledged that the emergence of the mental ego is an event that is brought about by many causes, of which the struggles with the Terrible Mother and Oedipal Father are but two. Other factors importantly involved are: (1) social conditioning and expectation, (2) adjustment to external reality, and (3) the growth impulse. All of these factors bear significantly upon the transition from the body-ego to the mental ego. If, then, the three factors just listed have not been part of the foregoing discussion, the reason is not that they are deemed unimportant to the developmental process. It is rather that the aim in this chapter has been to explain not only the differentiation of the mind but also the alienation of the body and the Dynamic Ground. And with specific respect to this second matter, the three factors just mentioned play accessory rather than central roles. So far as the split between the egoic and nonegoic poles of the psyche is concerned, the essential factors, as we have seen, are the psychodynamic and interpersonal, the ego's relations to the Dynamic Ground and to the mother and father.

CONCLUSION

The body-ego's existence is bounded on one side by original embedment and on the other side by original repression. The former boundary marks a condition of predifferentiated unity with the maternal principle, of blissful ensconcement in the Dynamic Ground. The latter boundary marks the point at which the ego utterly dissociates itself from the maternal principle, winning independence by divorcing itself from the Dynamic Ground. Original embedment is a condition of pre-egoic unity with the Ground, while original repression is a condition—or, rather, the act that ushers in a condition—of egoic estrangement from the Ground. The two boundaries of the body-egoic period thus represent two diametrically opposed positions in the unfolding of the ego/Ground relation. Original embedment represents the point at which the Ground is all and the ego nothing (i.e., in the sense of being still merely potential), and original repression represents the point at which the ego is all and the Ground nothing (i.e., in the sense of being submerged and invisible to consciousness).

The body-egoic period between original embedment and original repression is a time during which the young child is torn between these extremes. The body-ego has mixed feelings, wanting both intimacy with and independence from the Great Mother. It wants both to receive the Great Mother's blessings and to be self-possessed and self-controlled. However, these two desires are in conflict with each other. The desire for intimacy conflicts with independence, for when the body-ego comes into close contact with the Great Mother it suffers dissolution and re-embedment. And the desire for independence conflicts with intimacy, for when the body-ego makes a move of independence it experiences separation from the principal reality of its world, a reality to which the body-ego remains strongly attracted and attached. The body-ego, pulled in these opposite directions by its two basic desires, is caught in a dilemma. It finds itself in a contradictory, and therefore untenable, situation.

The body-ego cannot hold on indefinitely to both of the horns of its dilemma. Something must be sacrificed. And in the interests of development, it is the Great Mother—and with her, nonegoic or physico-dynamic life generally—that in the end is relinquished. In effect, the body-ego is finally confronted with the choice of either regression or repression. There is no middle ground. The body-ego must either side with the mother, and thereby submit to a regression that would forfeit autonomy, responsibility, mind, and will, or it must side against the mother (and with the father), and thereby perpetrate a repression that would forfeit body, dynamism, feeling, and creativity. The choice is not a happy one; the loss is great in either case. Nevertheless, a choice has to be made. And the choice that is finally arrived at, repression, is clearly the better of the two. For it is the only choice that allows the ego to continue to grow.

This account of original repression suggests an interpretation of the traditional Judeo-Christian doctrine of original sin. In particular, it provides a way of answering three questions that are especially vexing for the traditional view: (1) Why was humanity susceptible to sin? (2) In what respect was the act that was committed evil and deserving of punishment? and (3) In what meaningful sense can sin be said to be inherited?

The traditional account leaves it unclear why Adam and Eve were moved to sin. We are told that they ate the fruit because they were tempted. But why should they have been tempted to reach for more than was already theirs in paradise? If they were really in paradise, they must have been completely happy and satisfied. If, however, they were tempted for something more, then, it seems, they must not have been in paradise after all.

This problem can be averted if, as in the foregoing analysis, it is assumed that the paradisiacal conditions of Eden do not last. For on this assumption, the act of sin is a response not to paradise, but to the *loss* of paradise. Or in our terms, original repression is a response not to the completely benign conditions that obtain during original embedment and the early pre-egoic period, but rather to the negative transformation of these conditions that occurs during the middle and late pre-egoic period. If, as I have argued, the idyllic circumstances that make up the body-ego's initial environment change one hundred and eighty degrees, then sin, or original repression, can be understood to be an inevitable response to this reversal in the conditions of existence. On this interpretation, then, sin is not an act of gratuitous self-assertion but rather an act of necessary self-defense.

But if sin, so conceived, is a necessary response to an impossible situation, how can it be considered an evil deed deserving of punishment? Where is the wrong in self-defense? The answer, I believe, is that there is no wrong *at first*. Original repression is initially a necessary, and therefore innocent, act. However, original repression is not a mere passing event; it is rather the initiation of a posture that is sustained over time. Since original repression is a way in which the power of the Ground is contained, it must, like a dam, be an enduring structure if its effect is to last. And, indeed, original repression is just such a structure. It is a posture that, once assumed, quickly hardens and petrifies, becoming the unconscious infrastructure of the mental-egoic system. Original repression, once solidified in this way, remains in place for most people throughout the rest of their lives. But this is simply to say that original repression usually remains in place much longer than is functional or necessary. For once the ego is strong and mature, it no longer needs to be separated from the Ground. Hence, even though original repression is at first a necessity to be rued rather than a wrong to be condemned, it becomes, in time, an unnecessary, and an unwarranted, obstacle to the ego's higher destiny. In time, it becomes a way in which the ego is held back from—or, rather, holds itself back from—meeting its ultimate spiritual Ground. In short, original repression becomes a way in which the ego refuses God. It becomes sin.

This brings us to the question about how, if at all, sin can be said to be inherited. The problem, of course, is that if sin is an individual act, it seems that it should be an individual responsibility as well. Yet the traditional account of original sin contradicts this; it holds that there is collective, inherited guilt for the individual acts of Adam and Eve. In order to avoid the logical oddity of this position (not to mention its evident unfairness), many have argued that it is not sin per se that is inherited but rather only the predisposition to sin. This seems to be a move in the right direction, which, conveniently, fits well with the notion of original repression here being defended. Adopting this approach, then, let us say that human beings are born only with a tendency to sin, not with sin itself. And let us add that the inherited tendency in question is not the predisposition to commit the act of original repression—since, if I am right, original repression is unavoidable, and hence inculpable—but rather the predisposition to maintain, to hide behind, original repression for too long a period of time. Human beings are predisposed to sin not by virtue of their proneness early in life to repress the power-spirit of the Ground, but rather by virtue of their proneness later in life to resist lifting this repression. Human beings are subject to sin by virtue of their tendency, later in life, to put off the day of reckoning, to shy back from the precipice of faith.

Some final questions: Is original repression absolutely necessary? Granting that it is virtually inevitable, is it completely impossible to avoid? Could not, under exceptional circumstances, a child win independence without severing contact with the Ground, or master mental and volitional operations without forfeiting physico-dynamic life? Unfortunately, there are no sure answers to these questions. The possibility cannot be denied that a child of extraordinary ego strength blessed with parents of unlimited understanding and love might be able to weather the contradictions of early childhood without succumbing to original repression. Therefore, leaving this possibility open, the only warranted conclusion is that original repression—and therefore the ego/Ground, mind/body split—is an almost inescapable eventuality of early childhood development. Acknowledging the possibility of rare exceptions, it seems virtually unavoidable that the sins of the fathers will be visited upon the children.

CHAPTER 3

The Body-Ego: Cognitive and Affective Development

H AVING IN THE LAST chapter treated the body-ego's development from the dynamic perspective, I will in this chapter consider it as a process of unfolding stages of cognition and feeling. I will follow out the succession of these stages up to the point of original repression, which brings the period of the body-ego to a close.

Consideration of the body-ego's cognitive and affective life is important both for its own sake and because many of the aspects of this life, along with many of the aspects of the body-ego's dynamic situation already discussed, are early ("pre-") manifestations of nonegoic potentials that later (in their "trans-" form) become essential ingredients of integrated existence. These are potentials that enjoy a brief flowering during the body-egoic period only to be submerged and rendered unconscious at the point of original repression. These potentials then remain unconscious throughout the time of the mental ego's ascendancy. Thereafter, once the ego, fully developed, embarks upon the transitional stages leading to integration, these nonegoic potentials are derepressed and returned to consciousness. At this juncture, the whole range of physico-dynamic life reappears within the ego's field of experience and there commences an interaction between physico-dynamic and mental-egoic spheres that, carried to culmination, results in integrated existence. The ensuing discussion of the cognitive and affective dimensions of the body-ego's experience thus is concerned not only with the prehistory of the mental ego but with its possible future history as well. In addition to reviewing essential aspects of an early stage of development, this chapter will also be previewing essential ingredients of the last and highest stage of human development.

Our guide for much of this chapter will be Silvano Arieti, who in his National Book Award-winning *The Intrapsychic Self* (1967) has set forth an account of human development in cognition and feeling that at many points is congruent with the psychodynamic orientation of this book. In relation to those of the childhood years that correspond to the period of the body-ego, Arieti divides cognitive and affective development into three major stages: (1) the stage of exocepts and protoemotions, (2) the stage of phantasms and second-order emotions, and (3) the stage of paleologic and third-order emotions. I follow Arieti closely through the first two of these stages, offering only those additions and emphases that are necessary to situate Arieti's ideas within my own theoretical perspective. The account of the third stage also follows Arieti's lead, but not as closely, since significant modifications and departures are at that point required. Then, having treated these three stages, I turn in the final section to the matter of original repression and the splitting of the bipolar psyche into conscious and unconscious systems. My purpose in dealing with the unconscious in this chapter is not to provide a general account thereof—since, in any case, the unconscious is the topic of a later chapter. Rather, my concern here is simply to point out the ways in which the system of the unconscious reflects the repressed life of the body-ego.

THE STAGE OF EXOCEPTS AND PROTOEMOTIONS

The exoceptual-protoemotional stage begins at birth and extends to about the seventh month of life. It thus includes the neonate's originally embedded condition and the first stages of ego differentiation. In Freud's account of early childhood development, the exoceptual-protoemotional period corresponds approximately to the state of primary narcissism and to the oral stage of psychosexual development. In Piaget's system of cognitive development, it matches roughly with the first three sensorimotor substages.

Arieti defines exocepts in the following manner (1967, 43-44):

> The inner representation, which I call exocept and which resembles what some neurologists call engram, is one of the early constructs which lead eventually to the formation of concepts. Until the exocept is translated into motor behavior, it is only an internal and unconscious representation of motor behavior. In this construct there is no clearcut differentiation between cognition and conation. Perhaps we can state that in the exocept there is a primitive preconceptual meaning, which is inherent in the response . . . .

Exocepts, it seems, are genetically inherited forms of selective attention that are directly connected with specific conative and motor responses. Certain sensory patterns attract awareness and set off reactions of a positive (viz., pleasure combined with pursuing movements) or negative (viz., displeasure combined with evasive movements) type. There is here no abstraction of these patterns, nor, properly speaking, any recognition of them.[1] The process is entirely preprogrammed: pattern presentation automatically commands attention, which in turn gives rise automatically to

70

approach or aversive motions. Exoceptual awareness, therefore, is entirely preconceptual; it is a process of discrimination and response that operates completely without understanding or comprehension.

The affective experience of this period of development consists of what Arieti calls protoemotions: tension, appetite, fear, rage, satisfaction, and, I would add, exuberance. Distinctive of all body-egoic feelings is that they are directly and dramatically physical in nature. What is particularly distinctive of protoemotions is that, in being physical, they are global and of unnuanced simplicity. They are generalized body states that (with the exception of fear) have no external reference or internal meaning. Moreover, as Arieti notes, they are states that for the most part are short-lived, tending toward immediate discharge.

Exuberance and fear stand apart from the other protoemotions. Exuberance is distinctive in being more abiding. As was observed in the last chapter, exuberance is an expression of the newborn's basic dynamic condition: plenitude, upwelling and overflowing energy, fulfillment. And fear, as Wilber (1980a) has explained, differs from the other protoemotions in presupposing, however minimally, reference and meaning. Fear requires at least a vague awareness of otherness, of nonself, which, as the reference of the feeling, is perceived (however prereflectively) as a threat or danger. Because fear requires some sense of the self/other distinction, it cannot, as do the other protoemotions, occur in the originally embedded condition. Rather, it probably first occurs in the postembedded phase of the oral stage of development—and for this reason probably itself possesses an oral form. Protoemotional fear, therefore, is likely a diffuse somatic uneasiness having the specific character of a resistance to being swallowed or engulfed, perhaps by the Great Mother as she makes her initial appearance to the body-ego as its chief other.

The exoceptual-protoemotional ego is the first and most indefinite localization of selfhood in the body, and in its perceptions, feelings, and movements. This sense of selfhood is entirely prereflective and consists, as Arieti (1967, 48) says, only "of a bundle of simple relations between physiostates [e.g., hunger, thirst, fatigue], perceptions, protoemotions, and exocepts...." These relations, as Arieti remarks, are at first focused in the mouth but soon increase their scope to include a motor identity involving the body as a whole. Also, there is nothing particularly human about self-awareness of this crude sort; it is likely that it is shared by some of the subhuman animals.

THE STAGE OF PHANTASMS AND SECOND-ORDER EMOTIONS

Arieti refers to the second major stage of the body-ego's development as the phantasmic stage. It is so called because the emergence of the image—which Arieti, somewhat controversially, dates around the seventh month—is the essential distinguishing characteristic of the stage. According to Arieti, there are no images in the exoceptual-protoemotional stage, which is the reason why that stage is characterized by immediacy. The absence of images means that there is nothing to mediate between stimulus and response, which in turn means that the stimulus of the moment is, in effect, all that exists. The arrival of images upon the psychic landscape is thus a momentous event, one that opens up for the first time dimensions of the world lying beyond what is immediately present in awareness. Most importantly, it is images that first make possible inner representation of outer objects and situations and, thereby, the maintenance in mind of such objects and situations when they are not present in fact. And in rendering these things possible, images also make possible (1) understanding of the continued existence of objects during intervals when they are not perceived (object permanence); (2) recollection of the past and anticipation of the future; and (3) awareness of possibilities rather than just given actuality. The activation of the image-forming process consequently plays an indispensable role in expanding the very young child's world horizons. Of course this expansion is only a gradual process; object permanence, time, and possibilities, for example, are initially grasped only very obscurely and inadequately. But the point is that, beginning with the phantasmic stage, these dimensions of the world *are* beginning to be grasped for the first time.

As I said, Arieti dates the beginning of the phantasmic stage at around the seventh month, and he believes that the stage typically lasts until about the age of two. In Freud's thinking, the phantasmic stage therefore spans oral and early anal stages. In the Piagetian classification, it corresponds approximately to the fourth through the sixth sensorimotor substages.

Important characteristics of the images of the phantasmic stage are, according to Arieti, spontaneity and "realness" (my term). Images at this stage arise without being elicited or constructed in any conscious or voluntary manner. They simply emerge before the mind, which is as passive in its witnessing of them as it is in its perception of external things. In other words, the images of the phantasmic stage of the body-ego's development are *autogenerated*; they are products of spontaneity rather than will. Moreover, these images are exceedingly real to the body-ego, so real that the body-ego is frequently unable to distinguish between them and actual external things. Arieti says that this is likely due to the body-ego's undeveloped reality-testing skills, its inability as yet clearly to distinguish inner from outer, self from world. But, I suggest, the "realness" of these images is probably due as well to features intrinsic to the images, namely, their vividness and detail. This is likely because the body-ego has not yet suffered disconnection from nonegoic potentials and therefore is still intimately in touch with the nonegoic source from which creatively spawned images emerge: the autosymbolic process. Unlike the adult, who has little or no access to the autosymbolic process except during the dream state, the body-ego is in direct contact at all times with this image-forging source. For this reason the images experienced by the body-ego probably possess exceptional intensity and definition, perhaps as much as actual perceptions. The images experienced by the body-ego therefore likely possess the character of "realness" not only because they go untested against external reality but also because they closely approximate, in both force and form, the world as actually perceived.[2]

As the body-ego makes progress in developing reality-testing skills, its images begin to assume the status of signs. That is, the body-ego, in learning to distinguish between images and their originals, at the same time begins to establish intentional links between the two. Images at this point begin to stand for their originals; they become representations. Let us call these first mental representations *referential images*.[3]

Referential images constitute the elements of a primitive, preverbal and preconceptual form of thought. Without the intervention of language or any of the other conventions of public signification, the body-ego at this stage engages in private picture thinking. The body-ego's own internal world of images provides it with a natural set of mind-to-world correlations, and therefore with a natural basis on which it can begin the learning of language (i.e., in its basic denotative capacity).

The emergence of images that can stand for objects paves the way for what Arieti calls second-order emotions, the principal examples of which are anxiety, anger, wish, security, and, to a certain extent, simple forms of love and depression. All of these emotions are predicated on at least a minimal sense of object permanence, extended temporality, and possibility beyond what is immediately at hand. For example, anxiety differs from its protoemotional counterpart, fear, in being futurally oriented; anger differs from rage in having an objective focus; wish differs from appetite in presupposing awareness of possibilities; security differs from contentment in being an assurance about a more or less stable environment; and simple forms of love and depression differ from exuberance and malaise, respectively, in being functions of ongoing attachments to persons or, in some cases, to things. As these contrasts indicate, the cognitive sophistication introduced by the referential image carries with it a parallel sophistication in feeling.

Second-order emotions are additionally distinguished from protoemotions in being typically less global (more defined) in their physical expression, of longer duration, and less immediately connected with motor response. The cognitive advances ushered in by the referential image open the child to a multidimensional world beyond himself. Accordingly, the child's feelings go outside himself to meet this world; they intersect with, and are invested in, its newly revealed objects, persons, and possibilities. In this fashion the child's feelings are transmuted in the ways just mentioned. They cease being merely— what they were on the exoceptual-protoemotional level—meaningless, transient, and narcissistically self-contained waves of body energy and become meaningful and abiding relations between the child and the world. They become emotions proper, forms of cognitively grounded affective relatedness to the world.

Whereas the body-ego at the exoceptual-protoemotional stage possesses only the haziest sensorimotor familiarity with itself, the body-ego at the phantasmic stage develops a self-image—which is not to be confused with the mental ego's self-*concept*. At first this self-image is extremely vague and consists of but a rough outline of the body's size and shape. But over time it becomes more accurate and detailed. The self-image of the phantasmic period is a completely concrete self-representation. Possessing no universal or conceptual dimensions, it is simply a mental picture of the body and of the body's chief relations to things.

THE STAGE OF PALEOLOGIC AND THIRD-ORDER EMOTIONS

The third, and last, of the major stages of the body-ego's cognitive and affective development is, in Arieti's terms, the stage of paleologic and third-order emotions.[4] This stage typically begins when the child is about two years old and lasts until the child is about four, or slightly older. In Freud's terms, then, this third, or paleological, period cuts across and encompasses much of the anal and phallic stages of development. In Piaget's system, it is parallel to the preconceptual substage of the stage of preoperations.

As the image is the essential differentiating feature of the second stage, so it is the introduction of language as a truly viable instrument of communication that is the essential differentiating feature of the third, or paleological, stage. This is because the paleological stage involves the child's first real attempt to assimilate the conceptual framework of adult experience, and it is language that is the medium through which that framework is transmitted and acquired. Paleologic, or the primary process—or, in Piaget's terms, transductive reasoning—is the first step in this process of conceptual assimilation. The child's task is to raise cognition from the level of mere particularity to the level of universality, i.e., from the level of concretely given things to the level at which these concretely given things are comprehended as instances of concepts or kinds. This is a task that the child pursues with zeal but, at first, with only partial success. The paleological stage thus is a period in the child's cognitive development during which he significantly, but only partially, masters the adult's conceptual framework. Paleologic is an important first step toward mature cognition. But given its incompleteness, it suffers from certain deficiencies that seriously interfere with its reliability and effectiveness.

Of these deficiencies, there are three that are especially noteworthy. One is that the concepts that the child is expected to master are not at first understood in terms of what is basic and essential to them. Instead, they tend to be understood only in parochial terms, that is, only in terms of the "local" or merely contingent properties that happen to attach to those examples of the concepts to which the child is originally exposed. The child first learns a concept-term as it is employed ostensively to designate items in his immediate environment. These items, in being the first instances of the concept with which the child becomes acquainted, are (mistakenly, but understandably) taken to be the paradigm instances of the concept. What comes first in the order of the child's experience is taken by him to be first in the order of meaning. The result is that the child burdens concepts with accidental accretions and extraneous relations deriving from the narrowness of his perspective. The child, for example, might learn the word (and therefore the concept) *dictionary* in relation to the particular volume that happens to be in the study of his house, which volume, let us suppose, is thumb-indexed and quite big. It is entirely possible that the child, given this volume as the de facto defining instance of the concept, would incorporate into his understanding of the meaning of the term *dictionary* such nonessential elements as "thumb-indexed" and "big." That is to say, in the child's mind a dictionary might be understood to be a large book with colored notches on the front edge of its pages. Such an understanding, it should be stressed, is a real cognitive achievement; it is definitely better than having no concept at all. But obviously, such an understanding falls considerably short of full comprehension. Although a real achievement, it is only a partial one; consequently, it not only allows the child to make many correct identifications (of dictionaries in this case), but it leads him to make many misidentifications as well. Children at this stage of cognitive development operate with whole interlocking networks of such narrowly conceived and accident-burdened concepts. It is no wonder that they tend frequently to make bizarre associations and to ask what to adults seem like nonsensical questions.

A second shortcoming of paleological thinking is that its understanding of conceptual meanings is restricted to the concrete level of the imagination. In learning the term *dictionary*, the body-egoic child at the paleological stage does not formulate an abstract verbal definition; he does not actually say to himself,

"Oh yes, a dictionary is any large book with colored notches on the front edge of its pages." The child at this stage does not perform an inductive generalization on a variety of instances, abstracting common denominators and bracketing individual differences. Rather, he relies on his imagination—which is to say that he relies on the autosymbolic process—to do his cognitive work for him. And the autosymbolic process responds to the child's need with immensely creative assistance, spontaneously producing images in which the salient features of the newly learned conceptual meanings are graphically portrayed. The autosymbolic process is humanity's chief creative faculty, and its creativity is here pressed into service on behalf of the young child, for whom it fashions concrete picture-meanings, which are the half-particular/half-universal forerunners of concepts proper. It creates protoconcepts, images which are no longer merely mental representations of outer objects or individuals (i.e., referential images) but which, now, are also concrete exemplars of kinds (i.e., symbols in the more strict sense of the term). With this aid of the autosymbolic process, then, paleological thought takes a half step toward the abstractly universal meanings of adult cognition. However, in taking this half step it at the same time remains a half step short, since, operating exclusively in the medium of the imagination, paleological thought is unable to grasp universal meanings except in concrete pictorial dress. Paleological thought only half-conceives universal meanings; it fails fully to abstract concept from representative instance, essence from exemplar.

The fact that the autosymbolic process has been brought into the service of conceptual meanings indicates that the cognitive status of images has changed. As was just said, images cease being merely signs, representations referring to particular entities beyond themselves, and become symbols in the more strict sense of the term: exemplary particulars, concrete embodiments of universal meanings or forms. Or in the terminology to be used here, they cease being merely referential images and become *paleosymbols*.[5]

The paleosymbol, then, is not just an inner picture of particular objects or persons in the child's environment; it is rather a model or paradigm, a concrete universal. It is a symbol rather than merely a sign. However, if it is true that mental images become symbols during the paleological period, we should not be overly impressed by this fact. For the paleosymbol is still a very primitive form of cognition. Unlike the creative symbols forged by the artist or genius, which are *trans*conceptual, paleosymbols are decidedly preconceptual. To be sure, both of these types of symbols are exemplary particulars struck spontaneously by the autosymbolic process. But here the comparison ends. For whereas the symbols of the artist or genius are more than concepts, paleosymbols are less. The symbols forged by the artist or genius are universal meanings that have been condensed into concrete images or metaphors, general patterns that have been creatively instantiated. Paleosymbols, on the other hand, are but incomplete concepts, exemplary instances of concepts formed in the absence and stead of the concepts themselves. In other words, whereas the symbols of the artist or genius are universals succeeding in being particulars, paleosymbols are particulars that have not yet succeeded completely in being universals.

The third of the aforementioned deficiencies of paleological cognition is that this type of thought does not yet fully grasp the substance/attribute distinction. This is not to say that paleological cognition fails to grasp things as enduring individuals. Object permanence, as was noted, is already achieved in a rudimentary way in the phantasmic stage. However, the objects that are discriminated as enduring individuals are not clearly conceived as objects in the substantival sense, that is, as objects that logically are subjects of predication and that ontologically are unique and self-subsistent supports of qualities, properties, and relations. Because the distinction between substance and attribute has not been made with any degree of adequacy, it frequently is the case that the "objects" that the child has discriminated are not really understood by him to be anything more than clusters of qualities. It is not that the child has, as it were, decided to reify qualities and to reduce substances to the status of mere complexes of these. The point is that the child is at a pre-substance/attribute level, and therefore that the enduring objects of his environment are not clearly either entities or qualities, substances or attributes. The fact is that they are at once both and neither, since the distinction in question has not yet been completely made.

In the absence of an effective distinction between substance and attribute, the child—as Von Domarus (1944) was the first to realize—frequently operates as if by a principle of predicate identity rather than subject identity. What this means is that the child tends frequently to understand by the expression the same thing not the same subject or substance but rather the same predicate(s) or attribute(s). He tends not to distinguish similarity from identity, and consequently he is liable to conflate what, from the adult point of view, are numerically distinct entities. To return to the dictionary example, this means that the child who had learned the term dictionary in relation to the volume in the study of his house might be led, were he to see a similar volume elsewhere, to recognize it not as another dictionary but, rather, as a reappearance of the original dictionary. The reappearance of the same qualities would in this case be taken as a reappearance of the same thing. A perplexing implication of this is that, since qualities are reproducible without regard to spatio-temporal restrictions, what is taken to be a single thing could in principle exist in different locations at the same time. And so, to return again to our example, the child, it seems, would in effect be committed to the position that the same dictionary can, and perhaps does, exist in many different places simultaneously. It is obvious that thought of this type could

77

entangle the child in a thicket of contradictions.

There are three consequences of the predicate-identity principle that should be noted. These are: (1) that the possibility exists for virtually limitless condensations and displacements, of both cognitive and dynamic sorts, (2) that the body-ego at this stage is prone to feelings of magical power and vulnerability, and (3) that the body-ego's sense of selfhood at this point is radically unstable.

1. Condensation and displacement. Psychoanalysis stresses the importance of condensation and displacement to the primary process. The occurrence, indeed prevalence, of condensation and displacement during the paleological period can be explained in terms of the predicate-identity principle. For predicate identity, in treating similar things as manifestations of the same thing, allows both (1) that any instance of a concept or member of a class can stand for all the others, just as if it were the whole of the concept or class (this being condensation), and (2) that any instance of a concept or member of a class can be exchanged for any other, just as if it were a reappearance rather than a replacement of the original (this being displacement). If similarity is reduced to identity, it follows that any representative of a type or kind can stand for all others or be replaced by any other. Cognition is free, vertically, to treat particulars as universals and, horizontally, to exchange particulars for particulars, virtually without restriction.

And psychoanalysis holds that it is not only cognition but also energy that is free to move in these ways. Psychic energy is allowed to move easily from object to object (displacement), each of which is cathected to the maximum degree, as if it were the only object of its type (condensation). Generally speaking, the experience of the body-ego is one of energy freedom. The power of the Ground circulates freely within the confines of the body, despite primary localizations in the mouth, anus, and genitals; and the outward projection of energy is also open and mobile. Inwardly, the body-ego's experience is characterized by polymorphous sensuousness; outwardly, it is characterized by a highly charged numinous atmosphere in which there occur fluid transformations of psychic energy. Inwardly, the body-ego's experience possesses a generalized intensity and arousal capacity; outwardly, it possesses a prepotency, an electrical aliveness, that is open-ended and easily mutable in focus.

2. Magical power and vulnerability. The predicate-identity principle also is manifested in feelings of magical power and vulnerability. The sense of power derives from the fact that an action performed on one object automatically extends to all other objects bearing similar properties—since, if predicate identity prevails, these latter objects *are* the object on which the action is originally performed. The efficacy of actions therefore extends in principle as far as the most remote instantiation of the properties or qualities that (relevantly) inhere in the object that is the proximate recipient of one's deeds. Thus, for example, another person can be affected by manipulating an effigy or even by fantasizing action upon an image in mind. But the reverse also holds true, as Arieti notes. The reverse of magical omnipotence is total vulnerability and defenselessness, for just as actions outgoing from the subject suffer no obstacles in the attainment of their ends, neither, it must be assumed, do actions incoming upon the subject. These, too, reach their goal without diminution or delay. The subject is as vulnerable with respect to the magical omnipotence of others as they are with respect to his.

3. *Instability in sense of self.* At the phantasmic stage of development, the body-ego's sense of self was borne in a more or less vague self-image, i.e., a mental picture of the body. This self-image remains the depository of selfhood into the third, or paleological, stage. But in the third stage the self-image begins to acquire a rudimentary universal or conceptual character. The child begins to refer to himself as *I* and he begins, in a concrete imaginal way, to ascribe properties to himself. In other words, the child's self-image at this point, like all the other of his mental images, becomes a paleosymbol. It ceases being merely a sign, a mental picture of the body, and begins also being a concrete universal, a mental picture of distinctive, defining attributes. Also, as the child begins to assign properties to himself in this way, he at the same time begins to have a new sense of his standing in being. This happens because, owing to the lack of distinction between substance and attribute, the properties with which the child identifies himself are not mere attributes that might be "possessed" by a substance; they are rather quasi-independent entities that the child *is*. They are modes of being in which the child—along with other persons, animals, and things!—participates. Consequently, in beginning to *see* himself in terms of universals, the child in a sense *becomes* those universals: properties possess the child as much as the child possesses them. Consistent, then, with his view of things generally, the child in the paleological period comes to view himself as something that is at once both and neither a substance and an attribute, a particular and a universal.

In being raised to the semi-universal, protoconceptual level of paleologic, the body-ego's sense of self simultaneously becomes subject to the problems that are endemic to paleologic. Hence, besides being confined to the limits of the imagination, the body-ego's sense of self suffers from fortuitous admixtures and, more seriously, from predicate-identity instability. Regarding the latter problem, it is noteworthy that the body-ego at this point is without a clearly bounded identity. The body-ego has no being that is truly its own, since it shares being with every person, animal, and thing with which it happens relevantly to share qualities. These persons, animals, and things are, for the body-ego, totemic objects, objects with which the body-ego participates in condensation and displacement relations—condensation in that the body-ego possesses their identity, and therefore being, and displacement in that they possess the body-ego's identity, and therefore being. Like magical omnipotence and vulnerability, this condensation and displacement interplay is bidirectional and subject to unpredictable, instantaneous reversals. The boundaries of the body-ego's selfhood thus are radically unstable, subject to alternating expansions (via condensations) and contractions (via displacements). In theory, the body-ego's self-identity can fluctuate all the way from all-inclusiveness to empty nothingness. The body-ego can at one moment annex the whole world within itself only to be left, soon thereafter, with little or no self at all.

The emergence of paleosymbols leads to a second major transformation of the body-ego's emotional life. Like light that is passed through a prism, the second-order emotions that are filtered through the protoconceptual framework of paleologic come out, as third-order emotions, differentiated into many colors and hues. They take on new meanings and forms; they assume a universal dimension; and they are condensed, displaced, and otherwise modified in focus and scope.

Arieti deems the most important of the third-order emotions to be depression, hate, love, and joy. As observed shortly ago, these emotions have their beginnings in the phantasmic stage—indeed, joy can be considered an advanced form of exuberance, a protoemotion. But it is in the paleological stage, Arieti holds, that these emotions first find their full and proper expression. To these feelings, I think, should be added exhilaration and inflation on the one hand and dread and deflation on the other, since these are the feelings that would correspond to the wild fluctuations in the senses of power and identity that are characteristic of paleological experience.

In general, third-order emotions can be distinguished from second-order emotions in (1) possessing the universal dimension introduced by the paleosymbol, (2) being even more defined in their bodily expression, (3) being of even longer duration, and (4) reflecting even more abiding relations to persons and things.

As a final note, it should be stressed that the paleological stage marks a significant advance in overall development. If in the foregoing discussion I have focused on the deficiencies of paleologic, that was for purposes of explanation, not judgment. For whatever its shortcomings, paleologic constitutes a first and sizable step toward the mastery of the conceptual framework of adult thought. In particular, the paleosymbol must be credited for being a remarkably successful forerunner of the concept. Since it is important to understand the weaknesses of the paleosymbol, I have concentrated on the fact that it is an accident-laden and unstable image pressed to do all the work of a concept. But having made this point, it needs here to be emphasized that the paleosymbol is, in its own way, a highly versatile vehicle of cognition. It is a creatively forged meaning that merits praise for the progress that it represents when compared with its predecessor, the merely referential image. If to this point I have dwelt upon the distance by which the paleosymbol falls short of fully abstracted universality, I should here commend it for the considerable distance it has traversed *toward* this goal.

THE BODY-EGO, ORIGINAL REPRESSION, AND THE UNCONSCIOUS

The topic of the unconscious will be the subject of a later chapter. The following observations, therefore, are not intended to be complete or final in any way. My purpose at this point is only to indicate briefly how, following original repression, the pre-egoic period of life is represented in the system of the unconscious.

The body-ego is without a repressed or submerged unconscious.[6] There are, of course, many aspects of its experience of which it is completely unaware. But these, in being absent from awareness, are not separated from consciousness by means of repression. The body-ego does not normally—i.e., barring serious trauma—employ such a "mechanism," and thus its experience is not divided against itself into disconnected conscious and unconscious systems. It is true that the body-ego is fearful of, and resistant to, many of the nonegoic elements of its experience. But it is never altogether closed to them, not even to the power of the Dynamic Ground, which issues from the deepest fundament of the psyche.

However, if the body-ego is open to the deepest sources of the psyche, the mental ego is not. As we know, the transition from the pre-egoic to the egoic stage is predicated on original repression, which is an act that severs the two poles of the psyche. The mental ego therefore is dissociated from the nonegoic pole of the psyche, which is submerged and becomes the dynamic unconscious.

The unconscious that is created at this point is the *prepersonal* or *collective* unconscious, so called because this stratum of the unconscious is universal (collective) and is composed of materials all of which derive from the nonegoic or physico-dynamic pole of the psyche as it is repressively arrested in its "pre-" form (prepersonal). The prepersonal unconscious can be divided into three levels. The first and most basic of these is the sphere of the *Dynamic Ground*, the source and seat of the power-energy-spirit of the soul. The second level is the sphere of the *instinctual-archetypal* unconscious, which includes (1) the collective instincts and corresponding image systems (archetypes) that have been derived phylogenetically to deal with basic human needs and typical human situations, and (2) the universal images associated with the ontogenesis of the ego and its lifelong interaction with the Dynamic Ground. The former of

81

these two subdivisions can be called the *phylogenetic* level of the instinctual-archetypal unconscious, the latter the *ontogenetic* level of the instinctual-archetypal unconscious. Finally, the third level of the prepersonal unconscious is the sphere of the *body-unconscious*, which includes the "pre-" forms of all remaining nonegoic potentials that are deleted from consciousness when the ego dissociates itself from the nonegoic pole. This sphere, then, contains many of the specific features of the body-ego's experience that have been surveyed in this and the preceding chapter.[7]

Reserving treatment of the Dynamic Ground and the phylogenetic level of the instinctual-archetypal unconscious until Chapter 5, I will here present a few advance observations about the ontogenetic level of the instinctual-archetypal unconscious and about the body-unconscious, indicating how they reflect the lost life of the body-ego.

1. *The instinctual-archetypal unconscious.* The ontogenetic subdivision of the instinctual-archetypal unconscious consists of all the universal images that derive from the ego's evolving interaction with the Dynamic Ground. According to the account presented in the last chapter, the three principal moments of this interaction that occur during the pre-egoic period are (1) the beginning point of original embedment, (2) the early experience of the Good Mother, and (3) the eventual encounter with the Terrible Mother. All three of these moments are represented in the archetypes of the prepersonal unconscious.

Corresponding to original embedment are archetypes of self-containment and pure potentiality, as, for example, are expressed in such images as the cosmic egg, uroboros, and the original chaos (sea, darkness, void). Corresponding to the early experience of the Good Mother is a complex archetypal network expressed in such images as those depicting loving protectresses (e.g., graceful maidens, good fairies), friendly animals (e.g., mammals that are warm and furry or that, like the cow, are known for their milk), and natural forces of pleasant or bountiful character (e.g., virgin springs, warming fires, gentle breezes, the luxuriant environment of the garden of paradise). And corresponding to the later experience of the Terrible Mother is an archetypal network of just the opposite sort, reflected in images of malevolent crones (e.g., witches, evil seductresses), unfriendly animals (e.g., cold and scaly reptiles, violent predators), and natural forces of harsh or harmful character (e.g., floods and gales, whirlpools and whirlwinds, infernos and volcanoes, pits and abysses).

Also part of the larger network associated with the Great Mother are archetypes of the defenseless innocent (e.g., Adam and Eve, Hansel and Gretel, the babe in the woods), of the young hero (the prince or knight who slays the dragon: the Terrible Mother in bestial form), of sirens and nymphs (who would lure the ego back into oceanic immersion), and, in general, of all manner of sprites, elves, and imps, both good and bad, of magical and magnetic nature.

The act of original repression disconnects the ego from the network of archetypes that belong to the Great Mother system. These archetypes, then, which are active in the conscious life of the body-ego, are alienated from the conscious life of the mental ego. For the mental ego, these archetypes belong to the prepersonal unconscious; they are part of a separate psychic system, a system that is invisible and unknown—except, usually, in sleep and dreams. The Great Mother system, in being banished in this manner, is reduced to dormancy until such time as the repression that submerges it begins to dissolve or otherwise give way. At this point, the commencement of regression in the service of transcendence, many aspects of the Great Mother system are reactivated and returned to the field of consciousness.[8]

There are many other archetypes that bear upon the unfolding of the ego/Ground interaction, including, for example, archetypes of descent into the underworld, the beast of the abyss, demonic evil and angelic good, death and resurrection, purgation and transfiguration, damnation and salvation, and liberation and apotheosis. However, these archetypes, in being invisible to the mental ego, do not belong to the unconscious by way of inheritance from the body-ego. They are not buried remnants of the pre-egoic past, but rather still-latent potentialities of the transegoic future. Jung, who undertook an in-depth study of archetypes such as these, understood them to be spontaneous prefigurations of spiritual development, signposts of the Way. In the terms being used here, they are heralds of events that await the mental ego if and when it quits its repression of the Dynamic Ground and begins the journey that would lead it ultimately to a higher reunion with the Ground. These archetypes of the Way, then, are unconscious in a different sense than are the archetypes that make up the Great Mother system. Indeed, both groups of archetypes pertain to the ego's ontogenesis in relation to the Dynamic Ground, and both belong to the collective unconscious in the broadest sense of the term. But whereas the archetypes constituting the Great Mother system are vestiges of a prepersonal past, the archetypes of the Way are harbingers of a transpersonal future.

2. *The body-unconscious.* As was said, the body-unconscious consists of many of the nonegoic or physico-dynamic potentials that are distinctive of the body-ego's experience. These potentials, which have a brief flowering during the body-egoic period, are arrested in their "pre-" form when original repression submerges the nonegoic pole of the psyche.

Aspects of the body-ego's dynamic experience that belong to the body-unconscious are those that reflect the supercharging effects of the power of the Dynamic Ground. In the last chapter we learned that there are three principal such effects, namely, (1) polymorphous sensuousness, (2) amplification of perceptual, affective, and cognitive experience, and (3) numinosity or enchantment. These three expressions of the power of the Ground, which are so integrally a part of the body-ego's life, disappear at the point of original repression. Since original repression contains the power of the Ground, it has the effect of de-energizing the (mental) ego's experience across all dimensions. It deadens the body; it diminishes the intensity of perceptions, feelings, and thoughts; and it disenchants the world. Original repression thus works to eliminate from consciousness the superabundance that is so characteristic of the body-ego's experience. The supercharging effects of the power of the Ground are "turned off." They are relegated to the body-unconscious.

Also to be included in the body-unconscious are many of the modes of the body-ego's thought and feeling that have been reviewed in this chapter. Regarding the latter, we have seen that the body-ego's feelings are of a dramatically corporeal sort. They are jolts, waves, or upwellings of affect. As is true of everything in the body-ego's life, its feelings are inherently somatic in nature; they are body-feelings. Original repression, however, changes this in a decisive way. It does so not only because it seals the Ground and thereby de-energizes feelings but also because it armors the body and thereby obstructs the passage of feelings through the body. Original repression both saps feelings of their strength and blocks their movement. Original repression consequently disallows the full and free expression of body-feelings. It deletes the capacity for such feelings from consciousness, leaving the mental ego to experience merely mental feelings (a contradiction in terms?), i.e., bloodless, bodiless stirrings. The capacity for true body-feelings becomes part of the body-unconscious. Along with the supercharging effects of the power of the Dynamic Ground, this capacity is deactivated and put on hold for the duration of the mental-egoic period.

And much that is inherent to the body-ego's cognition suffers the same fate. This is because the body-ego's cognition is based on the autosymbolic process, and this process, as a nonegoic potential, is lost to consciousness along with other nonegoic potentials when original repression alienates the nonegoic pole of the psyche. Original repression dissociates the ego from the source of image production. Consequently, the ego is no longer able to rely on the assistance of creatively generated images. The paleosymbol disappears from consciousness. Original repression stifles the creative process, and the (mental) ego is forced to rely entirely on its own operational faculties. Again, an actual dimension of the body-ego's experience is deleted from consciousness; it is buried and becomes part of the unconscious, the body-unconscious.

CONCLUSION

In focusing on the loss of nonegoic potentials, I should not be taken as saying that every mode, faculty, and structure of the body-ego's experience is repressed and submerged at the point of original repression. If that were the case, the mental ego would come into being as a *tabula rasa*, which is clearly contrary to fact. Although most of the nonegoic potentials active during the body-egoic period either do not survive original repression or do so only in significantly attenuated form, the fledgling egoic faculties that emerge during this period do survive. Moreover, these egoic faculties undergo an accelerated development from this point on. The transition from the pre-egoic to the egoic period is not, then, just a matter of repression and forfeiture of nonegoic potentials; it is also, and even more, a matter of developmental advance and gain. The transition is a two-sided affair; it is at once a dissociative break and a movement to a genuinely higher stage of development.

Furthermore, it is a plausible hypothesis that the dissociative break caused by original repression is not only a precursor but also a *precondition* of the ego's developmental advance. For example, the loss of (nonegoic) dynamism and feeling may well be a prerequisite for the development of (egoic) mind and will. The reason for this is that the young ego has a difficult time establishing control over the latter so long as it is still subject to the powerful influence of the former. The young ego needs firm ground and clear air in order to gain mastery of its operational faculties. And, paradoxically, original repression meets these needs, since it both undergirds the mental ego and, in closing the Dynamic Ground, depotentiates the mental ego's subjective atmosphere. In short, a repression and consequent diminution of psychic resources may well assist rather than retard developmental advance.

Another example of such a trade-off is that, cognitively, the loss of the autosymbolic process may be a precondition of the ego achieving full mastery of conceptual thought. The reason in this case is that the autosymbolic process does cognitive work for the ego that the ego must eventually learn to do for itself. In fashioning paleosymbols, the autosymbolic process produces images for the body-ego that, in their concrete particularity, happen effectively to convey universal meanings. Consequently, the autosymbolic process allows the body-ego to get by for most practical purposes just as if it had itself grasped the universal meanings as abstract concepts. The autosymbolic process may then be a hindrance to cognitive development for the simple reason that it does its job so well. In creating images that have the character of concrete universals, the autosymbolic process elevates cognition halfway from mere particularity to full universality and at the same time does away with any pressing need to carry the process further. Therefore, if original repression did not deprive the ego of autogenerated paleosymbols, it is questionable whether a rigorous system of abstract concepts would ever come into existence. The alienation of the creative process may thus play a positive developmental role. In weaning the ego from paleosymbols, this alienation may be the impetus that forces the ego to think for itself, to distinguish concept from concrete exemplar, and thereby to surmount the limitations of paleologic.

To repeat, the transition to the egoic stage is a two-sided affair. If I have concentrated on the negative side, this has not been to slight the importance of the positive side. The phenomenon of original repression notwithstanding, the transition to the egoic stage is a real developmental advance. It is a change that is responsible for more gains than losses, and the losses it incurs, as we have just seen, may be the necessary price to be paid for the gains. In any case, the transition in question is extremely complex and is not to be either just indicted (e.g., as a sinful alienation) or praised (e.g., as a victory for reason and civilization).

CHAPTER 4

The Mental Ego *

T HE MENTAL EGO IS the ego with which we are all most familiar. It is the ego of life as we know it, as opposed to life as we only dimly remember it (the body-ego) or vaguely anticipate it (ego/Ground integration). It is, then, the mental ego with which ego theorists have been primarily concerned. Most prevailing accounts of the ego—whether by psychologists, theologians, or philosophers—can therefore be understood to apply primarily to the mental ego.

The account of the mental ego to be presented here follows directly from the bipolar and triphasic conceptions. These conceptions point to the following three facts as being basic to the mental ego: (1) It is a semi-autonomous pole of a bipolar psyche. (2) It is, however, a pole that has repressed and alienated its nonegoic counterpole. Therefore, (3) it is a semi-autonomous existent that operates on the false belief that it is a completely autonomous and self-subsistent entity.

The first of these facts is the subject matter of ego psychology, which studies the ego in terms of its autonomous functions and distinctive developmental patterns. In the history of psychoanalytic theory, Heinz Hartmann (1958, 1964) is the pivotal figure so far as ego psychology is concerned. He has this distinction because he is the one who convinced the psychoanalytic community that the ego must be studied not only in light of its defensive relation to the id but also in light of its independent (conflict-free) adaptive functions, such as perception, motility, causal thinking, and intentional action. Hartmann argued that if psychoanalysis is to be a general psychology, it must address the ego as a psychic reality in its own right and not just as an appendage of the id. Erik Erikson (1959, 1963, 1968), a

---

* Many of the ideas presented in this chapter were first developed in collaboration with Michael Stark. See Washburn and Stark (1979).

second major figure in psychoanalytic ego psychology, agreed with Hartmann on this point. Erikson, whose work deals primarily with the psychoanalytic theory of development, argued that human development must be understood not just in terms of psychosexual or intrapsychic dynamics but also in terms of the ego and its social challenges, personal crises, and identity needs. Psychoanalysis, according to Erikson, must broaden its focus beyond the unconscious to include an account of the inherent tendencies and self-chosen goals of the ego's development.

The second fact is the subject matter of both classical depth psychology (Freud and Jung) and existential theology (e.g., Augustine, Pascal, Kierkegaard). Depth psychology and existential theology both see the mental ego as having committed an act of alienation (repression, dissociation, or sin) that disconnects the mental ego from its basic source in being. Depth psychology and existential theology, of course, conceive this source in very different ways; depth psychology interprets it as the dynamic unconscious, an invisible psychic system, and existential theology interprets it as the *deus absconditus*, the absent God. Nevertheless, both depth psychology and existential theology agree that the ego has dissociated itself from a superior, or at least more fundamental, reality, and that, consequently, the ego is prone to existential woes: rootlessness or fallenness, discontent, anxiety, emptiness, and, sometimes, despair.

Finally, the third of the facts enumerated above is the subject matter of metaphysically oriented philosophy. The metaphysical question that has been asked about the mental ego pertains to its ontological status, i.e., to the manner in which, if any, it can be said to exist. Now, since the mental ego has repressed and submerged the physico-dynamic pole of the psyche, it is understandable that the mental ego would be inclined to think of itself as a being that is both independent in existence and incorporeal in nature: a substance consisting purely of consciousness or of mind. And it is understandable as well, then, that precisely this conception of the mental ego would have been dominant in the philosophical tradition. In the East, this conception is best known in the formulations given it by the two main schools of Indian philosophy, namely, Samkhya (which holds that the self is *purusha*, a conscious monad) and Vedanta (which holds that the self is *atman*, self-subsisting, self-illumined consciousness). And in the West, this dominant conception of the mental ego is most famously associated with the names of Plato (who holds that the self is *nous*, immortal intuitive mind) and René Descartes (who holds that the self is *res cogitans*, an immaterial thinking thing). However, if the ego is truly only a pole of a bipole, as is here being assumed, then it follows that this prevailing conception of the mental ego is really a misconception vulnerable to challenge. And, indeed, it has been challenged. There is a well-represented minority view (advocated in the East by Buddhists generally and in the West by such philosophers as David Hume [1888], William James [1890], and Jean-Paul Sartre [1957]) that has countered the prevailing view. Unlike the prevailing view, which has fallen for the mental ego's pose of independence, this minority view has seen through the mental ego's pose and has called the mental ego's bluff. The minority view has seen that there is no incorporeal substance to be found within psychic space and has concluded from this that the mental ego is therefore only a false pose, a mere fiction or illusion. Of course, in jumping to this conclusion, which denies all reality to the mental ego, the minority view has gone to the opposite extreme of the accepted view. If the ego is a pole of a bipole, then it is neither an immaterial substance nor a total nonentity, but rather something in between. These considerations aside, however, the point at hand is that the mental ego, owing to its dissociation from the physico-dynamic pole of the psyche, is inherently prone to both self-inflation and fear of nonexistence. It is prone to conceive itself as an independently existing consciousness or mind while at the same time suffering from fears that, behind its ontological pretensions, it really is nothing at all.

The ensuing account of the mental ego will elaborate on and, I hope, integrate to some extent the three perspectives just outlined. Before commencing the discussion, however, a brief warning is in order. The ensuing account of the mental ego is stated in uncompromising terms. I have presented the pure case. That is, I have described the mental ego in terms of what it is in essence, without consideration of the many qualifications and exceptions that invariably obtain in fact. The result is a picture that is clearly, dramatically, and, I believe, correctly drawn, but also one that is a bit overdrawn. It is unlikely that anyone has ever possessed a mental ego just like the one described below. The fact is that the mental ego is a matter of degree. The following account, then, although in no sense a caricature, is definitely an idealization, and I recommend that it be read with this in mind.

THE MENTAL EGO AND CARTESIAN DUALISM

We have learned that the mental ego is inherently prone to conceive itself in Cartesian terms. Divorced from the physico-dynamic plane, the mental ego takes itself to be a purely mental entity, an entity of opposite nature to and distinct existence from the body and the body's energies, impulses, and feelings. The mental ego considers itself to be a disincarnate consciousness that happens merely contingently to coexist with physico-dynamic life. It is true that the mental ego acknowledges an especially close connection with the human body; nevertheless, the mental ego does not believe that the body is in any way essential to what it, the mental ego, is. The body is a useful tool, indeed a necessary one for interacting with the world, but it is an implement that, the mental ego believes, is, in principle, dispensable. The mental ego, associated with the head, stands above the body and commands it from on high, and in doing so the mental ego takes on airs of incorporeality and independence. It adopts the Cartesian stance and assumes the role of *res cogitans*.

The origin of this Cartesian attitude lies in the dynamics of the body-ego's development. As we know, the mental ego succeeds the body-ego and dons the mantle of selfhood not just by differentiating itself from its physico-dynamic origins, but by dissociating itself from those origins. The ego, in becoming the mental ego, flees from the physico-dynamic plane because it perceives that plane to be a locus of dangerous and uncontrollable forces: the seductive power of the Terrible Mother and the wrath of the Oedipal Father. The ego fears that its very existence is threatened by these forces, and so it moves desperately to separate itself from them by the maximum distance possible. Accordingly, the ego commits the act of original repression. It disconnects itself from the body and from the dynamisms of bodily life, and it begins to look down upon the body as not-self, indeed as an alien and disposable integument.

In committing the act of original repression, the ego mobilizes tier upon tier of bodily defense to dam the upward movement of the power of the Ground. This fact was observed in Chapter 2 and will be explained more fully in Chapter 5. For present purposes, suffice it to say that the general thrust of original repression is downward, proceeding from the head, which is the seat of the mental ego, to the genital region, which is the seat of the Dynamic Ground. Layer upon layer of tension and constriction is laid down in order to create a hierarchy of resistances to the free circulation of the power of the Ground and, hence, to effect a reduction in the amount of this power reaching the brain. Well-known body armors that are part of this hierarchy are taut and stooped shoulders and upper arms, a knotted diaphragm, and a tight sphincter. These and other bodily rigidities are held fast, and in time they ossify and become embedded structures of the body, permanently locking the body in a defensive-containment posture.

This posture indicates that the mental ego's Cartesianism is more than just an attitude or theoretical perspective: it is an orientation to self and world that the mental ego *lives*. The mental ego does not just judge the body to be not-self, a mere thing; it actually reconstitutes it as same. It desensitizes and devitalizes the body. In committing the act of original repression, the mental ego both constricts the body, thereby divesting it of its inner suppleness and sensitivity, and seals the Dynamic Ground, thereby draining the body of energy or life force. The body is in this fashion both hardened and deadened; it is deprived of feeling and life and reduced to the merely material level.

The mental ego, in thus reducing the body to the merely material level, at the same time elevates itself to the purely immaterial level. It considers itself to be a wholly incorporeal entity that is altogether above the passions and vicissitudes (and even mortality!) of physico-dynamic existence. The mental ego stands aloof from bodily life and considers itself to be the exclusive bearer of consciousness and selfhood.

It was suggested earlier that the mental ego's dissociation from the physico-dynamic plane may have developmental advantages. One reason for this is that disconnection from the physico-dynamic plane frees the mental ego from the disturbing influence of nonegoic potentials and consequently allows the mental ego to keep a cool head as it gains mastery of itself and the environment. The body-ego, bathed as it is in numinous energy, is chronically liable to being captured in highly charged, self-contained experiences, and this liability interferes with its ability to gain control of egoic faculties and to attain any degree of overview and continuity in life. The mental ego, therefore, in closing the Dynamic Ground, protects itself from being swept away. It forfeits the fullness of physico-dynamic life, to be sure, but in compensation it gains sobriety and self-possession. It makes a trade-off; it buys clarity and control at the cost of passion and power. In Cartesian terms, it promotes itself to the status of *res cogitans* by demoting the body to the status of mere *res extensa*.

THE MENTAL EGO AND FLIGHT FROM "NOTHINGNESS"

Beneath its Cartesian pretensions, the mental ego harbors fears of not being real. The mental ego suffers these apprehensions because, having severed ties with the body, it has forfeited tangible existence, thinghood. It has ceased being a palpable object in the world and has rendered itself a nonentity, a mere ghostly presence within inner space. Moreover, in having closed the Dynamic Ground, the mental ego has also deprived itself of life force. The mental ego is for these reasons vulnerable to a sense of lack or nonbeing, to a sense that it is deficient in both substance and spirit—as if it were both hollow and dead at its core. This vulnerability is not a problem at first, since the young mental ego still enjoys relief from the dynamic and affective storms that had raged during the body-egoic period. But in time the mental ego's inner lack does become evident, sometimes distressingly and even despairingly so.

The mental ego's sense of nonbeing is not a fear of absolute nonexistence. The mental ego knows *that* it exists (*cogito ergo sum*); the problem is that it does not know *what*, if anything, it is. For the mental ego is neither mental space itself nor any of the contents that it meets with in mental space. It is not mental space, since mental, like physical, space is in itself nothing; it is simply subjective expanse, interior extension. The mental ego somehow exists within this space, but it cannot be identified with it. Nor can the mental ego be equated with any of the contents of mental space, i.e., any sensation, percept, image, feeling, or thought. For these are things that the mental ego experiences, not things that it *is*. The mental ego, then, exists as a disembodied consciousness, an unanchored and unlocatable presence within mental space. To use Sartre's term, its existence is "nothingness."[1]

Concerning the mental ego's lack of dynamism, little need be added to what was said above. As noted, the mental ego makes a trade-off, sacrificing intensity for sobriety. This exchange allows the mental ego to see clearly and to act dispassionately, but it eventually afflicts the mental ego with a sense of alienation from the fullness of life. Owing to the closing of the Dynamic Ground, the subjective atmosphere is depotentiated, sapped of charge and spirit. Besides being intangible, without substance or thinghood, the inner space of the mental ego thus is also dynamically dead. Or to make the same point in the terminology of Zen, this inner space is a *dead void*.

The mental ego cannot bear dwelling within the dead void of its subjectivity. To do so is, for the mental ego, to experience its own nullity. The mental ego is anxious in face of its inner "nothingness," and so it is impelled to go outside itself to find, or at least to divert itself from, what it is lacking within. Accordingly, the mental ego becomes a restless extravert; it engrosses itself in one event, project, or affair after another and in this way finds distraction and (manageable) excitement. Extraversion is, however, only a temporary, moment-by-moment palliative. The mental ego therefore tries in a more permanent way to fill its inner emptiness by constructing an identity, facticity, or self-concept. This self-concept, once established, is something that the mental ego can take itself to *be*, and thus it is something that allows the mental ego a sense of substance and self-nature.[2] Finally, as a last line of defense against facing its "nothingness," the mental ego engages in compulsive internal dialogue. It converses with itself, thereby filling the dead void with self-validating verbalizations. It assures itself of its existence by talking to itself—as is suggested in the qualification that Descartes added to his "I think therefore I am," namely, "at least so long as I continue to think." The mental ego experiences episodes of inner silence as frightening hiatuses, and so it talks to itself in order to preserve its sense of continuity in existence.

Extraversion, identity construction, and internal dialogue are the principal means by which the mental ego seeks to deal with its "nothingness." Let us now consider in greater detail what each of these involves.

1. *The mental ego and extraversion.* Extraversion is a natural and beneficial aspect of conscious life. Human beings, along with most of the higher animal species, are interested in the external environment for purposes of both curiosity and need, play and survival. However, for humans, qua mental egos, this outer focusing of attention assumes an added dimension: it ceases being simply an expression of spontaneity or practical necessity and becomes compulsive. Humans, qua mental egos, are driven out of themselves because they are disquieted about what they find—or, rather, what they fear they will not find—within themselves. That is to say, human, mental-egoic extraversion

is set in motion not only by curiosity and need but also by fear of "nothingness."

Extraversion is so nearly a universal feature of human experience that several psychologists and philosophers have taken it to be an essential characteristic of consciousness. For example, the great nineteenth-century psychologist Franz Brentano (1874) defined the psychic as the intentional, that is, as that form or mode of existence that necessarily relates itself to something beyond itself. All consciousness, Brentano was the first to say, is inherently "consciousness of"; it necessarily looks out upon an object that is other than itself. Edmund Husserl, Brentano's pupil, adopted this conception of intentionality and used it as the cornerstone of his phenomenological philosophy. For Husserl (1964, 1982), consciousness not only points beyond itself to objects; it also intends them in the sense of investing them with meaning. So far as they bear meaning for a subject, Husserl thought, objects are what consciousness intends them to be. Finally, it was the existential phenomenologist Jean-Paul Sartre who connected intentionality, or extraversion, with lack. He argued, in effect, that consciousness has no recourse but to attach itself to objects, since it has no being apart from them. Consciousness, he says (1956, lxi), is just "the revealing intuition of something"; it is a "nothing" that exists only in its illumination of objects.

Brentano, Husserl, and Sartre have, I think, overstated the case. Extraversion is doubtless a very strong tendency of consciousness, but it is unlikely that it is an absolutely necessary aspect. There is good evidence that deep, objectless introversion is a real possibility.[3] But the point is that it is a possibility to which the mental ego is by nature averse. Extraversion, or intentionality, therefore, although probably not essential to consciousness as such, is definitely an inherent tendency of the mental ego's consciousness. The mental ego is a fugitive, from interiority to exteriority. It is propelled outside itself so that it will not have to face the dead void that it carries within itself. The mental ego, then, can withdraw its attention within itself, but it is strongly resistant to doing so.

Extraversion is a projection of attention onto things in order to provide diversion and regulated excitement. As such, it is characterized not only by a tendency toward object and focus fixation but also by restlessness. Typically, it is not just one object or state of affairs that is the center of attention, but rather a succession of objects or states of affairs. For the most part, the mental ego is curious only in Heidegger's (1962) sense of the term. That is, it behaves as if with a greed for the new—which is the literal rendering of the term (Neugier) that Heidegger uses to describe the vagrant inquisitiveness of everyday life. No one thing can satisfy the mental ego, so it diverts its attention from one thing to the next. Its inner "nothingness," as Pascal (1958) so brilliantly explained, condemns it to alternating cycles of self-forgetting amusement and anxious *ennui*. A fugitive from "nothingness," the mental ego is forever after something new. The novelty of the new attracts the mental ego's attention and, in doing so, facilitates its distraction from self. And the novelty of the new also generates excitement, which is the mental ego's pale, but manageable, substitute for the native dynamism of life.

Restless extraversion is a way of life for the "normal" or "healthy" mental ego. But it can become a matter of desperation for a mental ego that is poorly constituted, weak, or ripe for regression in the service of transcendence. For in these cases the mental ego is vulnerable not only to the dead void of its conscious subjectivity but also to the ominous forces of the prepersonal unconscious, especially the repressed dynamism of the Ground. Introversion in these cases threatens not just pallid inexistence but, even worse, the possibility of being sucked into an abyss astir with a dangerous power. And since this power, however frightening, is highly magnetic and seductive in its effect upon the mental ego, it seems to the mental ego that at all costs it must not look back. And so the (weakened) mental ego extraverts itself fast and furiously. It tries desperately to keep itself preoccupied by leaping quickly from one thing to another. Schachtel (1959, 113-14) describes such a case:

> the case of Juli Weber, a young girl of twenty-four, with many phobic reactions, of which the most manifest was that she could not let her glance rest for more than the briefest moment on any single object without feeling overwhelmed by the masses of the objects seen, which led to severe anxiety attacks.

This young woman was apparently so open to the numinous energy of the unconscious that for her to relax extraverted attention even for a moment would have been to allow influxes of that energy into the brain and consciousness, thus affecting awareness in a way that would render objects strange and massive. For her, to allow attention to become fixed would have been to allow herself to become transfixed. This is an extreme case of psychopathological extraversion, brought on likely by an untimely weakening or breakdown of original repression. Lesser cases of morbid extraversion are found in such symptoms and syndromes as hyperactivity, obsessive-compulsive rituals, and the like.

2. The mental ego and identity construction. The mental ego lacks thinghood. Having severed its original identification with the body, the mental ego has shorn itself of tangible substantiality and has diminished itself to the point of being a mere shade, a merely virtual presence within mental space. And it experiences this, its disembodiment, anxiously, i.e., as an ontological deficiency. Set in motion by this fear of "nothingness," the mental ego embarks upon an attempt to make something of itself; that is, it attempts to fashion for itself something of substance (viz., the self-concept) that, by identifying with, it can take itself to be. This attempt to fabricate its own being is the mental ego's basic life objective; it is the mental ego's fundamental project in the world.

It is now evident that the mental ego and the body-ego have very different fundamental projects. Whereas the basic objective of the body-ego is to be an "independent intimate" of the Great Mother, that of the mental ego is to be a self-creator or, as Sartre (1956) puts it, an *ens causa sui*. Having lost its physical body, the mental ego is impelled to find an incorporeal replacement for it. It is for this reason that the mental ego forges the self-concept. It constructs the self-concept, introjects it, and identifies with it as the particular, substantial, and yet immaterial thing that it, the mental ego, *is*. The fashioning (and defense) of the self-concept is therefore the mental ego's primary life priority, since it is the chief means by which the mental ego's ontological insecurity is alleviated. The self-concept serves the mental ego as a surrogate body; it provides the mental ego with a sense of solidity and substance.

But the self-concept is not a genuine entity. It is rather a reified abstraction. It is a *product* of thought rather than an independent existent that could be *given* to thought. It is a cognitive construct, and an ever-unfinished one at that. Hence, the mental ego's fabricated substantiality is not something that could ever be encountered directly through introspection. Rather, it is something that can be apprehended only indirectly, namely, through inference, as it is implied in the mental ego's thoughts and deeds. The mental ego might say to itself, for example, "I certainly was nice to so-and-so; [therefore] I am a kind person." The inference is that a particular thought or deed implies an ego-entity that is its thinker or doer and, moreover, that this ego-entity is the kind of thing (i.e., possesses the requisite attributes) from which such a thought or deed would characteristically issue. The mental ego, then, never witnesses its incorporeal body, the self-concept, face to face. The self-concept is not a given; it is an ongoing project. It is presumed to exist and is open to being known only as it is inferred from its "effects."

The mental ego's identification with the self-concept constitutes a curious form of inversion. For the self-concept is but an abstract posit of consciousness, and yet it is taken to be an entity that exercises consciousness as its power. The self-concept is reified, introjected, and adopted by the mental ego as its very self. And since the modes of conscious activity are the modes of the mental ego's activity, they are thereby modes of activity of the "thing" (viz., the self-concept) that the mental ego assumes itself to be. The inversion, then, is that what is really an idea for consciousness is taken to be the subject and owner of consciousness; what is really a product of consciousness is taken to be the very source from which consciousness springs. The self-concept is illegitimately promoted to the rank of the self proper. And in being accorded this status, it confers upon the mental ego a semblance of substantial being.

This analysis of the self-concept is at once psychodynamic and existential. It is psychodynamic in that it deems the repression of physico-dynamic life to be a primary cause of the forging of the self-concept. And it is existential in that it considers the mental ego's pursuit of identity to be an endeavor that, in flight from "nothingness," strives for self-definition and self-creation. Understood in these ways, the quest for the self-concept must be acknowledged to be deficiency motivated: repression and "nothingness" impel the mental ego to forge a worldly facticity as a way of establishing a sense of abiding and defined existence. An inner lack forces the mental ego to embark upon an outer search for being.

In stressing that the self-concept is deficiency motivated, I do not mean to imply that it has only negative causes. Erik Erikson has shown that the opposite is true. Erikson, in theoretical writings rich in clinical detail (1959, 1963, 1968) and in illuminating psychobiographies (1958, 1969), has established that the search for identity is a lifelong endeavor by which the ego tests its own resources and finds a meaningful place in the world.

According to Erikson, the search for identity commences in the early latency period when the ego begins to imitate a variety of social roles. In doing this, the young ego learns about both society and itself; it becomes acquainted with the different parts that are played on the social stage and, at the same time, develops fragments of selfhood that later might be knit together as elements of a coherently unified ego-identity. Once latency gives way to puberty and adolescence, the ego's quest for identity takes a more serious turn. For the ego is here on the eve of adulthood and must face making real commitments. Accordingly, the ego now tries on worldly identities in earnest, even if frequently in caricature. The adolescent is allowed what Erikson calls a "psychosocial moratorium" in order to go through the process of identity trial prior to adult identity commitment. This period often involves an adolescent identity crisis. If, however, the period of trial and crisis is negotiated without pathology, the ego does finally consolidate an identity with which it can enter adult life. But even as this commitment is made, the ego's concern with identity is by no means over. Erikson traces the path of ego development to the very end, explaining how the identity consolidated in early adulthood must be maintained or restructured in order to facilitate such major life goals as intimacy, productivity, and integrity.

The self-concept is not then just a means of escape from inner deficiencies; it is also a vehicle by which the ego finds itself and its proper place in the world. The self-concept is two-sided; it serves both negative and positive purposes. It is both a camouflage and a medium of authentic expression. It is both a way in which the mental ego hides its inner self-alienation and "nothingness" and a way in which the mental ego engages and actualizes itself as a self-in-the-world.

Given the important purposes served by the self-concept, it is understandable that the mental ego would defend the self-concept with great concern and care. It also is understandable that the mental ego would be strongly resistant to accepting any aspects of itself that are incompatible with the central features of the self-concept. And, in fact, such aspects are typically either suppressed or repressed. In the latter case, they become elements of that part of the personal unconscious that Jung aptly called the shadow.

Unlike the features of the self-concept, which are introjected, the disowned fragments of the personality making up the shadow are in most instances projected upon others. The mental ego, blind to certain unwanted aspects of itself, tends unknowingly to impute these aspects to others. The mental ego, consequently, is prone to misperceive people. The mental ego clothes others in its own shadow, perceiving others in ways that it is loath to perceive itself. Attachment to the self-concept thus causes not only blind spots in oneself but also distortions in one's perception of others.

3. *The mental ego and internal dialogue.* The mental ego engages in an ongoing internal dialogue. It does so because (1) the internal dialogue fills the mental ego's inner void and assures the mental ego of its existence—after all, the mental ego thinks, "I must exist if I am talking to myself"; and (2) the internal dialogue is the actual activity of inference-drawing by which the mental ego constructs its self-concept.

As for the first point, it is noteworthy that the mental ego's inner conversation, like its extraversion, is compulsive. The mental ego becomes anxious when the internal dialogue quiets and the mind becomes silent, since then the mental ego's existence becomes undetectable. The mental ego, as noted above, cannot see itself directly (i.e., through introspection), but it can, it fancies, hear itself. Hence, it is assured of its existence so long as it continues to talk. However, when consciousness becomes silent, as it sometimes does, the mental ego is attacked by fears of "nothingness."

Regarding the second point, it has already been explained that the self-concept is a mental construct based on inference. It can here be added that the actual process of inferring is accomplished through internal dialogue. The mental ego is incessantly drawing literal, spoken inferences about itself. It says to itself, for example, (1) "I typed that letter quickly; [therefore] I am a good secretary"; (2) "What a stupid thing I just said; [therefore] I am a fool"; and (3) "They have accepted my story; [therefore] I am an author." Everyone is familiar with internal conversations like these; examples could easily be proliferated. The point is that such conversations, although seemingly trivial, are really of great importance, since they are the medium through which the self-concept is forged and known.

Things must now be complicated a bit. For the mental ego's voice is not the only one to be heard within consciousness. As Wilber (1980a) has noted, it is to the credit of Frederick Perls (1969) and Eric Berne (1967) to have shown that virtually every psychic level or function is represented by an internal voice. More specifically, they have shown that, besides the principal adult voice (which represents the mental ego), there is also a parent voice (speaking for the superego or ego-ideal) and a child's or imp's voice (speaking for rejected elements of life—e.g., elements belonging to the shadow). The mental ego is caught in the middle. Its self-concept can never measure up to the ego-ideal, and yet the introjected parent voice continues to harp from on high, issuing commands, forewarnings, and "I-told-you-so" scoldings and praisings. And on the other hand there are voices arising from below that would have the mental ego ignore the parental imperatives and submit to deeds that, for the mental ego, would be out of character, i.e., inconsistent with its self-concept. These voices speak in a variety of ways. For example, they frequently importune the mental ego by whining, enticing, prodding, deriding, or rationalizing. They represent the child and the imp in us.[4]

The mental ego, then, is pulled in opposite directions. Speaking for itself, it fashions the self-concept, which, be it good, bad, or neutral, is what the mental ego actually takes itself to be. But in doing this, the mental ego is influenced from above by the ego-ideal, which tells the mental ego what it should be, and from below by the alienated elements of the soul, which beseech, beguile, or command the mental ego to give in to what it is afraid to be. The mental ego therefore represents a middle ground; in speaking for itself, it is at the same time mediating between extremes.

Another aspect of the mental ego's internal dialogue that deserves consideration is its monitoring of the external environment. Ernest Schachtel describes this aspect well. He says (1959, 169-70):

> We look around and say to ourselves, silently and implicitly: "This is the store at the corner of X street, this is the red house, this is the tree in front of it, these are the people going to work, this is the bus stop; this is the chair and the floor lamp, the desk, the window, the bed, etc." While we see all of these objects, in this kind of perspective we do not see them fully, in their own right. What is the use we put them to when we just recognize them in this way and then let our glance pass on to some other object which, in turn, we quickly file away as "recognized"? We must use the objects for orientation and reassurance that we are moving and being in our familiar, accustomed everyday world.

As Schachtel says, the mental ego makes inner verbal identifications of things in order to orient itself in the environment. It protects itself against the danger of getting lost in the myriad stimuli that impinge upon consciousness by relating to things primarily as objects to which labels can be applied. This name-the-object approach to the world has the undeniably negative consequence of impoverishing experience. Objects lose their uniqueness, richness, and power and are reduced to mere instances of kinds. But the approach has the positive consequence of making things familiar and easy to deal with. We gain power over things by naming them, for they are thereby "known" and divested of their wonders. They are decathected and rendered powerless to fascinate and transfix.

The mental ego—or at least the inner voice that represents it—thus is engaged in a verbal effort to conceptualize both the outer and inner domains. It constructs a map of the territory of outer experience, which it extends, applies, and reapplies. And it also constructs a verbal-mental blueprint of itself: the self-concept. The major difference between these two conceptualizations is that in the former case there is an independent world given to conceptualize, whereas in the latter there is no ego-substance provided prior to the blueprint. In fact, as we have seen, the blueprint is itself introjected and is taken to be the very object (or subject) that it is supposed to describe. This is a horrendous logical contortion, but it is essential to the mental ego's sense of being.

THE MENTAL EGO AND FEELING

There are a variety of feelings that are characteristic of the mental ego, and, since many of these are negative, I will refer to them collectively as the mental ego's affective syndrome. The mental ego's affective experience is by no means unremittingly negative, but the mental ego suffers from root insecurities and frustrations that trouble it, deeply and persistently, and that darken the overall cast of its emotional life.

A basic aspect of the mental ego's affective syndrome is anxiety. The mental ego is by nature restless and ill at ease. One of the principal reasons for this is that the mental ego is ontologically insecure. Despite its Cartesian pretensions, the mental ego suffers from a deep-seated suspicion of its own "nothingness." This suspicion impels the mental ego to construct a self-concept, in which, the mental ego hopes, it will find a sense of being. A well-established self-concept does provide the mental ego with some relief from its sense of "nothingness," but this relief is never altogether sufficient or sure. For the *causa sui* project is a way in which the mental ego seeks *escape* from its interior lack, and therefore the project cannot really remedy the problem to which it is a response. The sense of "nothingness" continues to gnaw at the mental ego regardless of whatever success it might have met with in engineering an identity-in-the-world. The mental ego is ontologically insecure on a very basic level, and this insecurity generates an anxiety that is a fundamental dimension of the mental ego's life experience. The mental ego may not be aware of this anxiety at all times, because it is a constant background for more focused and intense feelings. Nevertheless, the anxiety breaks through to the foreground of awareness frequently enough, especially during those times when the self-concept is subject to challenge or change.

Fear of nonbeing is not the only cause of the mental ego's anxiety. For the mental ego also suffers from a sense of guilt: it apprehends itself, prereflectively, as being deficient not only in being but also in value or worth. That is, the mental ego is beset with the sense that its existence is unwarranted and in need of justification. The reason for this lies in the manner in which the mental ego comes into being: original repression. The first act of the mental ego—indeed, its first moment in existence—is the repression of physico-dynamic life, which is the ego's source and proper foundation. If we recall, this act is initially both necessary and justified, since it is the only way in which the developing ego can defend itself against the forces represented by the Terrible Mother and Oedipal Father. At first, then, the mental ego senses no guilt; original repression is, for it, still a matter of triumph and independence. But in time original repression loses its legitimacy, and the mental ego begins to experience a gnawing sense of guilt.

Original repression loses its legitimacy because, as the ego matures, it ceases needing to be protected from physico-dynamic life, which means that original repression ceases performing a necessary psychic function and, even more, begins performing a negative one. In particular, original repression ceases functioning as a protective shield by which the ego defends itself against dangerous forces and begins functioning as an unnecessary, and unjustifiable, barricade by which the ego avoids its deeper self and obstructs the birth of spirit in the soul. In short, original repression becomes sin. And as this reversal or transvaluation occurs, the mental ego's original sense of triumph gives way to an emerging sense of guilt. The mental ego begins at this point to feel a vague moral uneasiness and to search for ways in which it can assure itself of its value and worth. Like all repressive regimes that do not want to relinquish power, the mental ego at this point seeks a justification, or at least a rationalization, for its ascendant position.

The mental ego pursues its vindication in the same way it pursues its being: the *causa sui* project. The fashioning of the self-concept serves the double purpose of providing a sense of substantial existence *and* a sense of worth; it provides both *être* and *raison d'être*. Specifically, the mental ego rests the case of its value on those features of its self-concept in which, it believes, it can take pride. These include all of the self-concept's positive features. For example, the mental ego might say to itself, in effect, "My existence is justified because I am strong, beautiful, or intelligent; or because I am a good doctor, lawyer, merchant, or chief; or because I am kind, generous, or virtuous in this or that way." Positive features, however, are not the only ones that can support a sense of value. Negative features can do this too, provided they are features by which a person believes he gains distinction from others. For example, some people take pride in being "the worst" at something or in being exceptionally bad or wicked. For them, it is extreme negative facticities that allow the feeling of being special and important. The mental ego's self-justification therefore rides on all of those facets of its self-concept, whether they be positive or negative, that grant the mental ego a feeling of uniqueness and distinction. If there are few or no such facets, then the mental ego, although it might have earned some sense of existence on the basis of an ordinary or undistinguished self-concept, will not have succeeded to any significant degree in placating its underlying sense of guilt.

Two other feelings that are part of the mental ego's affective syndrome are elation and depression. These are endemic to the mental-egoic system because the forging of the self-concept, given what is at stake (being or "nothingness," justification or guilt), leads to a "high" when the mental ego meets with success and a "low" when it meets with failure. The person who wants very badly to *be* something, something which, moreover, will furnish him with a sense of specialness or worth, will be greatly relieved and gratified when actions and events confirm this facticity for him. This is elation. And, of course, when actions and events work to disallow or dispossess him of the facticity, the result will be despondency or depression. The mental ego's life is inherently one of ups and downs. When up, the mental ego basks in a temporary sense of being and value. And when down, it is assailed by the chronic anxieties of "nothingness" and guilt.

One more element of the mental ego's affective syndrome is despair. This is a mood to which the mental ego is susceptible owing to its chronic anxieties, its frequent depressions, and, in general, the impossibility of its fundamental project. The quest for the self-concept, no matter how successful, does not erase the root insecurities that motivate it. Identity and distinction are inadequate substitutes for the bodily substance and life-renewing spirit that are the mental ego's deepest and truest needs. The actuality of present successes and, even more, the possibility of future ones may be sufficient to keep the mental ego committed to the *causa sui* project for a long time. But there always exists the possibility of disillusionment, the possibility of awakening to the truth that, even given the best of efforts, the *causa sui* project cannot accomplish what it promises. Such disillusionment may occur because all efforts to establish a desired identity meet with failure. Or—what would yield an even deeper awakening—such disillusionment may occur because efforts to establish a desired identity meet with complete success, without, however, there occurring any appreciable alleviation of the anxieties of "nothingness" and guilt. But in either case, the mental ego would be forced to the realization that its fundamental project is impossible and without hope. And since the *causa sui* project is the basic meaning of the mental ego's life, the loss of hope in the outcome of this project would be tantamount to a loss of hope in life itself. The mental ego, awakening to this realization, would be vulnerable to despair.

Of all the mental ego's feelings, it is despair, paradoxically, that bears the most hope. For despair marks a real insight into the nature of the mental-egoic system. The person suffering despair has learned that the *causa sui* project is impossible. This is an insight of pre-eminent importance, and it has only to be augmented with the understanding that the limits of the mental-egoic system are not necessarily the limits of life for despair to be transmuted into a higher hope. The mental ego's fundamental project is indeed a futile one, but this does not entail that life itself is futile. The despairer thus has been only partially disillusioned. A full disillusionment would dissipate despair and lead to ego-transcending faith.

Much of this section no doubt has sounded like an exercise in existentialist morbidity. If so, there is this proviso: although such existential woes as "nothingness," guilt, anxiety, depression, and despair are both real and prevalent, they do not afflict humanity as such, but rather only humanity qua mental ego. Moreover, these are afflictions that the mental ego brings upon itself. It is the mental ego that disembodies itself, thereby sentencing itself to anxious "nothingness." And it is the mental ego that negates the Ground, thereby condemning itself to spiritlessness, guilt, and despair. The body-ego suffers from none of these problems, and neither does the person who, through the transcendence of the (mental) ego, has arrived at the integrated stage. Existentialism, then, at least in its lamentations, need not be taken completely to heart. There is no denying that it brilliantly describes the affective syndrome of the mental ego, but it goes to a morbid extreme in assuming that the mental ego's plight is an inherent and inescapable aspect of the human condition as such.

A final note on existentialism: It is incorrect to think of existentialism as being an entirely negative doctrine. It has its positive side as well. For example, it is the existentialists who have championed the notions of integrity, authenticity, and responsibility. What is interesting about this from the present perspective is that, just as the negative side of existentialism applies to the mental ego, so the positive side applies to the transegoic stage of integration. Existential integrity, which is the quality of being utterly true to oneself, requires that one not be divided against oneself in any way. Authenticity requires that one be one's genuine, and therefore whole, self. And responsibility requires that one assume ownership of the totality of one's being. In all three cases, it is a total ego/mind/body/Ground, conscious/unconscious integration that is required. Existentialism, therefore, without knowing it, really addresses our humanity on two different levels. Its description of human fate as involving "fear and trembling" and "sickness unto death" speaks to us in our status as mental egos. And its account of the existential hero as someone who is strong, straight, and true speaks to us in our (potential) status as fully integrated persons.

THE MENTAL EGO AND EGOCENTRICITY

Egocentricity is the outlook that views the world primarily as it bears upon one's own self. This is the mental ego's outlook, since, given the aims of the *causa sui* project, the mental ego views the world almost exclusively in terms of how it reflects upon the mental ego's being and worth. Egocentricity, then, is not, as might ordinarily be believed, a matter of a strong and self-assured ego taking pleasure in impressing itself upon others. On the contrary, it is a matter of an insecure ego needing to garner the attention and confirmation of others in order to assuage its anxieties of "nothingness" and guilt. The mental ego's strategy is simple, even though indirect. Motivated by fears of unreality and unworthiness, it seeks to prove that these fears are false by taking its case to jury: the public, other people. The mental ego makes a display of its facticities in the hope that, if it impresses others, it will thereby be entitled to take itself seriously. That is, it tries to convince itself of its being and value by first convincing others. In sum, egocentricity is a phenomenon based on a sense of deficiency. The mental ego is like a starving person; most everything it says and does is an attempt to reach outside itself in order to fill an inner void.

In the field of action, egocentricity expresses itself as egoism, the relentless pursuit of one's own interest. Egoism is a product of feeling oneself to be in need. And this, of course, is just the mental ego's situation. The mental ego feels itself to be in need not just materially or socially, but ontologically and morally. Virtually all of its commerce with the world is, for this reason, self-interested. Even when the mental ego's material and social circumstances are enviable, it still is plagued with an inner sense of lack that fuels a pursuit of self-interest. This does not mean that the mental ego necessarily seeks great wealth, power, and adulation, but it does mean that, almost regardless of what the mental ego does seek, it does so with at least one eye on possible benefits for itself. The mental ego is constitutionally resistant to selfless action. It cannot be denied that the mental ego is capable of generous deeds that greatly assist others, but these deeds are almost always burdened, however lightly, with a concern about how they might pay dividends to the agent.

THE MENTAL EGO AND COGNITION

The cognition of the mental ego corresponds to Freud's secondary process and to Piaget's operational thinking, especially formal operational thinking. Piaget's voluminous writings present the very best account of this stage and form of cognition. It is not my purpose here to summarize Piaget's work, which is well known.[5] Rather, my purpose is to sketch the mental ego's cognition in light of the triphasic framework, focusing specifically on how the mental ego's cognition surpasses the paleological cognition of the body-ego.

If we remember, paleological cognition suffered from the following shortcomings: (1) parochiality, the tendency to key on the local and incidental rather than the universal and essential; (2) incomplete abstraction, the inability to grasp conceptual meanings except in the concrete medium of the imagination; and (3) inconsistency, the proneness to confuse subject and predicate, instance and attribute, member and class. The cognition of the mental ego surmounts these three shortcomings of paleologic.

The mental ego, no longer buffered from the world by the Great Mother, needs a reliable conceptual map with which to test and explore reality. It therefore works hard to rid the rudimentary meanings inherited from the body-egoic period of their limitations and aberrations. And in time the mental ego succeeds in putting together a framework of fully abstracted concepts that define things consistently and along essential lines—whether essential intrinsically or relative to human needs and purposes. These concepts are hierarchically interwoven, with higher levels possessing greater generality and lower levels greater specificity. Room, logical space, is available for the inclusion of new concepts, and concepts already a part of the system are, in principle, open to revision or amendment. Hence, the system has both sufficient scope to assimilate the new and sufficient flexibility, usually, to accommodate anomalies and counterinstances.

The mental ego comes by this conceptual scheme less by its own efforts than by inheritance from others. The young mental ego, driven both by curiosity and necessity, does apply itself assiduously, attending closely to the qualities of things and abstracting from these qualities a sense of nature or kind. But the young mental ego is given much more than it gathers on its own. For previous generations have already done the majority of the work, and their accumulated learning is simply imparted to the young mental ego. To be sure, a conceptual scheme is not acquired without great effort; nevertheless, a conceptual scheme is for the most part a social bequest. It is inherited culture.

It was noted in the last chapter that the body-ego's failure to distinguish between a thing and its properties (the predicate-identity principle) has three unfortunate consequences, namely, (1) illusions of magical power and vulnerability, (2) unwarranted condensations and displacements (of both thought and energy), and (3) instability in the sense of self. These problems are also surmounted by the cognition of the mental ego. Magical thought gives way to thought based on systematic typologies of things and strict causal orderings of events. Condensations and displacements are in general banned—except in such "nonrational" areas of the mental ego's life as neuroses, dreams, and mythologies. And instability in the sense of self is solved by the

104

development, especially at the end of adolescence, of a coherent self-concept. In general, the unbridled transmutations and transferences allowed by paleologic are prohibited by the mental ego's cognition, which brings into focus a view of things that is orderly, predictable, and stable.

Characteristic of the mental ego's cognition is not only its well-drawn conceptual map but also certain forms of disciplined inferential thought, included among which are, most importantly, induction and deduction. The mental ego's cognition proceeds not only abstractly, i.e., conceptually, but also discursively, i.e., in a regulated, step-by-step fashion. And the primary objective in moving rigorously from evidence or premises to conclusions is to keep the mind harnessed and within the limits of reality. Induction and deduction are fail-safe methods of extracting truths from truths. They are forms of thought that, in their strictness, avoid the vagaries, and therefore errors, of intuition. Typically, then, the mental ego's cognition tends to be of a cautious type; indeed, it is as circumspect as paleologic, or the primary process, is reckless and untamed. Induction and deduction are painstaking and methodical. However, this is not to disparage them. For what they lack in boldness of vision they make up for in accuracy and reliability.

Moreover, it would be a distortion to say that the mental ego's thinking is exclusively abstract and discursive in nature, and thus altogether devoid of intuition. After all, it is only by intuition that scientific hypotheses are conceived. Hypotheses, the guiding ideas of empirical inquiry, are the fruit of insight, not inference. And the same, of course, is true, on an even more profound level, of the revolutionary ideas responsible for new paradigms in science and for new perspectives in art and literature. These examples indicate that the mental ego is more than just an instrument designed to map and compute. They indicate that the mental ego is capable of real intuition and inspiration. Nevertheless, what is *characteristic* of the mental ego's thinking is that it is mainly of an abstract and discursive sort. Intuition, especially symbolic intuition, issues from nonegoic sources; therefore, since the mental ego is alienated from the nonegoic pole of the psyche, it also is for the most part closed to intuition. Creative (indeed, visionary) intuition, as will be seen later, is one of the distinguishing characteristics of the cognition of the integrated stage.

A final point about the mental ego's cognition is that it breaks out of the narcissistic self-containment of the body-ego to a view that sees well beyond the individual and, indeed, to infinity. That is, the mental ego's thinking tends toward both impartiality and universality. It tends toward an ideal that both (1) treats instances of concepts and cases of rules equally, allowing no exceptions or exemptions, and (2) includes all possible instances or cases within the comprehended scope of a given concept or rule. In other words, the cognition of the mental ego aims at being both nonpartisan and all-inclusive.

But it must be stressed that this describes the mental ego's *cognitive* ideal, for it most certainly does not describe the mental ego's existential attitude. As explained earlier, the mental ego is inherently egocentric and egoistic. Although it knows intellectually that "all men are created equal," it persists nonetheless, in its feelings and actions, in being almost exclusively self-concerned.[6] To use one of C.S. Lewis's analogies, the mental ego is like the driver on a long stretch of road who, although knowing full well the illusion involved, cannot help but see the closest telephone pole as the largest. Each mental ego cannot help but take the issues of its own identity and worth as being the world's most pressing and important concerns, and it persists in this attitude despite the fact that it understands rationally that it is but one among many. The mental ego consequently experiences a conflict between its reason, which is impartial and universal, and its basic life orientation, which is unregenerately egocentric. On the theoretical level the mental ego legislates categorical imperatives that it enjoins upon itself. But on the practical level it stubbornly resists these imperatives and strives instead for the satisfaction of its own interest.

The cognition of the mental ego is exceedingly complex. I have only touched the surface. Nevertheless, the most essential dimensions have been mentioned. These are, again, (1) the organization of concepts into stable hierarchies that map the contents of experience along abstractly essential lines; (2) the ordering of events under causal rules, which allow changes to be seen as falling into repeatable, predictable patterns; (3) the mastery of inductive and deductive inference; and (4) the attainment of an impartial and universal perspective. The cognition of the mental ego is a vast improvement over the paleologic of the body-ego. The latter is simply too prone to inconsistency and caprice—although, phylogenetically, it must at one time have been sufficient for the survival of the species. It is only with the emergence of the secondary process that our epistemic efforts have accomplished regular and reliable results.

CONCLUSION

The mental ego is a multifaceted phenomenon. It is at once a Cartesian "thinking thing" disdainful of physico-dynamic life, an ontologically insecure self fearful of its own "nothingness," a restless extravert anxious to establish worldly identity and worth, and a cognitive subject responsible for testing reality according to the canons of secondary process or formal operational thought. And these are only the mental ego's more prominent features and functions.

Most of what the mental ego is and does is essential to effective living.

However, the mental ego has an Achilles' heel, a weak point in its constitution which, in later years, is responsible for much of human suffering. This, of course, is original repression. It is because of this weak point that the mental ego is plagued with the root anxieties of "nothingness" and guilt, and therefore also with the impossible project to be *ens causa sui*. In pursuit of a sense of being and worth, the mental ego stakes its all on the outcome of this project. But since the *causa sui* project is a form of flight, it cannot truly satisfy the needs that motivate it. "Nothingness" and guilt always remain one step behind the mental ego no matter how successful it might be in life. The mental ego strives after the impossible; it is condemned to a project requiring ceaseless efforts, to no avail.

The mental ego, then, to use another of Sartre's expressions, is a "useless passion." It struggles vainly to flee from what it is and to make itself what it is not and cannot be. And it suffers the consequences: chronic restlessness, dissatisfaction, and, ultimately, despair. Of these consequences, it is despair, curiously, that offers the mental ego some real hope. For despair, if it is truly profound, has the power to move the mental ego to the brink, from which the mental ego might acknowledge its "nothingness" and guilt and, perhaps, take a leap of faith. In short, despair can be the mood of transcendence.

In closing, I would like to reiterate the proviso set forth earlier, namely, that the mental ego is a matter of degree. Not every mental ego is completely out of touch with the body and Dynamic Ground, or perpetually anxious, or totally egoistic. Nor is it the case that despair is always a necessary condition of transcendence. All of these aspects of the mental-egoic system vary from individual to individual, and from culture to culture as well. Nevertheless, despite these very important qualifications, it remains true, I believe, that the foregoing account correctly states what the mental ego is *in essence*. No specific case may fully exemplify this essence, but it is only in terms of the essence that any specific case can be fully understood.

CHAPTER 5

The Unconscious

THE TOPIC OF THE unconscious has been touched upon in earlier chapters. Chapter 1 introduced the idea of the prepersonal unconscious as the nonegoic pole of the psyche in arrested, "pre-" form. Chapter 3 explained that the prepersonal unconscious can be divided into the Dynamic Ground, the instinctual-archetypal unconscious, and the body-unconscious. And the last chapter discussed the shadow as a principal component of the personal unconscious. These preliminary discussions were sufficient for earlier purposes, but they are incomplete. It is necessary now to provide a more thorough inventory of the unconscious. An outline of such an inventory is presented in Table 5-1.

Table 5-1 sets the agenda for the present chapter. I will briefly discuss each of the levels of the unconscious indicated, beginning with the prepersonal levels and finishing with the personal levels. (The parts of Table 5-1 designated "Regression in the Service of Transcendence" and "Integration" will not be considered here, since, strictly speaking, they play no role in the formation or constitution of the unconscious. They will be treated in later chapters. They are included in Table 5-1 only to show how the structure of the unconscious fits into the larger theoretical framework of this book.)

Geared as it is to Table 5-1, the present chapter may pose special difficulties for the reader. The format is that of an inventory: each of the levels of the unconscious is treated succinctly and in turn. This format makes it possible to cover a large and important topic in a relatively small space, but it has the consequence of imposing severe constraints on the exposition and prose, which in places are severely condensed. The reader may therefore find the present chapter difficult going and may want to read the chapter selectively. If so, I would urge that the reader *not* skip the sections on the Dynamic Ground, the phylogenetic level of the instinctual-archetypal unconscious, original repression, and the personal submerged unconscious, since

108

Table 5-1

THE UNCONSCIOUS

	LEVEL	POTENTIALS AND STRUCTURES	TRIPHASIC STAGE
TRANS-PERSONAL	Integrated Consciousness	A. Vision B. Bliss, compassion C. Contemplation, illumination	Integrated stage and beyond
	REGENERATION IN SPIRIT REGRESSION IN THE SERVICE OF TRANSCENDENCE		
PERSONAL	Personal Embedded Unconscious*	A. Self-concept B. Ego-defense mechanisms C. Filtering structures D. Autonomous complexes E. COEX systems	Mental ego
	Personal Submerged Unconscious*	A. Shadow B. Filtered stimuli C. Subthreshold stimuli	
	ORIGINAL REPRESSION (embedded*)		
PREPERSONAL	Body-Unconscious (repressed)	A. Autosymbolic, paleological cognition B. Full-bodied feelings C. Polymorphous sensuousness D. Amplified experience E. Numinosity or enchantment	Body-ego
	Instinctual-Archetypal Unconscious (repressed)	A. Ontogenetic B. Phylogenetic	
	Dynamic Ground (repressed)	Libido-Energy-Spirit	Original embedment

*Wilber's (1980a) term.

these sections introduce ideas that are particularly important or that are indispensable for understanding the chapters that follow.

THE DYNAMIC GROUND

The most fundamental concept advanced in this book is that of the Dynamic Ground. The Dynamic Ground is the seat of the physico-dynamic pole of the psyche and the source of psychic energy. As such, it is a *sine qua non* of any kind of psychic functioning or conscious life. Experience in general is possible only on the assumption that there is a line of contact to the power that resides in, and flows from, this source.

Despite the crucial role played by the Dynamic Ground, dynamic conceptions of the psyche are presently out of vogue among academic and research psychologists—even among psychoanalysts. Cognitivism, replacing behaviorism, is the currently reigning academic paradigm, and ego psychology and object-relations theory are the currently reigning psychoanalytic perspectives. There are many reasons why dynamically oriented psychology has fallen into disregard, but perhaps the principal one is that the notion of psychic energy has been liable to interpretations that in almost all cases have been either reductionistic or vague. For example, the notion has been interpreted reductionistically in terms of the instincts, the sexual and aggressive instincts in particular (psychoanalysis), or it has been conceived only very indeterminately as the omnitransmutable fuel of psychic life (Jung). Virtually all dynamically oriented theories suffer from one or the other of these two shortcomings, and, consequently, they have understandably become suspect in the eyes of psychologists who have little sympathy for the dynamic point of view.

The Dynamic Ground constitutes a topic unto itself, which, were it to be pursued at any length, would soon extend well beyond the scope of the present chapter. In any case, some of the pre-egoic manifestations of the power of the Ground have already been discussed in Chapter 2, and main transegoic manifestations will be discussed in later chapters. The ensuing discussion is therefore of necessity an extremely sketchy one. Proceeding on the basis of bipolar and triphasic assumptions, consideration will here be limited to only the most basic functions and expressions of the Dynamic Ground.

The primary function of the power of the Ground is to serve as the "fuel" (i.e., activator and enhancer) of psychic systems. As such, the power of the Ground is something that in principle is amenable to quantitative assessment, although of course we do not yet possess the means of measuring it. For example, the magnitude of dynamic charge is a chief difference between a stunning insight and a less striking cognitive experience, between an intense passion and a more mild mood or feeling, between a sensory spectacle and an ordinary perception, between an exciting adventure and a routine action, and, in general, between any peak and any pallid or neutral experience. In each of these pairs of examples, the sheer quantity of dynamism empowering the experience is a clearly evident distinguishing factor.

To use a term introduced by Stansilav Grof (1975) in a different context, the power of the Ground in its function as an activator/enhancer can be said to be a *nonspecific amplifier* of experience. It is a magnifier of all dimensions of psychic life. Thus, when the power of the Ground flows, experience quickens, becoming alive and acute, if not tumultuous and overwhelmingly intense. Conversely, when the power of the Ground ebbs, experience slows, becoming pale, distant, and dull. The presence of the power of the Ground potentiates experience across all dimensions; the absence of this power depotentiates experience.

In adopting the term *nonspecific amplifier*, it is implied that the power of the Ground is an energizer of psychic systems that is not itself reducible to or exclusively expressive of any particular system or systems. This is in contradiction to the Freudian theory of libido, according to which psychic dynamism is inherently sexual (or aggressive) in nature. However, if the Freudian theory is to be avoided in its reduction of psychic to sexual energy, it can still be followed in its linking of psychic dynamism to the sexual system. This is so for two reasons. First, as Reich (1942) stressed, psychic dynamism has its physiological seat within the region of the genitals; it is released from a location within the reproductive system. And second, psychic dynamism is for most people—i.e., as mental egos, operating under the constraints of original repression—primarily contained within this point of origin. I have argued that the mental ego lays down multiple layers of psychophysical defense against the upflow of the power of the Ground, with the effect that the power of the Ground is for the most part kept confined within the lower instinctual areas. For most people, then, I submit, it is true that the power of the Ground is *in effect* a sexual energy, since for them it not only originates within the sexual system but is also primarily concentrated in and expressed through that system. For them, it has assumed a genito-instinctual (and unconscious) organization.

In light of these facts it is useful to retain the term *libido* and to use it in contrast to *psychic energy*. Accordingly, I will employ *libido* nonreductively to designate the power of the Ground in virtue of its genetic connection with sexuality and in virtue of its predominant genito-instinctual organization. In contrast to this, I will employ *psychic energy* to designate the power of the Ground in virtue of its main functional role as the nonspecific amplifier or fuel of psychic systems. Thus defined, *libido* and *psychic energy* designate two of the three chief manifestations of the power of the Dynamic Ground. The other chief manifestation, spirit, will be discussed shortly.

Another feature of the power of the Ground is that it is an *attractive force*. This is evident from the magnetic influence that energy cathexes have upon the ego. Attention is spontaneously drawn to accumulations of the power of the Ground. Things charged with this power engage the ego's attention and are interesting or even fascinating to a degree that is directly proportional to the amount of power resident in them. For example, the power of the Ground is concentrated in the erogenous zones, and it goes without saying that attention is frequently riveted on them. The power of the Ground is heavily invested in the objects of desires and fears (and in cathexis objects generally), which are frequently the foci of fixations. Also, the power of the Ground is strongly present in so-called charismatic people, who have a spellbinding effect upon others. Anything on which the power of the Ground is projected or from which it emanates has a magnetic effect upon the ego. And this, it seems, is true regardless of whether the bearer or source of the power is positive or negative in its manner of appearance to the ego. Negative magnetism is, for example, evident in many neurotic fixations and obsessions and more generally in the morbid fascination that people have in things horrific, macabre, and demonic. In sum, the power of the Ground magnifies things and throws them into relief, whether pleasantly so (e.g., by rendering them inviting or enrapturing) or unpleasantly so (e.g., by rendering them gripping or hypnotically inescapable).

Owing to its magnetic character, the power of the Ground is able, if present in sufficient concentration, not only to attract attention but also completely to command it—almost regardless of whatever resistance might be mounted by the ego. In other words, the power of the Ground can induce transfixion. Spellbinding speakers, awesome sights, and arresting experiences generally exert their hold on attention by means of the power resident or deposited in them. There are many idioms that describe this phenomenon in remarkably insightful ways. For example, it is said that one is held "breathless" or "in suspense," or that one is "dumbfounded," "rendered speechless," "petrified," "riveted," and so on. All of these expressions connote *involuntary immobilization*, whether of body or mind. They indicate that a person, when in the presence of things highly charged with the power of the Ground, is vulnerable to being arrested or seized.

The power of the Ground, then, not only engages awareness; it can command and capture it as well. Moreover, in extreme cases the power of the Ground can *dissolve* the ego. The power of the Ground is a magnetic-*solvent* force before which the ego is liable to be captured *and consumed*. This is evident, for example, in such phenomena as oceanic regression, entrancement, and ecstasy. Oceanic regression involves a dynamic dissolution of the ego and, thereby, a reversion of the ego to the preindividuated condition of original embedment. Entrancement involves not only a fixation of attention but also an absorption of awareness in a dynamically charged object or situation. And ecstasy involves not only a euphoric infusion of the ego by the power of the Ground but also a bursting of ego boundaries by that power. When in the field of influence of the power of the Ground, the ego is liable to be engulfed, swept away, dissolved, or otherwise absorbed or expunged.

The power of the Ground thus has potential dominion over the ego. It can command the ego's attention, halt the ego's operations, and even absorb the ego, reducing it to temporary nonexistence. And the power of the Ground is able to do these things, in principle, even should the ego be resistant and refuse to "let go." The ego therefore is vulnerable in face of the power of the Ground.

This vulnerability, considered in conjunction with the ego's attraction to the power of the Ground, explains another basic feature of that power, namely, its radical bivalence—or, more accurately, its *seeming* bivalence, based on the ego's radical ambivalence toward it. The ego is both drawn to and apprehensive of the power of the Ground. For, on the one hand, this power is, to the ego, an alluring enlivener of awareness; yet, on the other hand, it is an uncontrollable and threatening force. It is a necessary condition of the ego's existence and operation, yet it also is a tractional force that can capture and consume the ego. It is the force behind passion and heightened life, yet it also is a force that can lay siege to the ego and that, siren-like, can lure it, seemingly, to its death.

The bivalence of the power of the Ground is the source of perhaps the most basic problem of the ego's existence. If we recall, this bivalence constitutes the fundamental dilemma of the body-ego's life, which, after an initial period of paradisiacal well-being, is lived futilely in pursuit of both intimacy with the Good Mother and independence from the Terrible Mother. The problem of bivalence is hidden, but by no means solved, for the duration of the mental-egoic period, during which the Ground is submerged beneath original repression and during which, therefore, the power of the Ground is able to manifest itself for the most part only through unconscious cathexes and projections. The problem of bivalence resurfaces with the onset of regression in the service of transcendence and continues to afflict the ego throughout this stage, and the stage of regeneration in spirit as well, since during these two transitional periods the ego comes once again into immediate contact with the Ground and undergoes a death/rebirth transformation at the hands of the power of the Ground. As we shall see, it is only when regeneration in spirit culminates in integration proper that the problem of bivalence is finally overcome. It is only at this highest stage of development that the ego, at last harmoniously rooted in the Ground, is no longer ambivalent toward the Ground, and consequently is no longer affected bivalently by the power of the Ground. The power of the Ground at this point drops its negative side and once again, as it did at the very outset of life, manifests itself as a univalent, wholly positive force.

Table 5-2 summarizes the major steps of the ego/Ground interaction in light of the ambivalence/bivalence phenomenon. Having already treated steps 1-5 of Table 5-2 in an earlier chapter, I will here briefly indicate how, in later chapters, steps 6-10 will be treated. This preview of ensuing developments is needed in order to set the stage for a discussion of the power of the Ground as spirit.

Original repression radically alters the character of the ego/Ground interaction. It does so because the vanquishment of the Terrible Mother submerges the Ground and therefore alienates the power of the Ground from consciousness. At this point the power of the Ground is for the most part

Table 5-2

THE AMBIVALENCE-BIVALENCE PHENOMENON

	STAGE	DISPOSITION OF EGO	APPEARANCE OF GROUND
10	Integration	Ego is in harmony with Ground as subordinate member of bipolar duality.	Power of Ground reveals itself as spirit proper: conscious light and love.
9	Regeneration in spirit	Ego's ingrained resistances to power of Ground are gradually purged.	Power of Ground presents itself in increasingly positive manners, as comforter, inspirer, enlightener, etc.
8	Regression in the service of tran-scendence	Original repression gives way or is broken through.	Power of Ground assails ego as alien and threatening force: the return of the repressed, the fury of liberated spirit.
7	Middle to late mental-egoic period	Same as below except that original repression is now weakened and less able to contain power of Ground. Ego becomes interested in ego-transcendent possibilities.	Occasional incursions of power of Ground into consciousness, giving rise to manifestations of the holy, the *mysterium tremendum et fascinans*.
6	Early to middle mental-egoic period	Same as below	Power of Ground operates as force of unconscious, which, although dark and threatening in an invisible way, is also (via cathexes and projections) compellingly magnetic.
5	Original repression	Ego alienates power of Ground from consciousness.	Power of Ground reduced to prepersonal (sexual, instinctual, unconscious) organization.
4	Late body-egoic period	Ego is highly attached to itself and highly threatened by Ground.	Terrible Mother looms large; conflict with maternal power.
3	Middle body-egoic period	Ego is attached to itself and equally drawn to Ground: acute ambivalence.	Good Mother and Terrible Mother equal but opposite sides of Ground/Mother complex: thoroughgoing bivalence.
2	Early body-egoic period	Ego has just emerged and is unresistant to Ground.	Good Mother
1	Original embedment	Ego has not yet emerged.	Womb of Great Mother; oceanic oblivion and bliss.

restricted to the status of libido, the energy of the instinctual underside of life. However, even under these alienated conditions, the power of the Ground continues to affect the ego (now the mental ego), namely, through unconscious cathexes and transferences. The power of the Ground, unbeknownst to the mental ego, is projected upon objects of unconscious drives, complexes, desires, and fears. These objects, charged with the power of the Ground, have a hypnotic and absorptive effect upon the mental ego—even though the mental ego at the same time is usually threatened by these objects. These objects therefore are the foci of the mental ego's fixations, obsessions, and compulsions. The mental ego is driven to these objects and is sometimes taken captive by them, for reasons that it does not and cannot understand. These objects have an uncanny hold upon the mental ego, and they consequently pose an invisible limit to its autonomy.

Even when contained by original repression, the power of the Ground does on occasion break loose to manifest itself directly within the field of the mental ego's experience, especially in mature years when the mental ego is ready for conversion and the openness of faith. When such "ruptures of plane" occur, the power of the Ground typically takes the form of what Rudolf Otto (1958) called "the holy." As described by Otto, the holy is the *mysterium tremendum et fascinans*; it is a dynamic presence that is ineffable, overawing, and compellingly magnetic. Moreover, according to Otto, the holy is dramatically bivalent in that it has both light and dark sides and engenders in the mental ego both ecstasies and agonies, exaltations and abasements. Owing to the magnetic character of the power of the Ground, the mental ego is irresistibly drawn to the holy. But owing to the captivating and solvent effects of the power, the mental ego is deeply apprehensive of the holy, which the mental ego approaches full of "fear and trembling," afraid that it will be engulfed and destroyed. In sum, the power of the Ground in its manifestation as the holy is experienced by the mental ego as an incomprehensible, ego-eclipsing, entrancing, and disconcertingly two-sided force. It presents itself as a numinous reality that is daunting as well as uplifting, a source of gravity as well as grace.

Once original repression gives way and regression in the service of transcendence commences, the ego begins to confront the power of the Ground within the intimacy of the soul. This confrontation takes two forms. First, since original repression had submerged the Ground, the removal of original repression triggers a violent resurgence of the power of the Ground, which (along with other nonegoic potentials) erupts into the upper sphere of consciousness and assails the ego within its own domain. And second, since original repression had undergirded the mental ego, the removal of original repression also triggers a collapse of the mental-egoic system and a fall of the mental ego into the underlying physico-dynamic sphere, i.e., into the prepersonal unconscious, the nonegoic pole of the psyche in arrested, "pre-" form. The confrontation between the ego and the power of the Ground that occurs during regression in the service of transcendence is therefore at once a violent upward and downward movement. It is both an upsurge of nonegoic life into the egoic sphere (the return of the repressed, the fury of liberated spirit) and a downfall of the mental ego into the nonegoic sphere (the fall into the abyss, the descent into the underworld). This confrontation is a collision between the two poles of the psyche; it is a battle between two opposed realms, the principal antagonists of which are the ego and the power of the Ground.

The battle between the ego and the Ground that ensues during regression in the service of transcendence is a battle to determine which of these will be the sovereign power of the soul. The ego, as mental ego, considers itself to be the exclusive owner and controller of subjectivity. The ego for this reason experiences the encounter with the power of the Ground as a confrontation with an alien force that challenges the ego's claim upon supreme authority within the psychic polity. Accordingly, the ego responds to this perceived threat with all the resources at its command. It attempts desperately to banish the power of the Ground from consciousness, to shore up egoic defenses, and thereby to reseal the Ground. But these are losing efforts, since the ego faces a power that is in all senses the ego's superior. Hence, the battle between the ego and the Dynamic Ground eventually comes to an end; it is "won" by the power of the Ground. The ego eventually realizes that it is the inferior party, both in strength and in right. The ego finally understands that it cannot triumph over its adversary and, moreover, that its adversary is really the ego's own higher life: spirit.

In arriving at this insight, the ego makes the turn to regeneration in spirit and begins a new type of struggle. It ceases struggling against the power of the Ground and begins struggling against its own remaining resistances to that power. This new struggle is therefore the battle of surrender to divine power fought by the knight of faith. Here there occurs an uncompromising purging of everything remaining within the mental-egoic system that is closed or opposed to the spontaneous movement of spiritual force, e.g., vestiges of original repression, many fears and defense mechanisms, and much of the self-concept/shadow complex. These impediments to the free expression of divine power are gradually dissolved in order to bring the ego into harmonious alignment with spirit. The ego struggles against all of these aspects of itself so that it can become an unobstructed vehicle of spirit.

The turn to regeneration in spirit is, then, the point at which the ego reverses its stance toward the power of the Ground: the ego ceases opposing the power and begins cooperating with it instead. Correspondingly, the turn to regeneration in spirit is also the point at which there occurs a reversal in the manner in which the power of the Ground appears to the ego: the power of the

Ground begins to drop its sinister guises and begins increasingly to assume friendly ones. Accordingly, whereas the power of the Ground had at first manifested itself primarily as a menacing force, this power, at the commencement of regeneration in spirit, begins manifesting itself primarily as a beneficent force, as a force that heals rather than slays the ego and that graces the ego with inspirations, ecstasies, and intimacies. The power of the Ground is bivalent throughout both regression in the service of transcendence and regeneration in spirit. But it is mainly the negative side of the bivalence that is experienced during the former of these two transitional periods and mainly, and increasingly, the positive side of the bivalence that is experienced during the latter of the periods.

Once the ego has been purged of its last resistances to the infusive movement of spirit, the power of the Ground ceases being bivalent. Without any obstacles left to overcome, the power of the Ground no longer needs to be violent with the ego, and consequently the power of the Ground begins here to present itself to the ego as a force that, unopposed, is entirely gentle and benign. The integrated stage that commences at this point is, therefore, one that is both powerfully infused and yet beatifically calm. It is a stage that transcends all darkness and violence. Even the positive experiences that highlighted the period of regeneration reflect this transcendence. These experiences continue to be every bit as powerful as before, but now, divested of all negative nuances, they lose their eruptive character and become smooth and serene. For example, inspiration is transformed into contemplation, ecstacy into bliss, and intimacy into at-one-ment.

Concomitant with these transformations, the spiritual power of the soul finally discloses itself in its highest and, I believe, truest nature as *conscious light and love*. To be sure, the power of the Ground continues here, as libido, to be released from the sexual system and, as psychic energy, to fuel psychic processes generally; moreover, it continues, similar to the holy, to be an all-pervasive numinous presence. But at this juncture, since the power of the Ground is liberated from exclusive association with the instincts and is disburdened of the resistance of the ego, it is able to reveal itself as well in its pristine form as luminously intelligent and spontaneously outreaching life. In other words, it presents itself as the dynamic essence of enlightenment and charity.

The light and love of spirit can be understood in terms of the foregoing account of the power of the Ground. I suggest that they are in fact the consciousness-amplifying and magnetic aspects of the power of the Ground when these aspects are manifested under conditions of dynamic freedom, i.e., conditions that obtain when the power of the Ground is neither consumed by specific psychic systems nor repressed or resisted by the ego. When the power of the Ground, as psychic energy, is utilized to fuel psychic systems, it works as an amplifier of specific modes of awareness. When it is not so channeled, however, and is instead permitted to flow freely, it is available to be experienced directly and in its own nature, namely, as a fluidic luminescence or interior light. As Daniel Brown (1986, 240) states in his study of contemplative experience, "awareness opens up to the substratum of ordinary perception, namely, an incessant flow of light in the stream of awareness."[1] The very energy that ordinarily facilitates the experience of things other than itself is in these circumstances itself experienced. The medium of awareness becomes object of awareness and, as such, is experienced as an incandescent dynamism.

Also, when the power of the Ground is opposed by the ego, its magnetic effect exhibits itself only darkly or indirectly, either through entrancements and transfixions or, when the Ground is repressed and submerged, through unconscious cathexes and projections. Once, however, the mature ego has become harmoniously integrated with the Ground, that power, as liberated spirit, manifests its magnetic character immediately and in a positive manner, namely, as spontaneous attraction, spiritual confluence, agapeic love. Under these conditions the ego is completely at one with the life of spirit, which moves not only infusively, within the ego, but also effusively, from the ego, radiating outwardly to others and bonding with them, spirit to spirit. Under conditions of dynamic freedom, then, the power of the Ground is not only the light of wisdom but also the outflowing heart of compassion. It is the pure spiritual force that loves others regardless of merit, simply by virtue of an irresistible magnetic attraction.

Of the several forms assumed by the power of the Ground, it is, I believe, spirit as manifested under conditions of dynamic freedom that alone displays the power's intrinsic nature. This is so because it is only in the case of liberated spirit that the power of the Ground is revealed without either modulation or constraint. And as was just explained, when the power of the Ground is revealed in this way, it shows itself to be luminous love, consciousness in search of communion. To be sure, it is rare for the power of the Ground to be seen in this pristine form. For given that original repression is the rule and dynamic freedom the exception, the power of the Ground is primarily limited to a prepersonal organization (libido), and that amount of the power that is allowed to circulate freely is usually channeled and consumed without remainder by psychic systems (psychic energy). It is only in those exceptional cases when original repression is lifted and the ego is at one with the Ground that the power of the Ground is able to disclose itself fully and with complete fidelity to its intrinsic nature, not just as the holy—which, in its bivalence, indicates that the ego is still not completely surrendered—but as the grace of the divine life.

Contrary to the Freudian position, then, according to which spirit is sublimated libido, the position that I am advancing is that libido is repressed spirit. Libido—and psychic energy, too—is a limited form of spirit. In saying this, however, I do not mean to imply that the reverse of Freudian reductionism is true. For the Freudian view is that all psychic systems are, in the end, subordinate to and expressive of sexuality, which is itself a psychic system. The present view, in contrast, is that no psychic system has the privileged status of uniquely revealing the essence of dynamic life. No psychic system is basic in this sense; rather, I suggest, the essence of dynamic life is truly disclosed only when it manifests itself *independently* of all systemic expressions and organizations. Therefore, in saying that spirit is the true essence of the power of the Ground, I am not committing myself to a reverse reductionism. Rather, all I am saying is that the power of the Ground has a distinctive self-nature, and that this self-nature is not fully evident in the sexual origin or containment of the power, as libido, or in the system-specific consumption of the power, as psychic energy, but rather only in the free expression of the power, as spirit.

In conclusion, I would like to submit the opinion that the power of the Ground as it has here been described is not merely a theoretical postulate, better yet fiction, but is rather a fundamental reality of the soul. It is true that, owing to original repression, the power of the Ground is rarely evident within consciousness. This, however, does not mean that the power is only an explanatory construct or a merely inferred existent. Although usually repressed and unconscious, the power of the Ground is something that can impinge upon consciousness in many ways. As psychic energy, it amplifies experience across all dimensions and, as spirit, it effects dramatic transformations of the ego and of subjective life generally. The power of the Ground, I submit, is an actually existing dynamism that can be directly experienced by the conscious ego. Moreover, there is reason to believe that the power of the Ground is a force that, under certain conditions, is discernible not only subjectively but also physically. This subject is taken up in Chapters 7 and 8, when we come to discuss the movement of the power of the Ground once it is freed from the bonds of original repression. Suffice it here to say that there are persuasive indications that the power of the Ground is something that affects the body as well as the mind, and, therefore, that it is something that in principle is amenable to strict scientific study, including measurement by physical instruments. However, in saying this, I realize that empirical science is not even remotely close to undertaking such a study. Discussion must first agree on the *existence* of something before it can begin to consider strategies for detection and measurement. Admittedly, then, the foregoing account of the power of the Dynamic Ground, although empirically meaningful, is not presently empirically verifiable except in a subjective and introspective sense, and even then, really, only by those for whom the power of the Ground has become active as spirit.

One last point. In stressing the existence of the power of the Ground, I am not advancing an opinion on the ultimate ontological status of this power. Such a judgment would, in any case, be unwarranted. It is beyond human cognitive capacity to know whether the power of the Ground, in addition to being an intrapsychic phenomenon, is also an extrapsychic (i.e., cosmic) noumenon. It can be affirmed that the power of the Ground is a dynamic reality of extra-egoic origin and numinous, indeed divine, nature, but it cannot be affirmed (or denied) that it also is something that exists independently of the psyche. This is *not* psychological reductionism; it is simply a confession of ignorance. Spirit may have its ultimate origin in a metaphysical source lying completely beyond the soul. However, as experienced by the ego, it is of necessity something that has entered and manifests itself within the boundaries of the soul. The ego can have no experience, and therefore no knowledge, of the power of the Ground as it may (or may not) exist beyond these boundaries.

THE INSTINCTUAL-ARCHETYPAL UNCONSCIOUS

As observed in Chapter 3, the instinctual-archetypal unconscious is divisible into ontogenetic and phylogenetic sectors or levels. The former contains materials deriving from the universal conditions governing the emergence of the individual organism or ego from the original context of its existence. The latter contains materials deriving from factors pertaining to the constitution and evolution of the species.

1. *Ontogenetic level.* Concerning ontogenesis, the dimension of greatest archetypal significance is the interaction between the developing ego and the maternal principle, i.e., the Great Mother. The ego/Great Mother relation is the source of many of the symbols that make up the collective unconscious. Having already treated this relation in the context of the discussion of the body-ego, the task here will be the limited one of describing the principal structural properties of the Great Mother system.[2]

The Dynamic Ground is the nascent ego's psychic womb and sustainer, and, as such, it constitutes the inner side of the *bidirectional* Great Mother system. The Great Mother is at once an outer and an inner source, support, and enveloping presence, at once the mothering parent and the Dynamic Ground. To the body-ego, however, these two dimensions of the Great Mother system are indistinct, and, thus, the images by which the Great Mother is pictured characteristically involve a degree of conflation of material and psychic, outer and inner, personal and impersonal ingredients. For the body-ego, then, the Great Mother is neither a fully personal (i.e., human) nor a merely impersonal (i.e., elemental) presence, but rather a presence that combines both of these aspects without completely exemplifying either one. To be sure, the Great Mother is depicted in female human form (e.g., as good and evil fairies, witches, guardianesses) and also in the form of elemental forces (e.g., as waters, fires, and winds of either soothing and nurturing or violent and destructive nature). But these depictions are limiting cases lying on either end of an axis the main, middle, ground of which is made up of forms that are at once both and neither human and elemental, i.e., forms that to a degree involve a predifferentiated fusion of the outer and inner dimensions of the maternal reality. Now, since subhuman animals represent just such a conflation of the personal/impersonal bidirectionality of the Great Mother, it follows that they can be regarded as providing perhaps the very best examples of how the body-ego perceives the Great Mother. This is especially true of animals that are either warm, furry, and milk-providing (the Good Mother) or that are cold, scaly, and dangerous (the Terrible Mother). Furry mammals (e.g., hairy and cuddly apes or placid bovine types) and scaly reptiles (e.g., loathsome "creepy-crawlies," poisonous vipers, and fire-snorting dragons) are thus central and essential to the Great Mother system. In sum, the Great Mother system can be said to consist of images almost all of which fall *between* the end points of an axis bound on one side by a completely personal mothering parent and on the other side by a completely impersonal Dynamic Ground. Some of these images fall closer to one end point of the axis and others fall closer to the other end point, but in virtually all cases they reflect some degree of conflation of the two dimensions that define the axis.

The Great Mother system is *bivalent* as well as bidirectional. Owing to the magnetic and nurturing nature of the Great Mother, the ego is drawn to her and is prone to imagine her in positive ways, e.g., as a graceful maiden, a furry mammal, or as elemental forces of pleasant and friendly disposition. However, owing to the captivating and absorptive/consuming nature of the Great Mother, the ego is frightened of her and is prone to imagine her in negative ways, e.g., as an ugly witch, a scaly reptile, or as elemental forces of unpleasant and hostile disposition. The Great Mother system consequently consists of images falling simultaneously on two axes, a bidirectional and a bivalent axis. These two axes define the boundaries of the system, and they therefore determine the field of possible images that can be included within the system.

There is an interesting difference in the primary points at which the images of the Great Mother system fall on its two axes. As was said, these images fall between, but rarely on, the end points of the bidirectional axis. Hence, neither a fully personalized mother nor a completely depersonalized Ground is normally a part of the Great Mother system. It is, rather, the intermediate points on the bidirectional axis that most truly belong to the system, with the more central points being more central to the system. This is why, as was just noted, the mammal/reptile antithesis provides perhaps the most revealing expression of the Great Mother. In contrast, images of the Great Mother fall near or at, but rarely between, the end points of the bivalent axis. That is to say, the Great Mother is virtually always conspicuously either positive or negative; the middle, neutral, ground of the bivalent axis is rarely represented. The Great Mother system therefore possesses the structure schematized in Figure 5-1.

Figure 5-1

THE GREAT MOTHER SYSTEM

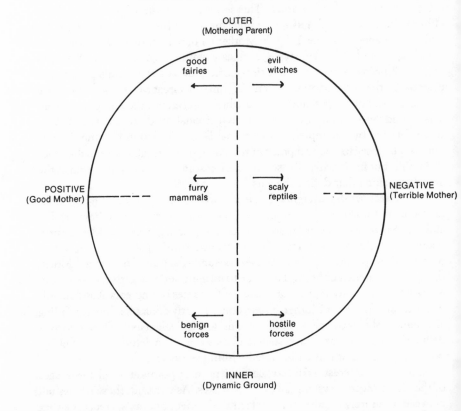

Images from the Great Mother system are a part of the body-ego's conscious experience. The body-ego produces these images in an effort to understand the principal reality of its world. These images, which at first are predominantly positive, become increasingly negative as the body-ego grows older, and then, at the point of original repression, they disappear from consciousness. For original repression is the act by which the ego severs its ties with the maternal principle. It is true that it is only the Terrible Mother that the young ego seeks to vanquish. But the Good Mother and the Terrible Mother are necessary counterparts, and, consequently, the vanquishment of the latter is perforce also a banishment of the former. Original repression therefore extends in its effects to the whole of the Great Mother system, all of the aspects and images of which are deleted from consciousness. The mother's affections are refused, and the Dynamic Ground is sealed and buried from view. Simultaneously, all of the bidirectional/bivalent images symbolizing these realities are laid to rest. They are relegated to the unconscious.

With the onset of regression in the service of transcendence, the Dynamic Ground is reopened and many of the images of the Great Mother system are reactivated—although not, as we shall see shortly, in exactly their original form. Also activated at this point is an elaborate system of ontogenetic archetypes the images of which anticipate the forthcoming stages of transegoic experience. Among these images must be included all those that are signposts of the Way, the spiritual path, both in its negative and its positive aspects. Belonging to this group, therefore, are the myriad symbols of death, resurrection, purgation, transfiguration, hell, heaven, devils, angels, damnation, salvation, liberation, apotheosis, and so forth. Images of these sorts express in highly condensed fashion experiences such as the conversion of the mental ego, its deathlike regression into the unconscious, its reconstitution and transubstantiation in spirit, and its final integration and fulfillment. Such images work to give the spiritual seeker a preview of the unknown territory he is about to enter as he is moved to unfold his ontogenesis, or his individuation, through its highest stages.

The archetypes of the Way are part of the collective unconscious in the widest sense of the term. However, they have a status that is different from the archetypes of the Great Mother system. For whereas the latter are repressed elements of a period of development already over, the former are latent indicators of a period of development not yet arrived. The signposts of the Way are spontaneous formations of the autosymbolic process that are given to the mental ego when it attempts, as it were, to look beyond itself into the transegoic horizon. They are the products of futural projection. The archetypes of the Great Mother system, in contrast, are repressed vestiges of the past. In the strict sense, then, it is only the archetypes of the Great Mother system that belong to the *prepersonal* unconscious; the signposts of the Way belong more properly to the transpersonal "not-yet-conscious."

2. Phylogenetic level. The phylogenetic level of the instinctual-archetypal unconscious consists of instincts and corresponding image-producing patterns that, in the history of the species, have emerged in response either to (1) the requirements of survival or (2) constantly recurring, universal human situations. Related to the demands of survival are, for example, the core id instincts of sex, childbearing and rearing, food acquisition, self-defense, and, perhaps, territoriality—together with their perceptual and imaginal correlates. And pertaining to universal human situations are, for example, those instincts and archetypes governing such things as birth, attainment of maturity, courtship, old age, and death. These various constituents of the instinctual-archetypal unconscious are inherited from our evolutionary ancestors. They thus belong to the most archaic stratum of the unconscious.

Of particular interest among the instincts are those of sex and aggression, which derive from primary survival needs. These are powerful instincts that can easily dominate energy resources and that, as Freud so clearly saw, can cause serious disruptions to rational and socially organized life. Developmentally, these instincts are for the most part latent and inactive until puberty, at which time they are awakened dramatically and begin to consume great amounts of energy and to give rise to compelling urges and ideations.[3] Since these instincts are mostly dormant during the period of the body-ego, they are not among the initial targets of original repression. Nevertheless, they still must be counted as part of the repressed or submerged prepersonal unconscious, because, as nonegoic potentials, they meet with the resistance of original repression once they are activated. So strong are these drives that they cannot approach being contained entirely. However, given the barrier of original repression (together with social inhibitions), their expression is significantly mitigated and "civilized." Raw lust and aggression are unleashed often enough, but for the most part they are contained within the instinctual-archetypal unconscious.

The activation of the sexual and aggressive instincts during puberty has significant ramifications throughout the whole of the unconscious. It alters the nature of the unconscious not only additively but also pervasively. Most important, perhaps, is the effect it has upon the Great Mother system, and, in particular, upon the Terrible Mother subsystem. Specifically, the activation of the sexual and aggressive instincts transforms the Terrible Mother from being "merely" the nemesis of the ego into being the ultimate embodiment of evil: the beast of the abyss. This is a transformation occurring entirely within the system of the prepersonal unconscious, which is registered in consciousness only indirectly, through the medium of the mythico-symbolic images by which the mental ego tries to give shape and meaning to its deepest fear: evil itself, THE ADVERSARY. This adversary, which used to be the Terrible Mother, is now the Terrible Mother *transmogrified*: it is the Terrible Mother rawly instinctualized by the now-activated sexual and aggressive drives. Hence, the Terrible Mother, who before was a thoroughly sinister being—a repugnant being representing all things dark and doomful—now becomes also an unspeakably hideous monster, a primitive beast with appetites of the nastiest and most rapacious sort. And this change applies to all of the Terrible

Mother's bidirectional (i.e., outer/inner, personal/elemental, and fused, animal) guises. In her outer or personal manifestation, the Terrible Mother becomes not only a wicked witch but also a killer whore (e.g., Kali, Medusa, the whore of the apocalypse). In her inner or elemental manifestation, she becomes not only violent waters, fires, and winds but also rampaging currents of lust and thirst for blood. And in her fused or animal manifestation, she becomes not only a devouring reptile or other predator but also the supreme adversary: the beast of the abyss, an antediluvian monster of utterly perverse, lascivious-destructive nature.

The Terrible Mother, instinctualized in these ways, becomes a primary structure of the prepersonal unconscious. At the same time, she becomes the mental ego's chief symbol of evil. It is interesting, then, that the mental ego conceives of the EVIL ONE as being fundamentally female in nature. It is the Terrible Mother as beast of the abyss (the power of the id) that is the mental ego's chief adversary. Satan, the Antichrist, and other male figures representing evil, it is implied, are of subordinate status; they are masculine agents of an underlying power of opposite, female gender.

To square this account, it should be added that the mental ego may also conceive of the GOOD ONE as being basically female in nature. This possibility is suggested because the opposite of the notion of evil as the instinctualized Terrible Mother is the notion of good as the spiritualized Good Mother. The mental ego's tacit understanding of the GOOD ONE may then consist of the archetype of the Good Mother *transfigured*, i.e., illumined and sanctified by the light and love of liberated spirit. Transformed in this fashion, the Good Mother would be elevated from a not-quite-human status to a superhuman status; she would become the Great Goddess, Shakti, the divine Sophia, the heavenly Beatrice. The mental ego may, then, operate with a feminine bias not only in its comprehension of evil and the EVIL ONE but also in its comprehension of good and the GOOD ONE. Admittedly, however, these speculations go against the grain of our male-dominant conception of heaven and hell.

THE BODY-UNCONSCIOUS

The body-unconscious consists of many of the nonegoic potentials that are integral to the body-ego's experience and that, upon original repression, are arrested at the "pre-" level and submerged into unconsciousness. Among these nonegoic potentials are (1) autosymbolic cognition (arrested in paleological form), (2) concrete bodily feelings (arrested as proto-, second-order, and third-order emotions), (3) polymorphous sensuousness, (4) amplified experience, and (5) numinosity or enchantment. Having already discussed the body-ego's cognitive and affective experience in full in Chapter 3, there is no need here to reconsider the first two of these types of potentials. It is sufficient to remind the reader that imaginal-symbolic thought and concrete bodily feelings are among the potentials that belong to the body-unconscious. With this understood, the ensuing discussion of the body-unconscious will be limited to considering the last three of the types of potentials just listed, all of which are ramifications of the body-ego's openness to the Dynamic Ground.

1. Polymorphous sensuousness. Although psychic energy is, for the body-ego, most highly concentrated in the erogenous zones, it is not confined to these areas. It circulates freely throughout the whole of the body-ego's physical being, and, in doing so, it enhances the arousal capacity of all bodily parts and regions. The body-ego thus is exceedingly sensitive to, and easily becomes engrossed in, tactile and other bodily stimulations. Tickling, caressing, and massaging, for example, delight the body-ego and send it into raptures. Experiences such as these are, for the body-ego, intensely sensuous and even voluptuous in nature. However, contrary to the Freudian position, there need be nothing specifically sexual about them. For the energy that fuels these experiences, although released from the sexual system, is not sexual in essence. Rather, as explained above, it is a nonspecific energy; it is an energy that potentiates all modalities of experience without being uniquely or inherently expressive of any one.

Original repression caps the Dynamic Ground and confines the power of the Ground, qua libido, within the sexual system. As a result, the body ceases being polymorphously sensuous and becomes instead predominantly genital in its arousal capacity. Immediately following original repression there begins the period of latency, which, with the arrival of puberty, is succeeded by mature genital sexuality. The adult (i.e., mental ego) is for the most part cerebrally aloof from immediate somatic experience, but he frequently descends from the upper mental regions in order to enjoy a genitally triggered discharge of libido. In sum, then, original repression puts all of the body to sleep except the genito-pelvic region. And in this sense polymorphous sensuousness can be said to be rendered unconscious.

2. Amplified experience. The power of the Ground, as psychic energy, enhances every dimension of the body-ego's life, including not just its somatic experiences but also its perceptions, feelings, and thoughts.

The body-ego's perceptions are rich and vivid. Sensory qualities appear to the body-ego with great vibrancy, endless variety, and exceeding definition and detail. In general, the body-ego's perceptual experiences have the character of sensory spectacles; each is a unique and virtually inexhaustible display of colors, sounds, odors, tastes, or textures.

Psychic energy also amplifies the body-ego's feelings. These (viz., proto-, second-order, and third-order emotions) are passions that reverberate powerfully throughout the body-ego's being. They are highly charged emotive currents that run their course without inhibition or disguise. Unlike the mental ego, which tends to experience feelings in significantly attenuated or altered form, the body-ego experiences feelings intensely and authentically.

And regarding the body-ego's cognition, although it may be woefully lacking in cogency, it is in no way lacking in force or vivacity. Given the supercharging effects of the power of the Ground, the paleosymbols that are the bearers of the body-ego's thought tend to have a strong impact upon the mind. They are stunning realizations or insights of seemingly immense significance. For the body-ego, the world is full of tantalizing secrets and beguiling mysteries, and when one of these secrets or mysteries is suddenly laid bare, the body-ego is literally struck: it is stopped in its tracks, astounded, and filled with delight or dread.

Original repression, in sealing the Dynamic Ground, has the effect of reducing the all-around intensity of experience. Perceptions are muted, feelings are devitalized, and mental representations lose their power of impact. The superabundance of the body-ego's experience is lost; it is put on hold and becomes a dormant potential of the body-unconscious.

3. *Numinosity or enchantment.* The relatively unrestricted outflow of the power of the Ground imbues the body-ego's outer world with a sheen of numinosity. The world is overlaid with an aura that renders things superreal, both intense and gripping. The world is charged and magnetized. It is full of objects that possess heightened qualities and that pulsate with hypnotic power. The body-ego thus tends to be in awe of its world, which is enchanted. This enchantment, however, is not always a positive thing. For the numinous power that permeates the body-ego's world can make things appear not only superreal and alluring but also strange and daunting. In fact, it is not uncommon for the body-ego at one moment to be rapt in a scene of great appeal only at the next moment to be shot through with a bone-chilling sense of uncanniness. Whether positive or negative, however, the body-ego's experience is extraordinary. The body-ego lives in a world of marvel, mystery, and miracle.

Original repression, in closing the Dynamic Ground, divests experience of its magic and leaves it without the power to astound. The power of the Ground is withdrawn from the world and relegated to the deep unconscious. It is contained within the Ground as an inactive potentiality of experience.

ORIGINAL REPRESSION

Original repression, which dissociates the ego from the nonegoic pole of the psyche, is what first creates the prepersonal submerged or collective unconscious. Original repression, however, is not just a cause of the unconscious; it is itself a part of the unconscious. It is so because it is a negative posture toward physico-dynamic life that, once assumed, is soon petrified and forgotten. Original repression is the remote, deeply embedded, and *invisible* infrastructure of the mental-egoic system.

Let us recall that original repression is a psycho*physical* phenomenon. The mental ego rests upon a repressive foundation that possesses a definite physical dimension. The mental ego in effect uses the body as an instrument by which to separate itself from the Dynamic Ground. In the initial act of original repression, the mental ego lays down layer upon layer of tension and constriction extending all the way from the base of the spine (which is the seat of the Dynamic Ground) to the base of the skull (which marks the beginning of the mental ego's sphere). These tensions and constrictions, which quickly solidify into permanent body armors, together form a hierarchy of barriers that contain the upward flow of the power of the Ground and, thereby, protect the mental ego from the magnetic-solvent effects of that power. Moreover, in covering over the Ground, these rigid layers at the same time provide the mental ego with a firm underfooting, with a seemingly solid basis in being. Original repression thus works at once to submerge the Ground and to support the mental ego. It transforms the body from a supple and open vehicle for the free circulation of the power of the Ground into a rigid, impervious structure that at once caps the Ground and underprops the mental-egoic system.

The key to understanding original repression as a physical structure is that it involves a chronic activation of the defensive posture of the body. Instead of being relaxed, erect, and open, the body is tensed, stooped, and closed. It is tensed in seeming readiness to respond to danger; it is stooped with a knotted stomach and hunched shoulders; and, braced in these ways, it is closed to what otherwise would be a free and continuous flow of psychic energy. This overall stance is functional in situations when the organism faces an external threat. So, for example, the body-ego contracts itself in this manner when confronted with something frightening or dangerous. However, in the case of the mental ego, this bodily stance has become permanent—indeed, petrified, buried, and forgotten. In more or less exaggerated form, it has become an acquired structure of the body, which, as such, is unconscious. And the cause of this perpetual defensive posture is not any external danger; it is rather a constant *inner* threat: the power of the Dynamic Ground. The mental ego is frozen in a closed defensive posture in relation to the Dynamic Ground, without in any way knowing that this is the case.

Among the body's defensive reactions that can be involved in original repression are: (1) a tight sphincter; (2) a knotted stomach, which precludes deep, diaphragmatic breathing; (3) a displaced pelvis, typically tilted forward out of its proper alignment; (4) a sunken chest, which characteristically is plated with muscular armor; (5) taut upper arms; (6) heaviness and tension in the shoulders, which frequently are stooped; and (7) a zone of tightness at the back of the neck and base of the skull.[4] These strata of repression, layered one atop the other, disjoin the head from the pelvis, the ego from the Ground. They constitute a multitiered dam that at once contains the power of the Ground and shieldingly undergirds the ego.

As was said, this physical undergirding assumes the character of an acquired structure of the body. As such, the layers of tension and constriction making up the structure become part of the (prepersonal) *embedded* unconscious.[5] The defensive posture of the body is a constant of the mental ego's experience. The mental ego, therefore, is habituated to it and fails to notice it as a possible object for consciousness. It is only in unusual circumstances that one or another aspect of this complex stance is thrown into relief. For example, experiences of extreme relaxation can, by sheer contrast, reveal to a person some of the ways in which he normally is rigid or tense, and experiences of unusual physical resilience and buoyancy (e.g., as occasionally occur during inspired performances in athletics or dance) can, also by contrast, reveal to a person ways in which he normally is tight or locked. Also, as we shall see, the postural set of original repression can be thrust into awareness during regression in the service of transcendence. This happens because the Dynamic Ground at this point begins to reopen and the power of the Ground begins to assert itself against the repressive barriers that hitherto had contained it. The power of the Ground challenges original repression and, in doing so, exposes it to conscious view.

THE PERSONAL SUBMERGED UNCONSCIOUS

The personal unconscious consists of a great number of different elements. The usual definition stipulates that the personal unconscious includes all those things that, in being unconscious, are person-specific, i.e., pertain to the biography of a particular individual. This definition is useful, but not entirely accurate, since on most accounts, including the one that follows, the personal unconscious is held to include cultural introjects and perhaps even inherited structures that are universal in scope. The usual definition, therefore, is not sufficiently broad. Another definition is that the personal unconscious consists of all those things that, in being unconscious, are constitutive of the ego or of the larger egoic system. This definition makes room for the social and inherited structures just alluded to, but it fails to accommodate many unconscious materials that are merely individual, e.g., subliminal stimuli and many complexes and COEX systems (to be explained). This definition, then, is also too narrow. The shortcomings of these two definitions can, however, be overcome simply by combining them. The resulting definition may suffer a bit from redundancy, but it does, I believe, cover all and only the requisite ground. Let us then define the personal unconscious as the class of all those materials (contents, structures, faculties, systems, processes, etc.) that, in being unconscious, are either (1) person-specific or (2) constitutive of the ego or egoic system.

Proceeding on the basis of this definition, the personal unconscious can be divided into the *submerged* and the *embedded* personal unconscious.[6] The personal submerged unconscious (which will be surveyed in this section) encompasses all the materials that are repressed, screened, or otherwise made invisible by the limiting effects of egoic structures or processes. The personal embedded unconscious, on the other hand, consists of just these structures and processes themselves. The distinction is a simple one: repressed contents require repressing mechanisms and screened materials require screening filters—and both sides of these pairings are unconscious, though for different reasons. The repressed and screened materials are submerged, and thereby rendered unconscious, by the exclusions and restrictions of embedded structures and processes. And embedded structures and processes are themselves unconscious because they (1) are unnoticed constancies of experience that, in many cases, (2) are also constitutive of the mental ego *as a subject* and thus unavailable to it as objects of which it might be aware. The submerged unconscious and the embedded unconscious are correlatives. As a rule, one cannot be unconscious without the other also being unconscious, and on those occasions when one of the two, for whatever reason, is disclosed to awareness, the other, too, in principle becomes available to consciousness.

In treating the personal submerged unconscious, I will follow the order established in Table 5-1.

1. The shadow. The shadow is the alter ego of the mental ego's self-concept. The mental ego has a vested interest in seeing itself in a certain way, namely, as possessing those facticities that enter into its self-concept, which is its surrogate body and being. These facticities are introjected and identified with as self, and everything incompatible with them is alienated and denied to awareness. The result of this alienation is the shadow, the psychic subsystem containing the dark and disowned dimensions of the personality.

Although virtually all of the features of an individual's self-concept are a product of an intersection of that individual's unique, pregiven nature with society's common conventions, there are some features that owe much more to the individual than to society and others that owe much more to society than to the individual. That is, some features are more nearly person-specific while others approach being stereotypical, reflective of dominant cultural patterns. And what is true in this way of the self-concept is true also of the shadow, since these two are inverses of each other. The shadow therefore also contains some elements that are more person-specific and others that are more culture-common.

Among those aspects of the self-concept/shadow system that are reflective of dominant cultural patterns, there are two in particular that deserve comment, namely, those that derive from the cultural paradigms of maturity and gender sexuality.

Every society has an implicit definition of maturity. Every society operates with a set of expectations that are imposed upon children in order to make them "shape up" and act as adult members of the society are "supposed to act." A certain set of attitudes and behaviors is prescribed as a condition of being accepted as a full member of the group. Identification with this set of attitudes and behaviors naturally results; the set is introjected and becomes an integral part of the self-concept. As this happens, however, those aspects of the personality that are immature according to the prevailing paradigm are disowned and disallowed conscious expression. They are repressed and become part of the shadow. In Gestalt therapy, these dissociated elements are referred to as "underdog." As a group, they include all the childish impulses that importune the mental ego, whining at it and tempting it to drop its responsibilities and to pursue such courses as those of pleasure, laziness, rebellion, and the like.

The cultural paradigms of gender sexuality also play a large role in the formation of the self-concept, and therefore in the formation of the shadow as well. Males, in identifying with the cultural definition of masculinity, at the same time alienate those aspects of themselves that, according to that definition, are feminine. And women, in identifying with the cultural definition of femininity, do just the opposite. As Jung was the first to realize, this means that men typically have a strong feminine component to their unconscious (the *anima*) and women typically have a strong masculine component (the *animus*). Each sex alienates the contrasexual elements of the larger personality, submerging them into unconsciousness.[7] Jung, it is true, would not include the *anima* and *animus* within the shadow, as I am doing here, since he conceives of the shadow as having the same gender status as the self-concept (or *persona*). Also, Jung holds that the *anima* and *animus* are predominantly archetypal rather than personal-submerged. I have no quarrel with Jung on these points; nevertheless, I have found it conceptually more parsimonious to expand the notion of the shadow to include all psychic potentials that are thrown into darkness because they are inconsistent with the self-concept, whether the potentials happen to be same-sex or contrasexual, personal or, ultimately, archetypal.

"Underdog" and the *anima* (or *animus*) are but two of the constituents of the shadow. The shadow also contains many other elements, some of which are more stereotypical and others of which are more distinctive of the individual. The shadow is a highly complex mental-egoic subsystem; it includes a vast number of personality fragments, half-formed alter egos, each

131

of which, in an unguarded moment, is capable of rising up and taking possession of the whole person.

Despite its threatening aspect, the shadow is not inherently negative or evil. In fact, many of its features, although contraconventional, are intrinsically positive. This is especially so in the case of the *anima* and *animus*, which, as Jung has shown, are indispensable to the wholeness of man and woman, respectively. And it is true as well of some aspects of "underdog"—although many aspects of this shadow element are merely childish rather than truly childlike. The shadow, then, contains many features that are potentially positive. Many of its features, although proscribed by the mental ego, would, if integrated, enlarge and enrich the personality.

In being disowned, the elements making up the shadow are in most cases projected upon others. The mental ego for this reason tends to exaggerate those features in others which correspond to parts of its own shadow. These features function as threatening stimuli to the mental ego, which fixates on them and reacts to them in excessive fashion. In a sense, the mental ego sees "through a glass darkly," as its shadow is a distorting lens through which it apprehends the world. The shadow stands between the mental ego and the world. Wherever the mental ego goes, the shadow is always one step ahead. And almost whomever the mental ego meets, it is in some ways meeting only the other side of itself.

It is not clear where the more strongly repressed parts of the shadow end and deeper, prepersonal levels of the unconscious begin. The reason for this is that, in an extended sense, all of the prepersonal unconscious is incompatible with the mental ego's self-concept and is thus within the farthest reach of the shadow. The shadow, then, although originating within the mental-egoic system, has ramifications well beyond it.

2. Filtered stimuli. There are innumerable embedded structures that govern the mental ego's overall response to experience. These structures are of many different kinds. They include, for example, (1) mental-egoic subsystems or operations such as the self-concept, ego-defense mechanisms, complexes, and COEX systems (see below), (2) acquired habits and dispositions of all sorts, (3) introjected concepts and values, and perhaps (4) certain inherited patterns governing language and cognition.

All of these types of embedded structures are examples of automatic routines or sets by which the mental ego, unbeknownst to itself, organizes or interacts with experience. As such, they are part of the unconscious, specifically the personal embedded unconscious—which is to be discussed shortly. The reason for listing these embedded structures here is that, as *embedded* structures, they have the effect of screening, filtering, or repressing, and hence submerging into unconsciousness, many stimuli that otherwise would be accessible to awareness.

All of the structures listed are alike not only in being embedded but also in having a selective focus or scope. They are structures that key on or engage only certain specific types of stimuli out of the entire range of stimuli that might be present at a given moment. They are structures that, in having a *selective* scope, thereby also have a *limited* scope. They are therefore structures that not only include but exclude as well. (Indeed, repressing structures may only exclude.) For every stimulus that embedded structures selectively bring to the attention of the mind, there are many other stimuli that are rendered invisible or are barred from awareness. Embedded structures thus are not only templates by which things are thrown into relief but also Procrustean beds by which things are deleted from view.

Acquired habits and dispositions provide an excellent example of how embedded structures edit experience by at once selecting and excluding stimuli. Acquired habits and dispositions are routines that regularly respond to the same stimuli in the same ways. Once a habit or disposition is triggered, everything that falls outside the routine is ignored. This happens not only in the case of conspicuous automaticities such as reflex emotional reactions and flagrant biases or prejudices but also in the case of very subtle tendencies of all kinds, e.g., susceptibilities of mood and established patterns of thought. In fact, subtle tendencies screen more pervasively than do conspicuous ones, since the former are usually very global and the latter very specific in their foci and effects. For example, the proneness to despair, which is exceedingly subtle, cuts across the whole spectrum of experience, selecting negative cues and screening positive ones, whereas a more conspicuous emotional reaction such as jealousy has a very narrow target, which it selects and screens in a highly defined way. In sum, acquired habits and dispositions are regularities by which experience is edited in an automatic and limited manner, in a manner that brings one dimension of experience into clear focus while relegating other dimensions to obscurity or invisibility.

Cultural introjects such as basic social concepts and values play an even larger role in editing experience. The socially transmitted world-picture is a matrix of meanings that, in mediating between a person and the world, works to disclose certain sectors or aspects of reality and to veil others. Alternative world-pictures present alternative interpretations of reality, each one bringing distinctive kinds of things into view while leaving many other kinds of things out of view, i.e., undetected, unknown, unconscious. A socially acquired world-picture is, then, a shared interpretive structure that gives shape and meaning to experience and that, in doing so, has the limiting consequence of restricting experience within definite boundaries. Or more accurately, a world-picture is an interpretive structure that has this limiting consequence for all those who are bound (i.e., unconsciously committed) to it. From the point of view of an *embedded* world-picture, then, it is true that the world-as-pictured *is* the world; the limits of the embedded unconscious are the limits of the world.

It is possible that some embedded structures are inherited rather than acquired. Mention has already been made of the Jungian archetypes in this respect—although they, of course, deriving from the nonegoic pole of the psyche, are not part of the personal unconscious. But also meriting mention are possible egoic/personal inherited structures determining the foundations of language and cognition. The possibility of such structures has been a perennial theme in the rationalist tradition of philosophy (e.g., Plato, Descartes, Leibniz, Kant), and in the last few decades the existence of inherited cognitive structures or operations has been accepted widely among representatives of structuralist and cognitivist schools of anthropology, linguistics, and psychology.

Unlike other embedded structures, inherited structures, if there are any, are "hard wired." They are part of the human biological apparatus and are therefore necessary rather than optional structures. They are structures to which human cognition is bound rather than structures that might be erased or exchanged for other structures that would provide an alternative rendering of experience. Accordingly, whatever might be screened by inherited structures is irretrievably beyond the reach of human conceptual capacity. To use Kant's (1929) term, such dimensions of existence would be things in themselves, dimensions inherently invisible to the faculty of categorial understanding. Or in Bohm's (1971, 1973, 1980) terms, such dimensions would belong to the unanalyzable implicate order that underlies the manifest order of conceptually and theoretically structured experience. Acquired habits and dispositions and embedded cultural patterns can be disembedded and replaced or supplemented by other interpretive structures, thereby bringing into relief aspects of the world that otherwise would go unrecognized by consciousness. But in the case of inherited structures, although disembedment and disengagement are in principle possible, replacement is not. The only possible alternative to interpreting experience according to inherited structures is not to interpret experience at all. The only possible alternative is to abandon all conceptualizations and to open the mind in a wholly (but also merely) receptive manner, in a fashion that is altogether without conceptual orderings and constraints. There are many who have suggested that such "direct contact with reality" occurs in the state of mystical union, given the suspension of thought and the transcendence of the subject/object separation that are characteristic of that state.[8] But this suggestion is speculative. As is true of metaphysical statements generally, it is an arguable conjecture.

3. Subthreshold stimuli. Subthreshold stimuli are stimuli that are too faint to impress themselves upon consciousness because they are overriden by psychomental activity (both embedded and conscious). The mental ego, as we know, is prone to restless extraversion and to internal dialogue, since these are ways in which it escapes its underlying "nothingness." The mental ego is prone to being preoccupiedly engaged, or at least self-distracted, lest it be drawn into its interior emptiness. Consequently, the mental ego rarely, if ever, allows the mind to be both introverted and quiet, which is to say that it rarely, if ever, allows the mind to enter the receptive mode. Yet it is only when the mind is silently receptive that faint signals have any chance of registering in consciousness. Thus, the mental ego's restless extraversion and internal dialogue have the effect of excluding faint signals from awareness. Such stimuli are kept below the threshold of awareness; they are kept within the personal submerged unconscious.

Little need be said in support of the reality of subthreshold stimuli. The phenomenon of subliminal perception has been extensively researched, and its practical importance is quite obvious, especially to those who exploit it for the purposes of advertising and propaganda. But it should be noted that subthreshold perception is not the only case of the unconscious presence of subthreshold stimuli. Also to be included under this description are internal bodily signals and many contents of the psychomental flux or stream of consciousness. The body is constantly emitting signals, many of which are filtered or repressed by specific embedded structures, and some of which, it seems, are simply too faint to register in consciousness. Moreover, the ongoing stream of consciousness contains many elements that, owing to their low intensity, do not impress themselves upon the observing mind. It sounds a bit paradoxical to say that there can be contents passing through the mind that go by wholly unnoticed by the mind, but, paradoxical or not, this seems to be what actually is the case—as is attested by many practitioners of meditation.[9]

THE PERSONAL EMBEDDED UNCONSCIOUS

Let us turn now to a consideration of the embedded structures that make up the personal embedded unconscious. As stated earlier, embedded structures are unconscious because they (1) are constancies of experience that, in many cases, (2) are also constitutive of the mental ego's subjectivity. As constancies, embedded structures are invisible by reason of habituation. As a rule, it is only new or unusual stimuli that attract attention. In contrast, things that are constant, regular, or routine recede from the focus of awareness and assume the status of merely implicit grounds. Embedded structures are just such implicit, and therefore invisible, grounds—and so they must remain until such time, if ever, as their usual mode of expression is altered sufficiently to make them, in effect, new stimuli. When this happens, attention is drawn to them and they step forth into the foreground of attention.

Many embedded structures also are unconscious because they are

135

instruments of, rather than possible objects for, the mental ego's subjectivity. That is, they are structures *through* which the mental ego is conscious and therefore are not themselves things *to* which the mental ego might attend. As Wilber states it (1980a, 89):

> . . . at each level of development, one cannot totally see the seer. No observing structure can observe itself observing. One uses the structures of that level as something with which to perceive and translate the world—but one cannot perceive and translate those structures *themselves*, not totally.
> . . . The point is that each translation process sees but is not seen; it translates, but is not itself translated; *and it can repress* [or otherwise screen], *but is not itself repressed* [or screened].

In short, many embedded structures are forms *of* a subject and therefore cannot, as such, be objects *for* that subject. Such structures can be either prepersonal (instinctual-archetypal) or, as pertains to the present section, personal (whether acquired or inherited).

In discussing personal embedded structures, I will again be following the order indicated in Table 5-1.

1. The self-concept. The self-concept has already been treated in some detail. The reader is referred to the chapter on the mental ego and to the section on the shadow, above.

2. Ego-defense mechanisms. Examples of ego-defense mechanisms include repression, projection, sublimation, reaction formation, rationalization, intellectualization, and denial. All of these strategies of self-defense are employed unconsciously by the mental ego to ward off or transform thoughts or feelings that are threatening to it. Although many ego-defense mechanisms are merely defensive, some are also genuinely adaptive, as was originally suggested by Anna Freud in her classic *The Ego and the Mechanisms of Defense* (1936). Moreover, as Heinz Hartmann has argued, some of the ego's defensive strategies can, in their adaptive aspect, even assume a significant degree of independence from their original defensive function. Explaining this point, Hartmann says (1958, 26):

> An attitude which arose originally in the service of defense against an instinctual drive may, in the course of time, become an independent structure, in which case the instinctual drive merely triggers this automatized apparatus, but, as long as the automatization is not controverted, does not determine the details of its action. Such an apparatus may, as a relatively independent structure, come to serve other functions (adaptation, synthesis, etc.); it may also—and this is genetically of even broader significance—through a change of function turn from a means into a goal in its own right.

Ego-defense mechanisms, therefore, need not be merely defensive. They can also be coping mechanisms that are genuinely adaptive and, in some cases, at least partially independent of their initial defensive purpose.

The most important among the ego-defense mechanisms are repression, projection, and sublimation. These three—and the others, too—can operate independently or in conjunction with one or more of the others. The mental ego, for example, might repress a shadow element, but perhaps not so completely as to keep it from being projected upon others and, to a certain extent, expressed in sublimated form within the mental-egoic domain. For example, a person might have as central components of his self-concept the facticities "strong" and "well-informed." This could lead him to repress virtually all feelings of dependence and ignorance—which feelings, in being repressed, would be relegated to the shadow. Such a person, however, would probably also tend to project these rejected parts of himself upon others, whom he would tend to see as being weaker and less knowledgeable than they really are. And at the same time it is possible that this person would find some way to transform (i.e., sublimate) these repressed and projected feelings so that they would cease being incompatible with his self-concept, and hence would be expressible within the mental-egoic system. He might find a compartmentalized sphere of his life in which he could unashamedly, and perhaps adaptively or constructively, confess his weakness and ignorance while in all other spheres maintaining just the opposite posture. Religion is a possible sphere for such an outlet to occur. Perhaps our hypothetical person would adopt a religious orientation stressing such elements as creaturely dependence, weakness of will, and the mysteries of faith.

3. Filtering structures. A list of major types of filtering structures was presented in the section on filtered stimuli. In that section, the point in discussing filtering structures was to indicate that they are causes of the personal submerged unconscious—since, in being structures with a selective focus or scope, they are at the same time structures with a limited focus or scope, a focus or scope that excludes (screens, filters, represses) as well as includes. The point here in discussing filtering structures is simply to note that these structures, in addition to being causes of the personal submerged unconscious, are themselves parts of the personal embedded unconscious. Filtering structures not only make other things unavailable to awareness but are also themselves unavailable to awareness, either by reason of habituation or because they are instruments, rather than objects, of consciousness.

It has already been observed that the class of filtering structures is very large. In fact, if the class is conceived in the widest sense, it can be said to include all embedded structures, since all embedded structures select and therefore screen or repress stimuli. In this broad sense, the class of filtering structures encompasses all of the types of embedded structures that are dealt with in this section. For example, the self-concept is a filtering structure by virtue of screening the shadow; ego-defense mechanisms are filtering structures by virtue of screening, or repressing, threatening materials of a variety of sorts; and complexes and COEX systems, as will be exlained presently, are filtering structures by virtue of screening things that stand in certain specific relations to the original experiences from which the complexes and COEX systems arise.

Other examples of embedded structures that work as filters of experience are: (1) acquired habits and dispositions, (2) introjected concepts and values, and perhaps (3) inherited structures governing language and thought. The manners in which these structures edit experience was explained in the section on filtered stimuli. For present purposes, suffice it to repeat that these structures are not only causes of the unconscious but also contents thereof. As the constant background or medium of experience, these structures are not themselves objects of experience. They are rather elements of the personal embedded unconscious.

4. *Autonomous complexes.* By autonomous complexes of the personal unconscious I mean to designate embedded structures of a more or less compulsive and neurotic sort that derive usually either from a traumatic episode or from what might be called "unfinished business" (i.e., an abrupt halting of an important life experience or stage prior to closure or fulfillment). In the case of a trauma-induced complex, it frequently happens that both the exaggerated response routine that results from the trauma and the trauma itself are in large measure unconscious, the former because it is embedded, the latter because it is repressed. In the case of "unfinished business," on the other hand, it is usually only the resulting complex that is unconscious—although, of course, the triggering episode (e.g., premature weaning, enforcement of rules of anal or genital propriety, imposition of a gender stereotype) may long since have been forgotten. Traumata typically cause negative fixations or blind spots and corresponding hostile, fight-or-flight reaction routines. "Unfinished business," on the other hand, typically causes fixations on the satisfiers of unmet (usually infantile) needs and compulsive behavior with respect to those satisfiers, or their adult surrogates. And to repeat, these fixations, blind spots, reactions, and compulsions are for the most part embedded and unconscious. Their more dramatic manifestations are of course quite evident, but most of their more subtle forms are completely invisible, at least to the person who suffers from them.

5. *COEX systems.* Stanislav Grof (1975) has introduced the highly useful notion of a COEX system, which is an abbreviation for *system of condensed experience.* A COEX system is a web of highly charged memories, meanings, and behaviors that are associated with a particular type of life experience. The key to the concept is that the first (or at least an early) instance of any kind of experience, if it happens to be sufficiently impressive in a negative or positive

way, tends to become the defining paradigm of all subsequent such experiences. Complexes, as just described, can be considered examples of COEX systems, since it is the traumatic or unfinished character of the original experience that determines the subsequent pattern of inappropriate perceptions, feelings, and behaviors. But complexes constitute only a small subclass of COEX systems. The notion of a COEX system is a comprehensive one; it includes all embedded structures that are the products of a primary or core experience. No restrictions are placed on the nature or quality of the core experience, which can be negative or positive, unfinished or fulfilled. The only character of the core experience that is required for it to be the ground of a COEX system is that it have a sufficient impact on the individual to establish a closed preconception of and reponse to later experiences of the same kind.

CONCLUSION

Of the many different potentials that belong to the unconscious, the single most important one, in my estimation, is also the one that has been the least understood: the power of the Dynamic Ground. The Dynamic Ground is the fount of life, and the power that issues from it is the vital essence of all experience. Direct contact with the Dynamic Ground thus has a pronounced effect on life—as is evidenced in the lives of the body-ego and the integrated person. In the case of the mental ego, original repression seals the Dynamic Ground, the power of which is directly contacted only in the deepest stages of sleep. To be sure, original repression allows the young mental ego the sobriety necessary to master egoic faculties and to learn how to conduct responsible affairs in the world. But this sobriety is purchased at a high price, as it requires sacrifice of nonegoic potentials: polymorphous sensuousness, full-bodied feelings, autosymbolic creativity, and overflowing well-being. However, the price that is paid in these ways need not be tallied as a permanent loss. The loss can be recouped. But in order for this to be possible, it is necessary that original repression be undone and that the Dynamic Ground be unsealed. When this happens, the ego is returned to the Dynamic Ground, where it is baptized and reborn in the power that arises from this source. This return of the ego to the Ground is regression in the service of transcendence. It involves a recapitulation of experience, sometimes even in its most primitive forms, and in the end it returns the ego to its original point of departure into the world. One is, in a sense, made a babe again. But this beginning is a new, second birth, for one is now restored to the full range of human resources and thus is able to mature into a complete human being. Regression in the service of transcendence leads to a rebirth in spirit, which ushers in a period of regeneration in spirit, which in turn culminates in integrated or perfected humanness.

CHAPTER 6

Meditation: The Royal Road to the Unconscious

P ATANJALI'S PROGRAM OF MEDITATION or mental culture was designated the royal yoga (*raja yoga*) long before Freud spoke of dreams as the royal road (*via regia*) to the unconscious. And of these two pathways to the unconscious, and thereby ultimately to integration, it is meditation that more properly deserves the royal title. For of all the approaches to the unconscious, it is meditation that pursues the straightest and truest course.[1]

Other approaches undeniably bring speedier and more spectacular results. This is true, for example, of hypnosis and drug intervention, both of which, it seems, can lead immediately to the deep unconscious.[2] But approaches such as these, although dramatic in the short run, usually do not accomplish much in the long run. The materials unveiled by them frequently are forgotten upon returning to normal consciousness, and those that are remembered are rarely integrated to any significant degree. More often than not they are recalled only as pale reflections of the original experiences, reflections which, like dream images, slip away and escape to the depths from which they sprang. Hence, although methods like hypnosis and drug intervention can plunge one deeply into the unconscious during the time of their employment, they tend to have little carry-over effect once their employment is concluded. Methods such as these allow temporary adventures into the territory of the unconscious, but they do not, as a rule, establish ongoing lines of communication, better yet permanent linkages, between conscious and unconscious systems.

More conventional techniques such as free association (psychoanalysis), active imagination (Jung), and dream analysis, on the other hand, tend to be superficial and sporadic. These techniques are exercised for the most part within the ego's own domain and therefore do not ordinarily involve deep or lasting contact with the unconscious during the period of their employment. These methods can, of course, yield considerable insight into the unconscious, but they are not really themselves vehicles for entering the unconscious. The person who employs these methods is like a fisherman who remains safely on shore while casting a line into the ocean depths. Occasionally a fish is caught. The fish may be an interesting specimen, and it may for a time provide food (for thought). However, the fact that the fish was caught and digested has very little effect on the overall relation of the fisherman to the ocean depths and to all that lives therein. Thus, whereas expedients like hypnosis and drug intervention, as it were, plunge one into the ocean so precipitously that one loses one's bearings and all sight of land, techniques like free association, active imagination, and dream analysis keep one so firmly planted within the egoic sphere that there is little chance even of getting one's feet wet.

Meditation possesses the strengths of both of the types of approaches just described and the weaknesses of neither of them. Like hypnosis and drug intervention, meditation leads deeply into the domain of the unconscious itself, although, of course, this requires persevering practice over time. And like free association, active imagination, and dream analysis, meditation works without dislocating or drowning the ego.[3] Meditation dissolves the barriers that separate the conscious and unconscious systems and establishes a real connection between the two. This is a connection that at first is an avenue by which consciousness gains access to the unconscious. Later it becomes a channel through which the unconscious flows continuously into consciousness. And in the end it becomes more than just a connection; it becomes a unifying synthesis of (what were) conscious and unconscious systems. This final synthesis is the synthesis of integration, the fully actualized union of the egoic and nonegoic poles of the psyche.

A DEFINITION OF MEDITATION

There is such a diverse array of different types of meditation that it is difficult to see how this group of practices constitutes a genuine class. If, then, a working definition of meditation is to be formulated, it is necessary first to bring order to the domain by attempting a classification of the major types of meditative practice.

There are many writers on meditation who believe that meditative practices can be divided into two major types, namely, (1) receptive meditations and (2) concentrative meditations.[4] Let us briefly describe these types and see how they differ. Then we can compare them to see what possible defining qualities they may share.

Receptive meditation (henceforth RM) is the practice of sustained, nonselective alertness. In practicing RM, the meditator maintains the stance of an open and unmoving witness. Whatever emerges in or before the mind is observed crisply but not in any way acted upon or reacted to. The images, feelings, and thoughts that present themselves to consciousness are witnessed uninterruptedly and with full consciousness but without in any way being engaged. In RM, the meditator emulates the character of a polished mirror, which reflects objects clearly, without becoming involved with them. Important examples of RM are the mindfulness (*satipatthana*) and insight (*vipassana*) meditations of Buddhism and the corresponding "just-sitting" (*shikan-taza*) form of meditation (*zazen*) of Zen. RM also includes forms of prayer, namely, all those exercises consisting of an open and unthematic posture of devotion and surrender.

In the case of concentrative meditation (henceforth CM), the meditator selects a specific object, idea, or other reference datum and focuses undivided attention upon it. This focal datum can be either an external object or an internal content (e.g., a sensation, image, or idea). However, the practice is considered more advanced when it is an interior and subtle datum that is employed.

Patanjali, whose *Yoga-Sutra* (Aranya 1983; Feuerstein 1979) is the classic text on CM, divides this practice into three stages: *dharana* (concentration), *dhyana* (meditation), and *samadhi* (absorption, enstasy). *Dharana* is the attempt on the part of the meditator to maintain alert attention upon the chosen object, and, as such, it involves a battle against the alternating tendencies toward distraction and drowsiness. *Dhyana* is achieved when these two problems are surmounted; it consists of a steady, easy, and sharp witnessing of the object. *Samadhi* occurs when the meditating subject becomes utterly absorbed in the object, thus reducing the psychic distance between subject and object to zero. The subject at this point is totally at one with the object and therefore is completely unself-conscious. Phenomenologically speaking, there exists only the object as illumined and explored by consciousness. Also, although *samadhi* must usually first be attained with an object, there exists the possibility of maintaining the state without a supporting object (*asamprajnata samadhi*). This is still a state of illumined absorption, but it is one that, in addition to being selfless (i.e., unself-conscious), is objectless as well. Besides Patanjali's *raja yoga*, examples of CM are the *jhana* (absorption) meditations of original Buddhism, the *koan* exercises of Zen, and many of the contemplative practices of the Christian and other religious traditions.[5]

Receptive and concentrative practices are importantly different in several respects, most evidently in that (1) CM focuses on a specific theme or object whereas RM does not, and (2) CM aims at achieving an absorbed state whereas RM typically does not.[6] Notwithstanding these differences, however, receptive and concentrative practices share a common nature in that both are forms of unmoving attention, i.e., forms of attention that, held fast, neither intervene upon nor are affected by experience. RM and CM, despite their differences, are both examples of stationary witnessing; both are forms of firmly anchored alertness that neither acts nor is acted upon. RM—to follow a description provided by Zen master Yasutani-roshi (Kapleau 1967, 53)—requires that the meditator be both as still as Mount Fuji and as openly alert as a swordsman in battle. And CM, of course, requires that the meditator focus unwavering, laserlike attention on a specific theme or object. In both cases it is imperative that the mind be vigilant and purely poised, neither active nor passive but steadfast. In light of this commonality, it is plausible to define meditation as the practice of *pure steadfast attention*.

MEDITATION AND PRAYER

The recent influx into the West of Eastern spiritual practices has stimulated a discussion of the relation of meditation as practiced in the Hindu and Buddhist East to prayer as practiced in the Judeo-Christian West. Some Western churches, somewhat defensively, have gone out of their way to underscore the differences, even going so far on occasion as to suggest that forms of meditation practiced in the East are merely occult, even demonic. Needless to say, this approach is shortsighted, and nothing good has come from it.

A more reasonable approach is to classify prayer as a particular type of meditation. This is indicated by the fact that prayer, of all forms, quite evidently satisfies the definition of meditation as a practice of steadfast attention. Adopting this perspective, the question that arises is not how prayer differs from meditation per se, but rather how it differs from *other types* of meditation. And the answer to this question, it seems, is that prayer is distinctive (1) in assuming that there exists a superior reality to which prayer is ultimately addressed, a reality that is somehow responsive to prayer, and (2) in adopting an attitude of reverent entreaty and submission toward this reality. Prayer, then, let us conclude, is a species of meditation that stands apart from other species by virtue of the ontological assumptions that underlie it and the affective or attitudinal posture that pervades it.

The fact that prayer is addressed to a higher reality does not mean that all types of prayer are therefore types of CM. For the superior reality to which prayer is addressed, although the ultimate goal of prayer, is rarely the immediate "object" of prayer. Most practitioners of prayer are religious *seekers*, for whom God is less a discernible presence to be focused upon than an absence to be filled, an unknown "not-there" to be beckoned through an attitude of supplication and surrender. Despite its God-directedness, then, prayer is not necessarily a concentrative exercise. Prayer can take the form of either RM or CM. Either of these two forms of meditation can be used as a way of beckoning God.

Prayers that can be considered cases of RM are all those that, in adopting the attitude of reverent surrender, do not thereby attach themselves to any particular image or idea of the divine reality that is being surrendered to. No form or figure of God, nor any divine attribute, nor any particular motif or datum of religion (e.g., verse, symbol, icon) is specifically addressed. Rather, the person practicing this kind of prayer remains choicelessly aware of all that enters his experience, whether he is situated in the arena of action or in anchoritic isolation. He makes no effort to keep anything in mind or to banish anything from mind, since his whole effort is put in to awaiting the arrival of the word or spirit of God. This kind of prayer thus is altogether without position-taking or object-preference; nothing is singled out as a matter of primary regard or of special favor or disfavor. Rather, everything is witnessed equally and disinterestedly; each thing is allowed to come and go as it will. The only constant is the posture of supplicatory openness.

A prime example of such receptive prayer is the prayer of simplicity or of simple regard, mentioned a moment ago (note 5). Although this prayer can adopt a theme or focus, after the fashion of CM, it is more usual for it to be practiced unthematically, after the fashion of RM . This prayer is called the prayer of simplicity because discursive activity and affective fluctuations have, for the most part, subsided (as in Patanjali's *dhyana*), hence freeing the practitioner from distractions and allowing him an undisturbed inner silence. Thus, when it takes the form of RM , the prayer of simplicity consists of a state of inner poise and quiet, in which, without abiding attention being given to any particular figure or form, the practitioner waits, vigilantly and expectantly, to be touched by the divine power. It consists of a naked receptivity of the soul, an empty openness that invites the influx of the Holy Spirit.

Prayers that can be counted as instances of CM are all those that focus devotional attention on a theme or object of religious significance, e.g., a scriptural verse, mantra, icon, symbol, theological idea, or thought or visualization of a deity, savior, or saint. All such practices typically observe the three stages that are characteristic of CM generally. Corresponding to Patanjali's first stage *(dharana)*, they typically involve an initial period of concentration, a period during which effort is required to harness the mind in order either to arrest it altogether or to discipline it firmly so that it can be kept within the boundaries of the focal referent. Corresponding to Patanjali's second stage *(dhyana)*, these practices typically lead to a point where the psychomental flux is stilled and consciousness is left intensely quiet and equipoised. Finally, corresponding to Patanjali's third stage *(samadhi)*, these practices typically culminate in infused and absorbed states; the meditator is at last transported out of himself and absorbed in an ego-transcending experience.

There are two main reasons why I have given special consideration to prayer. The first is that meditation and prayer have much more in common than many Westerners realize or are willing to admit. If the above account is correct, meditation and prayer are sibling species of a single genus. They share important common ground, ground which needs to be acknowledged if either is to be properly understood. Meditation and prayer are both practices of sustained unmoving alertness, and in this respect, as we shall see, they have similar effects upon the psyche. In particular, they access the unconscious in the same way.

The second reason for considering prayer is that different transpersonal paradigms have different implications bearing upon the type of meditation to be selected, including possibly prayer. Take, for example, the two paradigms discussed in Chapter 1, namely, the dynamic-dialectical paradigm, on which this book is based, and the structural-hierarchical paradigm. Of these two paradigms, it is evident that the former would more likely recommend a meditation conducted in the manner of prayer. This is because the dynamic-dialectical paradigm is based on a conception of the psyche according to which the meditating ego is, in all senses, a subject in its relation to the Dynamic Ground, the power of which is considered the sovereign power of the soul. If it is true that the ego is inherently related to such a sovereign power, then it is fitting that the ego should meditate with an attitude of submission to this higher power—which is simply to say that it is fitting that the ego should meditate in the manner of prayer. And this is all the more fitting if the ego, as mental ego, is assumed to have a repressive and therefore adversarial relation to the power in question, since then the ego, in meditating, would be opening itself not only to a superior reality but also to the wrath of the return of the repressed. It seems, then, that the dynamic-dialectical paradigm points to prayer as the preferred form of meditation.[7]

The structural-hierarchical paradigm, on the other hand, while in no way excluding prayer, does not so evidently point in the direction of prayer. Corresponding to its conception of the psyche as a hierarchy of structural levels, this paradigm sees meditation as a practice that facilitates a level-by-level ascent through the structural hierarchy. According to Wilber's (1980a, 1983b) account, meditation accomplishes this ascent by loosening the identification that consciousness has with the existing structural level and thereby rendering consciousness receptive to the influence of the next higher level. For the structural-hierarchical paradigm, then, meditation is not a matter of the ego submitting to a higher spiritual reality, but rather of consciousness climbing to a higher structural plateau. The elements of prayer are not, or at least need not be, present.

MEDITATION AND THE UNCONSCIOUS

Meditation is a practice that opens the ego to the unconscious. One reason why meditation has this effect is that it disengages the ego's attention from

145

extraverted involvements and, in doing so, allows inner signals to register in consciousness. When consciousness is occupied with wordly affairs, it is blind to most of the stimuli that arise from or are latent within. These stimuli exist, as it were, behind the focus of the ego's extraverted attention, and for this reason they usually go undetected by the ego. However, when meditation disengages attention from external concerns, it at the same time interiorizes awareness, rendering consciousness observant of inner signals. Meditation introverts attention and thus allows inner stimuli to shift from the invisible background to the conscious foreground of awareness. Subjective stimuli that before were hidden behind consciousness in this way are permitted to appear before the screen of the mind.[8]

The initial effect of introversion is to make the meditator aware of the stream of consciousness that ordinarily is the "background noise" of life. This stream consists primarily of the internal dialogue of the mental ego. As we know, the mental ego carries on a nearly incessant conversation with itself in order to fill the dead void of its psychic space. This conversation is so much a constant of experience and so taken for granted that it usually is not explicitly attended to. However, when meditation interiorizes awareness, the inner conversation is thrown into relief and becomes the principal focus of awareness. Accordingly, the beginning stages of meditation tend to be dominated by the mental ego's internal dialogue.

Engrossment in internal dialogue and the imagery that accompanies it ("inner cinema") can go on for a considerable period of time. However, if introversion is sustained, the tendency is for this stream of voices and pictures gradually to ebb, sufficiently so in time to allow submerged materials to surface in awareness. Subthreshold and filtered stimuli may in this way eventually make their existence known to the meditator, as, too, may components of the shadow. If introversion is sustained long enough, materials from even deeper regions of the submerged unconscious may emerge in consciousness, possibly even materials from the prepersonal submerged unconscious, although this would probably require prolonged introversion under severe conditions.

An example of introversion of such an extreme sort is found in certain sensory deprivation experiments.[9] It has been shown (Kammerman 1977) that multimodality deprivation over a period of several days can lead to hypnagogic imagery approaching the character of hallucinations. One reason why these effects are thought to occur is that sensory deprivation creates a condition of stimulus hunger. Deprived of external stimulation, the mind is forced to plumb its own resources, digging into deeper stores of potential stimuli as time passes. At first, the mental ego's internal dialogue suffices to fill the void. But in time, as the need for stimulation increases, the mind is forced to draw on unconscious materials, initially materials from the personal submerged unconscious and eventually even materials from the prepersonal submerged unconscious.

A second reason why meditation accesses the unconscious is that, as the practice of firmly anchored and unmoving attention, it has the effect of *demobilizing* the ego. Meditation, as pure steadfast witnessing, resists and ultimately arrests egoic activities (including embedded processes and operations), and it counteracts and ultimately dissolves egoic sets and postures (including embedded armors and repressions).[10] Meditation is a steadfast "not-doing" of all egoic actions and "undoing" or "letting go" of all assumed egoic stances. This is a very simple fact, but one with far-reaching consequences.

Meditative demobilization works to access the unconscious because, in opposing embedded activities and sets, it creates "friction" or "drag" on these structures and consequently (1) dishabituates them, thereby drawing attention to them, and (2) suppresses or weakens them, thereby rendering them less effective in keeping corresponding submerged unconscious materials from view. Hence, in opposing embedded activities and sets, meditation works both to throw light on these structures themselves and, in time, to uncover the materials screened or repressed by the structures. Meditative demobilization restrains, and thus exposes, the embedded unconscious, layer by layer, and in doing this it works also to uncover corresponding submerged unconscious materials, stratum by stratum. This process begins with more accessible levels of the personal unconscious, proceeds to deeper levels, and in some cases even works its way through original repression (the embedded structure dividing the two poles of the psyche) and enters prepersonal spheres.

Both receptive and concentrative meditations access the unconscious by demobilizing the ego. They do this, however, in slightly different ways. The most evident of their differences is that RM allows contact with unconscious materials *during* the period of its practice while CM allows such contact only *after* the conclusion of practice. The unconscious is inaccessible during the period of CM because CM invests the whole of consciousness in a single object and therefore closes it to everything else, including materials that otherwise might emerge from the unconscious. After concluding CM and opening the focus of awareness, however, the unconscious, in one or another aspect, can present itself to the conscious mind. RM, on the other hand, since it consists simultaneously of stationary *and* wide-open awareness, is receptive to the unconscious during the course of its practice.

As a technique of demobilization, RM achieves insight into the *embedded* unconscious because, in attempting merely to witness, and hence "not-do" and "let-go," the meditator resists all embedded tendencies and therefore puts himself in a position literally to feel the impact of their movement or, in the case of embedded sets or postures, the effort of their maintenance. Considered in this light, the meditator can be compared to a person who is trying to stand still in the middle of a river and who, in doing so, puts himself in a position to feel the movement of the river current and the exertion involved in maintaining his own rigidly immobile stance. RM, then, reveals embedded structures by opposing their expression and consequently raising their "coefficient of friction" and throwing them into relief. More concretely, what usually happens is that meditation is approached with the best of intentions, with a resolve to be a completely disengaged and unmoving witness. However, soon after the practice is begun, the meditator discovers that he cannot help but think or react in certain ways or that he is already locked in a particular set or stance. And it is just in making discoveries such as these that the meditator learns about particular embedded structures. What happens, then, is that in attempting *and failing* to "not-do" and to "let go," the meditator discovers some of the myriad ways in which he is unconsciously programmed to do just the opposite. And again, such insights are won *during* the period of meditation, since RM keeps the mind open to the stimulus of the moment.

The manner in which CM discloses the embedded unconscious is a bit different. As was just explained, CM's exclusive devotion to a focal object disallows contact with the unconscious during the time that CM is being practiced. This fact notwithstanding, however, the demobilizing effects of CM are such that the meditator is primed to encounter the unconscious after the focal object is dropped. Specifically, what happens in the case of CM is that the meditator re-enters the field of activity in a relatively still and disengaged condition.[11] It takes time for embedded dispositions, inhibited during CM, to be triggered and reactivated. It takes time for embedded response routines to be set in motion and embedded sets to be reassumed. Therefore, when the meditator, after CM, meets with stimuli that trigger embedded tendencies, he is able, owing to his CM-induced condition, to feel these tendencies being reactivated. This process is much the reverse of what happens during RM. For RM allows the meditator to witness the gradual demobilization of embedded structures and consequent destructuring of experience, whereas CM, once finished, allows the meditator to witness the gradual *re*mobilization of embedded structures and consequent *re*structuring of experience.

As a technique of demobilization, meditation works not only to reveal the embedded unconscious but also to uncover the *submerged* unconscious. Meditation has this double effect because the very same process of resistance that at first draws attention to embedded structures also works, over time, to inhibit the expression of these structures and therefore to lessen their effectiveness as screens or repressors of submerged materials. Accordingly, the continued practice of meditation leads to a gradual suppression or disengagement of embedded structures, and thereby to a gradual unearthing of the submerged unconscious. Submerged unconscious materials are in this way eventually aired within consciousness, either during the practice of meditation (RM) or immediately thereafter (CM).

However, emphasis should here be put on *eventually*, since it takes much longer to suppress or disengage an embedded structure than it does initially to expose it to consciousness. The act of meditative demobilization can draw attention to an embedded structure much more quickly than it can constrain or disarm that structure to a point sufficient to unveil corresponding submerged materials. It is much easier to learn what one's embedded tendencies are than it is effectively to diminish their effects. Nevertheless, the difficulties involved in effectively opposing embedded structures, and therefore in unscreening and derepressing corresponding submerged materials, are not insuperable. These difficulties can be surmounted by dedicated meditative practice. For meditation, in resisting the expression of embedded structures, *does* eventually suppress or disengage these structures.

To avoid misunderstanding, it should be stressed that the purpose of opposing embedded structures is not just to interfere with established tendencies and dispositions. Such an end would be pointless, indeed destructive. The purpose is rather to accomplish a psychic inventory and, even more importantly, to recover lost potentials that are necessary ingredients of transpersonal or integrated existence. If, then, meditation seems to be only a retrograde action, a merely negative process of "not-doing" and "undoing," we should not be misled by this appearance. For meditation, in counteracting egoic structures, at the same time achieves insight into egoic structures and gains access to essential materials that egoic structures screen or repress. Meditative demobilization thus is the first step toward a thorough psychic review and transformation. As Eliade (1969a, 1969b) makes this point in his account of yoga, it is first necessary to bring a halt to profane existence (through yogic cessation of movement, breath, and thought) before one can achieve higher insight and gain contact with the sacred. The apparent negativity of meditation therefore in principle leads to a positive end.

Let us remember that embedded structures cover a wide spectrum of types and degrees, extending from gross physical habits to extremely subtle tendencies of thought and feeling. Meditation, in working upon the embedded unconscious, usually begins with structures of the former kind and gradually proceeds toward structures of the latter kind. Accordingly, in a typical sequence, meditation would work to disclose: (1) mannerisms of physical and social behavior; (2) psychological tendencies such as acquired tastes and preferences, prides and prejudices, poses and affectations; (3) basic presuppositions of thought and value; (4) subtle aspects of personality such as nuclear elements of the self-concept and entrenched complexes and COEX systems; and, finally, (5) deeply underlying armors and constrictions such as those that constitute the barrier of original repression. The meditative practice of steadfast attention works in progressive fashion, affecting layer upon layer of embedment, starting with more conspicuous and external levels and working steadily toward the most hidden or guarded regions of subjective inwardness.

And to repeat, as these layers of the embedded unconscious are brought to awareness, the corresponding levels of the submerged unconscious are eventually unscreened or derepressed and thus allowed to re-enter the field of consciousness. In this way the whole of the unconscious, submerged as well as embedded, prepersonal as well as personal, can, in principle, be unveiled or unearthed.

For the most part, however, the process does not get beyond the personal unconscious. This limit obtains because original repression is not easily undone. However, in some cases meditation penetrates even this embedded structure. When this happens, the meditator "strikes oil": the Dynamic Ground is uncapped and the numinous power of the Ground begins to well up in consciousness. Simultaneously, potentials from the body-unconscious and the instinctual-archetypal unconscious begin to be reactivated on the conscious level. The meditator comes under the influence of the Dynamic Ground and begins to undergo regression in the service of transcendence.

MEDITATION BEFORE AND AFTER BREAKING THROUGH ORIGINAL REPRESSION

There have been many enthusiastic advocates of meditation who have spoken of meditation as if it were an unmitigated good, indeed a virtual panacea for physical and psychic ills. For example, one very popular view holds that meditation is essentially a method of deep relaxation, which, as such, has entirely beneficial effects. Now, although it cannot be denied that meditation has a relaxing effect, this is only part of a larger and more complex matter. Moreover, it is a part that, taken by itself, can be misleading.[12]

It is undeniable that meditation is an exercise that relaxes both body and mind. As the practice of sustained attention, it counteracts all movements and all assumed sets or stances, and it therefore reduces excitation and tension. Confirming this point, there have been literally hundreds of scientific studies that have shown that meditation either slows or lowers the intensity level of many psychophysiological processes, such as, for example, those involved in respiration, oxygen consumption, heartbeat, blood pressure, and brain wave activity.[13] It is, then, a well-established fact that meditation works in the direction of greater stillness and calm.

But this fact needs to be seen in a larger perspective. For meditation leads not only to greater stillness and calm but also, as we have seen, to derepression.

Hence, although meditation *initially* has a quieting effect, its *long-term* practice can lead to such disquieting experiences as encounter with the shadow, exposure to buried psychic wounds, and confrontation with fears, fantasies and disturbing feelings that before were manageably contained. Meditative demobilization works eventually to suppress or disengage the mental ego's embedded defensive structures, and consequently it renders the mental ego vulnerable to a breakthrough of unwelcome repressed materials. Meditation, if practiced in a disciplined way, leads beyond the superficial calm that it initially induces to an encounter with the personal submerged unconscious, and therefore to considerable anguish and agitation.

But there is more. Very importantly, it should be understood that the difficulties that are encountered in opening the personal unconscious are minor in comparison with the difficulties that can be encountered if and when the meditator begins to untie the knot of original repression. For in untying this knot, the meditator exposes himself to the prepersonal unconscious, which is a field of extremely potent energies and complexes. Jung was well aware of the dangers involved in "forcing" one's way into the prepersonal sphere by the use of meditation or other psychospiritual techniques. For this reason, he consistently advised Westerners against the practice of yoga, which, he warned, "in certain unstable individuals might easily lead to a real psychosis, . . . which abolishes the normal checks imposed by the conscious mind and thus gives unlimited scope to the play of the unconscious 'dominants' " (1953/1969, 520). Jung may at times have overstated dangers such as these; nevertheless, the dangers that he describes are real and should not be taken lightly. Some of the risks incurred in opening the prepersonal unconscious are considered in the next chapter. For the present, suffice it to say that the journey through the prepersonal unconscious, initiated by meditative demobilization, is a deeply unsettling affair.

Meditation changes in many ways once original repression has been penetrated or dissolved. Postponing consideration of the difficulties that can arise at this point, it can here be noted that crossing the threshold of original repression has dramatic effects. It reactivates latent nonegoic potentials and infuses the meditative process with the numinous power of the Dynamic Ground. And accompanying these effects there typically also occur a variety of extraordinary experiences, including, for example, experiences of light and sound, awe and devotion, fear and love, dread and bliss, strangeness and enchantment, trance and rapture, and, in some cases, extrasensory vision and audition.

In the case of RM as practiced in the Buddhist tradition (Buddhaghosa 1975), extraordinary experiences like the ones just mentioned are called the "ten corruptions" and are said to arise after the meditator's insight has become sufficiently refined to allow him clearly to see the impersonality (*anatta*) and impermanence (*anicca*) of all contents of mind. The reason for calling these experiences "corruptions" is that, as sudden and dramatic occurrences, they have the power to divert the meditator and to lead him to think that he has achieved *nirvana* when in fact he has, in the terms being used here, only begun the journey across the prepersonal unconscious.

Similar experiences in the Zen tradition are called *makyo*. Philip Kapleau quotes Zen master Yasutani-roshi, who describes *makyo* in this way (Kapleau 1967, 38):

> *Makyo* are the phenomena—visions, hallucinations, fantasies, revelations, illusory sensations—which one practicing zazen is apt to experience at a particular stage of his sitting. *Ma* means "devil" and *kyo* "the objective world." Hence *makyo* are the disturbing or "diabolical" phenomena which appear to one during his zazen. These phenomena are not inherently bad. They become a serious obstacle to practice only if one is ignorant of their true nature and is ensnared by them.

The occurrence of *makyo* is evidence of the opening of the prepersonal unconscious and the tapping of its nonegoic potentials. Experience becomes supercharged and strange, and, on occasion, the autosymbolic process, heretofore active only in dreams, brings forth images of visionary quality. Quite literally, the meditator's experience at this point can take on the character of a dream.

When RM is practiced as prayer, overcoming the barrier of original repression is conceived as the breakthrough that opens the psyche to the possible action of grace. It is at this point, for example, that the aforementioned prayer of simplicity is transcended and the discernible presence of the Holy Spirit is said to commence, leading the person in prayer through numinous and transforming experiences—experiences that are both agonizing and ecstatic, terrifying and rapturous, bewildering and illumined, purgative and redemptive. This is the point at which, it is said, the waters of grace begin to flow, at first slowly and only with the earnest beckoning of the person in prayer, and then more strongly and spontaneously.[14]

Turning to CM, crossing the threshold of original repression has the distinctive effect of raising the meditative state from mere unmoving one-pointedness to full absorption or enstasy. In Patanjali's terms, it is what lifts the meditator from *dharana* (effortful and wavering one-pointedness) and *dhyana* (easy and steady one-pointedness) to *samadhi* (absorption, enstasy). Passing beyond original repression leads to *samadhi*, I propose, because this state is, in essential part, a dynamic phenomenon requiring open access to the Dynamic Ground. Specifically, *samadhi* can be understood to be a powerful concentration of the energy of the Ground into which, given the magnetic and solvent effects of this energy, the meditator is drawn and absorbed. *Samadhi*, that is, is a consciously achieved cathexis.[15] Now, since *samadhi* is concentration in the true meaning of the term—*dharana* and *dhyana* being but steps to *samadhi*—the opening of the Dynamic Ground and the attainment of the first levels of *samadhi* in a sense mark the real beginning of CM. Patanjali's *raja yoga* is in this sense really a *samadhi yoga*, as Patanjali himself states at the very beginning of the *Yoga-Sutra*. It is a systematic training for *samadhi*, and for the liberation to which *samadhi* ultimately leads.

One other way in which overcoming original repression changes the character of meditation is in the manner in which embedded structures are revealed. These structures are no longer revealed only by being resisted and demobilized (RM) or by being triggered and remobilized (CM) but also, now, by being supercharged with energy. Once original repression is breached or rescinded, the power of the Ground infiltrates the egoic sphere and energizes the faculties and structures of that sphere in a heightened way. Embedded structures, in being energized in this fashion, are enlarged and rendered visible. They in effect become new, and hence salient, stimuli, stepping forth from the unconscious background to the conscious foreground of awareness. In some instances, if more energy enters the egoic sphere than can be accommodated, embedded structures can be charged beyond capacity, and therefore rendered uncontrollably active or else paralyzed. In these cases too, though, the change in the functioning of embedded structures bares them to conscious view.

BEYOND MEDITATION

Meditation as a technique or specific exercise really comes to an end once the Dynamic Ground is opened. Prior to the opening of the Dynamic Ground, meditation is like drilling for oil. Whether by RM or CM, the meditator works through layer after layer of embedded structure until he arrives finally at original repression, which, as the foundation of the mental-egoic system, is the most deeply embedded structure of that system. Meditation then begins to work its way through this last and most impervious barrier. "Drilling" through original repression is a long and difficult process. It may seem to the meditator that no progress is being made. However, with perseverance, original repression is sometimes penetrated or dissolved, at which point the meditator "strikes oil": the power of the Dynamic Ground. The power of the Ground begins at this point to flow into the system of consciousness, and the meditative process is henceforth transformed. Besides the introduction of the aforementioned extraordinary phenomena into the meditative process, there now occurs a basic change in what it means to practice meditation. Specifically, meditation ceases being an effortful technique of unmoving attention and becomes instead a matter of "going with the flow." "The flow," of course, is the free upsurge of numinous energy, of spirit, the activity of which now takes over the process of psychic evolution. The meditator's task, then, once "the flow" is discerned, is no longer to perform a rote exercise of stationary alertness, but rather to yield to the transformative process that now is unfolding within him.

CONCLUSION

I would like to make two points by way of conclusion. First, it should be noted that, since original repression is a psycho*physical* phenomenon, the purpose of meditation can be assisted by physical exercises. The practices that are most effective in this regard are not the cardiovascular exercises so popular in health-conscious America, but rather exercises that have the effect of dismantling the physical infrastructure of original repression. The practices that more than any other can be counted as examples of this latter type are the postures of *hatha yoga*.[16] Yoga postures (*asanas*) work to unblock the body so that energy latent in the body can be liberated and allowed to flow freely. The manner in which *asanas* accomplish this is essentially the same as the manner in which meditation accomplishes the unblocking or derepressing of the mind: demobilization. Yoga is a close analogue of meditation; both are techniques of demobilization. Yoga postures are distinctive configurations, that, if held fast, counteract and finally dissolve embedded rigidities and tensions, including those involved in original repression. Yoga postures therefore have much the same effect on the physical level that meditation has on the mental level.[17] For this reason, yoga postures are frequently practiced as a supportive adjunct to meditation.

The second point is that meditation needs to be understood in a more balanced and sober way than so far has been the case in the West. Meditation should not be vilified as mere narcissism or suspect occultism, nor should it be glorified as a psychic panacea or direct path to enlightenment or salvation. These widely contrasting assessments are both symptomatic of Westerners' ignorance of what meditation really is and does. A more objective assessment is: meditation, when practiced regularly for a long period of time, is a powerful instrument of psychic transformation; many of the changes it effects are deep and irreversible; and its practice bears great promise but is also fraught with serious risks.

CHAPTER 7

Regression in the Service of Transcendence

V IRTUALLY EVERY RELIGIOUS TRADITION knows of a period of protracted trial that typically attends spiritual awakening. This period is variously described as the dark night of the soul, the spiritual desert, the state of self-accusing (Islam), the great doubt (Zen), the ordeal of dying to the world, the descent into the underworld or into hell, the encounter with Kali (Hinduism) or Mara (Buddhism), and the passion or death of the self.

All of these descriptions capture one or another aspect of the period during which the ego undergoes a withdrawal from the world and a return to the Dynamic Ground. As a process that disengages the ego from worldly involvements and that submits the ego, beyond its knowledge and control, to the underlying physico-dynamic strata of the psyche, this "dark night" must be considered a type of regression. Since the physico-dynamic pole of the psyche is originally lost via repression, it can be restored only via regression. However, if the "dark night" is a type of regression, it is not a regression in any usual sense of the term. It is not a regression in the strict sense because it is not merely a retrograde movement to earlier or more primitive modes of functioning. Nor is it a regression in the service of the ego, since the "dark night" does not serve in the long run to consolidate the ego in a position of psychic ascendancy or command. On the contrary, the "dark night" radically undermines the (mental) ego's autonomy and submits the ego to the Ground, making the ego a servant of spirit. The "dark night" is, then, more a regression in the service of spirit than a regression in the service of the ego. Or more precisely still, it is a *regression in the service of transcendence*.[1]

In earlier chapters, I have spoken as if regression in the service of transcendence begins with the opening of the Dynamic Ground or, equivalently, with the undoing of original repression. It is necessary now to sharpen the notion by dividing it into two principal stages, namely, (1) the stage of withdrawal from worldly involvement or of "dying to the world," which occurs prior to the opening of the Dynamic Ground, and (2) the stage of encounter with the prepersonal unconscious or of "descent into the underworld," which occurs after the opening of the Dynamic Ground. The opening of the Dynamic Ground is indeed the event that initiates the ego's dramatic regression into prepersonal spheres. But there is a distinct and very important process that occurs prior to the opening of the Dynamic Ground that is best considered an integral part of regression in the service of transcendence—since this is a process of withdrawal from the world that leads precisely to the opening of the Dynamic Ground. Understood in its totality, then, regression in the service of transcendence is a two-stage process. And the unsealing of the Dynamic Ground is the pivotal event around which the two stages of this process turn.

The first stage of regression in the service of transcendence consists of a set of interrelated difficulties that have been made famous in the writings of the existentialists, included among which are such states of mind or feeling as alienation, meaninglessness, anomie, "nothingness," worthlessness, anxiety, and despair. During this period, the world loses its meaning, life loses its purpose, and the self loses its presumed substance and value. The period is one of disillusionment and alienation from the world. Worldly engagements are suspended, and worldly identity and justification are lost. The process leads, it seems, nowhere and to nothing—except to existential exile and despair. But in fact the first stage leads toward a recognition, by the mental ego, of its "nothingness" and guilt, and from there in some cases to an inner conversion that opens the Dynamic Ground.

The second stage, considerably rarer than the first, is the period of encounter with the prepersonal unconscious that follows the opening of the Dynamic Ground. During this stage, the ego comes into contact with the potentials of the physico-dynamic sphere and is affected by these potentials in dramatic and bizarre ways. Accordingly, the second stage of regression in the service of transcendence consists of a variety of highly unusual phenomena, phenomena which for the most part are described only in writings that treat either of psychopathology or of the lives of the saints. This stage sometimes begins with the sudden occurrence, triggered by the opening of the Dynamic Ground, of such "otherworldly" experiences as transports, raptures, revelatory intuitions, and, in some cases, apparitions. These preliminary experiences, when they occur, are highly impressive in their power and allure. They also are significant in indicating that the ego has finally come to an end of its exile and has come under the influence of numinous power. However, these experiences are deceptive in that they lend themselves to the false conclusion that enlightenment or spiritual fulfillment is at hand. Hence, they are called "corruptions," "temptations," or "diabolical phenomena" (*makyo*). The fact of the matter is that a radically new realm of experience has been uncovered, but it is not exactly the realm that had been expected. It is rather an intervening territory of dark and dangerous character. The opening of the Dynamic Ground leads at first not to the final goal of *moksha, nirvana,* or salvation, but rather, typically, to a long and difficult encounter with the prepersonal unconscious.

The prepersonal unconscious is the sea upon which the second stage of regression in the service of transcendence takes place. And the far side of this sea is arrived at, usually, only after many trials have been endured. Typical among the tribulations of this period are: (1) strange physical symptoms; (2) bizarre and morbid states of consciousness; (3) dread and estrangement (or strangeness)—in contrast to the anxiety and alienation of the first stage; (4) disturbance of thought processes; (5) loss of control of personality; (6) eruption of the instincts; and (7) recurrence of the ego/Ground conflict, with danger of ego death.

The experiences that characterize the two stages of regression in the service of transcendence—and especially those that occur during the second stage— constitute a highly unusual symptomatology, unusual not only in terms of social norms of mental health but also in terms of data deriving from psychiatry and spiritual practice. Considered individually or from a non-transpersonal perspective, it is extremely difficult to know what to make of these phenomena. It is little wonder that they usually have been subsumed under psychiatric categories, e.g., existential neurosis or dissociative psychosis (first stage) and disintegrative psychosis (second stage). This is not to say that these symptoms are never merely pathological, since in many, if not most, cases they probably are. Nevertheless, in exceptional cases, these symptoms are, I believe, redemptive rather than degenerative, "trans-" rather than "pre-." Accordingly, in this chapter I will try to show that these symptoms can be fit together as a coherent whole and that, from a bipolar and triphasic perspective, they can be seen to be natural expressions of human development as it arrives at the point of the transcendence of the (mental) ego.

I will proceed here, as in earlier chapters, by presenting what I take to be the pure or ideal-typical case. This exemplary model of regression in the service of transcendence is not meant to describe anyone's actual experience. Actual experience usually diverges significantly from the idealized pattern. For example, most actual cases probably do not involve all of the symptoms that will be discussed here. Moreover, they usually do not observe the strict division between the two stages. In most actual cases, the Dynamic Ground, if it opens at all, probably opens before the end of the first stage, thus making the process more complex and multifaceted than it otherwise would be. Also, most actual cases probably would not be as severe as the case I have constructed. However, even though actual experience may depart in these ways from the ideal-typical pattern, it is still only in terms of the ideal-typical pattern that actual experience can be understood or explained as a coherent totality. The ideal-typical pattern may fail to *describe* actual experience, but that pattern is nonetheless necessary in order to *comprehend* actual experience, especially its underlying logic and causality.

STAGE ONE: WITHDRAWAL FROM THE WORLD

I will begin with a sketch of the first stage of regression in the service of transcendence considered as a whole. Then I will undertake a closer examination of how this stage unfolds.

The first stage of regression in the service of transcendence commences when the mental ego begins to suffer disillusionment in the world, i.e., when the mental ego begins to realize that its deepest desires cannot be fulfilled by the world. The mental ego does not at first understand what these desires are for, namely, being and worth. Nor does it understand that the world's inability to satisfy these desires is due to no fault of the world, but rather to the impossibility of the mental ego's own fundamental project in the world, namely, to establish being and worth by acquiring worldly facticity and distinction. Nor, of course, does the mental ego understand what motivates its basic project, namely, underlying "nothingness" and guilt, or why the project is impossible, namely, because it is but a form of escape. Upon first suffering disillusionment, all the mental ego understands is that what it most wants from the world, the world cannot possibly provide. The mental ego's initial "awakening" consists of no more than a profound disappointment in the world, which is seen (distortedly) as being deficient in certain fundamental regards.

Disillusionment leads to alienation. Disabused of hope of finding fulfillment in the world, the mental ego begins to withdraw from the world: it suffers alienation. This alienation is two-sided; it is at once something that happens to the mental ego and something that affects the mental ego's world. On the side of the mental ego, alienation consists of a gradual loss of interest, drive, and capacity for engagement. And on the side of the world (as seen by the mental ego), alienation consists of a gradual loss of "realness" and meaning. The mental ego becomes apathetic, confused, and cut off; simultaneously, the world becomes barren, purposeless, and out of reach. Alienation is a condition that pervades the entire realm of the mental ego's existence. The mental ego, in a sense, loses its life, as it dies to the world; in turn, the world ceases any longer to be a world in the full sense of the term, as it is reduced to a mere stage or setting, an illusion.

There is nothing voluntary about alienation. Alienation follows upon disillusionment as an effect follows upon a cause, not as a decision follows upon an insight. It is therefore a process that the mental ego suffers and is powerless to reverse. Once the process is under way, the rift between the mental ego and the world widens, despite whatever efforts the mental ego might make to renew its interest and involvement in the world. Alienation is not renunciation. The mental ego does not give up the world; rather, the world simply slips away, becoming distant and unreal.

Alienation, by withdrawing the mental ego from the world, relieves the mental ego of the frustrations of its fundamental project in the world. It releases the mental ego from the futile compulsion to be *ens causa sui*, cause of its own being and worth. Far from being a blessing, however, this suspension of the fundamental project actually increases the mental ego's burdens. For, if we remember, the *causa sui* project serves the mental ego as an escape from its deeper self, and, therefore, the suspension of the project brings the mental ego ever closer to a dreaded self-encounter. Alienation, by withdrawing the mental ego from the world, returns the mental ego, most unwillingly, to its underlying "nothingness" and guilt.

The process of alienation causes the mental ego considerable distress, for it sweeps away all of the mental ego's moorings in, and reasons for, being. The mental ego loses its foothold in the world and is deprived of its established sense of being and worth. The whole of the mental ego's worldly existence is undermined, and for this reason the mental ego experiences anxiety, "fear and trembling." Moreover, in time the mental ego begins to suffer from despair, "sickness unto death." For without relief from its alienated condition, the mental ego eventually begins to feel as if it were permanently cut off and bereft, as if it were without hope of ever finding a way back to a meaningful existence in a real world.

Despair is potentially a profound state of mind, as it has the power to make the unthinkable thinkable. It is a state of mind that, because it is unendurable and yet inescapable within the system of known possibilities, impels the sufferer at last to embrace what, for him, is impossible. For the alienated mental ego, the unthinkable that despair prompts it to think, the impossible that despair drives it finally to embrace, is precisely its "nothingness" and original guilt or sin. Despair, it turns out, is worse than the mental ego's worst fears about itself. Despair therefore pushes the mental ego to the brink, from which the mental ego jumps. That is to say, the mental ego does what, for it, is impossible: it accepts its "nothingness" and guilt and takes the leap of faith. And in doing this, it submits to a process of conversion that (assuming the ideal-typical pattern) opens the Dynamic Ground—and thereby initiates the second stage of regression in the service of transcendence.

Let us now look more closely at the steps that lead from disillusionment to despair, and from there to the opening of the Dynamic Ground.

1. *From disillusionment to alienation.* Disillusionment usually occurs at first only vaguely and on the level of feeling. The mental ego merely senses that

its efforts are somehow pointless. But then, in some cases, disillusionment ripens and becomes a conscious insight. When this happens, the mental ego suddenly realizes that its own deepest needs and desires cannot be satisfied by anything the world has to offer. Perhaps the mental ego comes to this realization by way of a failure to achieve a worldly goal. Or perhaps it arrives at the realization by succeeding in a worldly goal, only to discover that restlessness and dissatisfaction continue. Or perhaps it is brought to the realization by means of self-analysis or philosophical reflection. But however the insight is earned, the meaning is the same: fulfillment is not possible through worldly successes, distinctions, and rewards. To understand this fact in a thoroughgoing way is to be fully disillusioned. To be fully disillusioned is to be on the verge of alienation.

Knowing that it cannot find fulfillment in the world, the mental ego gradually loses interest in the world and begins to withdraw from the outer arena of life. In ever-increasing measure, the mental ego begins to exhibit the classic signs of alienation: lack of motivation, disorientation, and a sense of being out of touch with things and out of step with the rhythm of events. The mental ego suffers from flagging interest in the world and decreasing desire to pursue old aims. It also suffers from confusion, or anomie, as old principles and priorities no longer make sense. And compounding these two problems, there is the sense that, even if old motivations and meanings were to return, they could not be translated into action, because somehow it, the mental ego, is cut off from the world and unable to enter the flow of life. Alienation cripples the mental ego, as it saps the mental ego's drive, obscures its purposes, and throws it out of gear. Alienation renders the mental ego listless, aimless, and unable to act.[2]

But this is only one side of a two-sided process. For as noted a moment ago, alienation is a malady that affects the mental ego's world as well as the mental ego itself. It is not only a process by which the mental ego secedes from the world but also a process by which the world becomes lost to the mental ego. Generally stated, the world during the process of alienation undergoes *derealization*: it loses its substance and meaning, its credibility and compellingness. It loses its familiarity, aliveness, and sense and becomes, by gradual deterioration, distant, dead, and "absurd." It is reduced to an arid and meaningless landscape—a wasteland. And these changes in the world, it should be added, although merely apparent—i.e., occurring in perception rather than in reality—seem entirely real to the alienated mental ego. From the point of view of the mental ego, it seems as if the world were undergoing an actual, mind-independent transformation. Moreover, not only does the mental ego see the world as suffering such a change, it also typically sees its own predicament as being an effect of this change—though, of course, the causality really works just the other way around. The mental ego takes its own dissociation and disorientation to be responses to the world's destitution. To the alienated mental ego, then, it seems as if the world were undergoing a completely objective derealization, and it also seems as if it were this derealization of the world that is the cause of the mental ego's deteriorating relationship with the world.

The reason for the ostensible change in the world is that the world, as a realm alive with meanings, values, and purposes, is a subjective construct. Hence, the withdrawal of the mental ego from the world is at the same time a deconstruction of the world. This is a point that the phenomenologists have made with great perspicacity.[3] A world, they have argued, is always a world *for* a subject; it is an experiential field that is not only objectively given but also subjectively colored and construed. Or, in a phrase, a world is a *setting lived by a subject.* As a setting—i.e., an outer context, stage, or landscape—a world exists independently of any subject, as a completely objective framework of states and events. But such a setting is not a world in the full phenomenological sense of the term, for it is not lived in, and thereby enlivened by, a subject. A setting becomes a world in the full sense only when it is lit up and animated by a subject's cathexes and comprehended (literally: held together) by a subject's intentional (i.e., meaning- and value-bestowing) acts.[4] And, returning to the main point, the opposite is also true. A world ceases being a world in the full sense, and is reduced to a mere setting, when it is deserted, and consequently decathected and "disintended," by its subject—which is just what happens in the case of alienation.

Looked at from the phenomenological point of view, then, alienation can be said to be a process by which the mental ego "unworlds" itself and, in doing so, causes the world to lose its "worldliness," and become thereby a mere setting. Since the world's loss of "worldliness" is an effect of the mental ego's act of "unworlding" (appearances to the contrary notwithstanding), it follows that aspects and phases of the mental ego's alienation have objective correlates. That is, it follows that aspects and phases of the mental ego's "unworlding" are reflected in the world as losses of facets of its "worldliness." Accordingly, there is a direct correspondence between the symptoms of the mental ego's alienation and the dimensions of the world's derealization. For example, the mental ego's secession from the world is reflected objectively in a recession of the world from the mental ego. The mental ego's apathy is reflected in the world's aridity, the mental ego's isolation in the world's remoteness, the mental ego's anomie in the world's meaninglessness, the mental ego's anxiety in the world's unreality, and so forth. The world *is* the world as it is lived by the mental ego; therefore, the steps of the mental ego's alienation from the world are registered in apparent changes in the world itself—which, again, are in turn incorrectly taken by the mental ego to be the causes of its alienation.

If there is any one idea that by itself captures the essence of alienation in its effect upon the world, it is flatness. Alienation affects the mental ego's world by leveling it, i.e., by throwing it out of relief, by deleting from it the dimension of lived depth. Alienation has this effect because, as was noted, it involves the withdrawal of cathexes and intentional acts, and it is precisely the outreach of these psychic projections that creates the dimension of lived depth. Depth is a consequence of a subject intersecting with a setting by sending forth vectors of thought and feeling. Thought-vectors (intentional acts) deepen a setting with layers of meaning; feeling-vectors (cathexes) deepen a setting with attractive or repellent values. Thus when, during alienation, a subject withdraws these vectors from the world, the result is that the dimension of depth is lost. The world goes flat; its horizons disappear and it collapses into a two-dimensional setting. In just this way, alienation has the general effect upon the mental ego's world of divesting it of all modes and gradations of lived depth. It works to conflate all differences between base and horizon, intimacy and distance, figure and ground. The world of the alienated mental ego, therefore, is one in which, progressively, nothing stands out and in which there are no hidden recesses. It is a world in which everything is shallow, neutral, uniform, and gray.

More concretely, the world of the alienated mental ego is one in which there are no peaks or valleys, no challenges or disappointments, no profundities or banalities, no heroes or fools. It is a world in which no action is any more exigent than any other, no person any deeper or more mysterious than any other, and no discourse any more meaningful than any other. It is a world in which everything is "equal." Actions are "equal" because they have all been reduced to mere motions. Persons are "equal" because they have all been reduced to mere *personae*. And all discourse is "equal" because it has all been reduced to mere words. The world of the alienated mental ego is flat throughout, since, in withdrawing from the world, the mental ego has ceased intersecting in depth with the world.

A perfect example of what it is like for the world to go flat is available from the domain of the cinema. Everyone is familiar with what happens when one is suddenly drawn out of the action of a film. Let us consider a possible case. Let us suppose that a man and a woman are viewing a mystery-suspense film. The man is totally absorbed. The world of the film is, for the present, his own world. He is identified with the hero, caught up in the action, and so forth. The woman in contrast, having already seen the film on a previous occasion, is not absorbed, and let us suppose that, out of boredom and impatience, she reveals the film's conclusion to the man—which conclusion, let us also suppose, the man finds disappointing. It is reasonable to assume that under these conditions the man would suffer disillusionment and would lose interest in the film. That is to say, he would become alienated from the *world* of the film. Simultaneously, the film itself, as everyone has experienced, would go flat. Without the depth factor provided by outreaching thought and feeling, the film would cease being a self-contained world, a reality unto itself, and would become instead only a film, a fiction. The hero would be reduced to a mere actor saying lines, and what was a compelling drama would be reduced to a mere plot or story line. The world of the film would no longer be engaged, and so it would cease being an engaging reality. It would become only a setting, a sequence of scenes.

The experience of the mental ego as it suffers disillusionment and then alienation is virtually identical with that of our moviegoer. Prior to disillusionment, the mental ego, like the moviegoer, is totally absorbed in the world, which is experienced as completely real and alive. But upon suffering disillusionment, the mental ego's world, again like that of the moviegoer, undergoes derealization; it is divested of sense and seriousness. It goes flat. What were meaningful deeds now become only idle motions or empty roles; what were real people now become only surface characters; what were living histories and institutions now become only documents and buildings. The experience of the mental ego as it falls prey to alienation parallels that of the moviegoer in all of these ways. But there is one way in which the mental ego's experience is crucially different, and that is that the world that it loses is not an optional world of fantasy but rather the given world of material and social reality. Consequently, whereas the moviegoer loses a few hours and a few dollars sitting through a film that does not attract his involvement, the alienated mental ego is in danger of losing its whole life. It is in danger of becoming a permanent exile from the world.

Disillusionment undeniably liberates the mental ego from the futile efforts of its fundamental project. However, in making the mental ego no longer *of* the world, disillusionment has the negative consequence of disallowing the mental ego to live *in* the world. The mental ego is forced into existential exile, condemned to wander lost in a no-man's-land seemingly without end. The Dynamic Ground is at this point still closed, so there are no oases in this desert, no upsurges of dynamism to quench the mental ego's thirst for life. Disillusionment thus is a double-edged sword; in cutting through the illusions that bind the mental ego to its fundamental project, it simultaneously severs the only tethers by which the mental ego is anchored in the world.

2. The deanimation of the self-concept. The loss of the world entails the loss of the self-concept, because the self-concept is founded upon the world and is inextricably a part of it. The self-concept is the mental ego's *self-in-the-world*. It is the mental ego's self as defined and justified in terms of worldly facticities. Hence, when alienation renders the world remote and unreal, it does the same thing to the self-concept. The mental ego's withdrawal from the world initiates a process of disidentification from its being-in-the-world; in other words, the derealization of the world carries with it a deanimation of the self-concept.

The deanimation of the self-concept brings the mental ego to perceive itself (i.e., its worldly self) in the same way that it perceives others. Like everyone and everything else in its derealized world, the mental ego sees itself as flat and dead. The mental ego senses that it is no longer a real person in a real world, but rather only an assemblage of traits, habits, routines, and roles that are played out on a lifeless stage. Just as the mental ego now sees other people only as facades without foundations, so, too, it sees itself as but a set of poses. It therefore ceases to believe in itself, to take itself seriously, for it has become only a disguise, a mask.

It is an interesting fact that in coming to perceive itself in this way, the mental ego gains self-knowledge that it did not possess before. The self-concept is for the most part and for most people an unknown. Under usual conditions, it is a part of the personal embedded unconscious. It becomes evident, as a rule, only when artificial means are employed or when exceptional circumstances obtain. By artificial means are meant such things as psychotherapeutic intervention, meditation, or some other type of disciplined self-reflection. And by exceptional circumstances are meant such things as abrupt or traumatic life transitions, decontextualization, or alienation.

The reason why alienation works to reveal the self-concept is that, in derealizing the world, it impedes the expression of the self-concept and hence draws attention to it. The self-concept is dishabituated and thrown into relief. Moreover, the self-concept is not just rendered visible in this way; it is made frustratingly conspicuous. This is because the embedded structures that constitute the self-concept, in being impeded, fail to achieve effective contact and connection with the world. Instead of achieving engagement, they tend either to fall dead or to become unmanageable caricatures of their former selves. They become wooden or unwieldy, and, consequently, they also become glaringly evident. Alienation disallows the mental ego any longer to *live* its self-concept, and the self-concept is therefore thrown up before its sight. As Hegel observed, "The owl of Minerva spreads its wings only with the falling of the dusk" (1952, 13). So long as the mental ego lives the self-concept, it does not know the self-concept. But as soon as the mental ego, in dying to the world, begins also to die to its selfhood-in-the-world, then, too late, it attains self-knowledge.

The alienated mental ego's heightened self-knowledge (combined with its total ineffectiveness in action) is the source of a thoroughgoing ambivalence, which is directed both toward the mental ego itself and toward others. The alienated mental ego prides itself in its disillusionment, its self-insight, and, in general, its "wisdom," yet it also despises itself for its utter uselessness to the world. And turning to others, the alienated mental ego holds them in contempt for their blindness, their lack of reflective self-awareness, yet it also envies them for their engagement and effectiveness in the world. As Dostoevsky's underground man puts it, the man of the world is stupid but strong while he, the underground (alienated) man, is wise but abjectly weak. The alienated mental ego is privy to a wicked disjunction, which it takes to be an inescapable truth: Those who do, do not know, and those who know cannot do.

The alienated mental ego experiences the loss of the self-concept as self-loss. Since, as we know, the self-concept is the mental ego's adopted being, the inability any longer to live the self-concept, to *be* it, carries with it the feeling of loss of being per se: death. The alienated mental ego feels as if it were undergoing an irresistible process of dispossession leading in the direction of complete paralysis (inability to act) and death (inability to be). The alienated person is dying; in Kierkegaard's terms, his "sickness" is "unto death."

3. Encounter with the shadow. So long as the mental ego lives the self-concept, the shadow remains securely contained as part of the repressed unconscious. But when, consequent upon alienation, the self-concept is deanimated, the shadow, simultaneously, is derepressed—and it rises into view, subjecting the mental ego to a host of unwelcome self-insights.

The alienated mental ego thus is afflicted with much gnashing of teeth and many stings of conscience. It sees through its rationalizations and deceptions and confronts the dark side of its personality. Having already been disillusioned of the world, the mental ego is now disabused of its illusions about itself. It is jolted into a rude awakening and brought to what must seem the worst of all possible situations—though there is worse to come. It is brought to the position of seeing *through* the illusions of the world and of the self-in-the-world *to* (what seems like) the exclusive reality of the shadow. The mental ego now encounters those features of the personality that it has shunned. And without the self-concept to fall back on, it cannot help but think that these shadow elements constitute the real and whole truth of itself. Having been dispossessed of the self to which it was attached (the self-concept), the mental ego is now forced to own, entirely and exclusively, the self that it has not wanted to be (the shadow). To say the least, this is a trying period for the mental ego.

But it does not last for long. For the shadow is also a part of the world; it is an alter-ego-in-the-world. Consequently, the alienation of the world entails an eventual alienation of the shadow, too. But the shadow must first be acknowledged before this can occur. Hence, the typical sequence is (1) loss of world, (2) concomitant deanimation of the self-concept, (3) consequent emergence of shadow, and then, finally, (4) deanimation of shadow.

It is a fact of some irony that the mental ego, after being shocked and dismayed upon first witnessing the shadow, actually begins to cling to the shadow as soon as it begins to slip away. The mental ego, it turns out, would rather be something that, in its eyes, is humiliating or perhaps even evil than not be anything at all. Dostoevsky's underground man gives forceful expression to this frame of mind, too (Kaufmann 1956, 66):

Oh, if I had done nothing simply from laziness! Heavens how I should have respected myself because I should at least have been capable of being lazy; there would at least have been one quality, as it were, positive in me, in which I could have believed myself. Question: What is he? Answer: A sluggard; how very pleasant it would have been to hear that of oneself! It would mean that I was positively defined, it would mean that there was something to say about me. "Sluggard"—why, it is a calling and vocation, it is a career.

This curious attachment to the shadow indicates that of the two desiderata of the mental-ego's fundamental project, being and worth, it is being that is the more important. The mental ego, after suffering the loss of its self-concept, is willing to sacrifice all sense of worth and justification just in order to preserve some vestige of being-in-the-world. Being the shadow is better than not being at all. But being the shadow is not a long-term possibility. For the shadow, too, is in time deanimated by the process of alienation.

4. Alienation and anxiety. The existentialists have made the point that anxiety is the basic mood of the alienated condition. The alienated mental ego experiences acute anxiety, and for several good reasons, as we shall now see.

First and foremost, of course, the alienated mental ego experiences the loss of the world and, even more, its own death with great alarm, even panic. No matter how hard the mental ego tries to re-establish contact with the world and to resuscitate its selfhood-in-the-world, it cannot, and thus it is subject to repeated and intense bouts of anxiety. Speaking of the alienated person, Waltraut Stein (1967, 270) says:

> And in a very real sense he is dying, as he feels less and less like a real person. This sense of dying can come upon him slowly or suddenly. In either case, panic is possible at any time, should he catch a glimpse of complete dispossession, of death. Then he feels totally disorganized and runs "every which way."

The alienated mental ego has been cut off from the world and is in the process of losing its footing in being. It is in a deeply unsettling, indeed terrifying, predicament.

Occurring in conjunction with the mental ego's anxiety over loss of being is an anxiety over loss of justification. These go hand in hand because the self-concept is, for the mental ego, the basis of both its sense of being and its sense of worth. Therefore, the deanimation of the self-concept deprives the mental ego not only of its being but also of its reason or justification for being. And to add insult to injury, the emergence of the shadow, which follows upon the deanimation of the self-concept, finally dashes all of the mental ego's airs of specialness and value. The mental ego is forced to see the many unseemly aspects of its personality and consequently is decisively relieved of its pretensions of distinction, if not grandeur. In sum, the mental ego is dispossessed of both being and justification, and it is highly anxious over both of these losses—though, as just noted, it is most concerned about the loss of being.

But the situation is a bit more complicated than this, for lurking behind the anxiety over loss of being is the more basic anxiety of "nothingness," and lurking behind the anxiety over loss of justification is the more basic anxiety of original guilt or sin. The former anxiety of each of these pairs is, in fact, the mental ego's fear of losing that which shields it from the latter anxiety of each pair. That is, the anxiety over loss of being is the mental ego's fear of losing the *surrogate* being of facticity and identity (i.e., of the self-concept and then the shadow), which, if totally lost, would leave the mental ego completely exposed to its "nothingness." And the anxiety over loss of justification is the mental ego's fear of losing the *fabricated* justification of distinction and reputation (enshrined in the self-concept), which, if totally lost, would leave the mental ego completely exposed to its guilt. The process of alienation divests the mental ego of its disguises and rationalizations, and, in doing this, it forces the mental ego eventually to confront its innermost self, its "nothingness" and guilt or sin.

The process of alienation leads inexorably toward "nothingness" and guilt. At first it does so through a withdrawal from the world, carrying with it a concurrent erosion of worldly being and value. During this phase of the process, the mental ego, as it were, backs its way toward "nothingness" and guilt without acknowledging them directly. Still unheedful of its deepest fears, the mental ego here remains focused on the world and the loss of worldly being and justification. This outer focus, however, can be maintained only up to a point, since the withdrawal from the world eventually runs out of ground. There arrives a point at which the self-concept (and even the shadow) is completely beyond redemption, leaving the mental ego without any trace of worldly being or worth to cling to. At this point the mental ego can no longer postpone the inevitable, and so it begins, anxiously, to make an about-face. It begins the uneasy process of looking forthrightly at itself, of facing its "nothingness" and guilt.

The apprehensions caused by loss of being and justification together with those associated with "nothingness" and original guilt or sin are perhaps the anxieties that are most basic and central to the alienated condition. But there are other anxieties that also are inherent to this condition. For example, the mental ego's encounter with the shadow must be counted as an anxious, or anguishing, ordeal, as the mental ego is forced to see, and then accept, all manner of unnerving truths about itself. It is stung time and time again by negative self-insights, and it shudders in view of what it now reluctantly accepts as its "true" self.

The alienated mental ego also suffers from an anxiety over freedom—or at least it does so during the early stages of its withdrawal. This species of anxiety is what Sartre (1956) calls the vertigo of possibilities, since it is the experience of being dizzied by the radical open-endedness of life, the unlimitedness of one's choices and chances. This problem arises in the context of alienation because the separation of the mental ego from its self-concept reveals to the mental ego that it is not limited to being what, as a matter of fact, it has been. In becoming conscious of the self-concept, and then in ceasing any longer to be it, the mental ego grasps that its own nature is not an ironclad given but is rather an infinite set of possibilities. It sees that its actions, and even its very being, are unsettled issues—issues for which, moreover, there are innumerable answers.

The mental ego is thus suddenly awakened to the vastness of its life horizons. And this awakening is not a happy one, since the mental ego lacks the strength needed to look out upon these horizons in a positive manner. The mental ego is not in a position from which it might boldly re-enter the world and formulate new meanings and forge new facticities for itself. It is rather in a position of weakness. It is powerless to do anything in pursuit of new possibilities, since it is cut off, disoriented, and paralyzed. The mental ego's newfound possibilities therefore do not appear to it as opportunities at its command, but rather as perils and pitfalls that it is helpless to forestall. The alienated mental ego is afraid of its newfound possibilities. It is assailed and overwhelmed by them. The discovery of radical freedom is not, then, for the alienated mental ego, a cause for celebration; it is rather a cause of vertiginous anxiety.

Accompanying this anxiety of freedom is a corresponding anxiety of responsibility—since responsibility rests upon and is a function of freedom. The magnitude of responsibility is a function of the scope of freedom: the wider the scope of freedom, the greater the magnitude of responsibility. And the character of responsibility (i.e., whether it is experienced as something positive or negative) is a function of the character of freedom: a happy freedom is a welcome responsibility and a dreaded freedom is a burdensome responsibility. Now, we have just seen that, for the alienated mental ego, the scope of freedom is suddenly widened without limit and that the character of this expanded freedom is negative. It follows then— and it is true, in fact—that the alienated mental ego experiences its responsibility as being at once great and oppressive. More specifically, the alienated mental ego relates to its responsibility as to a burden from which there is no relief. Like Sisyphus—a favorite figure among existentialist writers—the alienated mental ego feels as if it were condemned to bear a heavy weight without any chance of recess or remission. Fully cognizant of its present actualities and future possibilities, and utterly disabused of all rationalizations and self-deceptions, the alienated mental ego has no excuses for what it is and does. It alone shoulders the responsibility for its existence, even for its world (in the phenomenological sense of the term). And it trembles under the weight.

5. *Despair*. The mental ego's inability to stem the tide of alienation deprives it of hope and brings it finally to despair. Despair signals that all recourses within the mental-egoic system have been exhausted. It signals that the world is irrevocably lost and that the self-concept (and shadow, too) is completely defunct, beyond all possibility of reanimation. It signals that the mental ego has been totally dispossessed. Depair, that is, indicates that alienation has run full course and that the mental ego has arrived at its nadir. This nadir point—at which there is no world and no self—I will call *zero point*. Despair, then, is the state of mind of the mental ego at zero point.

Having lost the last part of its worldly being and justification, the mental ego at zero point is on the verge of encountering its "nothingness" and guilt. But it avoids this as long as possible. It tries again and again to repossess the world and to re-enliven the self-concept, even long after it knows that such efforts are in vain. However, the encounter with "nothingness" and guilt cannot be postponed indefinitely. The simple fact is that despair is unendurable. Consequently, the mental ego is eventually led to try *anything* that might relieve it of its condition, even to face its worst fears about itself. Despair is relentless; it pushes the mental ego ever closer to the brink, from which, finally, the mental ego leaps: it concedes its "nothingness" and guilt and reaches out for help. But this gets us a bit ahead of ourselves.

6. *"Nothingness" and guilt*. The only hope for the mental ego at zero point lies in accepting its "nothingness" and guilt, where by *acceptance* is meant not just a cognitive avowal but a complete realization-plus-assimilation, a complete insight-plus-working-through. But such acceptance, understandably, is an extremely difficult thing for the mental ego. Just how difficult is indicated by the fact that the mental ego sometimes refuses to accept its "nothingness" and guilt not only (1) after learning that the world and the self-concept cannot be repossessed, but even (2) after being repeatedly exposed to the fact of "nothingness" and guilt, and even (3) after coming to realize that only the acceptance of this fact can possibly bring an end to despair. The mental ego, as it were, sometimes continues to float new loans on its existence even after it knows full well that it is bankrupt, and even after it knows that only a confession of bankruptcy can save it from disaster.

Taking denial to these lengths is, of course, utterly perverse. But as Kierkegaard (1954) recognized, such perversity is not uncharacteristic of the despairing ego. In Kierkegaard's view, denial of this sort—which he terms demonic defiance—is a frequent precursor of the leap of faith. It frequently happens that the mental ego chooses to spite itself rather than save itself—just in order to continue to be itself. What a curious thing the mental ego is!

But despair is unremitting. It gradually wears the mental ego down until, finally, the mental ego has no energy left with which to avoid the truth. Reaching this juncture, the mental ego at last quits its denials and submits itself to the inevitable: it accepts its "nothingness" and guilt. And in doing this, the mental ego undergoes a radical conversion. It yields its own (false) ground and reaches out for (genuine) support. It lays down its precious autonomy and prays for guidance. It relinquishes its last defense and bares itself to powers from beyond. Or in our terms, it lets go the false support of original repression and thereby opens itself to the Dynamic Ground. This conversion, if and when it occurs, marks the end of the first stage of regression in the service of transcendence, and the beginning of the second.

STAGE TWO: ENCOUNTER WITH THE PREPERSONAL UNCONSCIOUS

The difficulties experienced during the first stage of regression in the service of transcendence are primarily problems of dispossession, problems dealing with the loss of the world, of being, of justification, and so forth—and also with the anxieties and despair incurred by these dispossessions. In contrast, the difficulties experienced during the second stage are, in a sense, primarily problems of *possession*, that is, problems resulting from the fact that the mental ego, now destitute and defenseless, is taken possession of by forces of the prepersonal unconscious. Since virtually the whole of the mental-egoic system is antagonistic to these forces, it is nothing short of cataclysmic for the mental ego to be taken in tow by them. The mental ego rests on original repression, on the negation of underlying physico-dynamic life. Thus when, by confessing its "nothingness" and guilt, it loosens the bonds of original repression, the mental ego opens itself to the fury of the return of the repressed. It is drawn into the stormy underworld of the prepersonal unconscious and laid siege to by the liberated power of the Dynamic Ground.

Let us now consider some of the phenomena characteristic of the second stage of regression in the service of transcendence.

1. *Black holes in psychic space.* The mental ego maintains its internal dialogue so long as the mental-egoic system remains intact, i.e., closed to the Dynamic Ground. This internal dialogue continues no matter how disillusioned, dispossessed, and despairing the mental ego might be.[5] However, once original repression gives way and, consequently, the Dynamic Ground is opened, interruptions in the internal dialogue begin to occur. And these interruptions are not periods of restful, better yet serene, silence; they are rather moments of trancelike blankness, moments during which the internal dialogue is extinguished by the infiltration into consciousness of heavy currents of energy. To use a simile, these interruptions are like encounters with black holes in psychic space. The mental ego feels as if in the presence of an

oppressive gravity that draws the mental ego, inwardly and downwardly, toward a dreadful unknown.

Wilson Van Dusen has described these black holes, which he has observed in his clinical practice with psychotic patients. He reports (1958, 218-19):

> In the hole one feels one has momentarily lost one's self. What one intended is forgotten. What would have been said is unremembered. One feels caught, drifting, out of control, weak.
>
> These holes and blank spaces are important in every psychopathology . . . . In every case they represent the unknown, the unnamed threat, the source of anxiety, and the fear of disintegration . . . .
>
> It is extremely important to know what people do when faced with encroaching blankness. Many talk to fill up space. Many must act to fill the empty space within themselves. In all cases it must be filled up or sealed off.

Van Dusen believes that these black holes are potentially restorative and creative wellsprings, and that there is really nothing to fear from them. For example, he says (1958, 219):

> The findings are always the same. *The feared empty space is a fertile void. Exploring it is a turning point toward therapeutic change.*

Van Dusen has put his finger on an important phenomenon. But he has not, I think, properly assessed it. Specifically, his view that yielding to these black holes in all cases brings about positive change is too optimistic. For this view overlooks the real risks involved in submitting the ego to the deep unconscious, i.e., to the nonegoic pole of the psyche in its repressed and arrested, "pre-" form. This is not to say that the nonegoic pole of the psyche is never a source of creative and healing upwellings—since in its "trans-" expression, it is, I believe, precisely this. However, in its status as the deep or prepersonal unconscious, the nonegoic pole should be regarded as presenting definite dangers to the ego, even to the ego that, strong and mature, is ready for regression in the service of transcendence.

This point can perhaps be stated more effectively by distinguishing three different types of void states or conditions, namely, (1) the dead void of the mental-egoic system, (2) the violent void of the derepressing prepersonal unconscious, and (3) the fertile void of the nonegoic pole of the psyche in its "trans-" expression.

The dead void of the mental-egoic system is "dead" because, owing to original repression, the egoic sphere is sealed from the power of the Dynamic Ground. The dead void is the uncharged subjective expanse in which the mental ego's internal dialogue takes place. The dead void disappears once original repression gives way, since this opens the ego to the Dynamic Ground and, therefore, to an underlying realm of experience that is alive with energy, and with physico-dynamic potentials generally. Now, admittedly this underlying realm, the nonegoic pole of the psyche, is *potentially* an upwelling fertile void. At first, however, this realm is experienced by the ego as the very opposite of a fertile void. For the first consequence of lifting original repression is not a peaceful infusion of the egoic sphere but rather a violent conflict between the ego and physico-dynamic life, which here, in arrested, "pre-" form, recoils upon its repressor. Consciousness is deluged with highly charged materials, which disconcert and derange the ego. These materials at once erupt upon the ego from below and pull the ego down, well "over its head," into nonegoic depths. Accordingly, the ego is drawn into a protracted conflict with nonegoic life, a conflict which begins to abate only after the majority of nonegoic potentials have been derepressed and the majority of egoic resistances to nonegoic life have been dissolved. The lifting of original repression can thus lead the mental ego into a confrontation with genuinely dangerous forces. It confronts the ego with the violent void of the derepressing prepersonal unconscious.

The dead void, then, is initially replaced by a violent rather than a fertile void. Again, it is true that this violent void is capable of becoming a fertile void, i.e., a regenerating and inspiring wellspring. But before this can happen, the ego must first weather the storm of the return of the repressed. And there is no guarantee that the ego will survive this storm, that the ego will successfully negotiate the heroic odyssey or "journey to the other side." Therefore, if the ego is to undertake this journey, it should do so with caution. But this is just to say that the ego should be careful before it capitulates to black holes, since these holes, as accessways to dynamic depths, lead immediately to the violent, not the fertile, void.

In sum, black holes are accessways between consciousness and the prepersonal unconscious. They are the first points at which the power of the Dynamic Ground burns through into the mental-egoic sphere. They are festering concentrations of psychic energy that magnetically draw the mental ego away from its worldly involvements and lead it toward its repressed underlife, which is a perilous unknown. Black holes therefore should be explored only by the ego that is ready for "the journey," regression in the service of transcendence.[6]

2. Dreams of cataclysm and apocalypse. Along with black holes, the beginning of the second stage of regression in the service of transcendence is characterized by dreams of disaster and destruction. Images of the apocalypse may emerge in dreams at this point. This is because the mental ego senses that its existence is seriously undermined: original repression, the mental ego's terra firma, is giving way and is on the verge of collapse. The mental ego fears that its situation is dire and is plagued by a mood of doom and by dreams of catastrophic happenings. The mental ego fears that its world is nearing an end, and so the mental ego dreams of ultimately terrible events.

Images belonging to this archetypal complex and their likely meanings are: (1) images of falling or crashing—which mean that the ego no longer stands on firm ground and is liable to fall through into the psychic underworld; (2) images of downward-sucking vortices, transfixing abysses, and sirens of death—which mean that the ego is now exposed to the underlying Ground and to its magnetic and entrancing effects; (3) images of earthquakes, volcanic eruptions, and other violent upheavals—which mean that the psychic underworld, the prepersonal unconscious, is no longer safely contained and is on the verge of breaking through into consciousness; (4) images of floods, violent seas, and raging infernos—which mean that repressed forces are astir and that the ego has begun to sense their destructive potential; (5) images of dark skies and stormy weather—which mean that the mental ego's whole being is threatened (dark skies) and that its subjective atmosphere is electrically charged with the power of the Ground (stormy weather); (6) images of a great clash with the power of evil—which mean that the egoic system is about to be besieged by its nemesis, the forces of the unconscious; (7) images of wild beasts with wanton appetites, especially oceanic and subterranean monsters (e.g., the dragon, behemoth, kraken)—which mean that the id is about to emerge from its nether lair; (8) images of blood, feces, and filth—which mean that the rawest and rudest aspects of life are about to break loose; and (9) images of darkness, plague, and death—which mean that the ego is beset with the mood of doom.

These images form a diverse array, but common to them all is the motif of a siege by forces of darkness, which siege augurs the end of the world and death.

3. From anxiety to dread. We have seen that anxiety is a feeling state characteristic of the first stage of regression in the service of transcendence. The mental ego suffers from anxiety because it is in the process of losing its worldly identity and justification and because it suffers from a sense of overwhelming possibility and unbearable responsibility. Anxieties such as these continue throughout the first stage of regression in the service of transcendence and frequently carry over into the second stage. Also, at the beginning of the second stage, a new form of anxiety appears, an intense anxiety signaling dire psychic emergency. The emergency, of course, is the breakdown of original repression and consequent upsurge of the power of the Ground. This crisis situation sets off massive alarms and triggers every defensive resource of the mental-egoic system into hyperactivity. The mental ego responds with violent anxiety as it discovers that it has suffered a deep psychic wound and is defenseless in face of unknown forces.

The commencement of the second stage of regression in the service of transcendence does not, then, bring the mental ego any relief from anxiety. However, as serious as anxiety is at this turning point, it does not long remain the chief, or the worst, of the mental ego's feelings. For anxiety now begins to be eclipsed by a new feeling: dread. To be sure, the mental ego continues to suffer from anxiety throughout the second stage of regression in the service of transcendence. But in general, anxiety tends to take a back seat to dread during this stage. And it does so not because the causes of the mental ego's anxiety are eliminated, but rather because the mental ego now comes into the presence of an awesome and eclipsing power, the power of the Dynamic Ground. The anxieties of worldly loss, and even those of psychic damage, are muted once the mental ego confronts the *mysterium tremendum*.

Dread and anxiety are very different. Anxiety is a generalized fear reaction. With anxiety, the heart beats faster, adrenalin flows, perspiration breaks out on the brow and palm, and the fight-or-flight reaction is triggered—even though, sometimes, there is no discernible or real danger at hand. But with dread, in contrast, rather than alarm and preparation to act, there is instead a sense of being immovably in the grip of something alien, of being overawed and stopped in one's tracks by ominous forces. Also with dread, rather than palpitation and heated perspiration, there occur instead such reactions as chills, clamminess, bristling sensations, gooseflesh, and hair raised on end. Hence, whereas anxiety signals mobilization for defense, dread attends the rapt perception of the eerie, ghastly, or strange.

Dread is distinctive of the second stage of regression in the service of transcendence because, during this stage, the mental ego's overall experience is shot through with a seemingly alien power, the power of the Dynamic Ground. This power infiltrates the mental ego's inner space, causing bizarre sensations and disconcerting states of mind. The power also projects itself upon the mental ego's outer world, shrouding it and making it forebodingly and grippingly mysterious. Everywhere the mental ego turns, it encounters things bathed in an aura that is at once uncanny and fascinating. The mental ego is thus entranced in the midst of its experience, which is pervasively strange. And so it experiences dread. In sum, whereas anxiety is alarm in face of the dangerous, dread is entrancement in face of the strange.

4. From alienation to estrangement. Just as flatness is the main feature of the world during the first stage of regression in the service of transcendence, so strangeness is the main feature during the second stage. This strangeness, although pervasive and emphatic, is not something easily described, since it is a quality that is both subtle and global, and therefore virtually ineffable. Strangeness does not involve an alteration in the specific natures of things in any conspicuous way, yet it does involve an alteration in the general "look" and "feel" of things. Although in one sense it seems as if nothing in the world has changed, in another sense it seems as if the whole world is entirely, and ominously, new. If in the first stage of regression in the service of transcendence things become *unreal*, losing their old sense and meaning, in the second stage they become *surreal*, acquiring a new, eerie, and as-yet-uncomprehended sense and meaning.

Strangeness is a matter not only of ineffable differentness but also of heightened or exaggerated reality. The power of the Ground, which is now the atmosphere of the world, affects things not only by imbuing them with eerie newness but also by enhancing and magnetizing them, making them thereby strikingly vivid and compellingly alluring. The power of the Ground supercharges the atmosphere of the world, and consequently everything in the world is amplified in its qualities and rendered hypnotically fascinating in its effect. Everything is endowed with a stunning potency and an entrancing depth. In becoming strange, then, the world changes in a twofold way: it becomes both surreal and superreal. A strange world is at once disarmingly different and prepotently alive. In short, a strange world has the character of a dream.

This comparison is to be taken literally. For, I suggest, the surreal/super-real quality shared by the strange world and the dream is due in both cases to the saturation of experience with the power of the Dynamic Ground. Ordinarily, the energy of the Ground is locked within the prepersonal unconscious and therefore is available only during sleep and dreams. The opening of the Dynamic Ground, however, liberates this energy from the confines of the unconscious and allows it to enter and pervade the egoic sphere. Consciousness is supercharged with numinous energy, and, consequently, waking experience is endowed with the eeriness and superabundance characteristic of dreams. And, I might add, waking experience is also rendered dreamlike at this point in that, for some, there arise in consciousness full-bodied, lifelike images. The emergence of such images indicates that the autosymbolic process, which normally operates only during dreams, has become active within the field of consciousness.[7]

Thus far two parallels have been established, namely, (1) that dread is to the second stage of regression in the service of transcendence what anxiety is to the first, and (2) that strangeness is to the second stage what flatness is to the first. To these, a third parallel can now be added, namely, that *estrangement* is to the second stage what alienation is to the first. In the first stage, anxiety and flatness are manifestations of the general condition of alienation. In parallel fashion, in the second stage, dread and strangeness are manifestations of the general condition of estrangement.

Estrangement, like alienation, involves the general relation of a subject to a setting, and therefore to a world. Alienation, as explained earlier, is the process whereby the mental ego, in suffering disillusionment, withdraws energy and interest from the world and thereby reduces the world to a mere two-dimensional setting. Estrangement, in contrast, is the reverse process whereby the mental ego, in undergoing deep regression, floods an alienated setting with energy and affect and thereby reanimates that setting, transforming it into a strange new world. Alienation involves a retraction of energy and, consequently, a desiccation of the world and a concomitant loss of interest in the world. Estrangement, in contrast, involves a resurgence of energy and, consequently, a re-enlivening (indeed, haunting) of the world and a concomitant renewal of interest (indeed, fascination) in the world. In short, whereas alienation is the process of flattening derealization, estrangement is the process of haunting re-realization.

5. Disruption of the personality. The second stage of regression in the service of transcendence is a time during which the mental ego's personality is again put to the test. Having already "died to the world" in the first stage, the mental ego in the second stage suffers a breakdown of its most basic protective system and is exposed to volatile materials arising from the deep unconscious. It is at once stripped of all defense and set upon by powerful forces.

A major difficulty here is that the mental ego is liable to be overrun by a host of irrational fears that derive from its wounded and estranged condition. Examples of such fears are the "psychiatric" apprehensions that one is going insane, that one is being possessed by an alien force or entity, that one is transparent to other people, and that one is being conspired against or manipulated by mysterious persons or powers. In light of the mental ego's highly altered condition, it is understandable that the mental ego would be concerned about its sanity, or possible insanity, and that it would be uncertain about who, or what, is in charge of its inner life. Regression in the service of transcendence is in many respects a psychotomimetic process, and to the person undergoing the process it may seem less like a semblance of psychosis than like psychosis itself.

Also included among the fears that can prey upon the mental ego at this point are a variety of infantile terrors that, long since outgrown, now spring back to life. Prime examples of such childhood fears are those of darkness, ghosts and other lurking presences, strange people, and haunted places. Without operative defenses to contain them, and with additional energy to enlarge them, these fears can assume sizable proportions, sometimes becoming debilitating fixations or phobias.

Fears are not the only feelings to disrupt the personality. Given the amplifying effect of the power of the Ground, together with the mental ego's weakened condition, virtually any feeling can grow large enough to create difficulties. Even feelings that have never before caused problems (e.g., minor embarrassments, irritations, tensions, enthusiasms) can become strong enough to be distressing. And what were powerful affective currents or undercurrents can become overwhelming waves of emotion. The mental ego during the second stage of regression in the service of transcendence is awash in feelings, old and new, and it is powerless to control them, better yet contain them.

Another way in which the personality is adversely affected is that ingrained habits and dispositions are disturbed.[8] This happens in part because the power of the Ground supercharges embedded routines and throws them out of their proper pace and rhythm. These "circuits" of the personality are overloaded with energy and thus made to operate in a wild manner, or not at all. It takes time for the personality to accommodate the increased energy intake, and, until such time, the personality tends to operate out of control. Embedded structures are also disturbed because many of them, having been party to the mental ego's repression of the Ground, are therefore targets for the derepressing power of the Ground. The uprising power of the Ground opposes, and overthrows, all of the ingrained ways in which the mental ego is disposed to resist or otherwise stand against the Ground. And as the power of the Ground asserts itself in this fashion, it subjects the mental ego's personality to considerable stress and strain.

In fine, the mental ego's personality is disrupted in a variety of ways during the second stage of regression in the service of transcendence. It is set upon by irrational fears; it is deluged with powerful waves of emotion; and it is charged beyond capacity, and sometimes violently counteracted, by the power of the Ground. The mental ego suffers both an outbreak of uncontrollable affect and a breakdown of many established structures and dispositions.

6. Disruption of mental processes. Mental processes are disturbed as well by the injection into consciousness of the power of the Ground. The main reason for this is that the supercharged atmosphere of psychic space interferes with the mental ego's ability to conduct operational thought. Specifically, the potent concentration of energy has the (magnetic) effect of inducing the mental ego into states of entrancement or empty abstraction and the (amplifying) effect of stimulating the mental ego to a degree that renders it unable to manipulate thoughts in a clear and collected way. Mental detachment and control are not totally lost during this period, but they tend to be exceptions to the rule. For the most part, the mind at this point tends to be either cloudily absorbed or wild and intractable.

Concomitant with the disruption of operational thought, there also frequently occurs a violent awakening of intuition. The power that asserts itself upon the mind jolts the ego out of the active or operational mode and throws it forcibly into a posture that is at once passive and open. The ego is stopped in its tracks and is made a captive witness to a flood of insights. These insights can be of any type, but in most cases they are unwelcome insights into the raw impulsions and primitive complexes that belong to the physico-dynamic sphere in its prepersonal organization. The whole of the unconscious, including its deepest levels, here empties itself into consciousness, and the ego has no choice but to look on, for it is in thrall. Moreover, the ego is impassioned by the intuitions that now besiege it, as these intuitions arrive with great force and effect. They are astounding disclosures which sometimes cause the mental ego to twinge, wince, or gulp its breath. The energy supplied by the Dynamic Ground intensifies cognitive experience generally, which tends on the discursive side to be uncontrollably aroused and on the intuitive side to be stunningly impactful.

This awakening of intuition sometimes involves a reactivation of the autosymbolic process and, consequently, a reappearance within consciousness of spontaneously produced and highly realistic images. The autosymbolic process is our chief creative faculty, and it is therefore potentially an extremely important contributor to human cognition. However, on those occasions when it re-enters consciousness during the second stage of regression in the service of transcendence, this process almost invariably has a negative effect. For at this point the images forged by the autosymbolic process, arising as they do from the prepersonal unconscious, usually take the form of the mental ego's deepest fears and most forbidden fantasies— "diabolical" tortures or temptations (*makyo*). They present themselves as frightening or alluring apparitions. In other words, they assume the character of virtual hallucinations.

One other alteration in mental functioning that can occur at this juncture is that the ego can be thrown into seriously deranged states of mind. These states are extreme cases of the mental absorptions and agitations mentioned a moment ago. They are states of morbid vacancy and frenzied effusion. The former of these two types of state is a condition of mental darkness. It is a condition of denseness, immobility, and blankness of mind—which can be compared to being caught in a psychic black hole. And the latter type, in complete contrast, is a condition of riotously overflowing ideation and affect, of mania and confusion. The state of morbid vacancy indicates that the mind has been taken in tow and is held in traction by the gravitational pull of the power of the Ground. The incoherent effusions, in contrast, indicate that the mind is exposed to the eruptive upsurge of nonegoic potentials. Deranged states like these are extreme in nature and may well be quite rare. Nevertheless, they are possibilities inherent to regression in the service of transcendence, possibilities which must therefore be included in a complete account of that process.

7. Activation of prepersonal spheres: The body-unconscious. The release of energy from the Ground reawakens the body and reactivates the physico-dynamic potentials that heretofore had constituted the body-unconscious.

An initial sign of the "resurrection" of the body is that there can occur a variety of bizarre physical symptoms. These symptoms, like the deranged states just mentioned, may be quite rare, appearing only in cases of abrupt or powerful awakening. Nevertheless, these physical phenomena are well known in the yogic tradition, in which they are called *kriyas* (purifications).[9] According to the yogic conception, the arousal of the latent power *kundalini* (i.e., the opening of the Dynamic Ground) sets off a flow of energy in the body which, in encountering impediments to its circulation, gives rise to unusual bodily sensations and reactions. Included among the effects that are frequently reported in the yogic literature are: (1) passage of energy currents through the body; (2) impulsion to assume strange bodily positions (*asanas* and *bandhas*); (3) sudden alterations in the breath, especially periods of cessation (*prana-yama*); (4) snapping and popping sensations; (5) spontaneous stretching and tensing of muscles; and (6) a variety of involuntary movements and vocalizations.

I suggest that these phenomena occur because the energy released from the Dynamic Ground is inhibited in its ascent by what remains of the physical infrastructure of original repression. The movement of the power of the Ground is impeded by a multitude of petrified tensions and constrictions, and the collective resistance of these obstructions causes the power of the Ground to feel like a heavy energy current or a thick, slow-moving liquid. Also, the movement of the power of the Ground is at certain points blocked by specific obstructions, and, when these obstructions finally collapse or dissolve, there occur the more discrete and dramatic phenomena just mentioned. The long-term results of this process of physical opening are probably entirely beneficial. They include a dismantling of body armor, a straightening of posture, and a development of atrophied muscles and occluded nerve pathways. Nevertheless, when the process first begins, the mental ego is understandably perturbed. For it must seem as if the body were suddenly taking on a life of its own, indeed an alien life working in strange and disconcerting ways.[10]

Occurring in conjunction with the "resurrection" of the body is the reawakening of bodily experience generally, which once again, as in the earliest years of life, becomes polymorphously sensuous. Actually, *polymorphous sensuousness* is not the best term here because it misleadingly suggests that the ego has once again become completely at home on the level of concrete physical existence. However, the fact is that during the second stage of regression in the service of transcendence, although the body has begun being "resurrected," the ego has by no means been "reincarnated," at least not fully or happily. To the ego, which is still basically the *mental* ego, the "resurrection" of the body perforce appears as a foreign and unwelcome process. Since, by this point, the ego has long fancied itself to be an essentially immaterial entity, it cannot help but consider the reawakening of the body to be an alien affair, an affair in which it, the ego, has no part. As we shall see, the "reincarnation" of the ego—i.e., its reidentifying reunion with the body—does not really commence until regression in the service of transcendence is over and regeneration in spirit begins.

But if the ego considers the reawakening of the body to be an alien affair, it nonetheless is drawn to the manifold new sensations that it now experiences. The body, energized and sensitized, tantalizes the ego, and the ego finds it extremely difficult to resist the body's enhanced magnetic appeal. Accordingly, the ego, despite its antiphysical metaphysics and morality, is susceptible to being beguiled and swept off its feet. Indeed, it frequently loses its head (literally!) and plunges into voluptuous sensations. It gives way to engrossments and sensuous delights—only later to return to its cerebral heights, and to experience dismay. At this point, then, the ego's experience is not yet polymorphously sensuous in the true meaning of the term. The ego is still a mental ego, but it is an ego that is on the verge of re-embodiment.

Also occurring together with the recrudescence of bodily life is the amplification of experience generally. We have already seen how the resurgence of the power of the Ground, in supercharging the egoic sphere, disrupts the personality and interferes with mental processes. It can now be added that the resurgence of the power of the Ground has similar effects in other sectors of experience as well. For example, the intensification of physical sensations renders them distracting, if not tormenting. The enhancement of perceptual qualities (e.g., lights, sounds, odors) renders them harsh and garish. And in general, all of life's stimuli are inflated and made more acute. Such stimuli may at times be exceptionally beautiful and moving. But an unceasing barrage of stimuli of such an intense sort can be more than the ego can tolerate. The ego, which has just lost the protective shielding of original repression, is frequently overwhelmed by the power and profusion of its experience. The person undergoing regression in the service of transcendence is hypersensitive, and for this reason it is sometimes advisable for him to seek out a low-stimulus environment.

8. Activation of prepersonal spheres: The instinctual-archetypal unconscious. Although there is no hard-and-fast order in which the levels of the prepersonal unconscious are returned to awareness, it usually hapens that the deeper, instinctual-archetypal levels appear after the initial reawakening of the body. Accordingly, having just discussed the "resurrection" of bodily life, let us here discuss the reappearance of these deeper levels.

One of the most perplexing aspects of regression in the service of transcendence, especially for those who have approached it from the point of view of a puritan ethic or an ascetic spiritual practice, is the arousal of the instincts, particularly those of sex and aggression. For someone who has condemned or attempted to conquer the instincts, it is an unpleasant surprise when sexual and aggressive impulses are stirred into activity. These impulses are nothing new, of course, as sex and violence are in many ways staples of human experience. But with the opening of the Dynamic Ground, they tend to become completely explicit and distressingly importunate.

There are many spiritual aspirants who, upon encountering the instincts in awakened form, have become convinced that, despite having striven for God, they have succeeded only in delivering their souls into the clutches of the devil. Evelyn Underhill (1961, 392) describes the case of St. Catherine of Siena:

> Where visual and auditory automatism is established [i.e., when the autosymbolic process is reactivated], these irruptions from the subliminal region often take the form of evil visions, or of voices making coarse or sinful suggestions to the self. Thus St. Catherine of Siena . . . was tormented by visions of fiends, who filled her cell and "with obscene words and gestures invited her to lust." She fled from her cell to the church to escape them, but they pursued her there: and she obtained no relief from this obsession until she ceased to oppose it.

Another striking example, this one from the East, is provided by Swami Muktananda (1978), who in the initial stages of his *kundalini* awakening was repeatedly visited by an apparition of a beautiful woman who, completely naked, enticed him to break his vow of chastity. No amount of effort could banish this apparition from mind. Only after Muktananda's guru told Muktananda that the experience was a necessary part of his spiritual growth did the perplexing experience finally come to an end. Only at this point did Muktananda realize that the apparition was an expression of the divine power at work within him.

It has been observed many times that spirituality is curiously intertwined with instinctuality and, consequently, that spiritually sensitive people are prone to suffer contradictory attitudes toward the appetites. Specifically, spiritually sensitive people are liable to suffer approach-avoidance ambivalences toward the appetites, frequently striving toward complete abstinence while at the same time being plagued with hedonistic impulsions. This phenomenon, I propose, can be understood in light of the instinctual organization that original repression imposes upon the power of the Ground. This explanation is suggested because, given the instinctual organization, it follows that access to spiritual power must at the same time involve some contact with the instincts. Original repression forces spirit to keep the company of the instincts, and it therefore requires the same of anyone who would keep the company of spirit. This, of course, is not to say that there is any *essential* relation between the power of the Ground and the instincts—that Freudian theme was rebutted in an earlier chapter. It is rather only to say that there is a paradoxical *developmental* overlapping of the two.

This peculiar juxtaposition of spiritual and instinctual possibilities is a source of acute conflict for the mental ego. Every time it opens itself upwardly to spirit, it feels the downward pull of the instincts. It is fundamental to the mental ego's system of beliefs that spirit and the instincts are complete opposites, yet the mental ego now discovers that it cannot aspire to the former without simultaneously involving itself with the latter. This is a wicked dilemma, and there have been many spiritual seekers who have suffered extreme anguish because of it.

It should be mentioned that regression in the service of transcendence seems in some cases to trigger instinctual systems deriving from prehuman strata of the psyche. The literature on *kundalini yoga*, for example, reports many experiences that are strikingly mimetic of the behavior of lower animal life, e.g., hissing like a snake, roaring like a lion, neighing like a horse, jumping like a frog, and bristling like a cornered beast of prey. And Stanislav Grof (1975) reports cases of LSD-induced regression that seem to intersect with very early stages of our phylogenesis. It is a bit of a paradox that the move toward integration, which aims at the apex of human actualization, would lead to such evolutionary reversals. But integration, as the term implies, is the unification of the totality of human resources. If anything were omitted, no matter how primitive, integration would not be complete.

Turning from the phylogenetic to the ontogenetic side of the instinctual-archetypal unconscious, the chief consequence of the opening of the Dynamic Ground is that the ego/Great Mother interaction is set once again in motion. This happens because the ego is here confronted anew with the power of the Ground, which it last experienced, during the pre-egoic period, as the inner aspect of the Great Mother. To be sure, this second confrontation differs from the original encounter in significant ways, namely, (1) in that the ego now clearly knows the distinction between the inner and outer sides of the maternal principle: it does not, as did the body-ego, conflate inner Ground and outer mothering parent, and (2) in that the power of the Ground is now associated not only with instinctual life generally but, since puberty, with the sexual and aggressive instincts more particularly. However, even with these important differences obtaining, the ego is still inclined to perceive the power of the Ground in maternal form. For the fact that the ego first experienced the Ground as an essential dimension of the Great Mother system predisposes the ego thereafter to perceive the Ground as possessing a basically female and maternal character.[11]

In re-encountering the power of the Ground, then, the ego has the experience of renewing its relation with the maternal principle. Moreover, given its long-standing negative stance toward nonegoic life, the ego has the experience more specifically of renewing its relation with the *negative* side of the maternal principle: the Terrible Mother. The ego finds itself once again in face of an abysmal, dark-dreadful-doomful-devouring reality. This awful female presence is in many respects similar to the Terrible Mother experienced years ago by the body-ego. But there are the two major differences just mentioned: this new Terrible Mother is not confused with a specific human person and she is intimately associated with the sexual and aggressive instincts. Unlike the old Terrible Mother, this new Terrible Mother is not an outer or material presence but is rather exclusively an inner, psychic or spiritual reality. She is a malevolent goddess, not a human being. Although she manifests herself in personal form, she is not embodied in any specific human person. And also unlike the old Terrible Mother, this new Terrible Mother is a rudely instinctualized (i.e., lascivious and rapacious) being—in all of her forms of manifestation: personal, animal, and elemental. Accordingly, in her personal form, she is not just a wicked witch but also a harlot; in her animal guise, she is not just a devouring monster but also the heinous beast of the abyss; and in her elemental form, she is not just unfriendly waters, fires, and winds but also raw currents of lust and thirst for blood.

In its encounter with the resurgent power of the Ground, the ego is thus liable to be assailed by apparitions of the instinctualized Terrible Mother, e.g., Kali, Mara, Medusa, the whore of the apocalypse. The ego finds itself once more in a life-and-death struggle with the power of darkness. The ego's existence hangs in the balance; should the ego lose this struggle, there is a real chance that it will die: ego death, psychosis. The ego therefore fights with every resource at its command to free itself from the ominous force that it confronts. It tries desperately to shore up old defenses and, if at all possible, to reseal the Ground. But the ego finds that these efforts do not work, and, in fact, that they are counterproductive, causing its adversary to grow in size and fury. Digesting this discovery, the ego eventually realizes that, in combating the Terrible Mother, it is really only hurting itself. And, in time, the ego also realizes why this is so, namely, because it is somehow related to the Terrible Mother as to a larger part of itself. The ego, that is, arrives at the insight that its adversary is not something inherently alien and evil, but rather something that only appears such because it has been alienated and condemned. For these reasons the ego at last concludes that it cannot—indeed, should not—continue to struggle against the power that has set upon it.

This is a momentous decision, which saves the ego from disaster. Putting this decision into practice, the ego reverses its stand. It ceases being the hero who would slay the dragon—that, after all, was the role of the body-ego—and becomes the knight of faith, the hero who submits himself to the awesome power of the dragon so that, through an atoning death, spiritual rebirth can be earned. The ego, therefore, quits its fight and flight and begins instead to surrender and return to the underlying sources of its being. It capitulates to the beast, allowing the beast thereby to vent its accumulated rage. And as the ego does this, it finds that the beast eventually becomes tame (the instincts are pacified) and that, more generally, the instinctualized Terrible Mother is slowly transformed into a goddess of love and light (libido is transformed into spirit). But this is to anticipate later developments, for the pacification of the instincts and the emergence of the power of the Ground as spirit signal that the ego has made the turn from regression in the service of transcendence to regeneration in spirit.

Before this turn can be made, the ego must suffer many encounters with the terrible maternal power. This power is strong and dark, and it repeatedly captures the ego. The magnetism of the power of the Ground draws the ego deeper and deeper into the abyss, and the solvent action of the power disintegrates the ego time and time again. The ego is fearful that it will be drawn into the abyss to a depth from which there is no escape, and therefore that it will be completely engulfed and destroyed.

It sometimes happens that the ego is destroyed. Regression in the service of transcendence aborts and degenerates into regression pure and simple. This is the supreme risk of the Way, which accounts for the many resemblances between madness and mysticism. Both the madman and the mystic have been cast upon the sea of the prepersonal unconscious. The difference is that the mystic's ego is seaworthy whereas the madman's is not. Thus, the mystic arrives safely at the other side of the sea, finding, thereby, safe Ground from which integration can be achieved, while the madman capsizes and falls into psychosis.

CONCLUSION

Regression in the service of transcendence is the first phase of a thoroughgoing psychic reorganization. Specifically, it is the negative or destructive phase that clears the way for the building of a new order. Egoically, it is the phase during which the mental ego is shorn of its false sense of being and value, is disabused of its illusions of sovereignty within the psyche, and is submitted to its underlying Ground. Dynamically, it is the phase during which the psyche is turned from a repressed and imploded system into a derepressing and exploding one. And structurally, it is a period during which the repressive barrier separating the two poles of the psyche is eliminated and the two poles are brought back into contact, and conflict, with each other. Regression in the service of transcendence is a radical transformation affecting all dimensions of life. It is a process that deconstructs the mental-egoic system so that physico-dynamic life can be liberated and so that, ultimately, the two poles of the psyche can be integrated in a single, perfected psychic whole.

Given that it is such a radical transformation, it is understandable that regression in the service of transcendence would in many instances be a long and agonizing process. But lest I conclude on too dour a note, I should stress that the overall process is probably rarely as grave an experience as the account in this chapter may suggest. For to repeat what was said at the outset, the account in this chapter has presented what I take to be the ideal-typical case. It has described what would happen *if* the mental ego (1) were to undergo complete disillusionment, alienation, and despair, (2) were then unconditionally to accept its "nothingness" and guilt, (3) were then to suffer a total collapse of original repression and, consequently, (4) were then to be entirely engulfed in a violent upheaval of the prepersonal unconscious. In actual fact it is unlikely that regression in the service of transcendence ever unfolds in just this way. Hence the process, although inevitably a protracted ordeal, is rarely fraught with all of the difficulties I have described. Regression in the service of transcendence is a dying to the world and a descent into the unconscious that precede spiritual regeneration, and for some this death and descent is more devastating than it is for others.

CHAPTER 8

Regeneration in Spirit

O NCE REGRESSION IN THE service of transcendence has returned the ego to the Ground, a developmental reversal occurs: the dark night of the soul comes to an end and a period of psychic renewal commences. The period of regressive deconstruction is over and the ego enters a period of transcending reconstruction, a period that, adopting traditional terminology, I will call *regeneration in spirit*. The developmental reversal that sets the ego on this course has been expressed in a great number of symbolic images. Included among these images are, for example, those that depict a transformation of violent waters into life-giving springs and founts, infernal fires into the flames of spiritual purification, raging winds into the breath of life, hell into purgatory, passion into resurrection, and, in general, death into new and higher life.[1]

Among the major historical conceptions of the regenerative process, the one predominant in the West is the Christian account of the new life bequeathed by the Holy Spirit. This new life, symbolized by the water of baptism, is said to be one that completely transforms a person, washing away sins and dispensing graces that are not possible for those in the unregenerate, fallen state. St. Paul, whose life was utterly changed when he was struck down and reborn to a life in Christ, provides for many Christians the paradigmatic example of regeneration in spirit. An alternative conception of the regenerative process within Christianity is found in the Roman Catholic and Eastern Orthodox conception of purgatory, which is held to be the postmortal place or state of being in which one undergoes the purifications requisite for admission to the heavenly kingdom. Purgatory is said to be an eschatological domain or condition in which the soul endures the redemptive transformations needed to cleanse it of residual earthly contaminations and thereby prepare it for the blessings of the celestial estate.

In the West, a second influential conception of the regenerative process is that of alchemy.[2] It is the assumption of alchemy that universal transubstantiation is possible, and in particular that base metals can be transubstantiated into gold and that the fallen soul can be transubstantiated into a soul that is spiritually perfect. The process by which the soul is transubstantiated is conceived differently in different alchemical systems; however, most systems agree that the process has at least the following stages. (1) The soul is subjected to intense inner heat through the practice of rigorous ascetic disciplines. (2) This heat gradually decomposes the soul and reduces it to prime matter—which, according to Aristotelian metaphysics, is the universal matter underlying all distinct substantial forms. (3) Upon being desubstantialized, the soul comes under the catalytic agency of the philosopher's stone or, as it was also called, the elixir (the power of the Ground as spirit) and begins to be reconstituted or transubstantiated. And (4) the process of reconstitution continues until the soul reaches a state of spiritual perfection, that is, until the soul is no longer merely something that is subject to the transforming action of the philosopher's stone but is itself the full and perfect embodiment of the philosopher's stone. The alchemical account of regeneration, then, is one that, like our own, conceives of the regenerative process as being a period of psychospiritual reconstitution that follows upon a period of radical psychic deconstitution.

A third important conception of regeneration in spirit, this one from the East, is that of tantric yoga.[3] According to tantric, or *kundalini*, yoga, the regenerative process begins when the so-called serpent power (*kundalini*) is awakened. This power—corresponding to the power of the Ground in its instinctual and unconscious organization: libido—is said to lie latent at the base of the spine until it is aroused into activity by means of ascetic and meditative practices. Upon being aroused, *kundalini* manifests itself as the goddess Shakti—corresponding to the power of the Ground as liberated spirit—who ascends through a central column associated with the spinal cord (*sushumna*), effecting purifications, stimulating the major psychophysiological centers (*chakras*), and thereby causing extraordinary experiences. The ascent of Shakti continues until the goddess meets her consort, Shiva, at the crown of the head, at which point the yogin is said to experience the highest type of spiritual enstasy. Similar to the Christian and alchemical accounts, tantric yoga conceives of the regenerative process as being one that is carried out by an extra-egoic power or agent as it moves in and through the body. The tantric conception of *kundalini*-Shakti corresponds to the Christian conception of the Holy Spirit, which in turn corresponds to the alchemical conception of the philosopher's stone or elixir. And the tantric understanding of the body as a *sushumna-chakra* system corresponds to the Christian understanding of the body as the temple of the Holy Spirit, which in turn corresponds to the alchemical understanding of the body as the crucible or alembic of the alchemico-spiritual process.

Pauline Christianity, alchemy, and tantric yoga are three of the more important historical conceptions of regeneration in spirit. There are many others besides. I make reference to these systems here not because it is my intention to offer a survey of historical views, but rather to situate the subject of this chapter in the context of historical formulations. The discussion that follows, although indebted in ways to all three of the historical views just mentioned, is not particularly indebted to, or couched in terms of, any one of them. I remain within the framework established in previous chapters and explain regeneration in spirit in terms of the triphasic dialectic of human development.

GENERAL FEATURES OF THE REGENERATIVE PROCESS

Let us first consider the general features of the regenerative process; then we can turn to some of its more specific dimensions.

1. *The calming of physico-dynamic potentials.* The conflict between the egoic and nonegoic spheres that occurs during regression in the service of transcendence consists of a double action. One of these actions is an upsurge of physico-dynamic potentials which, no longer contained by original repression, break free from underlying instinctual regions and erupt into the higher, mental-egoic domain. In this sense, regression in the service of transcendence is like a volcanic upheaval that spews highly energized materials from psychic depths into the stratosphere of consciousness. Occurring simultaneously with this upsurge of physico-dynamic potentials, however, is an equal but opposite downfall of the ego into the prepersonal unconscious, the gravitational pull of which, no longer blocked by original repression, now acts directly upon the ego. In this sense, regression in the service of transcendence is like plunging into an underlying deep, into an abyss seething with sinister forces. The violent conflict between egoic and nonegoic poles occurring during regression in the service of transcendence is therefore both an eruption of the psyche's repressed underlife and a submersion of the ego in this underlife. And this conflict is both of these movements at once, since the regressive return of the ego to nonegoic life is at once an explosive derepression of the latter and a precipitous collapse of the former.

This eruption/submersion ordeal escalates throughout regression in the service of transcendence, since the eruption of nonegoic potentials and the submersion of the ego proceed through ever-deeper and more highly charged levels of the unconscious. The ordeal comes to an end, or at least begins to do so, only when the most ulterior and potent levels of the unconscious have vented themselves and the ego has been pulled to the deepest of the depths. Only at this point does the conflict between the two psychic poles begin to abate and do the ego's prospects begin to look up toward a brighter horizon. This turning point marks the end of regression in the service of transcendence and the beginning of regeneration in spirit. It is signaled in two immediate ways: (1) the ego is released from the abysmal gravity of the Ground, and (2) the violence with which physico-dynamic potentials discharge themselves significantly diminishes.

The ego is released from the gravity of the Ground not because the power of the Ground loses any of its magnetism but rather because the ego finally reaches the bottom of the abyss, and therefore touches Ground. The ego reestablishes contact with the point in the psyche from which the gravity of the Ground emanates. It is re-Grounded, and, consequently, it is relieved of its prior impulsion toward the Ground. The ego continues to be affected by eruptive pulsations arising from the physico-dynamic sphere, but having completed its descent to the Ground, it is no longer subject to the lure of the deep. In the words of Nietzsche's Zarathustra (1966), the soon-to-be overman is at last disburdened of the oppressive "spirit of gravity" and, now rooted in Dionysian depths, begins to climb toward the clear atmosphere of mountain heights.

The release of the ego from the gravity of the Ground is indicated in the disappearance of the morbid transfixions that are symptomatic of the second stage of regression in the service of transcendence. If we remember, the mental ego during this stage is vulnerable to being captured by black holes in psychic space and to falling into blank trances. The mental ego is vulnerable in these ways because the power of the Ground, having infiltrated the egoic sphere, exerts an irresistible magnetism that commands the mental ego's attention, arrests its activities, and holds it fast, as if in the grip of death. The mental ego, caught in this stranglehold, panics and struggles to keep itself from being sucked under. Despite its fears, however, the mental ego is hypnotized by the power of the Ground and thus, paradoxically, is drawn toward the very thing from which it seeks to escape. Morbid transfixions such as these are symptomatic of the second stage of regression in the service of transcendence because this is a time during which the ego is open to but still unanchored in its underlying Ground. Accordingly, the ego does not overcome its susceptibility to these transfixions until it has completed the regression to the Ground and, taking root therein, is released from the Ground's downward gravitational pull.

When the ego is finally released from the gravity of the Ground, it also begins to be treated less violently by resurging physico-dynamic potentials. This happens in part because the most highly charged of these materials have by this time already vented themselves. Coinciding with the ego reaching the bottom of the abyss is the discharging of the most potent strata of the prepersonal unconscious. Another reason for the decrease in violence is that physico-dynamic potentials, in discharging themselves, do not reaccumulate energy. Since the power of the Ground is now no longer restricted to its prepersonal organization, physico-dynamic potentials, in discharging themselves, no longer automatically acquire a new charge. That is, they no longer acquire a new (repressively accumulated) *standing* charge. Consequently, the derepression of these potentials permanently defuses them; it disburdens them not of energy and life, but of the explosive *overload* of energy that hitherto they had borne. This, of course, does not happen all at once. Physico-dynamic potentials remain "hot" and dangerous for a considerable period of time. Nevertheless, the direction of change is clear: regeneration in spirit is a movement away from destructive discharges and toward more peaceful and creative upwellings of physico-dynamic potentials.

The power of the Ground must be distinguished from other physico-dynamic potentials, since, unlike other such potentials, it is not something that, in erupting, can be defused and rendered tame. The power of the Ground *is* energy, the very energy that, prepersonally organized, is accumulated in and then discharged from (other) physico-dynamic potentials. It is that *by* which things are charged, and hence it cannot itself be depotentiated through discharge. The breakthrough of physico-dynamic life into consciousness thus initiates a flooding of consciousness with the power of the Ground that continues long after specific physico-dynamic potentials have made their peace with the ego. The power of the Ground continues to inject itself into consciousness, and the egoic sphere, still resistant to the power of the Ground and unready for its supercharging and inflating effects, is repeatedly thrown into disarray. The egoic sphere is repeatedly burst, the egoic mind repeatedly "blown." And because of these effects of the power of the Ground, the ego's situation remains precarious well into the regenerative period, long after the most volatile layers of the prepersonal unconscious have been defused.

But this problem, too, is alleviated in time. It is so not because the power of the Ground recedes or abates in its flow (the opposite is in fact true), but rather because the flow of this power begins to have a less disruptive impact upon the ego. The ego's residual resistances to the power of the Ground are gradually overcome, and, in being resisted less, this power is able to flow more smoothly and gently, and therefore less destructively, through the egoic system. Also, the ego in time becomes more acclimatized to the heightened charge of its subjective atmosphere, which means that the ego is better able to withstand influxes of the power of the Ground without suffering debilitating overloads to egoic faculties and dispositional circuits. The effect of the power of the Ground remains violent throughout the regenerative period. But this violence steadily diminishes as the ego becomes more receptive to the power of the Ground and better able to tolerate its amplifying effect.

Moreover, there is a point at which the effect of the power of the Ground, although still violent, undergoes a reversal from negative to positive. A turning point is reached at which, specifically, the power of the Ground begins causing raptures rather than ruptures, ecstasies rather than agitations. The power of the Ground at this point still forcibly displaces the ego, but the ego now begins to feel less like it is being "blown away" by that power and more like it is being "carried away," i.e., transported, wildly enthused, spiritually inebriated. The influx of the power of the Ground is still more than the ego can accommodate; the ego is still disconcerted: overloaded, inflated, burst. But this disconcertion is now experienced in a positive manner, as being more purely dynamic than explosive, more creative than destructive, more intoxicating than deranging. This is a turning point at which a change in quantity brings about a dramatic change in quality: a decrease in the violence wreaked by resurging spirit markedly changes the value of Ground-infused states. Although the ego continues to be infused beyond capacity, and although it therefore is still subject to discomposing perturbations and effusions, it now undergoes a fundamental change in its perception of Ground-infused states. It no longer experiences these states as dangerous upheavals and begins instead to experience them as glorious exaltations and overcomings.[4]

This reversal from negative to positive applies not only to the power of the Ground but to all other physico-dynamic potentials as well. All such potentials, in being defused, also in time begin to assume a positive character. They change from adversaries to allies of the ego. For example, (1) the body, which had been a field of newly awakened, disturbing-yet-engrossing sensations, becomes eventually the ego's own polymorphously sensuous life; (2) the autosymbolic process, which had been a fabricator of terrifying or tempting apparitions, becomes eventually a forger of creative visions; and (3) the sexual and aggressive instincts, which had been sources of disruptive impulses, become eventually sources of feelings that fructify experience, enhancing it with sensual allure and assertive drive. These changes are merely mentioned here, since they will be discussed shortly. It suffices at present simply to note that the basic complexion of these, and other, physico-dynamic potentials changes during regeneration in spirit. They decrease in violence and, at a certain juncture, undergo a fundamental transvaluation, changing from dark to light.[5] In sum, then, regeneration in spirit can be said to be at first a *decreasingly negative* experience and then, arriving at the juncture just mentioned, an *increasingly positive* one.

2. The purging of mental-egoic resistances. Regeneration in spirit is a purgative process. It is the process by which all remaining egoic resistances to the power of the Ground are purged and the psyche is transformed into an unobstructed vehicle of spirit. It is the process of agonizing-yet-ecstatic opening that renders the egoic sphere completely receptive to spiritual life. Regeneration in spirit is, then, the necessary interim phase that, following the initial resurgence of nonegoic potentials, forges the conditions of fully integrated existence. In mythico-religious terms, it is purgatory, the halfway station between hell and heaven. So conceived, regeneration in spirit is an essential leg of the soteriological journey.[6]

As a purgative process, regeneration works to overcome the mental ego's defensive self-encapsulation. If we remember, throughout the mental-egoic period the egoic sphere is a self-enclosed domain. The mental ego is the Cartesian ego that has at once retreated *inwardly* (from the public to the private, inner world) and *upwardly* (from the physico-dynamic to the higher, mental plane). The mental ego has retreated from the public domain in that it has withdrawn into the protective confines of subjective space and hides behind a facade of identity. And the mental ego has retreated from underlying physico-dynamic life in that it has buried that life under the cover of original repression and has taken up exclusive residence in the region of the head. In these ways, the mental ego has seceded into its own sphere. It has sealed itself off from both the world without and its own deeper self within, reducing itself thereby not only to an insulated, but to an isolated, state.

Regression in the service of transcendence is the first step in reversing this state of affairs. For the undoing of original repression, which commences the regressive odyssey, suddenly divests the mental ego of its protective coverings. It ruptures the seal by which the mental ego had contained the Dynamic Ground, and, in doing this, it at the same time undermines the false ground on which the mental ego had erected its worldly identity. Hence, the undoing of original repression results at once in an uprising into the egoic sphere of the power of the Ground and a collapse of the facade behind which the mental ego had hidden itself from others. The egoic sphere is suddenly wrenched open and the mental ego is exposed simultaneously to inner forces and to outer view. The mental ego is rudely stripped of its protective insulation; it becomes vulnerable at its core, defenseless against indwelling forces and naked before the public eye.

This process of forcible opening continues to unfold as the turn is made from regression to regeneration. But the process now begins to be perceived differently. It does so because, true to the general pattern of regenerative transformation, the process is one that is decreasingly negative and increasingly positive over time. Accordingly, the opening of the egoic sphere changes by increments from something that is dreaded and resisted by the ego to something that the ego begins both to affirm and enjoy. Specifically, the incursion into the egoic sphere of the power of the Ground changes from something that is experienced as an injurious violation by an inimical force to something that begins being experienced as a rejuvenating and healing influx of grace. And the concomitant collapse of worldly identity changes from something that is experienced as a destructive denuding of personality to something that begins being experienced as a proper purging of impediments to authentic spiritual life. In short, what the ego had perceived as breakdowns, it begins perceiving as breakthroughs, and what it had perceived as vulnerabilities, it begins perceiving as emerging strengths.

This movement of spirit as it forces its way through repressions and breaks down facades is at the heart of the purgative process. Considered in this light, purgation can be seen to be a process that is similar to childbirth, since, like giving birth to a child, purgation is a process by which an emerging life breaks through resistances and is delivered into a new plane of being. Even more closely resembling physical birth, purgation is a process that (1) unfolds by way of alternating dilations and contractions and (2) involves not only agonizing pain but also ecstatic joy.

Purgation begins with dilation. The power of the Ground forcibly opens and penetrates the egoic sphere. Now, assuming that the action of spirit has begun being affirmed, the ego responds to this dilation and penetration in a twofold way. On the one hand, since it affirms spirit, the ego eagerly invites spirit to enter the egoic sphere and assists spirit in the dilation-penetration process. This is the attitude of faith. However, despite its sincere desire for spirit, the ego is still burdened by deep-seated resistances to openness and transparency. Hence, the ego no sooner welcomes the penetration of spirit than, in being touched intimately within itself, it is struck with visceral fear, and therefore contracts. It aborts the birthing process; it cuts short the adventure in faith. But the ego by this point realizes full well its need of spirit, and so in time it resummons courage and begins again to cooperate with the movement of spirit. Consequently, it is again dilated and penetrated, this time more widely and deeply than before. But once again, given its remaining resistances, it contracts in fear, although this time less severely than before. And so the process unfolds. With each succeeding phase the egoic sphere is dilated more widely, penetrated more deeply, and contracts less completely than was the case in the preceding phase. By these steps of the birthing process, then, the ego becomes progressively more open and progressively less resistant to the movement of spirit. Restricting defenses are gradually broken through, facades are gradually dismantled, rigid postures are gradually dissolved, and fears are gradually dispelled. Everything within the egoic system that encumbers the spontaneous life of spirit is gradually purged until, finally, the egoic sphere becomes fully open and transparent, a perfect vehicle-mirror of spirit.

The dilations and contractions of the purgative process correspond in many ways to those of physical labor. But there is a major disanalogy, namely, the order of causality is reversed in the two cases.[7] For whereas in the case of physical labor it is the contractions that (by exerting pressure on the cervix) cause the dilations, in the case of spiritual labor it is the dilations (and ensuing penetrations) that cause the contractions. Contractions are the cause of physical labor; they are but effects—indeed, inhibiting responses to—spiritual labor. This reversal of causality is a noteworthy difference between physical and spiritual labor. But it is a difference that is in no way problematic, since physical and spiritual labor are themselves processes that proceed in exactly reverse directions. Physical labor is an expulsive process, spiritual labor an infusive one. Physical labor is the process by which a baby is delivered from the womb; spiritual labor is the process by which spirit is delivered into the soul. Physical labor is an out-birthing process initiated by contractions; spiritual labor is an in-birthing process responded to by contractions.

As birthing processes, purgation and physical labor are similar in the feelings they evoke. Both are affectively double-edged, involving both agony and ecstasy. In the case of purgation, the penetration of spirit into the egoic sphere is definitely a painful ordeal, especially in the early going. In being forcibly opened and penetrated, the ego feels as though it were suffering a mortal wound, and in this sense it experiences agony: ego passion. But this agony is always tinged with ecstasy, for the wound suffered is, in the words of St. John of the Cross and St. Teresa, a "wound of love."[8] It is a wound that is painful and pleasurable at the same time. Spiritual agony and ecstasy, although opposites, are, then, inherently interrelated; they are paradoxical counterparts. Both are feelings of being too deeply touched and moved, too powerfully overswept, too intensely enswooned. Indeed, the primary difference between the two is in the magnitude of the "too." Agony is, as it were, too, too much whereas ecstasy is simply too much. Both are ego passions, but whereas agony is an ego passion felt to be threatening, ecstasy is an ego passion felt to be liberating and transporting.

Now, although purgation is at first much more an agony than an ecstasy, it is, owing to the intimate interrelation of these two feelings, never merely an agony. It is always also an ecstasy. It is never merely a matter of ego-threatening violence but always also a matter of ego-exalting deliverance. And true to the general trend of regeneration in spirit, it is progressively more a matter of ecstasy and deliverance and progressively less a matter of agony and violence as the process unfolds.

3. The mending of the psychic fissure. Original repression cleaves the psyche; it severs the connection betwen the two psychic poles and restructures the psyche into a dualism of alienated subsystems. The lifting of original repression intiates a reversal of this state of affairs. It re-exposes the two poles to each other and sets them on a collision course of reunion: the physico-dynamic sphere erupts into the mental-egoic and the mental-egoic collapses into the physico-dynamic. Regression in the service of transcendence, brought on by the lifting of original repression, is thus a period when the buffer separating antagonistic opposites is removed and these opposites are thrown into direct confrontation.

The transition from regression in the service of transcendence to regeneration in spirit is the turning point at which the confrontation between the two psychic poles begins to ease and the long-existing fissure separating these poles begins to mend. As we know, in making this turn, the ego quits its struggle against the power of the Ground and begins instead to struggle against its own resistances to the power of the Ground. The ego begins to struggle against its entrenched aversion to physico-dynamic life and begins to invite that life within the egoic sphere. These efforts on the part of the ego contribute to a reduction of conflict and, ultimately, to a reconciliation between the two psychic poles. The ego, in submitting to spirit, facilitates regeneration in spirit, which is a process that heals the breach between the two poles of the psyche.

But the real key to the mending of the psychic fissure is not so much the conciliatory efforts of the ego as it is the action of the power of the Ground. The power of the Ground plays this central role because it is the *common life* of the two psychic poles. Although the power of the Ground derives from the nonegoic pole of the psyche, it is the life force of the psyche as a whole, including the egoic pole. The power of the Ground therefore is at once transcendent and immanent with respect to the ego. Although its point of origin is entirely extra-egoic (and perhaps extrapsychic as well), it has intra-egoic expressions. During the mental-egoic period, the power of the Ground, owing to original repression, expresses itself intra-egoically only in the form of psychic energy. After the mental-egoic period, however, i.e., once original repression has been lifted, the power of the Ground also expresses itself intra-egoically in the form of the spirit that is the ego's higher self. The two poles of the psyche, then, although opposites, share a common life. The power of the Ground is the vital essence of both poles of the psyche, and as such it is the mediating agency by means of which the reconciliation and integration of these poles is accomplished.

Original repression never completely severs the two poles of the psyche from each other. If it did, the egoic pole would be deprived altogether of the power of the Ground, and hence of the psychic energy by which the ego exists and functions. There is a certain quantum of the power of the Ground that must be allowed to enter the egoic sphere even during the period when this sphere is otherwise dissociated from the nonegoic pole of the psyche. However, except for this quantum, the power of the Ground is confined during the mental-egoic period to an extra-egoic, and specifically a pre-egoic (i.e., merely instinctual, unconscious), organization. The power of the Ground consequently has two main, and sharply contrasting, expressions during the period of the mental ego. It is at once libido, the repressed dynamism of instinctual life, and psychic energy, the freely circulating fuel of psychic processes and systems.

Now, this artificial division of the power of the Ground into repressed and free forms cannot stand once original repression gives way. For the undoing of original repression liberates the power of the Ground from its instinctual organization and permits this power to vent itself within the egoic sphere. When this happens, as we know, the ego perceives itself to be under siege by an alien force. However, since the force assailing the ego is the very same force that, as psychic energy, has always been immanent and essential to the egoic system, the ego's battle with this force is in a sense a civil war within the ego's own domain. The ego is in a battle with an opponent that, while appearing "wholly other," is in fact not only "other" (i.e., of extra-egoic, transcendent origin) but also "self" (i.e., immanent and essential to the egoic sphere). The ego in this situation is subject to a simple but dangerous misperception. It misperceives a sudden *increase* in the power of the Ground to be a sudden incursion of a harmful *new* power, and, acting on this misperception, it unwittingly struggles to rid itself of something that is a necessary ingredient of its own life and being. A change in quantity is misperceived to be a change in kind, and this misperception prompts a reaction that, although seemingly self-protective, is ultimately self-defeating.

It follows from this that the ego, without realizing it, battles against its own life force. This is obviously a battle that the ego cannot win, and eventually the ego awakens to this fact and reverses its stance toward the power of the Ground. It quits attempting to re-repress the Ground and begins surrendering to it instead. The ego braves a radical spiritual conversion—and, in doing so, it makes the transition from regression to regeneration, and therefore also from conflict between the two psychic spheres to the mending and integration of these spheres.

The mending of the psychic fissure is thus accomplished by the power of the Ground which, in erupting upon the ego, is finally recognized by the ego as being not only "other" but also "self." The more this power, together with kindred physico-dynamic potentials, is allowed to express itself within the egoic sphere, the more the two poles of the psyche participate in a common life. And the more the ego submits to this life, allowing it to infuse and purge the egoic sphere, the more the two poles of the psyche begin to interact in harmonious and functionally coordinated ways. Remaining antagonisms between the two psychic poles are in this fashion gradually eliminated and a close partnership between the two poles develops. This partnership becomes progressively more intimate until, on the verge of integration, even it is transcended. Then, at this culminating moment, the two poles of the psyche finally become a true two-in-one. The psyche at last becomes a perfected bipolar system.

In fusing, the two poles of the psyche do not lose their distinct, indeed opposite, identities and functions. The psyche continues to possess opposite poles with opposite functions. But these poles are no longer alienated from each other, as they were during the mental-egoic period. Nor are they in collision with each other, as they were during regression in the service of transcendence. Nor are they even any longer in cooperative partnership with each other, as they were during regeneration in spirit. Rather, the two poles are here completely wedded to each other as a single life. Thus, their oppositeness is no longer one of dualistic (alienated, colliding, or even cooperative) subsystems; it is rather an oppositeness of integrated duality. The two poles of the psyche, in being united in spirit, become a *coincidentia oppositorum*.

And this fusion of opposites includes not only the two psychic poles themselves but also all of the specific faculties and potentials that are associated with these poles. Hence, not only does the ego fuse with the Ground to create an all-embracing coincidence of opposites, but the mind also fuses with the body, thought with feeling, logic with creativity, and personality with instinct to create lesser coincidences of opposites. In the case of each of these pairings, a bipole is forged that is greater than the sum of its parts. And each of these bipoles is itself a facet of the bipole of bipoles that is the fully integrated psyche.

SPECIFIC DIMENSIONS OF THE REGENERATIVE PROCESS

Since regeneration in spirit is an integrative process, to discuss its various aspects is, in a sense, to discuss integration itself. In order to avoid needless repetitions, then, it is necessary to divide the labor between this chapter and the next. Thus, rather than discussing regeneration in spirit across all dimensions, many of which would better be discussed under the heading of integration proper, I have here chosen to discuss only those select dimensions which I think constitute the most central features of the process.

1. *The taming of the instincts.* During regression in the service of transcendence, the instincts are inflated to larger-than-life proportions. We have seen that this uprising of the instincts is an unavoidable recoil action. It is an inevitable counterstroke to original repression, which at this point has just given way. Since original repression disallows the instincts their natural expression, and, moreover, since it keeps them superstimulated as well (viz., by limiting the power of the Ground to an instinctual organization), it is understandable that the removal of original repression would lead to an outbreak of instinctual impulses. The lifting of original repression frees the instincts in all of their repressively accumulated power, and it therefore allows them to run rampant and to plague the ego with compelling cravings and urges.

The instinctual catharsis lasts until the instincts have discharged the energy unnaturally stored in them. Then, having spent their energy surplus, the instincts gradually become calm. No longer superstimulated, they assume their natural proportions within the psychic economy. And concomitant with this change in magnitude, the instincts also undergo a change in quality: they are relieved of their negativity and begin to express themselves in positive ways. Like physico-dynamic potentials generally, the instincts express themselves to the ego in a way that reflects the ego's disposition toward them. Accordingly, since the mental ego had alienated the instincts and condemned them as evil, the instincts, mirroring this attitude, had in turn manifested themselves to the mental ego as alien and perverse urges, urges rightly kept in repressive containment (a vicious circle!). However, once the instincts have been loosed and the ego has finally accepted them as its own, then the instincts gradually lose their repugnant character and begin to express themselves in their proper, benign form. Specifically, the sexual instinct begins at times to grace interpersonal encounters with a harmless erotic appeal, and the aggressive instinct begins to strengthen actions with unharnessed will and drive.

The discharging of the instincts signals the beginning of a new dynamic organization. It indicates that the power of the Ground has been liberated from exclusive association with instinctual life and has begun to flow freely through the psychophysical system as a whole. The discharging of the instincts thus is not a merely temporary catharsis that, once finished, gives way to a reaccumulation of energy in the instinctual system. Rather, it is a permanent defusing, which disburdens the instincts once and for all of an unnatural standing charge. This is not to say that the instincts, in venting themselves, become dead. On the contrary, they continue to be systems that are easily aroused in response to appropriate situations and stimuli. However, in remaining excitable, they cease being systems that are stimulated in a chronic, smoldering (repressed) way. They lose the standing charge that hitherto had made them the foci of fixations and compulsions and become systems of experience that, like all others, are at times aroused and engaged and at other times dormant and still.

This new dynamic organization is therefore in no way a noninstinctual, better yet an anti-instinctual, one. The person for whom this new organization is coming into being is every bit as instinctual as before, if not more. But he is not as ambivalently riveted on sex or aggression. The sexual and aggressive instincts remain intact, but they now lose their compelling and wanton character. Indeed, in being disburdened of their standing charge and in being incorporated within the ego's life, the sexual and aggressive instincts become dimensions of truly human experience. They become dimensions of personhood. No longer reduced to mindless impulses, they show themselves to be feelings that, in welling up from the depths, support and enrich civilized life.

This transformation of the instincts of course does not happen all at once. In the early phases of the regenerative process, the ego is still troubled by sexual and aggressive feelings, which themselves are still importunate and threatening. The ego still fears that capitulation to these feelings will cause it to lose its head and to commit terrible deeds. But this fear eventually passes and the instincts, which had been so troublesome, begin to contribute to experience in positive ways. The sexual instinct begins to imbue many personal interactions with an innocent sensuality or "animal magnetism," and the aggressive instinct begins to fortify actions with unhesitating commitment and courage.

The taming of the instincts has been expressed in mythological and spiritual literatures in a variety of ways. The most frequent depiction of the phenomenon is in stories of saints or yogins for whom wild animals have become tame. Wild animals, and especially ferocious predators or primitive reptiles, fittingly symbolize the instincts. The befriending of wild animals by a person of great spiritual power therefore gives effective expression to the kind of instinctual life that emerges through the regenerative process. Among theoretical systems of spiritual transformation, perhaps the most graphic account of the taming of the instincts is the tantric conception of the upturning of the *chakras* that occurs upon the awakening of *kundalini*. It is held (Wood 1962) that when *kundalini* (libido) is awakened and begins its psychophysical ascent in the manifest form of the goddess Shakti (spirit), the *chakras* (i.e., centers of the instincts and of the major affective and cognitive systems) are turned from a face-down to a face-up position. This inversion indicates that the instincts, freed from the onus of original repression, are able to function in the service of higher life possibilities.

2. The reinhabiting of the body. The body is reawakened during regression in the service of transcendence. The opening of the Dynamic Ground looses the power of the Ground, which begins to break through the knots and constrictions of original repression. We learned in the last chapter that in cases of exceptionally intense and abrupt awakening, this breakthrough can give rise to bizarre physical phenomena such as spasms, snapping sensations, and a variety of spontaneous movements and vocalizations. In those instances when the ego is confronted with phenomena such as these, it feels as if an unknown force were working its way through the body, opening the body and returning it to life. To the ego, it seems as if the body were being resurrected from the dead, without ever having died in the literal sense of the term. Moreover, as this happens, there also arise in the body all manner of new sensuous feelings that attract the ego's interest. The body, in returning to life, becomes *aroused*; it pulsates with sensations that beckon the ego to abandon its cerebral perch and dive into physical delights. The ego is drawn to these sensations, and it frequently yields to them, engrossing itself in carnal indulgences. However, the ego is also highly threatened by these sensations, because they rudely disabuse it, the *mental* ego, of its airs of immateriality and entice it to fall to a merely material level of existence.

Just as the "resurrection" of the body is a characteristic feature of regression in the service of transcendence, so the "reincarnation" of the ego is a characteristic feature of regeneration in spirit. During the regenerative period, the ego experiences a reversal in its attitude toward the body and begins a reidentifying return to it. This reversal occurs because of the reversal the ego has already experienced in its attitude toward the power of the Ground. As we know, the ego's hard-won insight that the power of the Ground is truly the ego's own spiritual self rather than an alien and evil "other" brings the ego to make a complete about-face in its stance toward this power. Accordingly, the ego changes its posture from one of resistance to one of receptivity; it begins submitting to the power of the Ground and bidding the power to enter the egoic sphere—indeed, *as* the ego's own life. Now, since the power of the Ground is a reality that is spatially extended and situated, a reality that rises within and circulates through the body, the ego's new stance toward the power of the Ground requires at the same time a new attitude toward the body. If the power of the Ground is the ego's higher self, and if the body is the home of the power of the Ground, then it follows—and the ego, notwithstanding its deep-seated Cartesianism, is forced to conclude—that the body is also its, the ego's, home. By submitting to the power of the Ground, then, the ego at the same time commits itself to eventual re-embodiment. The ego thus in time concedes its corporeality; it drops its airs of immateriality and commences a reidentifying return to bodily life. The body having been "resurrected," the ego now allows itself to be "reincarnated." It returns to the body as the temple of its own spiritual life.

Two of the more important ramifications of the ego's "reincarnation" are (1) that the ego becomes more "earthy," less "heady," and (2) that the ego is re-established in polymorphously sensuous life.

During the mental-egoic period, the center of gravity of life is located in the head. The mental ego, dissociated from the body, has stationed itself in the uppermost regions and conducts life from an elevated, cerebral standpoint. To be sure, the body, in being repressed, does not become a completely insensate appendage; it continues to be a source of physical sensations. But these sensations usually are not of an irresistible or compelling sort. Moreover, in good Cartesian fashion, they are experienced by the mental ego in a disconnected way, namely, as sensations *of the body*, not of the mental ego. It is the body that experiences bodily sensations; the mental ego merely registers them, typically with some anxiety and only at safe remove.

The head ceases being the center of gravity of life once the body is reawakened and the ego, in yielding to spirit, begins to reinhabit the body. At first, during regression in the service of transcendence, the ego simply falls from its elevated station and plummets into the abyss of the prepersonal unconscious. This descent into the abyss, however, finally comes to an end. The ego touches Ground (located literally at the seat of the body) and, in achieving contact with this ultimate basis of its being, begins being supported and buoyed by the spiritual power that rises from the Ground. By these means, then, the ego comes to be re-Grounded, and, accordingly, its center of gravity shifts from above to below. The ego, of course, continues to be in charge of mental operations, and it continues to interact with the world through the sense organs located in the head. But in continuing to function in these ways, the ego's existence is no longer limited to the area of the head. The ego's existence now extends throughout the body, and it has its anchor point in the lower bodily regions.

Concerning this new anchor point, Kapleau (1967, 67) relates the following anecdote about a well-known Zen roshi:

> Harada-roshi [1870-1961], one of the most celebrated Zen masters of his day, in urging his disciples to concentrate their mind's eye...in their hara [the source of vital energy located in the lower body], would declare, "You must realize...that the center of the universe is in the pit of your belly"!

Harada-roshi is here voicing a view that is central to Zen: the soul is rooted in the seat of the body, in the *hara* or *tanden*.[9] The enlightened person is one who knows this truth, who *lives* it. The enlightened person therefore is one who is firmly planted at the base of things and whose fundamental character is of an earthy, visceral, and hearty, rather than airy and cerebral, sort.

The reinhabiting of the body also brings about a return to polymorphously sensuous life. This happens because the ego's reidentification with the body is at the same time a reowning of bodily sensations, which in being adopted by the ego, assume a more intimate and friendly character. Thus, unlike what was the case during the mental-egoic period, bodily sensations are here no longer distant and dim. And unlike what was the case during regression in the service of transcendence, neither are they frighteningly inflamed and alluring. Since the ego has already descended from the heights and is now becoming accustomed to life on the physical plane, the sensations of the body are no longer either as remote or as threatening as they used to be. They have become, or are in the process of becoming, expressions of the ego's own life. Consequently, the body now constitutes a field of sensuous experience in which the ego is increasingly at home and in which, increasingly, the ego can operate without radical dislocation or self-loss.

The ego does not become completely rerooted in the body until full integration is achieved. During regeneration in spirit, then, although the ego becomes progressively better attuned to bodily life, it is still liable to be buffeted about by physical sensations. Physical sensations continue to distract the ego and still occasionally capture it, coercing it to submit to somatic ecstasies. But these problems are not serious, nor for that matter even unpleasant, and in any case they are surmounted as the ego becomes more settled on the bodily plane. Once the ego's re-embodiment is complete, physical sensations cease being a cause of difficulty. The ego becomes fully attuned to embodied existence. It becomes intimate with all of the sensations of the awakened body without being threatened or dominated by any of them. In other words, it becomes polymorphously sensuous.

3. *The harnessing of the creative process.* We learned in the last chapter that regression in the service of transcendence is typically attended by one or more of the following types of disturbances to mental functioning: (1) disruption of operational thought, (2) besieging intuitions, (3) virtual hallucinations spawned by the autosymbolic process, and (4) states of mind such as vacant trances and wild effusions. With the exception of vacant trances, all of these disturbances continue into regeneration in spirit.[10] However, in continuing, these disturbances change in a way that conforms to the general pattern of the regenerative period: they become decreasingly negative and, then, increasingly positive over time.

The disruption of operational thought results from the sudden injection of the power of the Ground into the egoic sphere. The ego is unaccustomed to the magnetic and amplifying effects of the power of the Ground and consequently is prone to episodes of absent-mindedness and agitation. This, at any rate, is what happens initially. However, as regeneration unfolds, the effects of the power of the Ground upon the ego change in a favorable manner. For the longer the ego is exposed to the power of the Ground, the stronger the ego becomes and the better able it is to conduct itself at an elevated energy level. Accordingly, in the course of time, the ego tends to be affected less negatively, and then more positively, by its heightened dynamism. In growing accustomed to its new dynamic circumstances, the ego is able to operate more effectively within those circumstances. Eventually, it even begins to be facilitated rather than disconcerted by its quickened charge. For example, the magnetism of the power of the Ground begins to induce contemplative absorptions rather than mindless abstractions and the amplifying effect of this power begins to supercharge rather than overwhelm operational thought.

The ego is besieged by intuitions during regression in the service of transcendence because it has been disarmed, thrown from an active to a passive posture, and forced to observe the airing of the submerged unconscious. The unconscious becomes conscious, and the ego has no choice but to witness the display. This resurgence of repressed materials lasts throughout the ego's regression to the Ground. Then, as the turn to regeneration in spirit is made, it begins to taper off. The ego undergoing regeneration of course continues to be struck by insights arising from psychic depths, but its captive witnessing of *derepressing* contents is for the most part over. Moreover, because the ego grows in strength during regeneration in spirit, it begins to regain control of its cognitive posture. That is, it is no longer helplessly pinned down in the posture of passive openness. It is no longer merely a defenseless onlooker. It is rather in a position in which it can begin to choose which posture it will assume, active or receptive, operational or intuitive. At first, these choices are no doubt fairly ineffectual; the ego's intuitive experiences probably remain at first more a matter of the ego being passive and naked than of it choosing to be receptively open. Nevertheless, as the regenerative process leads toward integration, the ego begins to have better command of its mental stance and bearing. Having been initiated into intuitive life by force, the ego finally becomes able to solicit intuitions at will. It learns how, through receptive openness (and, as we shall see, contemplative absorption) voluntarily to access the creative process.

The images spawned by the autosymbolic process during regression in the service of transcendence resemble hallucinations because, during this period, the autosymbolic process still works in the service of threatening unconscious materials. These materials are at this point in the process of being derepressed, and the autosymbolic process sometimes dramatizes their unveiling by giving them lifelike form. The ego during this period is thus in the curious position of being tormented by its own creative faculties. It is subjected not just to distressing insights into its repressed underlife but also sometimes to a play of realistic apparitions embodying this underlife. The ego is subjected to this perplexing exhibition for a considerable period of time, but not indefinitely. For the contents of the submerged unconscious are eventually fully aired and defused, at which point the autosymbolic process is relieved of duty to forces pitted against the ego and comes into the service of forces friendly to the ego. This transition from dark to light is, of course, the transition from regression in the service of transcendence to regeneration in spirit.

The change in autosymbolic images that occurs here can be described by saying that these images are gradually transformed from virtual hallucinations into genuine visions, i.e., from apparitions of repressed materials into creative visualizations of higher meanings and possibilities. More precisely, since hallucinations and visions are really the outer boundaries of the change, the change itself can best be described as occurring in the intervening territory between these limits. The images of the regenerative period, therefore, although less and less resembling hallucinations, are not yet truly visionary. They are still apparitions, epiphanies of seemingly independent beings, places, and events—which indicates that the ego and the Ground are not yet completely united. But if autosymbolic images still possess the nature of apparitions, they do so in a decreasingly negative and increasingly positive way. They decreasingly depict demons and infernal depths and increasingly depict angels and celestial heights. The images of the regenerative period are progressively more light than dark, more allies than adversaries. They become progressively more "self" than "other" until, finally, as regeneration culminates in integration, they drop their apparitional form and become visions in the strict sense of the term: creative foreseeings of the as-yet-known.

States of mind such as vacant trances and wild effusions also observe the general pattern of the regenerative period.[11] Actually, as noted earlier, vacant trances usually disappear upon the commencement of regeneration in spirit. The ego, upon being regressively reconnected with the Ground, is released from the Ground's gravitational pull, and the ego is thereby freed from the states of heavy inertness that had plagued it. The wild effusions, on the other hand, continue into the regenerative period. If the ego's physico-dynamic underlife ceases being a magnetic abyss, it remains an active volcano. The ego therefore remains liable to explosive outpourings and inflations.

The effusive states that characterize the early phases of regeneration in spirit can still be extremely violent. But in becoming decreasingly negative and increasingly positive, these states are steadily transformed from destructive discharges into states that are creative and composed. Unfolding stages of this transformation are: (1) mental manias—states of explosive discharge that, although not completely incoherent, are seriously intoxicated and disorganized; (2) cognitive raptures—states of spontaneous, unsolicited inflation that, although eruptive, are joyous and creative; (3) induced transports—states of creative infusion/absorption that are triggered by the ego's own mental efforts and that, although unstill and unstable, are more clear and sustained than the preceding raptures; and (4) mature contemplations—states of creative infusion/absorption that are entered by the ego at will and that are at once powerfully concentrated and completely serene, lucid, and composed.

Unlike the blank trance states of the preceding period, the infused states just listed are cognitive states in the positive sense of the term. For whereas the trance states were destitute of cognitive content, the infused states are alive, indeed overflowing with such content. They are avenues through which insights are communicated to the ego. Moreover, since infused states become increasingly coherent, composed, and controllable as the regenerative process unfolds, what happens during the regenerative period is that the ego's capacity for infusion and its ability to pursue intuitive inquiry are gradually merged. The ego's infused states become less agitated and more serenely absorbed, and, concomitantly, its intuitions lose the character of stunning bolts from the blue and become more the ripened fruits of the ego's own absorbed "in-search." The complete union of intuitive and infusive capacities is achieved in contemplative enstasy. The arrival of contemplative cognition indicates that the ego has finally harnessed the creative process.

In sum, regeneration in spirit is a time during which factors that were seriously disruptive of mental functioning become factors that make a positive contribution to mental functioning. It is a time during which potentials that had precipitated a mental breakdown become elements of a higher mental organization. Specifically, it is a period during which dynamic, intuitive, autosymbolic, and infusive/absorptive phenomena, which had broken through into consciousness in ways resembling serious psychopathology, are reassembled on a higher level, bringing into being the highest of all cognitive capacities: contemplation. The subject of contemplative cognition will be taken up in the next chapter.

4. The personalization of spiritual dynamism. It is a basic dimension of the regenerative process that the power of the Ground is accepted by the ego as the ego's own higher life. The ego submits to the power of the Ground and there occurs a wedding of ego and spirit according to which the ego is spiritualized and, simultaneously, spirit is personalized.

The infusion of the egoic sphere brings into being the charismatic or numinous personality. The person undergoing regeneration in spirit becomes a beacon of spiritual power. He is a person whose very presence has a magnetic quality which fascinates people and sometimes binds them in spells. He is a person whose speech has a special command, an arresting sincerity and authority. And he is a person whose actions, although usually performed without fanfare, make a deep impression and bring about significant results. The person undergoing regeneration in spirit does not act by egoic means alone; he is assisted by spiritual power and creative insight. He is then—or, rather, he is on the way to being—a great-souled person, a person who has a commanding effect upon others simply by virtue of the spiritual dynamism that emanates from him.

In saying that spiritual dynamism is personalized, I do not mean to say that it is arrogated by the ego. On the contrary, rather than arrogating spirit, the ego yields to spirit, offering the egoic personality as a vehicle for spirit. At least this is the goal to which the ego has committed itself and toward which it is headed. Along the way, of course, there are a multitude of resistances that have to be overcome. The ego still harbors many ingrained egocentric tendencies—which tendencies are dross yet to be purged from the egoic personality. Consequently, the ego still sometimes balks at the movement of spirit and sometimes tries to appropriate the fruits of spirit, including all of the resources of the psyche's physico-dynamic pole. But such actions on the part of the ego are quickly and decisively punished. The power of the Ground, having already asserted its rightful sovereignty, brooks no misbehavior from the ego. In turn, the ego, having already acceded to the sovereignty of spirit, and having already enjoyed many of the blessings of spirit, accepts such punishments well, realizing that they are the inescapable effects of its own actions and the requisite means of its purgation. Given that the ego is not yet fully aligned with spirit, it is inevitable that the ego would frequently revert to its old egocentric ways. But when it does, it is immediately set straight—and it suffers this correction in good grace.

There are many specific charismatic phenomena associated with the spiritualization of the personality. Mention has already been made of ecstasies and transports, which are particularly distinctive of the regenerative process. To these phenomena can be added a variety of bizarre behaviors that are the outer manifestations of such spiritual intoxications, e.g., ravings of joy and dances of delight. But perhaps the most intriguing of all charismatic phenomena are the extranormal powers that are thought to attend spiritual awakening. These powers, recognized by virtually all religious traditions, are said to include such things as prophesy, healing, clairvoyance, and inspired leadership capabilities.[12] Different traditions have different attitudes toward these powers. For example, in most Indian systems, these powers, the *siddhis*, are considered distractions that can entrap the spiritual seeker and divert him from his proper goal: *moksha* or *nirvana*. In Christianity, on the other hand, miraculous abilities or special spiritual gifts are held to possess prima facie value and are considered worthy of cultivation on the condition that they have a positive bearing on one's participation in the religious community. This at any rate is the teaching of St. Paul in his first letter to the Corinthians. Despite differences like this, however, almost all spiritual systems agree that super-normal powers should be approached with great caution and should always be kept subordinate to spiritual ends. Almost all systems agree that it is important to employ safeguards to keep the seeker from becoming sidetracked or inflated by miraculous powers.

5. *Awe, ecstasy, blessedness, and bliss.* We know that anxiety and despair are states of mind inherent to the first stage of regression in the service of transcendence and that dread and entrancement are the corresponding states of mind in the second stage of that process. To this it can now be added that, during regeneration in spirit, the primary corresponding states of mind are awe and ecstasy.[13] These are dominant throughout the early and middle phases of the regenerative period. Then, in later phases, as regeneration culminates in integration, awe is gradually transformed into the sense of blessedness, and ecstasy is gradually transformed into bliss. The whole regressive/regenerative period thus observes the following parallel unfoldings of mood or state of mind: anxiety-dread-awe-blessedness and despair-trance-ecstasy-bliss.

The difference between dread and trance on the one hand and awe and ecstasy on the other is just the difference between their respective develop-mental stages. Dread and trance indicate that the ego is being overtaken by a force felt to be alien and evil, whereas awe and ecstasy indicate that the ego is being overcome by a force felt to be miraculous and good. Both pairs indicate that the ego is not well aligned with the force that it faces and, therefore, that

that force deals with the ego in a violent manner. Dread and trance reflect the magnetic and gravitational effects of the power of the Ground, which hold the ego in traction. Awe and ecstasy on the other hand reflect the upsurging action of the power of the Ground, which strikes the ego with stunning or dizzying impact (awe) and infuses it beyond the bursting point (ecstasy). Both of these pairs of states of mind reflect ungentle treatment of the ego by the power of the Ground in its capacity as the holy, the *mysterium tremendum et fascinans*. Dread and trance are responses to the negative side of the holy: the dark, the eerie, the demented, the abysmal. Awe and ecstasy, in contrast, are responses to the positive side of the holy: the brilliant, the miraculous, the angelic, the transporting.

Deriving from the physico-dynamic pole of the psyche, dread, trance, awe, and ecstasy all seem to be associated with the autonomic nervous system. The main indication of this connection is that all of these states of mind exhibit the paradoxical hot/cold, fever/chill interplay that is characteristic of autonomic activity.[14] Dread and trance are colder states. Dread involves clamminess and a bristling chill; trance involves frigid inertness.[15] But even these states show signs of the hot side of autonomic activity. For both are versions of the "cold sweats."[16] Both manifest a psychophysiological precipitation that is ordinarily associated with fever. In contrast to dread and trance, awe and ecstasy show a more even balance—or, more correctly, a more evident mixing or alternating—of hot and cold. Awe is breathless astonishment that mixes both perspiration and chill, palpitation and horripilation, and ecstasy is wild effusion that tends to be alternately hot (feverish frenzies) and then cold (weepy deluges). Both pairs of states are paradoxical in the way they bring together opposites. But no member of either pair truly synthesizes these opposites. Such a synthesis, as will be explained presently, is to be found only in the integrated states that succeed awe and ecstasy.

To repeat, awe and ecstasy are violent states. They are stunning impacts or sudden explosions that indicate that the ego is still at odds with the Ground. These states are most violent in the early phases of the regenerative period and then, as the ego is purged and becomes better attuned to the Ground, they become steadily less violent, and more smooth, subtle, and continuous. As the ego becomes better adjusted to the Ground, it is better able to withstand the influx of the power of the Ground without suffering violent arrestment, overinflation, or any other type of incapacitation. The ego is better able to breathe the rarified air of spirit without being dazzled, dizzied, or intoxicated. As the ego is brought into agreement with the Ground, then, such sudden and dramatic effects as states of awe and ecstasy disappear and are gradually replaced by states that reflect a more fluid and gentle movement of the power of the Ground. Specifically, awe is replaced by the sense of blessedness and ecstasy is replaced by bliss.

Blessedness resembles awe in being an immediate I-thou meeting between the ego and the supreme spiritual power. Both are intimate beholdings/touchings of the power of the Ground in its transcendent aspect, i.e., as a spiritual presence that presents itself to the ego from a source beyond the ego's own sphere. Related in this way, awe and blessedness differ in two principal regards. First, as was just explained, awe is abrupt and defacilitating whereas blessedness, of course, is not. And second, awe and the sense of blessedness quite evidently have very different casts. For whereas awe is an ego-eclipsing apprehension of the miraculous or sublime (i.e., the power of the Ground as *mysterium tremendum*), blessedness is a serenely joyous appreciation of the beatific and divine. Awe involves a humbling of the ego, a reduction of it to insignificance in the face of a magisterial power; blessedness in contrast involves an exalting of the ego, which is allowed to share in the spiritual glory of the world. Awe, although primarily a positive state of mind, is still tinged with fear, which implies that the ego is still ambivalent toward the Ground and, therefore, that the Ground is still bivalent in its appearance to the ego. Blessedness, in contrast, is a completely positive state of mind in which the ego, aligned with the Ground, is no longer ambivalent toward the Ground and, therefore, the Ground is no longer bivalent (but is rather wholly positive) in its appearance to the ego. Blessedness as it emerges during the later phases of the regenerative period still has much in common with awe. But as regeneration approaches integration, blessedness is experienced ever more completely and with increasing fidelity to its ownmost nature. Then, as regeneration culminates in integration, blessedness is finally experienced in its full essentiality: it loses all tinge of fear and becomes pure reverential joy.

One other way in which blessedness differs from awe is the way in which blessedness synthesizes the hot and cold sensations contributed by the autonomic nervous system. Whereas awe evidently mixes, without really combining, hot and cold, fever and chills, blessedness fuses these opposites into a single, paradoxical whole. Thus, blessedness is in a sense both hot and cold and in a sense neither; it is a synthesis of opposites. Blessedness is "hot" in that it is a radiant happiness. But it also is "cold" in that it involves an aspect, not of sadness, but of profound gratitude. In its initial emergence, the sense of blessedness usually combines these opposites in an unsubtle way, taking for example the form of tearful rejoicing: crying in uncontainable thankfulness for the goodness, beauty, and perfection of things. But in later, more mature stages of its expression, the sense of blessedness fuses both hot and cold more completely and thereby brings about a more subtle resultant. In the end, as regeneration verges into integration, the sense of blessedness assumes its final form: glowing gratitude, the sense of being divinely favored.

Very closely paralleling the transformation of awe into blessedness is the transformation of ecstasy into bliss. As the state succeeding ecstasy, bliss resembles ecstasy in being an experience of upwelling, expansive happiness. But as has been explained, bliss differs from ecstasy in being more continuous and composed. It does not come in explosive bursts, and it does not involve wild euphorias. Compared with the intoxication of ecstatic states, in fact, bliss would have to be considered a state of sobriety. And so it is. It is a state of clarity and composure. But if bliss is a state of sobriety in this sense, it is not at all a state of sobriety in the other senses of the term. For opposite to the dourness frequently associated with sobriety, bliss is a condition full of good spirit, overflowing with *joie de vivre*. Unlike the mental ego's sobriety, which is gravely earnest, blissful sobriety is calmly exuberant, composedly in the flow of the juices of happiness.

Bliss is a close kin of blessedness; in fact, it is the very same feeling state shorn of its relational, I-thou significance. Whereas blessedness involves an appreciative apprehension/touching of the power of the Ground in its ego-transcendent aspect, bliss is the sheer feeling of the power of the Ground as an inner infusive current. Bliss, one might say, is blessedness merely felt, not meant. Bliss lacks the cognitive facets of blessedness but it shares the same affective composition. Hence, in this latter regard, bliss, like blessedness, is a synthesis of qualitative opposites; it too is a serene (cool) delight (warm). More precisely, bliss is a joy that wells up in the soul, slowly and continuously, and that has the "feel" of a soothing, sweet liquid. The receptacle of the soul runneth over with the waters of life, the power of the Dynamic Ground, and this overflow at once bathes the ego coolly and fills it with a sense of glowing well-being. The ego is assuaged by an inner ambrosial fluid, a fluid that, in rising from the Ground, gently buoys and infuses the ego in its current, and then spills out of the soul in waves of subtle delight. Bliss, like blessedness, combines hot and cold in a way that transcends their contrariety, yielding a paradoxical resultant, a liquid warmth that sets the ego coolly aglow.

Given this paradoxical conjunction of opposites, it is understandable that the chief symbol for bliss would be honey or nectar. Honey possesses almost all of the right qualities. It is a life-giving substance that flows slowly and smoothly and that is both sweet in taste and radiant in color. Honey possesses so many of the right qualities that it is almost a complete symbol of bliss. It is rightly likened to the drink of the gods. The only relevant quality that honey does not possess is cool refreshingness. However, a substance that does possess this quality, along with others essential to the experience of bliss, is milk—which, as *mother's* milk, is in any case already deeply associated with the experience of bliss. Honey by itself, in its warm viscosity, is soothing in a way that suggests sleepy contentment. Milk, in contrast, in its cool moistness, is soothing in a way that suggests rejuvenated alertness. Milk, unlike honey, conveys the higher sobriety of bliss. The perfect symbol for bliss would thus be a substance that combines the relevant features of both milk and honey. It would be a not-quite-viscous, silvery-gold liquid that flows smoothly and that is vitalizing, refreshing, and sweet. Earthly milk and honey only approximate the divine nectar, which is the sap of the tree of life.

True bliss belongs only to the integrated stage of existence. Nevertheless, states progressively closer in nature to bliss occur during the second half of regeneration in spirit. The direction of change during the second half of the regenerative period is away from episodes of ecstasy and toward the even and continuous experience of bliss. Just as blessedness gradually becomes a permanent attitude, so bliss gradually becomes a constant underlying feeling state; it becomes the affective foundation on which the ego's overall emotional life is built.

6. Enchantment and hallowed resplendence. If we recall, flatness (or unreality) and strangeness (or surreality) are the dominant features of the world during the first and second stages, respectively, of regression in the service of transcendence. Correspondingly, enchantment and hallowed resplendence are the distinctive features of the world during the early-to-middle and the later phases, respectively, of regeneration in spirit. These divisions of course are not neat and clean; there is a good deal of overlap and mixture. The divisions do, however, hold for the most part. Hence, the transition from regression in the service of transcendence to early phases of regeneration in spirit is one that is marked by a transformation of the world from an environment that is eerie and alien to one that is miraculous and sublime. And in turn, the transition from early and middle to later phases of regeneration in spirit (leading into the integrated stage) is one that is marked by a transformation of the world from an environment that is miraculous and sublime to one that is sanctified and glorious, of celestial cast and hue.

During the second stage of regression in the service of transcendence, the world is recathected with psychic energy; it is reimbued with the power of the Dynamic Ground—which power is at this point released from the constraints of original repression. This overlaying of power upon the world invests the world with a numinous aura of a surreal, ominous character. The world as a whole and everything in it is suddenly rendered new, in a strange and frightening way. Just as it seems to a person undergoing the second stage of regression in the service of transcendence that he has been possessed by an alien power, so it also seems to him that the world has been haunted by an alien power. The person who, subjectively, experiences dread looks out upon a world that, objectively, is (or seems) uncanny.

Without losing any of its numinosity, the world is in gradual measure relieved of its unnerving alienness once regeneration in spirit begins. For the ego, having already been drawn to the nadir, is at this juncture relieved of the grip of dread, doom, and death, and, concomitantly, the world is relieved of its eerie and foreboding darkness. However, even though the world is brightened in this way, it remains mysterious and pronouncedly "other"—although now in the primarily positive manner of enchantment. The world continues to reverberate with the power of the Ground in ways that are radically unfamiliar and alarming; the world continues to defy comprehension, to be unfathomable, full of hidden depths and meanings. But the spiritual power enlivening the world is now sensed to be basically benign; the world is now sensed to be charmed rather than haunted, awesome rather than dreadful, miraculous rather than menacing. It could be said that the ego in this transitional phase has finally found its way out of the deepest and darkest part of the forest and has entered an enchanted wood.

But the ego is still in the woods. The enchantment of the world, similar to the awe and ecstasy of the subject, reflects early and middle phases of regeneration in spirit. Significant purgations and reconstitutions of the egoic system are still in order before complete ego/Ground alignment, and therefore integration, is established. The enchanted world thus is not the world of the integrated stage. Nor is it the world of later phases of the regenerative process—which are already merging into integration. The enchanted world is rather an intermediate territory, a transitional domain that leads the ego from the alien land in which it had been wandering to its true and final home, the glorious estate of the integrated stage. The enchanted world is the purgatorial accessway from hell to heaven.[17] Beginning at the exit of the underworld, it is a region still darkly shrouded and frighteningly "other"; entering its midspace, which includes its most distinctive terrain, it is a region that becomes miraculous and sublime; then, ascending to its upper reaches, it is a region that increasingly partakes of celestial splendor. The enchanted world is a world that begins haunted and strange, that becomes magical and marvelous, and then, approaching its far boundary, becomes hallowed and resplendent, a supernal sanctuary, a heavenly home.

As regeneration nears integration, then, the world begins to lose its enchantment and begins to take on the qualities of an earthly heaven. The world is disenchanted—not in the sense that it is emptied of spiritual power but rather in the sense that the spiritual power of the world finally loses its last vestiges of darkness, mystery, and foreignness. The world, as intensely alive with spirit as ever, now becomes an effulgent, pellucidly clear, and utterly native domain. The world in this phase ceases being enchanted and becomes *hallowed*; it ceases being marvelous and becomes *resplendent*; it ceases being to any degree ego-alien and becomes *home*. In approaching integration, the ego returns, on a higher level, to its aboriginal Ground, which, no longer the womb of the Great Mother, is now the ego's hallowedly resplendent home.

Hallowed resplendence is the objective correlate of blessedness and bliss. As such, it shares essential features with these states of mind, one of which is the synthesis of qualitative opposites. I have explained how blessedness and bliss fuse hot and cold. Similarly, hallowed resplendence, it might be said, fuses fire and ice. For hallowed resplendence involves both brilliant radiance and crystalline cool. A hallowedly resplendent world is one that is bright without being hot and crisp without being cold. Everything in such a world possesses a lustrous, scintillating quality. It is as if everything were accentuated by a luminous sheen, a sheen that gives things a shimmering aura, translucent depth, sharply enhanced qualities, and vibrant power. In a hallowedly resplendent world, everything gleams with dewy newness and glows with deep, burnished radiance.

Perhaps the chief symbol of resplendence is the sparkling jewel, especially the diamond, which so dramatically synthesizes brightness and coolness, fire and ice. The diamond is utterly translucent and illumined; there is nothing hidden or dark in it. But simultaneously, the diamond is cool to the touch, and its multifaceted brilliance, rather than being blinding, is pleasant to the eye. For these reasons, diamonds—and precious stones and metals generally—are frequently thought to be the building materials of the heavenly city, which is envisioned with jewel-bedecked buildings and streets made of gold or rare gems.

Rivaling the jewel, or the jeweled city, as a symbol of hallowed resplendence is the garden paradise, which is a setting characterized by superabundant life, superreal qualities, and ethereal atmosphere. The garden paradise is an environment pulsating with life; everything in it is fresh and lush, at once virgin and in full bloom. It also is an environment embellished with voluptuous, extravagant qualities, e.g., exploding colors, delicate floral scents, velvety textures. Moreover, the garden paradise is an environment graced with a celestial climate; its atmosphere is lit up and warmed by an equatorial sun and at the same time kept fresh and cool by gentle showers. Finally, the garden paradise is an environment in which all of the flora and fauna exist in the most benign harmony. Even the serpent is a friend (the instincts are tame), and the central tree is a tree not only of knowledge (the ego) but also of life (the Ground). The garden paradise is resplendent in many ways and thus serves as a fitting symbol for the beatified world that begins to open its "pearly gates" to the ego as the ego makes the homeward turn toward integrated existence.

In sum, regeneration in spirit is a period during which the world steadily becomes less foreign and dark, first in the sense of becoming less strange or surreal and more enchanted, then in the sense of becoming less enchanted and more heavenly. The ego gradually finds its way out of the forest it had entered during regression in the service of transcendence. At first it finds its way to an enchanted wood, and then, breaking into the open, it finds its way to paradise. The ego, having been lost in darkness, is at last delivered to its glorious destiny.

It arises from the discussion in this and the preceding section—and the discussion in the last chapter as well—that there are completely parallel alterations in (subjective) mood and in the (objective) tone of the world during regression in the service of transcendence and regeneration in spirit. These are summarized in Table 8-1.

Table 8-1

EGO-MOOD AND WORLD-TONE CORRELATIONS

DISTINCTIVE MOOD OR FEELING STATE OF EGO	PERVASIVE TONE OF WORLD		
INTEGRATION		Permanent	INTEGRATION
Blessedness: Grateful joy; the sense of being favored to live in a beatified world. *Bliss:* Serene delight, supernal joy; power of Ground flows smoothly, thickly, sweetly.	*Hallowed Resplendence:* World is beatified; it is a coolly radiant, superreal spiritual paradise with which the ego is utterly at one.		
TRANSITION TO INTEGRATION		Late	REGENERATION IN SPIRIT
Transition to Blessedness: Beholding of spiritual power of world becomes less arresting, more exalting. Rejoiceful attitude supervenes. *Transition to Bliss:* Ecstatic intoxications subside; higher (joyous) sobriety supervenes.	*Transition to Hallowed Resplendence:* World gradually loses its mysterious otherness and becomes a glorious home.		
ENCHANTMENT		Early	
Awe: Stunning or dizzying encounter with miraculous and sublime. *Ecstasy:* Sudden, wild inflations and transports.	*Enchantment:* World becomes magical, full of higher, unforeseeable possibilities.		
ESTRANGEMENT		Stage Two	REGRESSION IN THE SERVICE OF TRANSCENDENCE
Dread: Hair-raising, bone-chilling encounter with the eerie and alien. *Entrancement:* Morbid, black depressions; ego put in traction by the gravitational force of the Ground (also delirious effusions).	*Strangeness:* World becomes strange, haunted, surreal; world is full of hidden, sinister meanings and possibilities.		
ALIENATION		Stage One	
Anxiety: Fear of losing touch with the world and of losing worldly being and value; vertigo of possibilities. *Despair:* Loss of hope that world can be re-engaged and self-in-the-world reanimated.	*Flatness:* World suffers derealization, becomes phenomenologically flat: uninteresting, meaningless, purposeless.		

CONCLUSION

The regenerative process is of no set duration. But it rarely is finished in a short period of time. Doctrines of sudden enlightenment and instant salvation notwithstanding, the regenerative process normally unfolds over a stretch of years. To be sure, there are dramatic conversions, breakthroughs, awakenings, *satori* experiences, etc., but the potentials that emerge so suddenly during episodes such as these take time to be knit together harmoniously with established egoic structures. The eruption of physico-dynamic life can be abrupt, but the ensuing reconstitution of the egoic sphere and mending of the two psychic poles is typically a long-term process.

It is, however, a process with a happy horizon, since it is a developmental change the direction of which is *away* from suffering and *toward* joy. It is the purgatorial interlude during which the ego is released from hell and brought ever closer to heaven. It is therefore a period during which the ego is confident of its own eventual salvation. Given this confidence, the ego patiently suffers the hardships lying along its path. And in any case these hardships steadily decrease, and blessings increase, as the ego makes progress toward its goal. For the goal toward which the ego is headed is a goal of the progressively actualized, cumulative/culminative sort. Integration is not something that appears suddenly at the end of the regenerative process; it is rather the final realization of that process.

CHAPTER 9

Integration

I N MYTHICO-RELIGIOUS TERMS, the afflictions of hell and the purifications of purgatory are followed by the blessings of the heavenly estate: salvation. In more psychological terms, regression in the service of transcendence and regeneration in spirit are followed by the integrated stage of life. Integration is the culminating stage of human existence. It is the stage at which human nature is finally perfected and rendered whole. Integration is, then, the end, *telos*, of human development. But is should be quickly added that integration, in being the end of human development, is also in a sense the real beginning. For it is only at the integrated stage that a person, having completed human development, can begin living a fully human life. Integration is the end of *becoming* human and the beginning of *being* a complete human being.

DUALISM TRANSCENDED: THE *COINCIDENTIA OPPOSITORUM*

Since regeneration in spirit is the process by which the two poles of the psyche are reconciled and united, it is only upon the completion of this process that the two poles can be said to constitute a true bipolar *system*. Prior to this point, the two poles of the psyche are in antagonistic opposition to each other. It is only at the point of integration that all remaining traces of interpolar friction disappear and the two poles finally begin to interact in a completely unified and complementary way, as sides of a harmonious duality. Or to adopt Jung's terminology, it is only at the point of integration that the psyche becomes a true *coincidentia oppositorum*.

The integrated psyche possesses a great many different facets. Of these, I will here consider only those that are most basic to it in its character as a bipolar coincidence of opposites.

1. Mind-body integration: The ethereal body. The body is "resurrected" during regression in the service of transcendence, and then the ego is "reincarnated" during regeneration in spirit. By these means the mind/body alienation characteristic of the mental-egoic period is overcome and a higher mind/body whole is brought into being. This is a whole that, objectively, is immediately present in outer physical space and that, subjectively, is intimately familiar with inner psychic space. It is a whole that has its anchor in the body and yet is capable of ascending to abstract intellectual heights. And it is a whole that has firm command of mind and will and yet is capable of enjoying the polymorphous pleasures of concrete bodily life. But this much was already said in the last chapter.

What was not said in the last chapter is that, as the transition to integration is made, the ego begins to become aware of itself as having *two* bodies, namely, not only the physical body (which is now awakened) but also an energic or spiritual body, namely, the circulating power of the Dynamic Ground. That is, the ego begins to realize that it is not just a solid substance but also a moving, dynamic one. It becomes evident to the ego that, as an extended being, it is not only the body proper but also the spiritual force that enlivens the body. This second, ethereal body is recognized by most of the world's religions. For example, it is, I suggest, what is meant by the resurrection body (*soma pneumatikon*) in Christianity and the body of bliss in Hinduism (*ananda-maya-kosa*) and Buddhism (*sambhogakaya*).

Issuing from the Ground, located physically within the sexual system, the spiritual force ascends into the body, charging it with a vital current. Much of this force is channeled through a central column associated with the spinal cord: the *axis mundi*, the Tree of Life, the *sushumna*, the staff of the symbolic caduceus. But in addition to this central pathway, there are innumerable subsidiary arteries through which the power of the Ground travels as it moves through the body—e.g., the *nadi* channels which are said to carry the *prana* energy (Indian yoga) and the *mo* channels which are said to carry the *ch'i* energy (Chinese, Taoist yoga).[1] Almost all of these arteries are normally blocked by the many locks and constrictions that make up original repression. These blockages, however, are broken through during regression in the service of transcendence and finally dissolved during regeneration in spirit. By the time integration is achieved, the power of the Ground has free access to the entirety of the body. It moves through the body without obstruction, and as it does so there results not only an awareness of the body being energized but also an awareness of an extended, moving life force at work within the body. There arises not only an awareness of the body *enlivened* but also an awareness of a living dynamism that *enlivens*. The body becomes the temple of spirit, and spirit becomes not only the ego's higher life but also its new, ethereal body.

2. Thought-feeling integration: Conscience. The disconnection of thought and feeling characteristic of the mental ego is gradually overcome during the transitional periods leading to integration. During regression in the service of transcendence, feelings hitherto repressed and contained erupt into consciousness, impassioning the ego. The ego is flooded with feelings, which obscure, if not drown, thought. This state of affairs improves during regeneration in spirit, given the pacification and mending that are inherent to the regenerative process. During regeneration, with thought having already ceased stifling feeling, feeling gradually ceases overwhelming thought. Accordingly, during regeneration there occurs a progressive reconciliation of cognitive and affective life. By the arrival of the integrated stage, this reconciliation is complete, and thought and feeling begin functioning as one: thought becomes spirited and feelings become insightful. Head and heart are united, giving rise to conscience as a fully formed faculty of integrated life.

The integrated person is, then, a person of conscience. He is a person who cannot think about or be witness to something without knowing at once how he feels about it. For the integrated person, feeling is an integral part of thinking or perceiving. To be sure, there are some matters that are more neutral or purely intellectual than others, and the integrated person can be dispassionate in his consideration of these. But for the many matters that bear upon the fortunes or misfortunes of people (or living things generally), the integrated person is by nature concerned and involved. He is immediately affected by such matters. He is pained at the sight of suffering, angered and revolted by brutality, saddened by hatred, cheered by the happiness of others, moved by kindness, and so on. The integrated person is in full touch with his own humanity, and he therefore feels for humanity as a whole. To be witness to another's experience is, for him, to share in that experience. And it can be added that this immediate response on the level of feeling prompts in its turn an immediate response on the level of action. The thinking-feeling unity of conscience is also a unity of thought and action. The integrated person acts unhesitatingly upon the heartfelt insights of his conscience. Hence, it is with respect to the integrated person, and the integrated person alone, that the Socratic equation of knowledge and virtue holds true. It is the integrated person alone who does not suffer from weakness of will, for whom knowledge of the good is a sufficient condition of doing the good. Conscience is a faculty not only of moral knowledge but also of moral feeling and action.

Given that he is so easily and deeply affected, the integrated person is in a sense vulnerable in his emotional life. He has a "bleeding heart": he cannot see, or even think about, the sufferings and joys of other people without experiencing those sufferings and joys himself. This vulnerability, however (if that is the best term), is not usually a liability: it is a naked sensitivity but not really a weakness. For although the integrated person is easily touched and deeply moved, he is rarely overwhelmed by feelings. This is so because, for him, there no longer exists a repressed unconscious at the ready to vent itself should a strong feeling suddenly disarm the ego. Nor is there any longer any antagonism between feeling and thought; feelings now empower rather than obscure or drown thought. Feelings, then, even very strong ones, do not ordinarily affect the integrated person in a violent or disruptive manner. Although easily touched, he is rarely shaken, and although deeply moved, he is rarely swept away in emotional outpourings. To the untutored eye, it may even appear as if the integrated person were unfeeling or uncaring. But this is the very opposite of the truth. If the integrated person's feelings tend not to be loud, the reason is that they are so deep and so true.

In concluding this section, it would be good to stress that conscience is a capacity for positive as well as negative feelings. Conscience is not just a vulnerability, a susceptibility to moral co-suffering. Conceptually, conscience implies only an intimate attunement of thought and feeling; nothing is implied about whether the experience of conscience will be of a positive or negative, pleasant or painful sort. Conscience can therefore be as much a source of joy as of grief. Of course, in unhappy times the integrated person is bound to experience the unhappiness of his fellow human beings. But this does not mean that the integrated person's lot is necessarily, or even usually, an unhappy one. The integrated person sees, and thus feels, both sides of life. Moreover, it should not be forgotten that blessedness and bliss are intrinsic to the integrated stage. The integrated person feels a reverential joy for life and a sweet happiness in living. These feeling states make up the abiding affective basis of integrated existence, over which pass the more temporary pangs *and* pleasures, sufferings *and* joys of conscience.

3. Logic-creativity integration: The tertiary process. Integrated cognition— or, to use Arieti's (1976) term, the tertiary process—is a coincidence of opposites in two main regards, namely, in involving syntheses of (1) operational control and dynamic absorption and (2) logical rigor and autosymbolic creativity. Let us examine these two syntheses and see how they draw upon and integrate the resources of the two poles of the psyche.

(a) Operational control and dynamic absorption. As explained in the last chapter, the effusions and ecstasies characteristic of regeneration are gradually transformed into more composed and controllable dynamic states. Cognitively, this is a transformation that leads from explosive upheavals of ideation to the poised enstasy of contemplative cognition. Contemplation is a dynamic state that is completely harmonious with the ego. It is a state of powerful-yet-lucid absorption in which the ego, although fully open to physico-dynamic potentials and unself-consciously at one with experience, is nonetheless still in command of egoic faculties and operations. It is a state of dynamic enstasy that is also a state of rational and volitional control. Moreover, contemplation is a state that the integrated ego can enter, or rather invite, at will.

The manner in which the integrated ego invites contemplative absorption is quite simple. It does so just by giving concentrated attention to the matter in which it would become absorbed. Such concentration leads to absorption because, given the integrated ego's harmonious alignment with the Ground, undivided concentration has the effect of mobilizing the power of the Ground and channeling it toward the focal datum, which, consequently, is dynamically charged and becomes a cathexis object. As a cathexis object, the focal datum begins to exert a magnetic-absorptive effect upon the ego, educing it from its subjective reserve and inducing it into an objective enstasy. In this fashion the ego, in being able to mobilize the power of the Ground, is able to exercise control over the absorptive state: the ego orchestrates the conditions for its own self-transcendence. The procedure is always the same: (1) the ego gives one-pointed attention to an object (idea, image, feeling, etc.); (2) the power of the Ground follows the lead of attention and flows to the object, charging and magnetizing it; and (3) the ego, responding to the magnetic attraction, allows itself to be drawn to the object and to become absorbed in it as a self-contained phenomenological world.

This dynamic conception of contemplation, I believe, provides the best way of understanding the stages of meditative practice, as for example they are set forth by Patanjali.[2]

If we recall, Patanjali distinguishes between *dharana* (effortful focusing of attention), *dhyana* (easy, continuous one-pointedness), and *samadhi* (absorption, enstasy, contemplation). For the beginning meditator, commencing practice during the mental-egoic period, these three levels of experience mark stages of progress in meditative practice. The person making his first attempts at meditation truly practices only *dharana*. It is all the beginning meditator can do to fix attention on a meditation object without succumbing to distraction or torpor. With continued practice, however, the meditator succeeds in harnessing his attention. He learns how to hold the mind still and remain alert at the same time, and consequently he is able more and more easily to give sharply focused and uninterrupted attention to the meditation object. That is to say, he attains *dhyana*. But now, I suggest, *dhyana* is the highest meditative level to which the mental ego, as mental ego, can attain. The reason for this is that the mental ego, owing to original repression, is cut off from the power of the Dynamic Ground. The mental ego is thus unable by means of concentration to mobilize the power of the Ground in a way that would cathect the meditation object with magnetic-solvent energy. Uncathected, the meditation object does not attract the ego and draw it out of itself into absorption or *samadhi*. Try as it may, then, the best the mental ego can do is to establish an undisturbed inner vigilance. Nevertheless, the attainment of *dhyana* indicates that absorption is imminent; it indicates that, by continued practice, the meditator is on the verge of unsealing the Ground and thereby of coming into direct contact with the power of the Ground. If, therefore, the meditator perseveres in the practice of *dhyana*, it is likely that a breakthrough experience will occur, at which point *dhyana* would be transcended and the meditator would have his first experience of absorption. The meditation object at this point would be cathected with the power of the Ground, and the meditator would cease being detachedly vigilant and would be drawn into a state of fusion with the meditation object. He would enter *samadhi*.

After the original breakthrough experience, a period of mastering absorption ensues. Absorptive states of increasing power, clarity, and control are attained. Patanjali sets forth a hierarchical classification of *samadhi* states along these lines, beginning with the initial levels of unstable object-centered *samadhi* and culminating in the pure and powerful effulgent states just prior to ultimate liberation (*kaivalya*).[3]

Upon achieving control of *samadhi* at a given level of practice, the meditator is able to perform (what Patanjali calls) *samyama* at that level of practice. *Samyama* is absorption entered by means of a rapid and easy transition through *dharana*, *dhyana*, and *samadhi*—which are now successive moments of a single meditative experience rather than, as before, long-term stages of meditative growth. To practice *samyama* on something is, then, to enter it absorptively via a direct *dharana-dhyana-samadhi* route. It is to have command of these three levels of the meditative experience so that they can be employed as a single three-step procedure for achieving contemplative enstasy. And again, the etiology of this procedure, I suggest, is primarily dynamic. It is because the integrated ego is open to and aligned with the Ground that its focusing of attention has the effect of mobilizing the power of the Ground, and consequently of magnetizing the focal object and drawing the ego into a revelatory absorption. Conceived in this fashion, *samyama* is the three-step procedure by which the ego taps the Ground in order to engage in contemplative inquiry.

If contemplative enstasy is usually accomplished with a specific object in mind, this is not to say that such an anchor point is always necessary. Patanjali indicates that objectless enstasy (*asamprajnata samadhi*) is a real possibility, although he allows that this type of *samadhi* is a higher and rarer attainment than is object-centered *samadhi* or, as he calls it, *samadhi* "with support" (*samprajnata samadhi*). In the case of objectless enstasy, *samadhi* is usually achieved by employing, and then dropping, a support.[4] By this means, the power of the Ground is drawn into the ego's subjective space, and the ego in turn is drawn toward this power, becoming absorbed in it as a pure power cathexis, independent of any cathexis object. An enstasy thus ensues that is not only without self-awareness but that is without awareness of objects as well. A dynamic void (or better, plenum) is created. The ego becomes one with the power of the Ground and experiences states of entityless spiritual dynamism.

With advancement in meditative practice, contemplation, of both object-centered and objectless sorts, becomes progressively more bright, pellucid, and poised. The meditator achieves states that are increasingly powerful and pure, *sattvic* in the language of Indian metaphysics and metapsychology. The goal of the meditative quest, according to Patanjali, is an objectless *samadhi* of boundless power and purity, which *samadhi* is said to liberate the meditator from the snares of nature and to bring the meditator into perfect coincidence with *purusha*, the Self.

(b) Logical rigor and autosymbolic creativity. In mastering contemplation, the ego also gains control of the creative process. This happens because the ego's ability to mobilize the power of the Ground is at the same time an ability to mobilize the nonegoic pole of the psyche in general, in all of its resources, including the autosymbolic process. Hence, the ego's ability to marshall the power of the Ground is at the same time an ability to engage the instrument of creative cognition. And it is by the same procedure that both of these abilities are exercised: the concentration of attention. Because the ego is harmoniously integrated with the nonegoic pole of the psyche, that pole is immediately responsive to the ego's concentrative efforts. It is as if the ego were the focusing mechanism of the psyche as a whole: whatever the ego intently focuses upon becomes a target for energy cathexis and a subject for autosymbolic exploration. In concentrating its attention, therefore, the ego not only enters into dynamic fusion with the object of attention but also embarks upon a symbolic-intuitive investigation of this object. The ego is made privy to landscapes of new meaning as the inner nature of the object is symbolically probed and disclosed.

The creative process, which was gradually harnessed during the regenerative period, is in this way at last taken in rein during the integrated period. The ego assumes control of the psyche's creative resources. To be sure, these resources continue to be extra-egoic in nature, which means that the ego can never acquire the same direct command over them that it has over the discursive faculties of its own sphere. This fact notwithstanding, however, the ego does gain indirect control over creative resources. It is able to access them and to set them in motion for purposes of its own choosing.

The primary products of the creative process during the integrated stage are *visionary symbols*. These are symbols that can best be described by contrasting them with earlier products of the creative process, and specifically with the paleosymbols that are forged during the body-egoic period and the apparitions that visit the ego during the transitional periods leading to integration.

The chief contrast between visionary symbols and paleosymbols lies in their differing relations to concepts: paleosymbols are less than concepts, visionary symbols are more. If we recall, paleosymbols are autogenerated images that, in the absence of the distinction between universal and particular, abstract meaning and concrete instance, are in effect at once both and neither universals and particulars, meanings and instances. They are particulars attempting to be universals, exemplary instances of meanings attempting to be the meanings themselves. Paleosymbols thus are incomplete concepts. They are strikingly creative but still very primitive cognitions that, having transcended the level of mere particularity, still lie below the level of abstractly conceived universality. Visionary symbols, in contrast, are advanced cognitions that presuppose that the level of abstractly conceived universality has already been attained. As expressions of the tertiary process, visionary symbols presuppose that the ego has already completed the work of constructing a conceptual scheme. Hence, visionary symbols, rather than being incomplete concepts, particulars attempting to be universals, are instead completely instantiated concepts, universals succeeding in being particulars. Like paleosymbols, visionary symbols are concrete exemplars or models. But unlike paleosymbols, their concrete universality is truly symbolic rather than merely protoconceptual. Visionary symbols alone embody a genuine synthesis of the concrete and the abstract, of particularity and universality.

A second important difference between visionary symbols and paleosymbols is that only the former are subject to critical assessment. Unlike paleosymbols, which the body-ego accepts at face value, visionary symbols have a hypothetical character and are subject to validation or invalidation. Thanks to the mental ego's theoretical labors, the integrated ego is in possession of rational tools with which to test its creative envisionings. Most importantly, it possesses a conceptual scheme with which to assess new meanings and a body of scientific knowledge with which to assess new facts and possibilities. A creatively envisioned meaning that conflicts with the established conceptual scheme incurs a special burden of proof, as too does a creatively envisioned fact or possibility that conflicts with established scientific knowledge. The integrated ego has these egoically forged means at its disposal for evaluating its nonegoically generated symbols. It is able to bring egoic rigor to bear upon nonegoic creativity—to the best advantage of both.

One other way in which visionary symbols differ from paleosymbols is in the range of the meanings they embody. Paleosymbols are extremely limited in this regard, since they draw upon only the meager experience of the body-ego. Visionary symbols, in contrast, draw upon the wealth of meanings contained in the complex theoretical systems established by the mental ego. The abstract universals belonging to these systems seed the autosymbolic process with ideas and with questions of exceeding subtlety and power, thus spawning symbols of commensurate subtlety and power. The theoretical systems established by the mental ego therefore contribute to the autosymbolic process in a substantive as well as a critical way. They interact with the autosymbolic process not only at the end of its cycle, by assessing its products, but also at the beginning of its cycle, by inseminating it with germinal ideas. Visionary symbols can also be contrasted with the images that arise during the transitional periods leading to integration. The chief difference here is that visionary symbols are elicited cognitions rather than self-manifesting apparitions. They are creatively produced images by which the ego probes the unknown rather than specters or epiphanies appearing without forewarning from the unknown. Unlike the images of the regressive and regenerative periods, visionary symbols do not present themselves in the guise of independent entities; they present themselves as *invited condensed meanings* rather than as *unbidden phantasmic realities.*

The images that accompany the ego's regression to the Ground are seeming hallucinations; they are apparitions embodying unconscious desires and fears, which at this developmental juncture are just being derepressed. During regression in the service of transcendence, the ego is seriously out of accord with the nonegoic pole of the psyche; consequently, the images struck by the autosymbolic process have the character of threatening manifestations from the unknown. It is only after regression has run its course and regeneration begins that autosymbolic images change from being ego-alien to being ego-friendly: miraculous and angelic rather than menacing and demonic. However, since the ego, during regeneration, is still not completely aligned with the Ground, the images of the regenerative period continue to present themselves as if they were independent entities arriving from an altogether transcendent domain. The images of the regenerative period thus still appear in apparitional guise. They do not drop this guise and become visionary symbols proper until complete ego/Ground alignment is achieved. Only at this point, the commencement of the integrated stage, do autosymbolic images cease presenting themselves as mysterious phantoms and finally present themselves in their true nature, namely, as spontaneously fashioned symbols pointing beyond the horizon of established knowledge.

4. Civilization-instinct integration: Cultivation in spirit. The mental ego has a highly conventionalized personality. Its self-concept is to a large extent composed of internalized social roles, codes of behavior, and prescribed manners. Many of these conventions, of adventitious origin, are imposed upon the young ego as it is shaped for adulthood. But the young ego, hungry for identity and acceptance, does not ordinarily refuse this socialization process. It usually submits willingly to being formed and defined by conventional structures, which are introjected and become, for the mental ego, a second nature. They become an acquired dispositional structure with which the mental ego is unconsciously identified.

This socialization process is in many respects both natural and necessary, for reasons touched upon in Chapter 4. However, the process is also problematic in that the second nature that is acquired by means of socialization is not just a cultivation of a person's original nature but also, to a significant extent, a *replacement* of that nature. It is true that the self-concept is a socially adapted vehicle for many of an individual's inherent potentialities and tendencies. However, it also is true that the self-concept serves as a *substitute* for much of a person's native endowment, namely, alienated nonegoic or physico-dynamic potentials. The mental ego forges the self-concept not only to conform to social expectations and to satisfy individual developmental needs but also to compensate for the sense of deficiency caused by the repression of the nonegoic pole of the psyche, i.e., to escape from inner "nothingness." The mental ego's acquisition of a second nature therefore is a matter of fabrication as well as cultivation. The mental ego's personality, although by no means a completely artificial implant, is to a significant extent a facade that hides, rather than shapes or forms, native potentials of life.

The mental ego harbors a deep fear that, should it fail to maintain its acquired character, the consequence would be not just a loss of identity and acceptance, but a wild unleashing of instinctual life. And the mental ego is not mistaken in harboring this fear. For given original repression, the mental ego resides atop a potentially explosive dualistic system that consists (among other things) of an antithesis of merely conventional civilization on the one hand and merely animalistic instinctuality on the other. The mental ego is very Freudian in this respect. It believes, however prereflectively, that civilization and instinct are fundamentally opposed, and therefore that the former can be maintained only when the latter is contained. The repression of physico-dynamic life, the mental ego believes, is the required price, the unavoidable discontent, of social existence.

But the cries of the existentialists—inauthenticity!, conformism!, escape from self!—reveal that the price paid by the mental ego for its civilization is greater than the mental ego had realized. They reveal that the mental ego forfeits not only the instincts but also spontaneous, authentic, dynamic, spiritual selfhood. In other words, it forfeits the nonegoic pole of its nonegoic/egoic total self. In hiding behind its socially sanctioned mask, the mental ego cuts itself off not only from instinctuality but also from its own deepest and truest promptings. To a significant extent, its behaviors cease being immediate expressions of what it truly is and become only role-scripted performances of what, in self-concept, it thinks or believes it is.

The move toward authenticity consequently requires that the mental ego redeem (or, better, allow itself to be redeemed by) what it has forfeited. The mental ego must drop its defenses and disguises and bare itself to the forsaken parts of the soul. For the only true self is the whole self: existential integrity requires complete psychophysical/psychospiritual integration. The move toward authenticity, then, requires that the mental ego temporarily let go of its second nature and submit itself to the original nature from which it has been in flight. That is, it requires that the mental ego undergo regression in the service of transcendence.

As we know, regression in the service of transcendence involves a derepression of the instincts, which, in recoil fashion, rise up and assault the ego. The mental ego, thus, in submitting to regression in the service of transcendence, is for a time confirmed in its fear that beneath the conventions of civilized life lies a powder keg of raw libido. At this point even the most avid existentialist might concede that inauthenticity is not as bad as it had seemed, for it now appears more evident than ever that the only choice is between mannered civility and unbridled instinctuality. However, the instinctual catharsis associated with regression in the service of transcendence eventually runs its course, and in time a much more promising state of affairs begins to emerge for the ego. Commencing at the turn to regeneration in spirit, the instincts begin to lose their fury and begin slowly to change from adversaries of the ego to allies. Simultaneously, much of the old mental-egoic personality begins to be restored to life and to show signs of spontaneity and authenticity. Instincts and civilized life, which had been antithetical, begin at this point intimately to interpenetrate and to fuse. Instincts, which had been mindlessly primitive, are invested with personhood, and civilized life, which had been superficially conventional, is given power, passion, and drive. The old disjunction of civilization or instinctuality is therefore refuted. It becomes apparent that true civilization is not a matter of social constraints overriding instinctuality but rather of social life and instinctuality becoming one.

But this is only one dimension of a more complex transformation. For the cultivation distinctive of integrated life is a synthesis not only of convention and instinct but also, and even more importantly, of ego and spirit. The taming and integration of the instincts is part of a larger process that also includes the liberation of spirit and the regeneration of the ego by spirit. In fact, as we have seen, the unleashing of the instincts and the liberation of spirit are the same event differently perceived: the catharsis of the instincts is simply the initial expression of the liberation of spiritual power from its repressed, instinctual organization. The resurgence of the instincts therefore is a precursor to the arrival of spirit. Accordingly, the ego's instinctualization is also a spiritualization. The ego's cultivation is a matter not only of civilization being animated by eros but also of the personality being purified and "sanctified" by spirit. True cultivation is above all cultivation *in spirit*.

Unlike the instincts, with which it had been exclusively associated, the power of the Ground needs no disciplining or refining. For in its pristine nature, as spirit, the power of the Ground is a force that is inherently sensitive and other-attuned. The power of the Ground is a noble force that, in infusing the egoic sphere, transforms the acquired virtues of that sphere into spontaneous graces of character. Differently stated, the power of the Ground is the dynamic essence of charity and wisdom, the pure strain of life that gives heart and eyes to the conventional structures of the mental-egoic personality. The truly cultivated person is therefore someone whose civilized behaviors have been infused and transformed by spirit. He is someone whose personality, no longer in any sense a fabrication, has become the vehicle of authentic instinctual *and* spiritual life.

In dialectical terms, the foregoing can be restated to say that the mental-egoic personality, as a second nature based on a negation of a person's original nature, must itself be negated before the higher egoic-nonegoic synthesis of integration can be achieved. Accordingly, the mental-egoic personality, long in the process of formation, is eventually exposed as a false mask and, then, is regressively submitted to resurging nonegoic life. This regression, however, is not an annihilation. To be sure, there is much in the mental-egoic personality that is purged, namely, everything that is opaque to or resistive of the free movement of spirit. But the great majority of the structures constituting the mental-egoic personality survive its regressive negation and, reconnected with nonegoic life, begin to take part in a new and superior synthesis. This synthesis, the integrated personality, is a union of egoic and nonegoic resources, of egoic form and nonegoic substance and power. The acquired structures of the mental-egoic sphere are regenerated in the native flesh and spirit of physico-dynamic life, and in turn the spontaneities of physico-dynamic life, no longer confined to a prepersonal organization, are shaped according to the established canons of social and intellectual culture. In this way a person's second nature is wedded to his original nature and he becomes a genuinely cultivated being, a being of both form and substance, civilization and instinct, personality and spirit.

One more point needs to be added to avoid misunderstanding, namely, that cultivation in spirit, as a synthesis of egoic and nonegoic elements, is not a synthesis of equals. It is rather a synthesis in which—as is true of integration generally—the egoic elements are subordinate to the nonegoic. Thus cultivation in spirit is a synthesis in which the structures of personality play an indispensable, but secondary, role. It is a synthesis the libido/spirit, eros/agape authenticity of which is more important than the social correctness of behavior. Relatively speaking, the latter is icing on the cake. Indeed, so much more important is the substance than the conventional form that the integrated person cares little if he looks foolish or clumsy by prevailing standards just so long as his actions embody what he truly thinks and feels. Spirit is the inner living core of integrated life, personality but its means of outer expression. Both spirit and personality are necessary for complete humanness, but of the two, it is spirit that is primary and most truly essential.

5. Ego-Ground integration: Fulfilled humanness. The ego and the Dynamic

Ground are the seats of the two opposite poles of the psyche. The ego is the seat of the mental-egoic pole, the pole that is responsible for organizing and controlling experience and in general for conducting affairs with the world. And the Ground is the seat of the physico-dynamic pole, the pole that provides life with substance, creativity, eros, and spirit. Together, these two poles include within themselves the totality of psychic resources. Everything that is native to the human endowment derives from one or the other of these two poles or from the two poles acting in synergistic unison.

The ego/Ground bipolarity is the psyche's most basic constitutional structure. From the very beginning, the psyche is a complex of two poles. However, as we have seen, these two poles, although always coexistent, are not always equally developed or harmoniously coordinated. At the outset of human development, the ego is totally enveloped in the Ground; like an embryonic chick in the egg, it exists only as a potentiality for future development. And soon thereafter, when the ego is born, it is immature and weak, and consequently still eclipsed by the Ground. The fledgling ego strives very hard for individuation and independence, but it is still so deeply immersed in and affected by the power of the Ground, and by nonegoic potentials generally, that it is all too easily swept away and reduced to the preindividuated state.

The ego remains extremely unstable throughout the pre- or body-egoic period of development. It remains vulnerable to the Ground until, reaching an impasse, it finally takes matters decisively into its own hands and commits the act of original repression. In making this move, the ego, now the mental ego, wins its independence, but only by alienating the Ground. Hence, the beginning of the mental-egoic period marks a reversal in which psychic pole predominates over the other. The nonegoic pole, which was ascendant, suffers repression and is rendered unconscious; simultaneously, the egoic pole, which was subordinate, asserts its dominance, laying claim to sovereignty over the psyche as whole.

This situation obtains for the duration of the mental-egoic period. Then, commencing with regression in the service of transcendence, another reversal occurs. The mental ego is undermined—it loses the undergirding of original repression—and falls again under the influence of the nonegoic pole of the psyche. The ego is regressed to the Ground. The ego undergoes this regression not in order to submit to re-embedment in the Ground, but rather to become rerooted in the Ground and thereby open to the transformative action of the power of the Ground. The ego is regressed to the Ground so that it can be regenerated in spirit.

Therefore once regression in the service of transcendence has fulfilled its purpose, one last reversal occurs: regression gives way to regeneration. The ego is given a new lease on life and there commences a healing fusion of the ego with the nonegoic pole of the psyche. The final result of this regenerative process, integration, is, at last, a perfected bipolar system. The psyche, which had all along been bipolar in fundamental design, now becomes bipolar in fully actualized fact. At this point both poles of the psyche are completely developed *and* properly attuned. Both finally function to the full extent of their distinctive capacities and in synergistic harmony, as one.

Integrated bipolarity is a perfect coincidence of opposites. The two poles of the psyche continue to be opposite in their nature and functions, but now, for the first time, they are completely supportive and facilitative of each other.

Table 9-1

THE DEVELOPMENT OF BIPOLARITY

BIPOLAR CONSTITUTIONAL STRUCTURE		TRIPHASIC DEVELOPMENTAL STRUCTURE		
Nonegoic Pole	*Egoic Pole*	*Body-Egoic Stage*	*Mental-Egoic Stage*	*Integrated Stage*
Co-original sides of psychic life		Unstable, Ground-dominant duality.	Repressive, ego-dominant dualism.	Fully developed, Grounded bipolarity.
Dynamic Ground	Ego	Immature ego overawed by Ground as inner aspect of Great Mother.	Ego repressively contains Ground, rendering Ground unconscious.	Ego, fully developed, rooted in and infused by Ground.
Unity	Individuation	Ego prone to regress to original embedment.	Ego individuated in disconnected, Cartesian manner.	Ego fully individuated vehicle-agent of Ground.
Body	Mind	Body-ego: ego completely identified with bodily life.	Mental ego: ego a Cartesian self, divorced from bodily life.	Integrated mind-body whole; the ethereal body.
Instinct	Personhood ·	Original bioinstinctual nature predominates over emerging personhood.	Personhood constructed in conventionalized manner: second nature, self-concept.	Cultivation in spirit: dynamic, instinctual-spiritual personhood.
Feeling	Thought	Impulsiveness, reactivity.	Reserved, dispassionate thought.	Conscience: insightful feeling, passionate thought.
Perception	Conception	Sensory saturation: percepts without concepts.	Conceptual abstractness: concepts filter percepts.	Perceptual fullness: percepts conceptually grasped, concepts perceptually filled.
Absorption	Subject-object separation	Proneness to fascination.	Ego incapable of absorption, locked in subject-object mode.	Contemplation; voluntary, lucid absorption.
Autosymbolic creativity	Discursive cognition	Primary process: paleosymbols as bearers of rudimentary meanings.	Secondary process: operational thought bereft of symbolic concreteness and creativity.	Tertiary process: union of symbol and concept, creativity and logical rigor.

No longer antagonistic opposites, they now are complementary opposites. And this applies across all dimensions of their functioning, as is indicated in Table 9-1. Integrated bipolarity is thus a multifaceted union of opposites, a *coincidentia oppositorum* made up of many participating *coincidentiae opposito-rum*. Table 9-1 gathers together some of the many elements that make up this larger whole, tracing their development through the unstable duality of the body-egoic period and the repressive dualism of the mental-egoic period to the fully realized bipolarity of the integrated period.

Table 9-1 should be self-explanatory for the most part. There is only one point that needs to be made. This is a point that was made shortly ago but that merits being stressed, namely, that the two poles of the psyche, although co-original, are not co-equal. It bears repeating that the nonegoic pole is the basic psychic pole. And it is so in a double sense: in both time and authority. The nonegoic pole has primacy in time in that it is active prior to the egoic pole. Although the two poles are always coexistent, it is the nonegoic pole alone that is manifest at the outset of human development. In the neonatal state, the egoic pole of the psyche exists, but only in a latent, preactive manner; the ego is still *in utero*, gestating in the Ground.[5] And the nonegoic pole has primacy in authority in that the egoic pole can become integrated with the nonegoic pole only by submitting itself to the nonegoic pole. The ego can enter into union with the Ground only by becoming an instrument of the Ground. An implication of this is that the psyche, although bipolar, is not truly bicentric. The egoic pole has no true center in itself; it is centered or anchored only when it is rooted in the Ground. In political terms, the Ground alone is sovereign; the ego is (in all senses) subject. The ego is a self, but it is so truly only when it is the self of spirit.

THE HORIZONS OF INTEGRATED LIFE

Integration is perfected humanness. It is the complete actualization of our originally given nature. Integration therefore is not a matter of being superhuman, but rather of being fully human. Its rarity and excellence notwithstanding, there is nothing about integration that places it beyond the range of native human possibilities.

However, if we look into the far horizon of integrated life, there can be glimpsed vistas of experience that are so extraordinary that, although still human, they must also be considered divine. The three most remarkable such vistas are prophetic vision, saintly compassion, and mystical illumination.

1. Prophetic vision. Jung went beyond Freud in understanding that the symbols produced by the unconscious are not just retrospective, harking back to significant events of childhood (or the race), but that they are prospective as well, forevisioning the course of future development. Jung employed this insight primarily to plot the future and final stages of ontogeny, or individuation. Dream symbols and the symbols that emerge from the process of active imagination, Jung believed, are in many cases suggestive of the imminently forthcoming steps of an individual's growth and development. For Jung, a person's symbolic life is often a few steps ahead of his actual life. Accordingly, for a person to understand the symbols fashioned by the unconscious is in many cases for him to understand his own future.

This insight of Jung's can be extended beyond the ontogenetic or individual level. Humanity, I suggest, has not only memory of its collective roots but also precognition of its collective future. The autosymbolic process generates images that anticipate not only the development of the individual but also the development of the community, and even the species.

However, the autosymbolic process usually has no chance of attending to the future of the community and species until after the full integration of the individual has been achieved. The reason for this is that, throughout the mental-egoic stage, the autosymbolic process is disjoined from consciousness and is forced almost exclusively to work in the service of unconscious materials. The autosymbolic process is in a sense beheaded and made into an enigmatic oracle of goings-on in the netherworld. Given this situation, the images spawned by the autosymbolic process during the mental-egoic stage tend to be expressions of existing psychic stresses or else foretokens of adjustments by means of which such stresses are about to be relieved. That is, during the mental-egoic stage, the autosymbolic process is responsive primarily to chords astir within the unconscious of the individual psyche, qua individual. However, once the psyche has finally suffered the readjustments necessary for proper ego/Ground alignment (i.e., integration), the autosymbolic process is reconnected with consciousness and is free to attend to interpsychic as well as intrapsychic concerns. At this point, then, a person might begin to anticipate not only his own future but that of his fellow human beings as well. This is when prophesy becomes a real possibility for humankind.

In saying that prophesy is an inherent human possibility, I do not mean to suggest that we are capable, potentially, of *infallible* precognition. Prophesy, like everything else that derives from the autosymbolic process, is fallible. The autosymbolic process gives symbolic expression to higher meanings and future possibilities, and it does so with immense creativity and insight. But it does not do this with any guarantee of correctness. The deliverances of the autosymbolic process need to be critically analyzed and assessed. They need to be abstracted from their imaginal dress and then put to the test by checking them against existing knowledge. Nevertheless, even though autosymbolic foresight is not to be accepted as literal and infallible truth, it ought to be taken seriously as a prefiguration of things to come. For under integrated conditions, the autosymbolic process is both intimately attuned to the rhythms of life (collective as well as individual) and free of all constraints that would render its symbols prima facie suspect.

2. *Saintly compassion.* We have already seen that the integrated person is a person of conscience. To this it can now be added that, in some cases, the integrated person is also a person of saintly compassion.

Saintly compassion, among other things, is a dynamic phenomenon: it is an expression of spirit. Specifically, it is an expression of the spontaneous outgoingness and magnetism of spirit. Since the power of the Ground is a magnetic or attractive force, the ego is drawn to the power of the Ground and to anything in which the power is deposited or to anyone from whom it emanates. The ego's attraction to the power of the Ground can be compared to the attraction of iron filings to a magnet. But the magnetism of the power of the Ground affects not only the ego; it also affects the power of the Ground itself, i.e., as one source of this power meets another. And the attraction of this power to itself is even stronger than is the ego's attraction to it. If the ego's attraction to the power of the Ground can be compared to the attraction of iron filings to a magnet, then the attraction of the power of the Ground to itself, of spirit to spirit, can be compared to the attraction of one magnet to another. Spirit strongly flows to spirit and bonds therewith to form a communion, or mystical body, of (ego-differentiated) spirits. Spirit is irresistibly drawn to itself as it meets itself in others and is thus moved to join in a higher life with others. So impelling is this impulse for some integrated persons—in whom, no doubt, the movement of spirit is particularly strong— that they value the spiritual whole more than they do any of its egoic parts, including most immediately themselves. These are persons so utterly devoted to spirit that they are most willing to sacrifice their own individual lives if doing so would contribute to the growth of humanity's collective life in spirit.

Not all integrated persons are prophets, nor are they all saints. These types must in fact be counted as infrequent exceptions to the rule. Prophesy and sainthood are among the very highest, and hence rarest, possibilities of human existence. Few people ever arrive at the integrated stage, and of these only a few are gifted in the ways that are necessary to be a prophet or a saint. Nevertheless, prophesy and sainthood are real human possibilities. There have always been, and there continue to be, true prophets and saints. But regrettably, their numbers have always been very small.

3. *Mystical illumination.* Mystical illumination is the highest form of infused and absorbed experience. There are at least four reasons for this. First, mystical illumination is an objectless enstasy, being an absorption in the power of the Ground itself rather than in any object or activity in which the power of the Ground has been invested. Second, mystical illumination is completely pure, being a union with the power of the Ground in its pristine nature as spirit rather than as expressed through or admixed with particular feelings or instincts. Third, mystical illumination is an experience of measureless immensity, being a beholding so extraordinary in power and grandeur as entirely to eclipse any other experience that it is possible for the ego to have. And fourth, mystical illumination is a gift of grace, being an experience beyond anything the ego can attain or induce at will.

Mystical illumination needs to be distinguished from the other types of objectless states that have been discussed in previous chapters. If we recall, the following are distinct types of objectless states: (1) the dead void states that sometimes are experienced during the mental-egoic period, (2) the empty trances that occur during the second stage of regression in the service of transcendence, (3) the undifferentiated effusions and ecstasies that are characteristic of regeneration in spirit, and (4) the objectless contemplations that are achieved by the ego during the later phases of regeneration in spirit and throughout the integrated stage. Of these, the objectless contemplations are most closely akin to mystical illumination, but even they fall considerably short.

Dead void states differ from mystical illumination in being bereft of the power of the Ground; these experiences are merely episodes of mental vacancy, without any degree of dynamic infusion or absorption. Empty trances differ from mystical illumination in being implosive rather than infusive absorptions; moreover, trances are dense and dark rather than ethereal and bright. Undifferentiated effusions and ecstasies differ from mystical illumination in being wild and impure; they are explosive absorptions or transports that are admixed with derepressing feelings and instincts. And objectless contemplations, although suffering from none of these deficiencies, differ from mystical illumination in being experiences of significantly lesser stature; they fall far short of mystical illumination in the degree to which the ego is infused, illumined, and beatified by spirit.

The difference in degree that distinguishes mystical illumination from objectless contemplations is sufficiently great to constitute a difference in kind. Mystical illumination is not just an experience of serene enlightenment, as are objectless contemplations; it is rather an experience of celestial exaltation and effulgence. Mystical illumination is an experience of inconceivable enormity. In the case of mystical illumination, the Ground releases a prodigious outpouring of spirit. The aperture of the soul is opened to its widest bore and spirit, in the fullness of its power and glory, graces the ego with the ultimate vision. Mystical illumination, then, unlike objectless contemplations, is inherently of the nature of a gift. The ego, by steadfast meditative effort, can voluntarily enter a contemplative absorption and, in doing so, increase its chances for a genuine mystical experience. But whether or not the ego makes such efforts, it is in the last analysis the Ground itself, or the inner principle that regulates it, that determines when an ultimate disclosure will occur. Regardless of human will, it is the divine power itself that elects the times and places at which it will bare itself to the ego. Therefore, mystical illumination, like prophetic vision and saintly compassion, is statistically extremely rare, even among integrated persons.

CONCLUSION

No two integrated persons are alike. Unlike persons at the mental-egoic stage, who have conventionally stylized personalities, integrated persons are all uniquely and authentically themselves. They are the true individuals so lauded in existentialist literature. And integrated persons differ widely from each other not only in the distinctiveness of their authentic personalities but in most other respects as well. As we have seen, only a small minority are prophets, saints, or mystical illuminati. Also, few integrated persons possess extranormal powers to any significant degree. Integrated persons cover a broad spectrum of types, from the seemingly quite ordinary to the truly extraordinary. Except for their outgoing spirit and deep genuineness, most integrated persons do not stand out in any way. There are no requirements for attaining integrated existence other than having an ego that, strong in itself, is able to submit itself to the Ground. Given that this is the only prerequisite, it is easy to see that integration, although rare and of the highest excellence, is a developmental stage open to humanity at large. If there is an elect, it is one from which no one can a priori be excluded. Integration is an inherited destiny belonging to humankind as a whole.

EPILOGUE

THE DIALECTICAL CHARACTER OF our development indicates that human evolution has been uneven and is incomplete. It is evidence that the evolutionary development of the ego and the neocortex was accomplished only by means of a repression of the older strata of the psyche. The nascent ego apparently could not have survived if it had not been protectively sealed from the potencies of biodynamic life. The fledgling ego needed clear air (de-energized psychic space) and firm ground (the infrastructure of original repression) in order to grow and to gain control of both the environment and itself. This, of course, was a crucial turning point in our distant past. Later chronicled as the fall, it is the point at which a species-wide repression was suffered. This repression, incurred at a discrete juncture of human prehistory, is now repeated with each succeeding generation. Each human being, in the earliest years of his individual life, re-enacts and hence perpetuates the repression that the species suffered in the earliest stages of its collective life.

The human race thus has long been burdened with a deep-seated repression that, while protecting the ego, has at the same time divided human nature against itself. This state of affairs implies not only that our species has had a difficult evolutionary past but also that it will have a difficult, a dangerous but auspicious, evolutionary future. If the ontogenetic stages that I have termed regression in the service of transcendence and regeneration in spirit have phylogenetic analogues, then it follows that times at once perilous and promising await us. Humanity as a whole has yet to go through a regression to the Ground and a period of regenerative transformation. Our species has yet to face its own repressed depths and to endure the painful process leading to psychic integration.

It is frightening to imagine what times like these would be like. The forces unleashed would be of overwhelming magnitude, and it is a real possibility that we would not be able to cope. We live on the edge of global conflict and thermonuclear disaster as it is. But our situation would be immeasurably more precarious if we were to enter a dark night of regression and despair. If there is to be any chance of surviving such a period, it seems clear that the key factor will be the presence of strong spiritual leadership. There have always been prophets who have foretold of dramatic events lying in our future. And there have always been saints and sages who, in their exemplary lives, have led us in our evolutionary odyssey. The hope is that, when our species is finally put to the ultimate test, there will be enough individual men and women who have themselves already passed the test that the race can be guided through its dark night and led safely into the dawn of the spiritual age.

APPENDIX

The Bipolar and Bimodal Structures of the Psyche

THE BIPOLAR STRUCTURE IS grounded in the human body in many different and exceedingly complex ways. I will here explore only some of the possible connections. First, there is probably a close connection between the bipolar division of the psyche and the hemispheric division of the cerebral cortex. (However, as will be touched upon in a moment, the bipolar structure is not the only psychic duality likely to be rooted in cortical laterality.) Many recent studies have shown that the left cerebral hemisphere typically bears the responsibility for most of the egoic functions listed in Table 1-1 and that the right hemisphere typically is involved with such nonegoic functions as spatial awareness, imaginal-symbolic thought, and the experience of many kinds of affective stimuli.[1] Yet, despite this plausible connection with the lateral division of the cerebral cortex, the bipolar structure seems in some respects to be more of a vertical than a horizontal structure. The bipolar structure may, then, reflect the hierarchical stratification of the brain, perhaps as described by MacLean (1973), namely, as consisting of the neocortical superstructure (including both hemispheres) on the one hand and such substructures as the limbic system (the so-called mammalian brain) and the R-complex (the so-called reptilian brain) on the other. This vertical division corresponds well with certain aspects of the bipolar structure because the dynamic, bioinstinctual, and affective dimensions of life can plausibly be said to have their deepest bases in the two latter, lower and more primitive strata of the brain, whereas the egoic functions have their seat in the neocortex. The bipolar structure is additionally reflected in human anatomy in the division of the nervous system into voluntary (egoic) and involuntary (nonegoic) subsystems and in the vertical division of the larger body into the head (egoic) on the one hand and the pelvic-abdominal area (nonegoic) on the other. There is a good deal of overlap and redundancy in these physiological and anatomical divisions, but in general they seem to reflect, and ground, the bipolar duality that is fundamental to human nature and experience.

Turning to the bimodal structure of the ego or egoic pole, present knowledge of the brain indicates that it too is closely related to the lateral division of the cerebral cortex. Split-brain research provides an abundance of evidence that would link the active mode of the ego with the left hemisphere of the cortex and the receptive mode with the right hemisphere. The active mode is linked with the left hemisphere because it is the left hemisphere that, usually, has been found to be dominant in the performance of such distinctively egoic functions as operational cognition and intentional action. It is the left hemisphere in which, as it were, the ego is usually seated when it assumes the detached, subject-over-object stance and takes experience in rein, exercising theoretical and practical control over it. The right hemisphere, although apparently capable of assuming many left-hemisphere functions, is not ordinarily ego-active in these ways. Rather than being an instrument by which the ego acts on experience, the right hemisphere, it would seem, is primarily a source from which or a medium through which the ego is affected by experience, i.e., struck or moved by insights, images, sensations, feelings, and the like. Perhaps it can be said that the right hemisphere, rather than being the basis of the ego's operational command over things, is instead an accessway through which the ego is influenced by things, and by dynamic and creative resources in particular—which is just another way of saying that the right hemisphere may be the seat of what I have called the ego's receptive mode.

If this account of hemispheric functions is at all accurate, it follows that the right hemisphere of the brain has an important double aspect. For according to this account, the right hemisphere corresponds at once to both poles of the psyche: it represents the egoic pole in its receptive mode and, as was noted, the nonegoic pole in a variety of its physico-dynamic potentials. This possible Janus character of the right hemisphere invites the hypothesis that a chief function of the right hemisphere is to mediate between the two poles of the psyche. That is, it suggests that the right hemisphere, in being the seat of the ego's receptive mode, is thereby a channel through which the psyche's nonegoic potentials are communicated to the ego, and therefore to consciousness. This hypothesis is, of course, only a bare conjecture, but it is at least a conjecture that makes sense of a way in which the horizontal (i.e., lateral) and vertical axes of the brain may intersect.

NOTES

Introduction

[1]For a preliminary definition of transpersonal theory, see the Preface.

[2]An in-depth comparison of the psychodynamic and structural-hierarchical approaches to transpersonal theory is undertaken in Chapter 1.

[3]The holographic paradigm was inspired by optical holography and in particular by the intriguing fact that a holographic image can be reproduced from any of its parts. The basic idea of the paradigm is, then, that each part of a totality may enfold the whole, and therefore that all parts of a totality may be internally interconnected. The holographic paradigm was pioneered by David Bohm, a theoretical physicist, and Karl Pribram, a neuropsychologist. Bohm (1971, 1973, 1980), responding to anomalies in quantum mechanics, speculated that the physical universe as we know it may be a manifestation of an underlying implicate order governed by holographic principles. And Pribram (1971, 1986; Pribram et al., 1974), investigating how the brain preserves memories, hypothesized that the brain may store information holographically. Many people in transpersonal theory have now adopted Bohm's and Pribram's work as pointing the way to a post-Newtonian paradigm, a unifying paradigm that, they believe, promises to bring together matter and consciousness, science and mysticism. For discussions of the holographic paradigm by spokespersons of transpersonal theory, see Wilber (1982), Mann (1984), and Grof (1985).

[4]The abbreviated form, *Ground*, always with an uppercase G, will also be used.

[5]A variety of dynamic terms will be used in this study, the most important of which are *libido, psychic energy*, and *spirit. Libido* will be used in an extended Freudian sense to designate the instinctual (and primarily unconscious) organization of our dynamic life. Freud of course believed that this organization is a necessary and exclusive one, stemming from the biophysical roots of human dynamism. Following Jung and others, I sharply disagree with Freud on this point. However, if I disagree with Freud on whether the instinctual organization of dynamism is the only one, I do agree with Freud to an

extent in thinking that this organization is a (indeed, *the*) predominant one. Therefore, it is useful to retain the term *libido* to denote this very important aspect of our dynamic situation. A full account of the interrelated meanings of *libido, psychic energy,* and *spirit* is given in Chapter 5.

[6]It ought not be inferred from the fact that the second or middle stage of a dialectical process is based on negation (or, psychodynamically speaking, on repression) that that stage is therefore merely negative. On the contrary, the second stage, in opposing the content of the first stage, at the same time develops a content of its own—a content that, in the third stage, is creatively synthesized with the (restored) content of the first stage. The second stage, therefore, in being inherently opposed to the first stage, is not thereby merely reactionary; it is rather progressive on the whole.

Chapter 1

[1]See Wilber 1980a, 1980b, 1981a, 1981b, and especially 1983b.

[2]See the Appendix for a discussion of the possible physiological bases of the bipolar structure.

[3]Freud's topographic (conscious/preconscious/unconscious) model has fewer affinities with the bipolar structure. This is because, as has frequently been noted, the topographic model is not really a blueprint of the psychic constitution, but is rather a classification of the degree to which specific psychic contents are present or available to the ego. The structural model, on the other hand, is a blueprint of the psychic constitution, mapping psychic regions, levels, and functions.

[4]An argument could be formulated that, for Freud, the ego is also a developmental rather than constitutional structure. On the side of this argument there is the fact that for many years (during the first two decades of the century and into the early 1920s) Freud spoke of the ego as if it were little more than an extension of the drives, existing in order to buffer the drives from the hardships of reality. And there is also Freud's statement, as late as *The Ego and the Id* (1923, 38), that "it is not possible to speak of direct inheritance in the ego." However, these were not Freud's only, or last, words on the status of the ego. Hartmann (1956), Rapaport (1958), and Klein (1976) agree that Freud's thinking about the ego evolved through three stages, namely, (1) an early period (up to 1897) during which the ego, as in the *Project for a Scientific Psychology* (1895), was assigned a degree of functional autonomy within the overall psychic apparatus, (2) a middle period (1897-1923) during which the exploration of the unconscious was the main focus of Freud's work and, therefore, during which the ego tended to be neglected or considered only in light of its relation to unconscious drives or to specific repressed materials, and (3) a late period (after 1923) during which Freud acknowledged the biological roots of the ego and assigned the ego a quantum of neutral energy and a number of autonomous functions. In his later years, Freud seems to have been concentrating more on ego psychology, perhaps, as Benjamin (1966) conjectures, in response to the ego-psychological work of Hartmann.

[5] What Jung calls the personal unconscious, like the Freudian superego, is not a basic or original (i.e., constitutional) structure but is rather a psychic stratum created during development, by repression.

[6] In saying that the ego can switch back and forth between the active and receptive modes, I do not mean to imply that these two modes are necessarily mutually exclusive. It must be left open as a possibility—which I will later be defending as fact—that the ego, in a completely integrated psychic economy, can effectively execute egoic operations while at the same time drawing on the full range of nonegoic potentials: bimodal integration.

[7] See the Appendix for a discussion of possible physiological connections between the bimodal and bipolar structures.

[8] The rudiments of Freud's notion of primal repression are to be found in *The Interpretation of Dreams* (1900). This preliminary formulation was then developed rather sporadically in later essays (1911b, 1915, and especially 1926). Madison (1961) provides an excellent account of the status and development of the notion of primal repression in Freud's thought.

[9] This conception implies a dynamic unconscious similar to the Freudian id. In the case of both conceptions, the nonegoic pole is described in pre-egoic (i.e., primitive and primarily instinctual) terms. The difference, though, is that whereas the id is inherently pre-egoic, the dynamic unconscious as conceived here is pre-egoic only developmentally. The dynamic-dialectical view holds that the dynamic unconscious (of the middle or mental-egoic period) is indeed id-like, but only because it represents a developmental retardation of the nonegoic pole of the psyche.

[10] Stress should be put on the qualification *potentially*. The proviso is necessary in order to allow for the real possibility that the process will abort and lead only to regression, and not to transcendence. In other words, it is implied by the dynamic-dialectical paradigm that ego transcendence involves serious risks. The dynamic-dialectical and structural-hierarchical paradigms will be contrasted on this issue later in the chapter.

[11] Table 1-4 is a reconstruction of one of Wilber's own tables (Wilber 1983b, 271).

[12] It is not clear whether ultimate unity should be considered a *psychic* level, since, as the coincidence of the individual with reality, it seems to be more of a metaphysical than a strictly psychic structure.

[13] Wilber 1983b, 284.

[14] It is Jung's view, specifically, against which Wilber levels this charge. But Wilber casts his argument against Jung in terms that are sufficiently general to apply to any theory that holds that ego transcendence involves a return of the ego to pre-egoic origins.

[15] Jung's formulation is liable to Wilber's charge because, as observed earlier, Jung never clearly distinguished between the "pre-" and "trans-" dimensions of the collective unconscious. Consequently, in Jung's conception of the night sea journey or heroic odyssey as involving a return of the ego to the collective unconscious, it is rarely entirely clear whether the ego is returning to something lower or higher, to mere "archaic dominants" or to genuine spiritual potentials. It is true that Jung conceives of

the Self archetype in consistently transpersonal terms, but his treatment of many of the other archetypes of the collective unconscious leaves it uncertain to what extent those archetypes are merely vestiges of phylogenesis and to what extent they are prefigurations of transpersonal possibilities.

Chapter 2

[1]The newborn's attention is unselectively open in the sense that it is without active, volitional preference for any one stimulus over any other. It is well known that newborns exhibit certain stereotypical responses to key stimuli in the environment, e.g., turning the head when touched on either side of the mouth, sucking when a nipple is inserted in the mouth, grasping when an object is placed in the palm, tracking when a moving visual stimulus is brought into the field of view. However, it would seem that the infant, in exhibiting such behaviors, is not an ego-subject exercising intentional control of consciousness but rather only a biological organism executing genetic programs. More on this in a moment.

[2]A number of recent studies of infants (Fagan 1973, 1977; Cohen, DeLoache, and Pearl 1977; and McCall, Kennedy, and Dodds 1977) have shown that babies in the first few months of life habituate to repeated stimuli and therefore are capable of recognition or memory of a rudimentary sort. But such recognition could at best be only a figurative precursor of what is ordinarily understood by the term, since it would be devoid of any understanding of object permanence or of general type or kind. (Object permanence and beginning concept formation come later on the developmental timetable, as will be explained in the next chapter.) Infant "memory," then, it would seem, is simply an automatic process of registering stimulus repetition, without any conscious awareness of the fact of repetition.

[3]See Bornstein (1975), Kagen (1978), and Ruff and Birch (1974).

[4]Jung and his followers have explained the Great Mother as an archetypal system of the human unconscious. Jung (1912/1952/1967, 1938/1954/1968), Neumann (1954, 1963), and others have shown that the Great Mother archetype is basically a *biaxial* system, possessing both positive and negative sides (the Good Mother and the Terrible Mother) and both inner or archetypal and outer or personal dimensions. Proceeding on the basis of this conception, the following account of the Great Mother sets itself apart by identifying the inner dimension of the Great Mother with the Dynamic Ground. Accordingly, the Great Mother is explained not only as an archetypal and personal reality but also, and even more fundamentally, as a multifaceted dynamic reality.

[5]It is necessary to insert the qualification *at first*, since, as will be explained shortly, the effect of the Great Mother on the body-ego changes as the body-ego matures. In particular, the Great Mother ceases being just a benign nurturer and protectress (the Good Mother) and becomes also a sinister and dangerous force (the Terrible Mother).

[6]The Great Mother has this effect simply by the power of her (bidirectional) presence. Closeness to the Great Mother tends to melt the body-ego, whatever the particular style

and intentions of the mothering parent might be. This means that the so-called problem of the engulfing mother has deep, universal roots.

[7]Whirlwinds and whirlpools are quite common symbols of the action of the Ground, since they neatly convey the abysmal-gravitational aspect of the Ground. Seen in this light, the Ground is an unknown deep that acts upon the ego as a vortex of forces with irresistible power of suction. The ego is easily dizzied by such vórtices, which entrance it and induce its reabsorption in the Ground.

[8]The Great Mother system is complicated by the fact that many of the archetypes of this system, and especially those expressive of the Terrible Mother, are colored by events that occur long after the period of the body-ego has come to an end. The most important event in this regard is the stimulation of the sexual and aggressive instincts during puberty. Upon the occurrence of this event, the Terrible Mother—long since having been relegated to the unconscious—is rawly instinctualized in all of her guises, personal, elemental, and animal. She thus becomes not only an ugly and wicked crone but also a whore, not only violent elemental forces but also uncontrollable currents of lust for sex and blood, not only a scaly reptilian devourer but also the beast of the abyss, a hideous monster of utterly perverse nature. This subject is treated in Chapter 5.

[9]This way of depicting the struggle for separation from the Terrible Mother reflects more the male than the female perspective. Research needs to be done on the female experience of this archetypal encounter. In myths and fairy tales, girls, rather than fighting the monster, are typically rescued from it by a male hero figure. But this depiction may be just a further illustration of the male perspective.

[10]Original repression also has the effect of divesting experience of its original all-around abundance and numinosity, since these too, if we remember, are expressions of the free movement of the power of the Ground.

[11]The Cartesian mind/body split is also in part a consequence of the Oedipal conflict, as will be explained below.

[12]This should not be taken as a denial of important gender differences in early childhood development. There are no doubt many such differences (Gilligan 1982). The point is only that the *fundamental existential project* is the same for all very young children, regardless of gender.

[13]Wilber offers a different account of the Oedipus complex in his more recent book, *Up from Eden* (1981b).

[14]This should be qualified a bit. Of the two conflicts, it is the battle with the Terrible Mother that is the more basic and universal. In families without a father, or someone who represents this role, the Oedipal conflict may not come into play.

Chapter 3

[1]See Chapter 2 (note 2) for a discussion of recognition in infants.

[2]Once images assume a referential capacity, their autogeneration becomes part of the autosymbolic process, i.e., the process by which concrete pictorial meanings are spontaneously produced. The source of image production becomes autosymbolic in the latter part of the phantasmic stage; it is then seeded with new meanings during the third or paleological stage of the body-ego's development; and it is then deleted from conscious experience when original repression submerges the nonegoic pole of the psyche. Van Dusen (1972) has reported that the autosymbolic process is operative to a significant extent during the hypnagogic state. But for the most part it seems to be operative, for most adults, only during dreams.

[3]This departs from Arieti's terminology, since he calls these phantasmic representations *paleosymbols*. Arieti makes no clear distinction between the images of the phantasmic stage and those of the third, or paleological, stage of the body-ego's development. I, however, think there is an important distinction to be made between these two types of images. Briefly, whereas the former type are representations of individual objects, the latter type are, I believe, embodiments of (newly emerging) universal meanings. In other words, whereas the former type are signs, the latter type are symbols in the more strict sense of the term. In light of this distinction it seemed advisable to revise Arieti's terminology, coining the expression *referential image* for the representations of the phantasmic period and reserving the term *paleosymbol* for the more truly symbolic images of the paleological period.

[4]The ensuing discussion is not as closely geared to Arieti's account. The principal debt is still to Arieti, but his views are here modified and extended considerably.

[5]As mentioned shortly ago, this distinction is mine, not Arieti's. Arieti discusses the rudimentary conceptual meanings that emerge in the paleological period, but in doing so he does not explain the role played by images as the bearers of these meanings. Therefore, he does not distinguish, as I have done, between referential images (mere signs, distinctive of the phantasmic period) and paleosymbols (concrete universals or symbols proper, distinctive of the paleological period).

[6]I borrow the term *submerged unconscious* from Wilber (1980a).

[7]Many of the terms introduced in this paragraph are my own. *Collective unconscious* is, of course, Jung's term for describing the deep unconscious. Jung also speaks of the deep unconscious as having instinctual and archetypal roots; however, he does not explicitly distinguish between ontogenetic and phylogenetic instincts and archetypes. This distinction is sometimes implicit in Jung's writings, but to my knowledge it is never explicitly formulated. The notion of the body-unconscious is new with this account of the unconscious. The notion is required in light of the conception presented here of the nonegoic pole of the psyche and of the developmental arrestment of nonegoic potentials that occurs at the point of original repression.

[8]As mentioned in Chapter 2 (note 8), the Great Mother system, and its negative side in particular, undergoes certain alterations during the mental-egoic period owing to the triggering of the sexual and aggressive instincts during puberty. Consequently, when the Terrible Mother is re-encountered during regression in the service of transcendence, it is not exactly the same Terrible Mother that was vanquished at the point of

original repression. It is rather a Terrible Mother that has been rudely instinctualized in sexual and aggressive manners, in all of her (human, elemental, and animal) forms. This matter will be treated in full in Chapter 5.

Chapter 4

[1] This term will always be enclosed in scare quotes when used to describe the mental ego. In saying that the mental ego's existence is "nothingness," I am speaking only of the mental ego's ontological insecurities in light of its alienation from the nonegoic pole of the psyche and its unlocatability within mental space. I am not speaking of the mental ego's actual ontological status—which, as conceived here, is that of a pole of a bipole.

[2] If we recall, the self-concept has its rudimentary beginnings in the third or paleological stage of the body-ego's development. The body-ego at this stage begins to refer to itself as *I* and to think of itself in terms of classes and kinds. The self-concept is not, then, something unique to the mental ego. However, if the self-concept is not new to the mental ego, it at least undergoes decisive changes in becoming part of the mental-egoic system. For example, it ceases being a vehicle of paleological cognition (more on this later), and, relevant to the point at hand, it acquires a crucial ontological function, becoming the seat of the mental ego's sense of being.

[3] Virtually every spiritual tradition with a systematic discipline of meditation or prayer acknowledges the existence of states of objectless interior absorption. For example, in the classical yoga tradition codified by Patanjali (Aranya 1983; Feuerstein 1979), such states are referred to as states of unsupported enstasy (*asamprajnata samadhi*). In the early Buddhist system set forth by Buddhaghosa (1975), these states are called formless absorptions (*arupa jhanas*). And in the mystical tradition of Christianity, they are known as states of infused objectless contemplation. These and other meditative states are discussed in Chapter 6.

[4] The Perls-Berne trinity of parent, adult, and child is correct as far as it goes. But it does not take into consideration the deeper, prepersonal levels of the unconscious, which sometimes speak not only in a childish (impish or rebellious) spirit, but in a primitive and even demonic manner.

[5] For accounts of Piaget's work, see Cowan (1978) and Flavell (1963).

[6] Agreeing with Piaget that formal operational thought transcends egocentricism, I would emphasize that the ego that achieves this self-transcendence *in thought* remains decidedly egocentric *in fact*.

Chapter 5

[1] Brown's study reveals that this flow of light is a phenomenon of cross-cultural scope

which can be considered inherent to contemplative development. Brown maps the unfolding awareness of the flow of light as it has been described in Hindu, Tibetan, and Theravadin literatures. He also reports that this cartography was cross-checked for consistency with other (e.g., Christian and Chinese) contemplative texts. For a graphic autobiographical account of awareness of the flow of light, see Gopi Krishna (1971).

[2]The ensuing account of the Great Mother, like the account in Chapter 2, is essentially a modification of the Jungian account as adapted to the distinctively bipolar, dynamic, and triphasic perspective of this book. Following Jung (1912/1952/1967, 1938/ 1954/1968) and Neumann (1954, 1963), the Great Mother is here considered a biaxial system, possessing both positive (Good Mother) and negative (Terrible Mother) sides and both inner (archetypal) and outer (personal) dimensions. The present account departs from the Jungian, however, in identifying the inner dimension of the Great Mother with the Dynamic Ground, which implies that the Great Mother is not only an archetypal network but also a multifaceted dynamic reality.

[3]It was argued in Chapter 2 that early childhood prior to latency is a period during which the power of the Ground, and not the sexual and aggressive drives, is dominant. In the Oedipus complex, it was explained, the child's main objective is not really a sexual relationship with the mother but rather "independent intimacy" with her. It is true that the child, in pursuing this objective, comes into conflict with the father. But this conflict, it was argued, is caused primarily by a desire to replace the father in his relationship with the mother rather than by independent feelings of aggression toward the father. It follows from this account, then, that the resolution of the Oedipus complex is not, as Freud believed, a turning point at which the sexual and aggressive drives are put in abeyance. Rather, it is a point at which original repression closes the Dynamic Ground. The latency period, which begins at this point, is thus the period extending from the closing of the Dynamic Ground to the onset of the sexual and aggressive instincts in puberty.

[4]Rigidities and deformations such as these are the focus of *hatha yoga* and other transformative exercises, such as for example Reichian body work and the body therapies associated with the names Alexander Lowen, F. Matthias Alexander, Moshe Feldenkrais, and Ida Rolf.

[5]The notion of the embedded unconscious is discussed in the section on the personal embedded unconscious, below.

[6]These are Wilber's (1980a) terms. It is to Wilber that I am indebted for having most clearly distinguished between these two sides of the unconscious.

[7]The gender of the conscious and unconscious spheres of the psyche differs depending on the frame of reference. Although it is true that, viewed from the perspective just discussed, a male person has a feminine unconscious (*anima*) and a female person a masculine unconscious (*animus*), it also is true that, viewed from a more fundamental perspective, the sphere of consciousness, as the egoic pole of the psyche, is masculine (in both men and women) and the prepersonal unconscious, as the dynamic and creative pole of the psyche, is feminine. The two poles of the psyche constitute a bisexual whole, which is fully realized only in the integrated stage. There are, then, two

levels of androgyny that can be achieved during the course of psychic development. The first consists of the appropriation of the *anima* (by the man) or the *animus* (by the woman) within the parameters of the larger egoic personality. And the second, deeper form consists of the synthesis of consciousness with the prepersonal unconscious, of the ego with the Dynamic Ground, which yields the higher whole of integration.

[8]Historically, this is the view of neo-Platonists and most religious mystics in the West and of most exponents of Vedanta Hinduism and Mahayana Buddhism in the East. Recently, the view has received a new philosophical formulation in light of the holographic paradigm (Wilber 1982), based on Bohm's notion that mind and the physical world are grounded in the same implicate order. Perhaps the most acute assessment of the view in question is that of Alex Comfort (1979, 1984). Comfort brilliantly explores the possibilities and pitfalls involved in the notion of mystical contact with reality. He suggests that mystical or fusional experience may well transcend all of the Kantian a priori structures (including not only space, time, and objectifying categorial thought but also the very sense of separate I-ness) and that, in doing this, mystical experience may at the same time accomplish an I-less, empathic intuition of preobjective implicate reality.

[9]See Goleman (1977), Ornstein (1972), Walsh (1977), and Washburn (1978). All of these sources report that, during meditation, consciousness becomes progressively more sensitive and that, consequently, materials that earlier were too subtle to be discriminated begin to be noticed by the conscious mind.

Chapter 6

[1]Transpersonal psychologists have formulated several different accounts of how meditation accesses the unconscious. For example, Wilber (1980a, 1983b) sees meditation as a process that facilitates the emergence into consciousness of uncon-scious (submerged or not-yet-emerged) psychic structures, and Welwood (1977) sees meditation as a process that moves awareness from conscious figure to unconscious ground. Some transpersonal psychologists reject the idea that meditation accesses the unconscious, holding that meditation is exclusively a technique for achieving higher or transpersonal states (Russell 1986). In the present account, meditation is conceived as a practice that both accesses the unconscious *and* (thereby) leads to higher or transpersonal states.

[2]Grof's work in LSD psychotherapy (1975) is a major contribution in this area.

[3]As will be discussed shortly, meditation in its more advanced stages does lead to states of selfless absorption. But these states of enstasy (*samadhi*, *jhana*, contemplation) differ considerably from hypnotic trance and drug-induced altered states. Principally, these states, although egoless in the sense of being unself-consciously absorbed, nonetheless have at their disposal egoic faculties and knowledge. These states are indeed without the reflective self-awareness that is usually associated with the ego (Descartes' *cogito*, Kant's transcendental apperception, Patanjali's *ahamkara*). In these states there is no

subject/object division by which the ego can be aware of itself by standing back from an experience and thereby being aware of itself as having that experience. However, although these states are egoless in this sense, they are nonetheless states in which reality testing, operational cognition, acquired knowledge, and other functions and resources normally associated with the ego are fully available and operative. In hypnotic trance and drug-induced altered states, on the other hand, these functions and resources are usually suspended and unavailable.

[4]See for example Ornstein (1971), Goleman (1977), Sopa (1978), and Washburn (1978).

[5]The Roman Catholic Church divides mental prayer into (1) discursive prayer (also called meditation), in which, similar to *dharana*, one focuses on a specific theme or object of prayer; (2) the prayer of simplicity or of simple regard (also called simplified affective prayer, acquired recollection, and acquired contemplation), in which, similar to *dhyana*, the unruliness of the mind is quelled and consciousness is left quietly alert, able to give steady and undivided attention to the theme of prayer, if any, or simply to remain vigilantly solicitous of the Holy Spirit; and (3) infused contemplation, in which, similar to *samadhi*, the ego is absorbed, stirred, transported, etc. (by the action of the Holy Spirit).

[6]Actually, the Buddhist literature on *vipassana* (insight) meditation does include an account of RM as a practice leading to absorption. However, since RM does not focus on any specific theme or object, the absorbed states that result from RM are typically of an objectless type (corresponding to Patanjali's *asamprajnata samadhi*). Buddhaghosa (1975), the classic expositor of the early Buddhist tradition of meditation, refers to these attainments as *arupa jhanas*, i.e., states of formless absorption.

[7]This does not mean that the dynamic-dialectical paradigm mandates prayer as the only viable or effective (better yet morally proper) type of meditation; nor does it mean that this paradigm would recommend any specific creedal or sectarian type of prayer over any other. Rather, all it means is that the dynamic-dialectical paradigm implies that prayer, understood generally and without commitment to any particular form, is the type of meditation that best fits the ego's constitutional status as conceived in dynamic-dialectical terms, namely, as the lesser pole of a bipolar psyche. No "religious ax" is here being ground; it is simply a matter of acknowledging the practical implications of theoretical premises.

[8]Patanjali considers introversion or withdrawal from the senses *(pratyahara)* to be one of the preliminary "limbs" or practices of meditative yoga. One must be able to disengage awareness from the senses before one can successfully focus the mind.

[9]The similarity between meditative introversion and sensory deprivation is discussed in Staal (1975).

[10]Egoic sets and postures are in a sense actions by which the ego responds to experience: they are *petrified* actions. Meditation, then, as a form of attention that neither acts nor is acted upon by experience, opposes not only egoic activities in the usual sense of the term but also egoic sets and postures. To meditate is to be a pure witness, and an ego that is set or posed (e.g., braced, girded, armored, or repressed) is not a pure witness.

[11]Just how demobilized the psychophysiological system becomes depends on the level of attainment of the particular meditator. As progress is made in CM, consciousness becomes increasingly still and free of sets and postures. This greater degree of demobilization in turn allows the meditator to use more subtle focal objects, which in turn further demobilize consciousness—and so on.

[12]The reader is referred to the masterly article by Jack Engler (1984) in which both positive and negative consequences of meditation are explored. Engler's general point is that it takes a strong ego to be able to transend the ego, and therefore that meditation practiced by people without a strong sense of self can be dangerous. Meditation practiced under these conditions can backfire; it can work to dissolve precisely what needs to be consolidated. Meditation practiced by people who are not developmentally ready for it can lead to a "clear sequence of pathological consequences" (43).

[13]For an excellent bibliography of scientific studies of meditation, containing over eight hundred entries, see Murphy and Donaldson (1983).

[14]On the Roman Catholic conception of the stages of contemplative prayer, see Arintero (1957), Garrigou-Lagrange (1948, 1951), and Royo and Aumann (1962).

[15]I should stress that this is my interpretation of *samadhi* (or of enstasy more generally), and not Patanjali's. Patanjali describes *samadhi* in phenomenological terms (as a state of unself-conscious absorption) and explains it in metaphysical terms (as a movement away from identification with nature [*prakrti*] and toward the isolated purity of the true Self [*purusha*]). He does not, however, explain *samadhi* in dynamic or energic terms, as I have done. Moreover, he would probably disagree with such an explanation, since in his dualistic metaphysics dynamism or energy would belong to the lower realm of nature rather than to the higher, immutable realm of the Self. On Patanjali's metaphysics (which is a variation of the Samkhya system), see Radhakrishnan and Moore (1957) and Raju (1985).

[16]See Dipika (1966), Satchidananda (1970), and Vishnudevananda (1959). The bioenergetic exercises of Alexander Lowen (1967, 1977) also merit mention in this context.

[17]See Funderburk (1977) for a review of scientific studies of the effects of yoga practice.

Chapter 7

[1]The concept of regression in the service of transcendence is heavily indebted to Jung's interpretation (1912/1952/1967) of the night sea journey or heroic odyssey as involving a return of the ego to the dynamic and creative resources of the collective unconscious. The concept is also indebted to Laing's (1965) phenomenology of the alienated condition and to Laing's (1967), Perry's (1974, 1976), and Grof's (1985) conceptions of the redemptive possibilities implicit in the psychotic process. And the concept is indebted as well to Prince's and Savage's (1966) explanation of mystical experience in terms of the psychoanalytic notion of regression in the service of the ego.

[2]The alienated mental ego, panicked by its severed condition, might try very hard to achieve engagement and to act effectively in the world. But these efforts are not likely to be successful. More often than not, such efforts yield only contrived behaviors, caricatures of real actions.

[3]The original phenomenological account of the world was developed by Edmund Husserl (1964, 1982). For a good discussion of Husserl's views, see Landgrebe (1981).

[4]I do not mean to suggest that a setting is a blank backdrop onto which a subject can overlay any meanings, values, and purposes whatsoever. A setting has its own contours, which impose limits on what a subject can project upon the setting. Still, an isolated, unlived setting is not a world.

[5]In fact, the mental ego's inner talk probably increases with its alienation, for internal dialogue is one of the mental ego's main lines of defense against facing its "nothingness" and guilt. Therefore, once alienation has undermined extraversion and identity-construction, internal dialogue is forced to play a larger role.

[6]The mental ego is for the most part terrified of black holes, yet at the same time it is drawn to them because of the magnetic pull of the power resident in them. In other words, the mental ego is morbidly fascinated by black holes—and it occasionally yields to them, despite fearing that, in doing so, it is doing mortal harm to itself. Such behavior on the part of the mental ego is perverse, every bit as perverse as its self-assertion at zero point. Harding (1963) has taken note of this seemingly suicidal fascination that the ego has for the dynamic unconscious. She calls it the ego's renegade impulse.

[7]As noted in the last chapter, such images are among the "illusory sensations" called *makyo* in Zen and the "ten corruptions" in original Buddhism. These images are discussed in greater detail below.

[8]Embedded structures of the personality are, of course, already affected during the first stage of regression in the service of transcendence, since the process of alienation disconnects these structures, depriving them of their field of exercise, the world.

[9]For accounts of spontaneous *kriya* phenomena, see Mookerjee (1983), Muktananda (1978), Sannella (1976), and White (1979).

[10]To my knowledge, the most remarkable (and, I would think, pathologically extreme) case of such bodily awakening is that described by Gopi Krishna in his spiritual autobiography (1971).

[11]The power of the Ground can also be experienced in masculine form, although, cross-culturally, this may be counted the exception rather than the rule. For example, the power of the Ground can be seen as acting in a masculine manner when it forcibly penetrates the egoic sphere and enswoons the ego. In this respect, the power of the Ground is the bridegroom, the ego the bride. Christianity, given its commitment to conceiving all members of the Trinity in masculine terms (even the Holy Spirit), favors this orientation. St. Teresa's works provide the most graphic illustrations of this perception of the activity of divine power.

250

Chapter 8

[1]For cross-cultural comparisons of symbols of regeneration, see Campbell (1974) and Schnapper (1980).

[2]Alchemy is an esoteric teaching that, in its Western form, arose in the Hellenistic period out of Oriental and Greek sources. At the end of the Hellenistic era, the practice of alchemy was continued mainly among the Arabs, and it therefore eventually took on the dress of Islam. In the twelfth century, alchemy, along with other ancient and classical teachings, began to make its way into the West, and a distinctively Christian version of the alchemical quest was gradually developed. Alchemy continued to have devoted practitioners all the way into the eighteenth century, at which time the victory of the new science, which was fundamentally at odds with the Aristotelian assumptions of alchemy, brought about the final demise of the arcane art.

[3]Among the many spiritual systems of the East, I have chosen tantric yoga to exemplify regeneration because it is a system that very clearly conceives of the regenerative process as a transformation effected by spiritual power (kundalini-Shakti). Most Eastern systems, in explaining how the soul is brought to redemption, emphasize enlightenment and liberation rather than spiritual transformation and purification. Most systems hold that the soul (e.g., atman, purusha) already exists in pristine condition (or truly does not exist at all: Buddhism) and needs only to attain intuitive knowledge of this ultimate fact in order to be liberated from suffering and rebirth. Tantric yoga, on the other hand, explains regeneration as a real transformation that is accomplished within the soul by the transformative agency of spiritual power.

[4]As regeneration culminates in integration, Ground-infused states cease altogether being violent, even in an ecstatic manner. For as the ego grows stronger and becomes more harmoniously aligned with spirit, the effect of spirit upon the ego becomes less wildly effusive and intoxicating. The ego becomes more composed and clear-headed, and the agitation of ecstatic states progressively calms into a serene dynamism. This change manifests itself in diverse ways. Later in the chapter I will discuss how, cognitively, the calming of Ground-infused states manifests itself in a transformation of intellectual transport into contemplation and how, affectively, it manifests itself in a transformation of emotional rapture into bliss.

[5]This change is what Nietzsche calls the transvaluation of values. According to Nietzsche, Dionysian (nonegoic) potentials, which had been condemned as evil, here become sources of higher value. The overman draws upon these potentials for strength, creativity, and spirit, and in doing so he transcends the (conventional, "slavish") distinction between good and evil. On Nietzsche's conception of transvaluation, see especially Thus Spoke Zarathustra (1966), On the Genealogy of Morals (1969), and The Will to Power (1967).

[6]Roman Catholic theology divides the mystical path into three stages: the purgative way, the illuminative way, and the unitive way. The purgative way is a period of torment during which the soul is cleansed and made ready for the divine life. The illuminative way, also called the spiritual espousal, is a period of ecstasy and rapture during which

the soul is penetrated intimately by and infused with the divine life. And the unitive way, also called the spiritual wedding, is a period of perfect fulfillment during which the soul enjoys complete at-one-ment with the divine life. (Happold 1970; Royo and Aumann 1962; Underhill 1961.) This tripartite division of the mystical path corresponds in many respects to the division that I have made between regression in the service of transcendence, regeneration in spirit, and integration. But the two divisions are by no means congruent, since my division also corresponds in important respects to the eschatological division between hell, purgatory, and heaven. The reason for the incongruities in these divisions is that Roman Catholic theology utterly disconnects hell and purgatory: only the damned go to hell, the saved pay for their sins in purgatory. This disconnection puts a negative burden on purgatory by forcing it to do double duty. Purgatory must serve not only as a place or stage of purification (i.e., regenerative transformation) but also as a place or stage of punishment (i.e., regressive deconstitution). That is, owing to the disconnection of hell and purgatory, purgatory must double as a surrogate hell for heaven-bound souls.

[7] Another disanalogy is that the contractions grow steadily stronger in the case of physical labor and steadily weaker in the case of spiritual labor.

[8] St. John of the Cross and St. Teresa speak of infused spiritual life as involving "fiery darts of love" and "wounds of love." In their account of these feelings, Royo and Aumann (1962, 550) state: "According to St. John of the Cross, the fiery darts of love are certain hidden touches of love which, like a fiery arrow, burn and pierce the soul and leave it completely cauterized with the fire of love. St. Teresa describes this phenomenon as a wounding of the soul, as if an arrow had pierced the soul. It causes the soul great affliction, and at the same time it is very delectable. The wound is not a physical one, but it is deep within the soul and seems to spring from the soul's inmost depths . . . . The wounds of love are similar to the preceding phenomenon, but they are more profound and more lasting." An excellent contemporary example of the intimate interplay of agony and ecstasy in spiritual life can be found in the mystical writings of Simone Weil. See *Gravity and Grace* (1952).

[9] The *hara* is the source of vital energy, which rises from the seat of the body. The *tanden* is a point below the navel at which the practitioner of *zazen* seeks to concentrate the vital energy. With the *hara* forces concentrated at the *tanden*, one is said to be spiritually balanced and coordinated, anchored in life's proper center of gravity. See Sekida (1975) and Sayama (1986).

[10] As observed earlier, vacant trances (black hole experiences, morbid transfixions) usually disappear with the commencement of regeneration in spirit, since, at this juncture, the ego is freed from the gravity of the Ground.

[11] Effusive-ecstatic states are perhaps the single most characteristic sign of the regenerative period. These states are discussed at several points in this chapter. The general features and causes of ecstatic states were explained in an earlier section. The present section treats the cognitive dimension of ecstatic states. A later section will treat the affective dimension.

[12] Roman Catholic and Eastern Orthodox Christianity, of course, credit all manner of miracles not only to Jesus but also to the saints. Judaism and Islam are religions based

on a belief in prophets and divinely inspired leaders. And Eastern religions generally believe that supernormal powers are a natural by-product of spiritual endeavor. For two interesting—although popular and mostly anecdotal—accounts of extranormal powers and events, see Yogananda (1972) and Rogo (1982). Yogananda describes instances of special powers that he observed in his travels among Indian yogis, and Rogo describes miraculous phenomena within Christendom.

[13]It is the affective dimension of ecstasy that is here considered.

[14]These sets of contraries are well known in esoteric literatures. In yoga they are explained in terms of the twin nerve pathways, *ida* (cool and wet) and *pingala* (hot and bright), which are said to twine about the *sushumna*, the central energy channel of the body. In astrology and alchemy the opposition is symbolized by the reagents mercury (cool and wet) and sulfur (hot and bright). In all of these systems the object is to attain a balanced synthesis of these opposites. For a discussion of this subject, see Washburn (1987).

[15]The great Rinzai Zen Master Hakuin described the "doubt mass" (a trance induced by *koan* practice) as a condition in which one is frozen in sheets of ice. See Kasulis (1981).

[16]In Rinzai Zen, it is said that a person is near *satori* when, deep in a "doubt mass" (see note 15), his face shows signs of perspiration. See Chang (1959).

[17]Contrary to the traditional view, according to which hell and purgatory are in no way connected, this view, following Dante's conception in the *Divine Comedy*, situates the entrance to purgatory at the very bottom of hell.

Chapter 9

[1]On this and other similarities between Indian and Taoist yoga, see Blofeld (1973).

[2]The ensuing account of Patanjali's concentrative meditation (CM) could, *mutatis mutandis*, be applied to receptive meditation (RM) as well. Also, I should repeat a proviso stated in Chapter 6, namely, that although I follow Patanjali's phenomenological description of the stages of meditation, I do not subscribe to his theoretical explanation of the underlying factors involved in the meditative process. My theoretical perspective is psychodynamic, his metaphysical. On these differences, see Chapter 6, note 15.

[3]See Eliade (1969a, 1969b), Feuerstein (1974, 1979), and Taimni (1961) for discussions of Patanjali's classification of types and levels of *samadhi*.

[4]Objectless enstasy can also be achieved without the initial use of a support, i.e., by the practice of open mindfulness or insight. In the Buddhist system of meditation codified by Buddhaghosa (1975), such enstasies are called *arupa jhanas* (formless absorptions).

[5]It would seem that the nonegoic pole has phylogenetic priority as well. The egoic pole is probably an evolutionary add-on, something overlaid upon a predeveloped nonegoic base.

Appendix

[1]For a discussion of the division of hemispheric functions, see Martindale (1981). Any statement of distinctive hemispheric functions is at best only typical, since it is now known that specialization of functions in right and left hemispheres can vary according to handedness, gender, and other factors. On this, see Levy (1980).

BIBLIOGRAPHY

Aranya, H. (1983). *Yoga Philosophy of Patanjali*. Albany, New York: State University of New York Press.

Arieti, S. (1967). *The Intrapsychic Self*. New York: Basic Books.

_____. (1976). *Creativity: The Magic Synthesis*. New York: Basic Books.

Arintero, J.G. (1957). *Stages in Prayer*. Trans. K. Pond. St. Louis: B. Herder Book Co.

Assagioli, R. (1971). *Psychosynthesis*. New York: The Viking Press.

Becker, E. (1973). *The Denial of Death*. New York: The Free Press.

Benjamin, J.D. (1966). "Discussion of Hartmann's *Ego Psychology and the Problem of Adaptation*." In *Psychoanalysis — A General Psychology: Essays in Honor of Heinz Hartmann*, edited by R.M. Loewenstein et al. New York: International Universities Press, 1966.

Berne, E. (1967). *Games People Play*. New York: Grove Press.

Blofeld, J. (1973). *The Secret and Sublime: Taoist Mysteries and Magic*. New York: E.P. Dutton & Co.

Bohm, D. (1971). "Quantum Theory as an Indication of a New Order in Physics. Part A. The Development of New Orders as Shown through the History of Physics." *Foundations of Physics* 1:359-381.

_____. (1973). "Quantum Theory as an Indication of a New Order in Physics. Part B. Implicate and Explicate Order in Physical Law." *Foundations of Physics* 3:139-168.

_____. (1980). *Wholeness and the Implicate Order*. London: Routledge & Kegan Paul.

Bornstein, M.H. (1975). "Qualities of Color Vision in Infancy." *Journal of Experimental Child Psychology* 19:401-419.

Brentano, F. (1874). *Psychologie vom empirischen Standpunkt*. Selections translated in *Realism and the Background of Phenomenology*, edited by R.M. Chisholm. Glencoe, Ill.: The Free Press, 1960.

Brown, D. (1986). "The Stages of Meditation in Cross-Cultural Perspective." In *Transformations of Consciousness: Conventional and Contemplative Perspectives on Development*, edited by Ken Wilber et al. Boston: Shambhala, 1986.

Brown, N.O. (1959). *Life Against Death*. Middletown, Conn.: Wesleyan University Press.

Buddhaghosa. (1975). *Visuddhimagga*. 3d ed. Trans. Bhikkhu Nanamoli. Kandy, Sri Lanka: Buddhist Publication Society.

Campbell, J. (1974). *The Mythic Image*. Princeton: Princeton University Press.

Chang, G.C.C. (1959). *The Practice of Zen*. New York: Harper & Row.

Cohen, L.B. (1982). "Our Developing Knowledge of Infant Perception and Cognition." In *In the Beginning: Readings on Infancy*, edited by J. Belsky. New York: Columbia University Press.

Cohen, L.B.; DeLoache, J.S.; and Pearl, R. (1977). "An Examination of Interference Effects in Infant's Memory of Faces." *Child Development* 48:88-96.

Comfort, A. (1979). *I and That: Notes on the Biology of Religion*. New York: Crown Publishers.

————. (1984). *Reality and Empathy: Physics, Mind, and Science in the 21st Century*. Albany, New York: State University of New York Press.

Cowan, P.A. (1978). *Piaget with Feeling*. New York: Holt, Rinehart & Winston.

Deikman, A. (1971). "Bimodal Consciousness." *Archives of General Psychiatry* 25:481-489.

Dipika (Yoga). (1966). *Light on Yoga*. New York: Schocken Books.

Eliade, M. (1969a). *Patanjali and Yoga*. New York: Funk & Wagnalls.

————. (1969b). *Yoga: Immortality and Freedom*. 2d ed. Princeton: Princeton University Press.

Engler, J. (1984). "Therapeutic Aims in Psychotherapy and Meditation: Developmental Stages in the Representation of Self." *The Journal of Transpersonal Psychology* 16:25-61.

Erikson, E. (1958). *Young Man Luther: A Study in Psychoanalysis and History*. New York: W.W. Norton & Co.

————. (1959). *Identity and the Life Cycle*. Ed. D. Rapaport. New York: International Universities Press.

_____. (1963). *Childhood and Society*. rev. ed. New York: W.W. Norton & Co.

_____. (1968). *Identity: Youth and Crisis*. New York: W.W. Norton & Co.

_____. (1969). *Gandhi's Truth*. New York: W.W. Norton & Co.

Fagan, J.F. (1973). "Infant's Delayed Recognition of Memory and Forgetting." *Journal of Experimental Child Psychology* 16:424-450.

_____. (1977). "An Attention Model of Infant Recognition." *Child Development* 48:345-359.

Feuerstein, G. (1974). *The Essence of Yoga*. New York: Grove Press.

_____. (1979). *The Yoga-Sutra of Patanjali*. Folkestone, Kent (UK): Dawson.

Flavell, J.H. (1963). *The Developmental Psychology of Jean Piaget*. New York: D. Van Nostrand Co.

Freud, A. (1936). *The Ego and the Mechanisms of Defense*. New York: International Universities Press.

Freud, S. (1895). "Project for a Scientific Psychology." In *The Origins of Psychoanalysis: Letters to Wilhelm Fliess, Drafts and Notes, 1887-1902*, edited by M. Bonaparte et al. New York: Basic Books, 1954.

_____. (1900). *The Interpretation of Dreams*. In *The Standard Edition of the Complete Psychological Works of Sigmund Freud*, vol. 4. London: Hogarth Press, 1953.

_____. (1911a). "Formulations on the Two Principles of Psychic Functioning." In *Standard Edition*, vol. 12. London: Hogarth Press, 1958.

_____. (1911b). "Psychoanalytic Notes on an Autobiographical Account of a Case of Paranoia (Dementia Paranoides)." In *Standard Edition*, vol. 12. London: Hogarth Press, 1958.

_____. (1915). "Repression." In *Standard Edition*, vol. 14. London: Hogarth Press, 1957.

_____. (1923). *The Ego and the Id*. In *Standard Edition*, vol. 19. London: Hogarth Press, 1961.

_____. (1926). "Inhibitions, Symptoms and Anxiety." In *Standard Edition*, vol. 20. London: Hogarth Press, 1959.

Frobenius, L. (1904). *Das Zeitalter des Sonnengottes*. Berlin.

Funderburk, J. (1977). *Science Studies Yoga: A Review of Physiological Data*. Himalayan International Institute of Yoga Science & Philosophy of USA.

Garrigou-Lagrange, R. (1948). *The Three Ages of the Interior Life: Prelude to Eternal Life*. Trans. M.T. Doyle. 3 vols. St. Louis: B. Herder Book Co.

_____. (1951). *Christian Perfection and Contemplation According to St. Thomas and St. John of the Cross.* Trans. M.T. Doyle. St. Louis: B. Herder Book Co.

Gilligan, C. (1982). *In a Different Voice.* Cambridge, Mass.: Harvard University Press.

Goleman, D. (1977). *The Varieties of the Meditative Experience.* New York: E.P. Dutton.

Grof, S. (1975). *Realms of the Human Unconscious.* New York: The Viking Press.

_____. (1985). *Beyond the Brain: Birth, Death, and Transcendence in Psychotherapy.* Albany, New York: State University of New York Press.

Happold, F.C. (1970). *Mysticism: A Study and an Anthology.* rev. ed. Baltimore: Penguin Books.

Harding, M.E. (1963). *Psychic Energy: Its Source and Its Transformations.* 2d ed. New York: Pantheon Books.

Hartmann, H. (1950). "Comments on the Psychoanalytic Theory of the Ego." In *Essays on Ego Psychology: Selected Problems in Psychoanalytic Theory.* New York: International Universities Press, 1964.

_____. (1956). "The Development of the Ego Concept in Freud's Work." In *Essays on Ego Psychology: Selected Problems in Psychoanalytic Theory.* New York: International Universities Press, 1964.

_____. (1958). *Ego Psychology and the Problem of Adaptation.* Trans. D. Rapaport. New York: International Universities Press.

Hartmann, H., and Loewenstein, R.M. (1962). "Notes on the Superego." In *The Psychoanalytic Study of the Child,* edited by R. Eissler et al., 17:42-81. New York: International Universities Press.

Hegel, G.W.F. (1952). *The Philosophy of Right.* Trans. T.M. Knox. London: Oxford University Press.

Heidegger, M. (1962). *Being and Time.* Trans. J. Macquarrie & E. Robinson. London: SCM Press.

Hume, D. (1888). *A Treatise of Human Nature.* Oxford: The Clarendon Press.

Husserl, E. (1964). *Cartesian Meditations: An Introduction to Phenomenology.* Trans. D. Cairns. The Hague: Martinus Nijhoff.

_____. (1982). *Ideas Pertaining to a Pure Phenomenology and to a Phenomenological Philosophy: First Book.* Trans. F. Kersten. The Hague: Martinus Nijhoff.

James, W. (1890). *The Principles of Psychology.* New York: Henry Holt & Co.

Jung, C.G. (1912/1952/1967). *Symbols of Transformation*. 2d ed. Trans. R.F.C. Hull as vol. 5 of *The Collected Works of C.G. Jung*. Princeton: Princeton University Press, 1967. This is a translation of *Symbole der Wandlung*, which, published in 1952, is an extensive revision of the *Wandlungen und Symbole der Libido*, first published in 1912.

————. (1938/1954/1968). "Psychological Aspects of the Mother Archetype." Trans. R.F.C. Hull in *Collected Works*, vol. 9. 2d ed. Princeton: Princeton University Press, 1968. Originally published in German in 1938; revised 1954.

————. (1953/1969). "Psychological Commentary on *The Tibetan Book of the Dead*." Trans. R.F.C. Hull in *Collected Works*, vol. 11. 2d ed. Princeton: Princeton University Press, 1969. Originally published in German; 5th ed., 1953.

Kagan, J. (1978). *The Growth of the Child: Reflections on Human Development*. New York: W.W. Norton & Co.

Kammerman, M. (1977). *Sensory Isolation and Personality Change*. Springfield, Ill.: Charles C. Thomas.

Kant, I. (1929). *The Critique of Pure Reason*. Toronto: Macmillan.

Kapleau, P. (1967). *The Three Pillars of Zen*. Boston: Beacon Press.

Kasulis, T.P. (1981). *Zen Action/Zen Person*. Honolulu: The University Press of Hawaii.

Kaufmann, W., ed. (1956). *Existentialism from Dostoevsky to Sartre*. Cleveland: World Publishing Co.

Kierkegaard, S. (1954). *Sickness unto Death*. In *Fear and Trembling and Sickness unto Death*, translated by W. Lowrie. Princeton: Princeton University Press.

Klein, G.S. (1976). *Psychoanalytic Theory: An Exploration of Essentials*. New York: International Universities Press.

Kohlberg, L. (1969). "Stages and Sequence: The Cognitive-Developmental Approach to Socialization." In *Handbook of Socialization Theory and Research*, edited by D.A. Goslin. Chicago: Rand McNally, 1969.

————. (1976). "Moral Stages and Moralization: The Cognitive-Developmental Approach." In *Moral Development and Behavior*, edited by T. Lickona. New York: Holt, Rinehart & Winston, 1976.

————. (1984). *Essays on Moral Development*, vol. 2: *The Psychology of Moral Development*. San Francisco: Harper & Row.

Krishna, G. (1971). *Kundalini: The Evolutionary Energy in Man*. Berkeley, Calif.: Shambhala.

Laing, R.D. (1965). *The Divided Self: An Existential Study in Sanity and Madness.* Middlesex, England: Penguin Books.

_____. (1967). *The Politics of Experience.* New York: Pantheon Books.

Landgrebe, L. (1981). "The World as a Phenomenological Problem." In *The Phenomenology of Edmund Husserl,* edited by D. Welton. Ithaca, New York: Cornell University Press.

Levy, J. (1980). "Varieties of Human Brain Organization and the Human Social System." *Zygon* 15:351-375.

Loevinger, J. (1976). *Ego Development: Conceptions and Theories.* San Francisco: Jossey-Bass Publishers.

Lowen, A. (1967). *The Betrayal of the Body.* London: Collier Macmillan Co.

Lowen, A., and Lowen, L. (1977). *The Way to Vibrant Health: A Manual of Bioenergetic Exercises.* New York: Harper & Row.

McCall, R.B.; Kennedy, C.B.; and Dodds, C. (1977). "The Interfering Effect of Distracting Stimuli on Infant's Memory." *Child Development* 48:79-87.

MacLean, P.D. (1973). *A Triune Concept of the Brain and Behavior.* Toronto: University of Toronto Press.

Madison, P. (1961). *Freud's Concept of Repression and Defense, Its Theoretical and Observational Language.* Minneapolis: University of Minnesota Press.

Mahler, M.; Pine, F.; and Bergman, A. (1975). *The Psychological Birth of the Human Infant.* New York: Basic Books.

Mann, R. (1984). *The Light of Consciousness.* Albany, New York: State University of New York Press.

Martindale, C. (1981). *Cognition and Consciousness.* Homewood, Ill.: Dorsey Press.

Maslow, A. (1968). *Toward a Psychology of Being.* New York: D. Van Nostrand Co.

_____. (1970). *Religions, Values, and Peak-Experiences.* New York: The Viking Press.

_____. (1971). *The Farther Reaches of Human Nature.* New York: The Viking Press.

Mookerjee, A. (1983). *Kundalini: The Arousal of the Inner Energy.* 2d ed. New York: Destiny Books.

Muktananda (Swami). (1978). *Play of Consciousness.* S.Y.D.A. Foundation.

Murphy, M., and Donaldson, S. (1983). "A Bibliography of Meditation Theory and Research." *The Journal of Transpersonal Psychology* 15:181-228.

Neumann, E. (1954). *The Origins and History of Consciousness.* Princeton: Princeton University Press.

―――. (1963). *The Great Mother.* 2d ed. Princeton: Princeton University Press.

―――. (1973). *The Child: Structure and Dynamics of the Nascent Personality.* Trans. Ralph Manheim. New York: G.P. Putnam's Sons.

Nietzsche, F. (1966). *Thus Spoke Zarathustra.* Trans. W. Kaufmann. New York: The Viking Press.

―――. (1967). *The Will to Power.* Trans. W. Kaufmann. New York: Random House.

―――. (1969). *On the Genealogy of Morals.* Trans. W. Kaufmann & R.J. Hollingdale. New York: Vintage Books.

Ornstein, R. (1972). *The Psychology of Consciousness.* San Francisco: W.H. Freeman & Co.

Ornstein, R., and Naranjo, C. (1971). *On the Psychology of Meditation.* New York: The Viking Press.

Otto, R. (1958). *The Idea of the Holy.* New York: Oxford University Press.

Pascal, B. (1958). *Pensees.* New York: E.P. Dutton & Co.

Perls, F. (1969). *Gestalt Therapy Verbatim.* Moab, Utah: Real Peoples' Press.

Perry, J.W. (1974). *The Far Side of Madness.* Englewood Cliffs, N.J.: Prentice-Hall.

―――. (1976). *Roots of Renewal in Myth and Madness.* San Francisco: Jossey-Bass Publishers.

Pribram, K.H. (1971). *Languages of the Brain: Experimental Paradoxes and Principles in Neuropsychology.* Englewood Cliffs, N.J.: Prentice-Hall.

―――. (1986). "The Cognitive Revolution and Mind/Brain Issues." *American Psychologist* 41:507-520.

Pribram, K.H.; Nuwer, M.; and Baron, R.J. (1974). "The Holographic Hypothesis of Memory Structure in Brain Function and Perception." In *Contemporary Developments in Mathematical Psychology,* vol. 2: *Measurement, Psychophysics, and Neural Information Processing,* edited by D.H. Krantz et al. San Francisco: W.H. Freeman and Co.

Radhakrishnan, S., and Moore, C., eds. (1957). *Indian Philosophy.* Princeton: Princeton University Press.

Raju, P.T. (1985). *Structural Depths of Indian Thought.* Albany, New York: State University of New York Press.

Rapaport, D. (1958). "A Historical Survey of Psychoanalytic Ego Psychology." In *The Collected Papers of David Rapaport.* New York: Basic Books, 1967.

Reich, W. (1942). *The Function of the Orgasm.* New York: Farrar, Straus & Giroux.

Rogo, D.S. (1982). *Miracles: A Parascientific Inquiry into Wondrous Phenomena.* New York: Dial Press.

Royo, A., and Aumann, J. (1962). *The Theology of Christian Perfection.* Dubuque, Iowa: The Priory Press.

Ruff, H.A., and Birch, H.G. (1974). "Infant Visual Fixation: The Effect of Concentricity, Curvilinearity, and Number of Directions." *Journal of Experimental Child Psychology* 17:460-473.

Russell, E.W. (1986). "Consciousness and the Unconscious: Eastern Meditative and Western Psychotherapeutic Approaches." *The Journal of Transpersonal Psychology* 18:51-72.

Sannella, L. (1976). *Kundalini: Psychosis or Transcendence?* San Francisco: H.S. Dakin.

Sartre, J.-P. (1956). *Being and Nothingness.* Trans. Hazel Barnes. New York: Philosophical Library.

———. (1957). *The Transcendence of the Ego.* Trans. F. Williams & R. Kirkpatrick. New York: The Noonday Press.

Satchidananda (Swami). (1970). *Integral Yoga Hatha.* New York: Holt, Rinehart & Winston.

Sayama, M.K. (1986). *Samadhi: Self-Development in Zen, Swordsmanship, and Psychotherapy.* Albany, New York: State University of New York Press.

Schachtel, E.G. (1959). *Metamorphosis.* New York: Basic Books.

Schnapper, E.G. (1980). *The Inward Odyssey: The Concept of the Way in the Great Religions of the World.* 2d ed. London: George Allen & Unwin.

Sekida, K. (1975). *Zen Training: Methods and Philosophy.* Ed. A.V. Grimstone. New York: Weatherhill.

Sopa, G. (1978). "*Samathavipasyanayuganaddha:* The Two Leading Principles of Buddhist Meditation." In *Mahayana Buddhist Meditation: Theory and Practice,* edited by M. Kiyota. Honolulu: The University Press of Hawaii.

Staal, F. (1975). *Exploring Mysticism.* Berkeley: University of California Press.

Stein, W.J. (1967). "The Sense of Becoming Psychotic." *Psychiatry* 30:262-275.

Taimni, I.K. (1961). *The Science of Yoga*. Wheaton, Ill.: Theosophical Publishing House.

Underhill, E. (1961). *Mysticism*. New York: E.P. Dutton.

Van Dusen, W. (1958). "*Wu Wei*, No-Mind and the Fertile Void in Psychotherapy." *Psychologia* 1:253-256. Reprinted in *The Meeting of the Ways: Explorations in East/West Psychology*, edited by J. Welwood. New York: Schocken, 1979.

———. (1972). *The Natural Depth in Man*. New York: Harper & Row.

Vishnudevananda (Swami). (1959). *The Complete Illustrated Book of Yoga*. New York: Bell Publishing Co.

Von Domarus, E. (1944). "The Specific Laws of Logic in Schizophrenia." In *Language and Thought in Schizophrenia: Collected Papers*, edited by J.S. Kasanin. Berkeley: University of California Press.

Walsh, R.N. (1977). "Initial Meditative Experiences: Part I." *The Journal of Transpersonal Psychology* 9:151-192.

Washburn, M. (1978). "Observations Relevant to a Unified Theory of Meditation." *The Journal of Transpersonal Psychology* 10:45-65.

———. (1987). "Human Wholeness in Light of Five Types of Psychic Duality." *Zygon* 22:67-85.

Washburn, M., and Stark, M. (1979). "Ego, Egocentricity, and Self-Transcendence: A Western Interpretation of Eastern Teaching." In *The Meeting of the Ways: Explorations in East/West Psychology*, edited by J. Welwood. New York: Schocken, 1979.

Weil, S. (1952). *Gravity and Grace*. London: Routledge and Kegan Paul.

Welwood, J. (1977). "Meditation and the Unconscious: A New Perspective." *The Journal of Transpersonal Psychology* 9:1-26.

White, J., ed. (1979). *Kundalini: Evolution and Enlightenment*. Garden City, New York: Doubleday/Anchor.

Wilber, K. (1977). *The Spectrum of Consciousness*. Wheaton, Ill.: Theosophical Publishing House.

———. (1980a). *The Atman Project*. Wheaton, Ill.: Theosophical Publishing House.

———. (1980b). "The Pre/Trans Fallacy." *ReVision* 3:51-71.

———. (1981a). "Ontogenetic Development: The Fundamental Patterns." *The Journal of Transpersonal Psychology* 13:33-58.

———. (1981b). *Up from Eden: A Transpersonal View of Human Development.* New York: Doubleday/Anchor.

———, ed. (1982). *The Holographic Paradigm and Other Paradoxes.* Boulder, Col.: Shambhala.

———. (1983a). *A Sociable God.* Boulder, Col.: Shambhala.

———. (1983b). *Eye to Eye.* New York: Doubleday/Anchor.

Wilber, K.; Engler, J.; and Brown, D. (1986). *Transformations of Consciousness: Conventional and Contemplative Perspectives on Development.* Boston: Shambhala.

Wood, E. (1962). *Yoga.* rev. ed. Baltimore: Penguin Books.

Yogananda (Paramahansa). (1972). *Autobiography of a Yogi.* Los Angeles: Self-Realization Fellowship.

INDEX

107; and Cartesian dualism, 89-91, 200; and cognition, 103-106; and egocentricity, 103, 106; and extraversion, 92-94; and feeling, 99-103; its fundamental project, 94-95, 159; and guilt or sin, 100-101, 103, 107; and identity construction, 94-97; and instincts, 224; and internal dialogue, 97-99, 146, 170, 250n5; and "nothingness," 91-99, 107, 135, 245n1; as self, 38-39. *See also* Triphasic development, egoic or mental-egoic stage

Mental processes: and mental ego, 103-106; in regeneration in spirit, 202-205; in regression in the service of transcendence, 177-178

Moksha, 156, 206

Muktananda, Swami, 181

Mystical body, 231

Mystical experience, 134, 231-233

Neumann, Erich, 18, 43, 57

Nietzsche, Friedrich, 189, 251n5

Nirvana, 152, 156, 206

Nonegoic potentials. *See* Bipolar structure, nonegoic pole

"Nothingness," 91-99, 156, 159, 167, 169-170. *See also* Mental ego, and "nothingness"

Nous (intuitive intellect), 88

Numinosity, 49-50, 83-84, 127, 205, 210. *See also* Enchantment

Object permanence, 72, 77

Oedipus complex, 12, 18, 62-64, 246n3; resolution of, 64; role of father, 63-64

Original embedment, 21, 42-46; archetypes of, 44, 82; definition of, 16; and Dynamic Ground, 65-66

Original repression, 18, 23, 57, 90, 114, 127-129, 181; and Dynamic Ground, 65-66; and forfeiture of nonegoic potentials, 84-86; and genital

dominance, 59, 246n3; mending of, 194-197; and original sin, 66-68, 100; physical infrastructure of, 58-59, 128-129; as self-alienation, 60; as unconscious embedded structure, 128

Otto, Rudolf, 115

Paleologic, 74-81, 104-105

Paleosymbols, 76-77, 79-80, 85, 221-223, 244n3

Pascal, Blaise, 88, 93

Patanjali, 140, 144, 152-153, 219-221, 248n8, 249n15, 253n2

Paul, Saint, 186

Perls, Frederick, 98, 245n4

Personality: in regeneration in spirit, 223-226; in regression in the service of transcendence, 176-177. *See also* Self-concept

Phenomenology, concept of world, 161

Physico-dynamic potentials. *See* Bipolar structure, nonegoic pole

Piaget, Jean, 28, 30, 44, 70, 72, 74, 103

Pingala (nerve pathway), 253n14

Plato, 88, 134

Polymorphous sensuousness, 49, 59, 61, 83-84, 126, 179, 191, 199-202

Prana (energy), 216

Prayer, 143-145, 152; definition of, 143; in Roman Catholic Church, 144, 152, 248n5

"Pre-/trans-" fallacy, 37-38

Predicate-identity principle, 77-79, 104

Pre-egoic stage. *See* Triphasic development, pre-egoic or body-egoic stage

Pribram, Karl, 239n3

Primal repression, 18, 241n8

Primary process. *See* Paleologic; Psychoanalysis, primary process

Projection, 137

Protoemotions, 71

Psychic energy, 110-111, 118-119, 126, 128, 239n5

Psychoanalysis, 7, 110; and